HISTORICAL ATLAS

OF THE

BIBLE

A CARTOGRAPHICA BOOK

This updated edition published in 2010 by:
CHARTWELL BOOKS, INC.
A Division of BOOK SALES, INC.
276 Fifth Avenue Suite 206
New York, New York 10001, USA

Copyright © 2006 Cartographica Ltd

Reprinted in 2011 twice

ISBN-13: 978-0-7858-2627-9
ISBN-10: 0-7858-2627-0

QUMBMINI

This book is produced by
Cartographica Ltd
6 Blundell Street
London N7 9BH

Design & Cartography:
Red Lion Mapping

Printed in Singapore by
Star Standard Industries Pte Ltd.

THE
HISTORICAL ATLAS
OF THE
BIBLE

BY
DR IAN BARNES

CHARTWELL
BOOKS, INC.

CONTENTS

INTRODUCTION

THE WORD "BIBLE" COMES, THROUGH LATIN, FROM THE GREEK WORD *BIBLIA*, MEANING "BOOKS," WHICH IN ITS TURN COMES FROM *BYBLOS*, MEANING "PAPYRUS," THE MATERIAL FROM WHICH BOOKS WERE MADE.

We are used to speaking of the Bible as a single book, but, in fact, it is a collection of works, of different authorship and written at different times, and selected from a wider range of writings to make up the Bible as we know it. The books of the Old Testament were written over centuries and some of them were added to or changed their form over many years. None of the original manuscripts has survived, but by the 2nd Century BC the Old Testament had been organised into the 24 books that make up the Hebrew Bible.

The earliest translation of the Hebrew scriptures was the Septuagint, a Greek translation of all the Old Testament canonical books and some of those that are regarded by many as apocryphal. The Jewish translators—traditionally, they are 72 scribes—started work on the Pentateuch (Genesis, Exodus, Leviticus, Numbers, and Deuteronomy) in Alexandria in the first half of the 3rd Century BC. The other canonical books appear to have been translated by the end of the 2nd Century BC. The Septuagint forms the basis for several subsequent translations. In AD 382, St. Jerome made a Latin translation, called the Vulgate, which is still used by the Roman Catholic Church.

Where translations of the Old Testament books are taken from the Hebrew, the source is generally what is known as the Masoretic text or Masorah. The Masoretes (transmitters) probably started their work around AD 500 and did not finish it until the 10th Century.

Most biblical texts have come down to us as a result of repeated copying in a perishable medium, such as leather or papyrus. The latter was made from the pith of the papyrus plant, cut into strips and glued together cross-wise like plywood. The single sheets of papyrus were normally joined together to form rolls up to 30 feet (9.8 m) long. These were inscribed on the inner side only, where the fibers ran lengthwise. The text was written in narrow parallel columns, with a reed pen trimmed at the top, which was dipped into ink made from soot or gall. Another form of book commonly chosen by Biblical scribes was the codex, which in its basic form corresponds to a modern book. Four or more double-size sheets were laid on top of each other and folded in the middle, forming a "codex" that then needed binding. The page of a codex was written in one to four parallel columns.

After AD 200, the more expensive, but much harder wearing, parchment gradually supplanted papyrus, though the latter continued to be used up to the 8th Century for the production of New Testament manuscripts. Parchment is animal skin (from sheep, goats, calves, or antelopes) with hair and grease removed, and then smoothed and bleached. Parchment could be scraped and written on again. In the late Middle Ages, parchment was gradually replaced by paper.

The greatest archaeological breakthrough in discovering texts was undoubtedly the discovery of the Dead Sea Scrolls in 1947. The Scrolls were found in a cave near the Dead Sea and finally identified as Hebrew texts. One of them was a copy of the Book of Isaiah. When compared with the Masoretic texts, various differences were found, but on the whole there were no major changes and the discovery tended to give greater authority to the accuracy of the Jewish copyists. The books of the New Testament were written in Greek in the 1st Century AD, but the earliest manuscripts date from the 3rd and 4th Centuries AD. There are about 175 manuscripts dating from this period, written on papyrus or parchment, most of them very well preserved.

Two developments stimulated the reading of the Bible: the printing press and the rediscovery during the Renaissance of the authors of classical antiquity. The scholarly study of Greek and

THE SCROLL OF ISAIAH
Part of many of the texts known as the "Dead Sea Scrolls" were found at Qumran in 1947. This particular scroll represents the oldest complete book of the Old Testament, and dates from around 100 BC.

Latin was extended to Hebrew and Aramaic. As early as 1477, the Psalms were printed in Hebrew in Italy; the complete Old Testament followed in 1488. An impressive early scholarly edition is the famous Bombergiana (1516–17), edited by Felix Pratensis and named after its Antwerp printer, Daniel Bomberg, who had set up his Venetian printing house in 1515. The Bombergiana is what is known as a rabbinical Bible, because each page has a Hebrew text of the Old Testament with its Aramaic translation, and commentaries by famous Jewish scholars above, below and alongside the Bible text. The text of its second edition of 1524–25 has remained the basis of all printings of the Hebrew Bible.

Equally important is the impressive Complutensian Polyglot, which appeared in Alcalá in 1520. This opus has Hebrew, Aramaic, Latin, and Greek text and marginal notes on each page of the Old Testament. The printing of the New Testament was complete in 1514, but the Papal imprimatur did not arrive until 1520, so the Basel printer Froben preceded the publication of the Complutensian Polyglot with a less thorough edition of the Greek New Testament in 1516, the work of the famed Erasmus of Rotterdam.

In the history of the Greek New Testament, the most significant edition is the Editio Regia of the Paris printer, Robert Stephanus. It contains the Erasmus text corrected in accordance with the Complutensian Polyglot and other manuscripts and is the first edition to possess a critical apparatus. The next edition of this publication in 1551 originated the division of the text into the verses we use today. The traditional division into chapters had appeared soon after 1200 and is attributed to Archbishop Stephen Langton of Canterbury, England. The second edition of the Stephanus text in 1633, printed in Leyden, was regarded as the "textus receptus" until the 19th Century.

The Renaissance made a highly dramatic contribution to Bible study—the Reformation. The reformers thought the Bible had been closed to far too many Christians and claimed that people should learn to live again by the Bible, *sola scriptura* – "by the scriptures alone." Hence, the Bible was translated into English by John Wycliffe (c. 1382), William Tyndale (1525) and Miles Coverdale (1535).

The Bible is the best selling and most widely distributed book in the world. In 1988, the United Bible Society reported that the number of languages and dialects into which complete books of the Bible had been translated had reached 1,907. This includes complete bibles in 310 languages and New Testaments in 695 languages.

Why has the Bible, a collection of ancient and diverse writings, achieved such a status in the modern world? There is no single answer, just as there is no single attitude to the Bible. To some it is the supreme holy book, the inspired word of God, still relevant as a guide to faith and conduct. To others, it is primarily of great historical interest, charting the history of the Jewish people over centuries, and the origins and growth of the Christian Church. To some, it is essentially a myth, a collection of stories that evolved to explain natural phenomena and events.

For many people, the Bible has no particular significance. It is a book that they own but never read, believing it to be of little interest or relevance. They are missing out on a wealth of information and entertainment. Whatever the reader's religious views, the Bible remains an important record of ancient history and ideas, whose significance on Western culture, language, and thought is

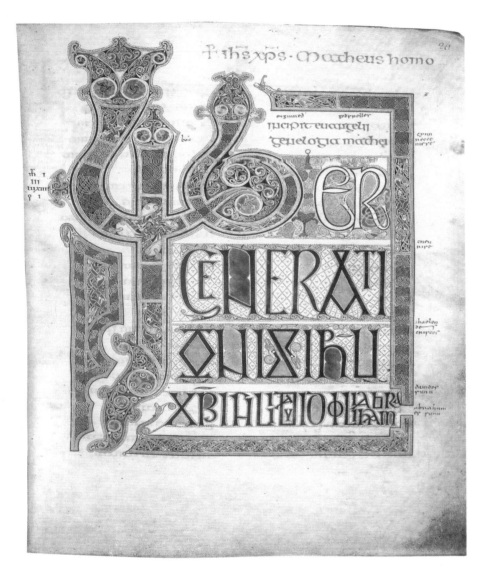

incalculable. It is also a considerable work of literature, containing beautiful poetry, exciting stories, and inspirational characters. It has not been possible to include all the fascinating Bible narratives here, but it is hoped that the tales and facts related in this book might send its readers back to the original work with renewed interest.

THE ANCIENT NEAR EAST

THE GREAT EGYPTIAN AND MESOPOTAMIAN RIVERS SUPPORT AN AGRICULTURE OTHERWISE IMPOSSIBLE IN THE DRY, HOT CLIMATE. IN PALESTINE ALMOST ALL THE LAND IS FERTILE IF IRRIGATED. THROUGHOUT THE REGION CEREALS ARE A STAPLE CROP. SHEEP AND GOATS—EITHER TENDED BY NOMADS OR FARMED—ARE THE MAIN LIVESTOCK.

Scientists believed that in ancient times the climate of the Near and Middle East was wetter than in recent centuries. This is supported by evidence that in the central Sahara Desert plants were growing that are characteristic of the Mediterranean region and also that the area is cut by dry water courses, which must once have carried water. Though more evidence exists, ranging from silt deposits to pollen analysis, the debate remains controversial since the caravan routes of ancient times passed through the same oases as now. Perhaps the best explanation is that there were fluctuations in climate with a general move towards arid conditions, but with periods of wetter conditions. During wetter periods it would have been possible for certain areas to be occupied that could not support a population of any number today.

However, it was human occupation rather than climate changes that had the most drastic effects on the region by changing the conditions necessary for successful occupation. Human activity such as tree felling has had a dramatic impact in terms of soil erosion and changes in the water-table.

Although the the hottest part of the earth's surface should in theory be the Equator, it is in fact the area from the Sahara through central Arabia to the Punjab, a little to the south of the Near and Middle East. This is due to the large land masses and their effects on heat radiation. Heat transfer is by air currents, particularly the jet streams. These are winds high in the atmosphere blowing at extremely fast speeds. Major jet streams from the Mediterranean are responsible for bringing very warm air from

SYMBOL OF PEACE
Human intervention created
major changes to the land and
water-table of the Near and
Middle East, when hillsides were
terraced for the planting of olive
trees. Many of these trees still
survive and bear the fruit that
has become a symbol of
peace worldwide.

PLANTS OF THE BIBLE
Date palm (*top*) and barley
(*bottom*) are among the
100 plants referred to by
name in the Bible, and are as
commonplace and vital today
as they were in biblical times.

the Sahara to the cold mountain ranges of western Asia. This warm air, combined with the melting snow in the Taurus Mountains of Turkey and the Zagros Mountains of Persia, creates the conditions for the annual flooding of the Tigris and Euphrates rivers. The agricultural cycle in Mesopotamia was dependant upon this.

Similarly, the unique pattern of air currents over the north-east Indian Ocean creates the conditions for the annual flooding of the River Nile. During the summer months, an easterly air flow at high altitude creates turbulence at lower levels and carries moist air from the Indian Ocean to the mountains of Ethiopia and the Sudan in eastern Africa. The heavy rainfall of the monsoon flows into the Blue Nile, eventually depositing silt in the enormously long, level stretch below the First Cataract, where the Nile flows through Upper and Lower Egypt to the Mediterranean Sea. By contrast, westerly jet streams prevail from November to March, in association with an air current that peters out by the time it reaches the coasts of southern Arabia, which are amongst the most arid in the world.

Whatever the minor changes in climate may have been, these very broad patterns have controlled the weather of the Near and Middle East during historical times. If anything, the area was rather more moist within the historical past, and able to support the size of population needed for the initial draining of the river marshes and the rise of civilizations in the two main river valleys.

Most of the Near and Middle East experiences a dry, hot climate, with large variations of temperature between day and night. As the great river systems of Egypt and Mesopotamia draw their waters from mountain ranges well beyond their main valleys, they can support agricultural economies that would otherwise be impossible. However, even in much of the desert there are marginal areas that can support sheep and goats on sparse areas of pasture.

There are therefore two distinct types of livestock production—wandering herds led by nomadic herdsmen and shepherds, and the settled livestock farming with which the modern, developed world is more familiar. The two systems can exist happily side by side, for the shepherds are not competing with the farmers for land. A further factor in ancient times lay in the different social structures of nomadic tribes and farming communities. The latter often lived in fortified settlements from which they farmed the surrounding agricultural lands, while the nomads traveled through the marginal lands and semi-desert areas without any close association with fixed settlements.

This accounts for tribal groups such as the Hebrews of patriarchal times (Genesis 12 onwards) that traveled over large distances and across "national" frontiers without much apparent hindrance from the settled peoples. The nomadic shepherds had to ensure that they were not competing with each other for routes to pasture lands, for it would have been fatal for one group to enter a marginal area where the ground had recently been grazed bare by another group. This explains why, in Genesis 13, Abraham and Lot agreed to take different parts of Palestine—they were nomads, rather than occupiers. To this day sheep and goats are still important and herded in large numbers in this area, for their milk and fleeces, and because they are able to travel over fairly long distances.

Cereals were the main agricultural crops, as wheat and barley are indigenous to the region. Barley was a currency in Mesopotamia as early as 2000 BC. Modern bread wheat is a hybrid crop, but the ancient native *emmer* wheat is still grown widely because it is a much hardier type.

When the flooded rivers of Mesopotamia and Egypt returned to their beds each year, they left a rich

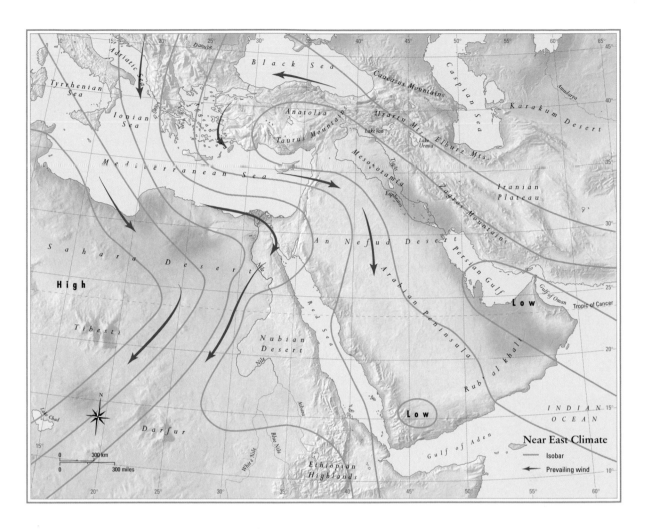

Near East Climate
— Isobar
← Prevailing wind

deposit of silt that formed the basis of the agricultural economy. As the ground dried, it was ploughed and irrigated by cutting water channels through the river banks. Unfortunately, this technique tended to divide the land into small squares, which encouraged salt formation when the water evaporated. As the salt content of the land increased, harvest yields diminished—a proportion of 0.5 percent salt prevents wheat growing, while 1 percent prevents barley growing, and 2 percent stops date palms from fruiting. Records from the 2nd Millennium BC show that this was a serious problem in Mesopotamia. In addition to cereals and dates, other indigenous crops of the Near and Middle East include olives, grapes, apricots, figs, pomegranates, cherries, and peaches. They were all cultivated together with vegetables such as lettuces and onions.

The Hebrew feast of Tabernacles, or Booths, was once a great feast of thanksgiving, marking the end of one year and the beginning of a new one. By modern reckoning, it falls in the autumn, in the months of September or October. It no longer marks the new year in Palestine, but its old significance

WEATHER PATTERNS
Prevailing weather patterns over the Middle East and northeast Africa create conditions where the annual flooding of the three main rivers—the Nile, Euphrates, and Tigris—produce an environment where consistent agriculture thrives, supporting a large population.

lingers on. A keen watch is kept for rain during the eight days of its harvest festivities. The long, dry summer of Palestine should be ending and the first rains falling to show that the agricultural year can start all over again.

The Mediterranean Sea is a small body of water compared with the Indian or Atlantic Oceans, so the weather in Palestine is influenced more by the great land masses of Asia and Africa than by the sea. Most of the rain that falls on Palestine comes from the Atlantic, carried on the predominantly westerly air flow, with support from the Mediterranean. Much of the moisture has been lost by the time the stream of Atlantic depressions reach the eastern end of the Mediterranean. Seasonal weather patterns determine whether the moist winds will reach Palestine at all, and if they will release their moisture in the area.

In winter, the Mediterranean had its own distinctive weather system. Atlantic depressions cross north-west Africa, Spain and Europe into the Mediterranean basin and on as far as Pakistan. As they travel, they become more constricted in area and more intense, even though they may not be as deep as the depressions with which northern Europe is so familiar. Rainfall results from warm, moisture-laden air hitting cooler air streams, producing water vapor. Very little of the moisture trapped in the Atlantic depressions is released in Egypt as there is no high ground to force the air up to cooler levels. But the mountains of northern Palestine, and the ridge stretching from Mount Carmel down to Judea, do so. Consequently there is a marked contrast in annual rainfall between the dry desert area south of Beersheba, which receives little rain, and the mountainous area of Upper Galilee where 55 inches (140 cm) falls, mainly between the months of November and April.

A different pattern prevails in summer. An area of high pressure, the "Azores High," extends across north-west Africa to as far as Libya and Egypt in the north-east. There, its edges meet a characteristic area of low pressure over Cyprus and southern Turkey. This blocks the Atlantic depressions or forces them further north, and the area of low pressure draws dry air from central Asia, which reaches Palestine as hot, dry south-westerly winds. These seem to come from much the same direction as the

A TIMELESS SCENE
For millennia, the River Nile has been an area of great fertility. These flood plains receive rich silt deposits from the annual flood every wet season for the growing of varied crops.

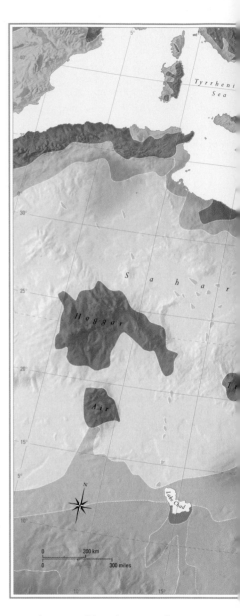

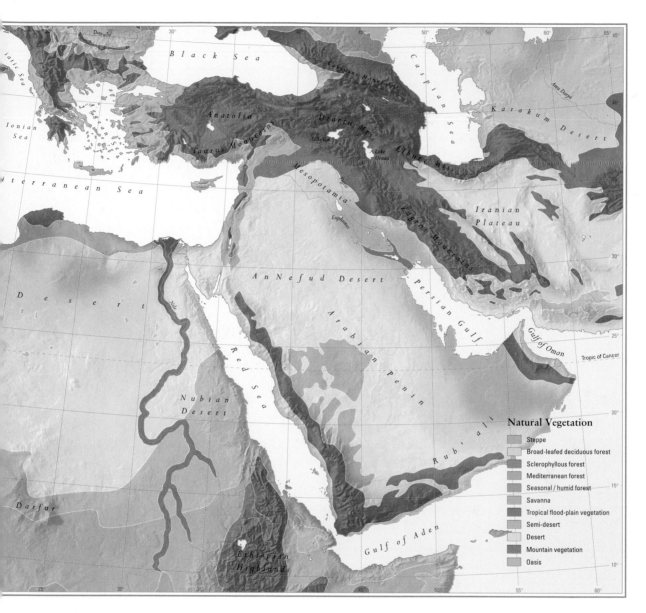

Natural Vegetation

- Steppe
- Broad-leafed deciduous forest
- Sclerophyllous forest
- Mediterranean forest
- Seasonal / humid forest
- Savanna
- Tropical flood-plain vegetation
- Semi-desert
- Desert
- Mountain vegetation
- Oasis

wet, winter winds, but the air carries little moisture and no rain falls.

In the wet months, the rain usually takes the form of heavy cloudbursts, which produce deep gullies in the steep sides of the Jordan Valley. Roadside notices warn of flash floods, which occur because the sun-baked ground is unable to absorb the deluge of water that falls in a short period. As a result, the roads are flooded over long distances. Under such conditions, it is essential to dam gullies and direct the water into irrigation channels.

The significance of water for Palestinian agriculture is dramatically demonstrated by the effects of

NATURAL VEGETATION

The vegetation types of the Bible Lands are predominately influenced by the weather patterns created by the land masses of Asia and Africa.

irrigation—crops grow to a sharp boundary where the irrigation ceases, to be replaced by brown, parched earth. Almost everywhere that water can be taken proves to be fertile land. An exception is the area around the Dead Sea, called the Salt Sea in ancient times. It lies only some 50 miles (80 km) from the Mediterranean, but is 128 ft (400 m) below sea level and has no exit for the incoming waters of the River Jordan. Instead, the water evaporates at a fast rate, causing high salt levels.

Yet even here, the abundant freshwater springs of Jericho, only 9 miles (15 km) north in the same deep rift valley, provide luxuriant oasis conditions for one of the oldest of all settlements. Springs make occupation possible down the western shores of the Dead Sea in biblical times, supplemented by dams in the deep gullies from the Judean hills. Such centers of population ranged from the great fortress of Masada, with its deep water cisterns on the top of the crag, to the Essene community at Qumran, where ritual bathing was an important part of life in the community.

Only the northern highlands of Palestine and the coastal area, as far as about 35 miles (60 km) inland, receive any appreciable and dependable amounts of rainfall. South of Gaza and Beersheba, rainfall is negligible, but evidence of ancient settlements in the Negev, the area south of Beersheba, suggest that it was either wetter in biblical times or very efficiently irrigated. Tree felling during historical times has also increased aridity and erosion, just as it has in Greece.

In the Bible, the area is described as "... a land of wheat and barley, of vines, of figs, of pomegranates, a land of olives, of oil, of honey, ... a land where the stones are of iron, where the hills may be quarried for copper ... your flocks and herds increase" (Deuteronomy 8:8–13). The farming Canaanites tended the fertile areas by day, returning at night to fortified centers that could withstand long sieges. Thus, when the Hebrews began their occupation in the 13th Century BC, Canaan formed a patchwork of city states combined in various alliances. The nomadic Hebrews soon adopted the Canaanite way of life, but this placed considerable strain on their religious traditions as they adapted them to agricultural needs.

Nomadic shepherds continued to graze sheep and goats through the marginal areas, as part of their long routes from Egypt to Mesopotamia. The area was also able to support a larger population than might be expected because of the great international trading routes that passed through it. The region exported grain, oil, wine, and honey, and was famous for the healing properties of the "balm of Gilead" (Genesis 37:25; Jeremiah 8:22). Luxuries and raw materials such as metals and wood were exported to Egypt.

Trading began to increase during the biblical period. However, the Philistines hindered Hebrew participation in this business by occupying the southern coastal area until the Hebrew King David gained control in about 1000 BC.

Palestine, which was settled by the Sea Peoples, was part of the so-called "Fertile Crescent" linking the vast, rich valleys inhabited by two ancient civilizations—the Egyptian and Mesopotamian. The Hebrews were one of the nomadic groups grazing their flocks on the sparse pastures between desert and fertile land.

In the Fertile Crescent, the two great civilizations of the Near and Middle East in ancient times grew up in two vast river valleys. The Nile supported the ancient Egyptians while the Mesopotamians

RAINFALL IN PALESTINE

Water is the key to agriculture in Palestine. Areas of higher rainfall along the coastal strip and the hill country of Judah and further north, support most kinds of agriculture, vines, wheat, olives, and dense woodland, especially in the north.

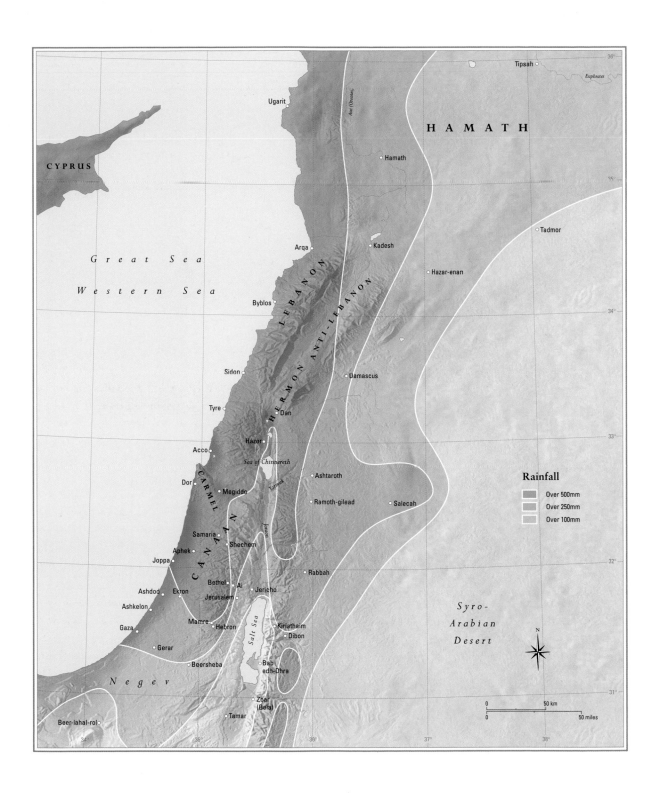

Tipsah

Euphrates

Ugarit

HAMATH

Hamath

Tadmor

CYPRUS

Arqa

Kadesh

Hazar-enan

G r e a t   S e a

W e s t e r n   S e a

Byblos

L E B A N O N

A N T I - L E B A N O N

H E R M O N

Sidon

Damascus

Tyre

Dan

Hazor

Acco

Sea of Chinnereth

Dor

C A R M E L

Megiddo

Yarmuk

Ashtaroth

Ramoth-gilead

Salecah

Rainfall

Over 500mm

Over 250mm

Over 100mm

Samara

C A N A A N

Shechem

Aphek

Joppa

Rabbah

Bethel

Ai

Jericho

Ashdod

Ekron

Jerusalem

Ashkelon

Syro-

Arabian

Desert

Mamre

Hebron

Salt Sea

Kiriathaim

Gaza

Dibon

Gerar

N

Beersheba

Bab edh-Dhra

N e g e v

Zoar (Bela)

Beer-lahal-rol

Tamar

0   50 km

0   50 miles

THE NILE
The annual flood of the
Nile provides continuing
fertility, the basis for creating
a vibrant civilization.

lived on the banks of the Tigris and Euphrates rivers. Between the two lies desert, the Dead Sea and Palestine. This tiny corridor of land provides the only fertile strip from the Persian Gulf to the Nile Valley. Its position was vital, as it linked the two valleys forming a long stretch of fertile land from one end of the region to the other. It became the major trade route between the civilizations.

Rising in the complex of great African lakes that straddle the Equator, the River Nile winds down through the Sudan and the eastern end of the Sahara Desert until it sprawls out into the fan-shaped swamp of river mouths and marshes that make up its delta. For most of its journey, it flows through desert, with minimal rainfall and no tributaries to feed it. The people who drained the marshes around the delta and learned to make use of the great river formed one of the oldest civilizations of the ancient world. The pyramids they built had been standing for more than 2,500 years when Jesus Christ was born.

The River Nile was the unifying factor for the peoples who lived along it. Its waters and the mud it left behind after the annual floods from the mountains of Ethiopia turned the desert into rich agricultural land and made Egypt the most dependable source of food in the eastern Mediterranean. Power shifted between the delta cities—Memphis in Lower Egypt, and Thebes, the capital of Upper Egypt, which ended where the First Cataract interrupted navigation from the coast. Beyond the First Cataract lay Nubia and, eventually, tropical Africa.

Beyond the desert to the east of Palestine was Mesopotamia—drained by both the Tigris and Euphrates, which in ancient time entered the Persian Gulf separately—some 125 miles (200 km) north-west of the present coastline. To the east, the area is bordered by a long mountainous region stretching from India to Turkey. Between the mountains and the desert, Mesopotamia was peopled, like Egypt, by civilizations that had learned to control the river waters and use them for their agriculture. Power was located at several centers—Sumer and Babylonia near the Persian Gulf, straddling the River Euphrates, and Assyria about 435 miles (700 km) to the north on the River Tigris. Beyond Assyria was Mitanni. For all its apparent strength, Mesopotamia was frequently threatened by incursions from eastern mountain tribes, and no single power managed to dominate all of Mesopotamia for long.

Beyond Syria to the north, the Hittites inhabited the area that is now Turkey. The Hittites briefly extended their power into the Fertile Crescent, but their land had nothing comparable to the great rivers to give continuity, and they were overrun by migrants from the west.

Throughout the Fertile Crescent, from the Persian Gulf to the borders of Egypt, independent nomadic shepherds grazed the sparse areas of pasture between the desert and the fertile land. The Hebrews were originally such a group.

The name Palestine is derived from the Greek for Philistine; the Philistines were among the the waves of Sea Peoples who arrived from the west at the end of the 2nd Millennium BC. They briefly dominated the southern part of the land bridge from the Jordan Valley to the Mediterranean. Before the Philistines, it was mainly occupied by the Canaanites and is referred to as Canaan by the Hebrews. Its long desert frontier to the east exposed it to penetration from the nomadic desert people, including the Hebrews themselves, while its strategic position between Egypt to the south and the Mesopotamian and Hittite peoples of the east and north made it a politically sensitive area. It seldom enjoyed peace, but its peoples profited from the international trade routes that passed through it.

From the south, the route from Egypt passed into the coastal area. Here the shifting sands forced travelers inland for some 12 miles (20 km), to pass through the town of Aphek and northward to the ridge of Mount Carmel.

The Philistines settled in this coastal plain, establishing themselves at Gaza, Ashkelon and Ashdod near the coast, and at Gath and Ekron further inland to the south of Aphek. From this coastal plain, minor roads led eastward up through the lowland hills of the Shephelah, which was densely populated, to the hill country of Judah and the deep rift valley of the Dead Sea, some 1,285 ft (400 m) below sea level. Beyond the Dead Sea lie mountain ridges, with steep gullies running down into the rift valley, and beyond these mountains the desert begins.

The Judean hills run northward, parallel with the Jordan Valley, until they turn north-west to meet the Great Sea, as the Mediterranean was called in biblical times, at Mount Carmel and form the northern limits of the coastal plain.

The major coastal route crosses the Carmel ridge to enter the Plain of Jezreel at the ancient fortress of Megiddo, where it then splits in to two routes. A western branch hugs the coast, and an eastern branch goes on to Hazor and Damascus. Jezreel means "God sows" in Hebrew, reflecting the fertility of this valley running from the Great Sea to the Jordan Valley, which is still more than 600 ft (180 m) below sea level where the River Jordan leaves the Sea of Galilee. This lake is called the Sea of Chinnereth in the Old Testament, and variously the Sea of Galilee, Lake of Gennesaret, and Sea of Tiberias in the New Testament.

Northward again, between the upper Jordan Valley and the sea, the land rises steeply into Upper Galilee. Above the Sea of Galilee was Lake Hulek, a small expanse of water now only marshland, just about at sea level. At the eastern side of the very top of the Jordan Valley is Mount Hermon with its snow-covered peak that marked the northern limits of Palestine or Canaan. The road to Damascus and Mesopotamia passes south of Hermon. The King's Highway, a route used mainly by nomads, ran from Damascus southward to Elath, situated on the Red Sea.

The towns of Beersheba in the south and Dan in the north marked the traditional limits of the ancient land of Israel. That area contains extreme geographical contrasts, including mountain ridges and the lowest point on earth, extremely fertile land, and desert-like terrain. Such conditions led to many kinds of peoples with vastly different ways of life settling there. The international trading routes through the region remained its most important feature.

The Ancient Near East in the Third Millennium

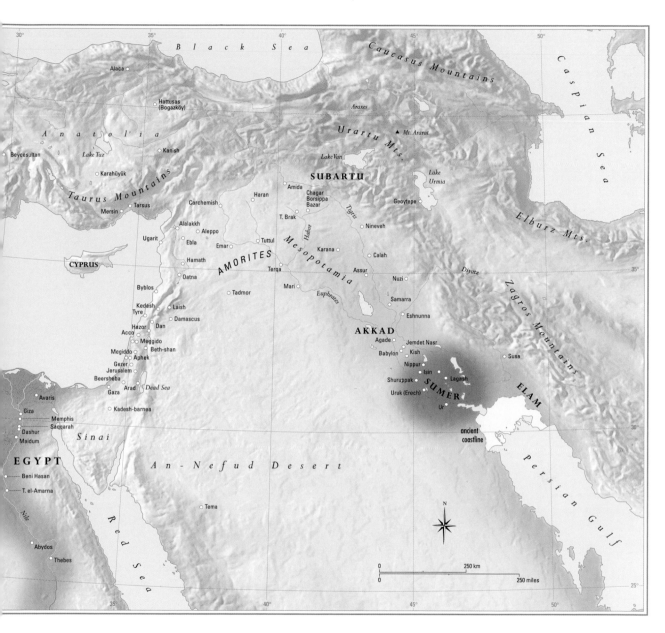

Black Sea

Caucasus Mountains

Alaca

Hattusas
(Bogazköy)

Araxes

Urartu Mts.

▲ Mt. Ararat

Caspian Sea

Lake Van

Lake
Urmia

Beycesultan

Anatolia

Lake Tuz

Kanish

SUBARTU

Amida

Geoytepe

Karahüyük

Chagar
Borsippa
Bazar

Elburz Mts.

Mersin
Tarsus

Taurus Mountains

Carchemish

Haran

T. Brak

Tigris

Nineveh

Alalakkh
Aleppo

Ugarit
Ebla
Emar
Tuttul

Habur

Karana

Calah

Assur

Nuzi

Diyala

Zagros Mountains

CYPRUS

Hamath

AMORITES

Mesopotamia

Terqa

Oatna

Byblos

Tadmor

Mari

Euphrates

Samarra

Eshnunna

Kedesh
Tyre
Laish
Damascus

Hazor
Acco
Dan

Meggido
Beth-shan

Megiddo
Aphek

Gezer
Jerusalem

Beersheba

Gaza
Arad
Dead Sea

AKKAD

Agade

Babylon
Kish

Nippur

Isin
Lagash

Shuruppak

Uruk (Erech)

Ur

SUMER

Jemdet Nasr

Susa

ELAM

Avaris

Giza

Memphis
Saqqarah

Dashur
Maidum

Sinai

Kadesh-barnea

ancient
coastline

EGYPT

An - Nefud Desert

Persian Gulf

Beni Hasan

T. el-Amarna

Nile

Tema

Red Sea

Abydos
Thebes

N

0 ____ 250 km

0 ____ 250 miles

**NEAR EAST IN THE 3RD
MILLENNIUM** By this date
powerful civilizations had
become well established in the
Fertile Crescent. Egypt traded
with Akkad and Sumer, in the
east along busy trade routes
leading through Palestine.

ARCHAEOLOGY OF THE BIBLE

TWO BRANCHES WITHIN THE SCIENCE OF ARCHAEOLOGY FOCUS ON THE BIBLE: BIBLICAL ARCHAEOLOGY, IN WHICH THE BIBLE LANDS AND SURROUNDING AREAS ARE SELECTED FOR STUDY, AND THE ARCHAEOLOGY OF BIBLE TEXTS, WHERE THE RESEARCH IS CENTERED ON ACTUAL MANUSCRIPTS.

Biblical archaeology is primarily a source of historical information. Taken in conjunction with the Bible itself and other evidence, it helps us to ascertain and understand the sequence of biblical events, and to build up a picture of what life was like in Bible lands in those times.

Many of the problems of biblical archaeology are those that are common to all branches of the science: the randomness of which items happen to survive, and the fact that organic materials such as leather, wood, and textiles generally fail to survive over such long timescales. The sheer vastness of potential sites for investigation, combined with limited resources, also presents problems. Further difficulties are raised by the inaccessibility of many sites because they are inhabited, or because they are sacred to Christians, Jews or Muslims—or all three. Political tensions in the area persist, and cause misery on every level. Despite these difficulties, impressive finds have been made and, as the science of archaeology has become more exact, these have contributed greatly to Bible scholarship.

Mesopotamia

The Fertile Crescent stretches from Sumeria at the top of the Persian Gulf, up the Euphrates and the Tigris rivers through Babylonia and Assyria, westward along the southern edge of the Armenian Mountains, southward through Syria and Lebanon to the Jordan Valley and down to the Dead Sea. This is the route that Abraham took, and it could be said that the civilizations of the Middle East followed the same path. The archaeological sites in Mesopotamia are rich sources of evidence, given their long history of occupation by technically and culturally advanced peoples with a well-developed social organization.

The ancient civilizations of Assyria and Babylonia dominated this area for centuries. Although both were occupied from prehistoric times, probably the most interesting archaeological work had been concentrated on the period when the city states of these empires were flourishing.

Excavation on the site of the city of Nineveh began in the middle of the 19th Century, and it was not long before reliefs and inscriptions were found, which clearly came from the palaces of Sennacherib and Ashurbanipal. Huge numbers of inscribed tablets were subsequently found, providing invaluable information about Assyrian literature and civilization.

The site at Calah, south of Nineveh, has revealed the ruins of ziggurats, and enough of the remains of the temple of Nabu and the palace of Ashurnasirpal II (879 BC) to enable scholars to construct accurate plans of the original buildings. Scriptures, ivories, and weapons were found in the outer town, and are thought to be booty captured by the Assyrian army.

Babylon was always a center of interest to explorers hoping to find the remains of the legendary Tower of Babel, described in Genesis 11:1–9. This has never been found, although some have identified it with the ruins of a ziggurat found a few miles to the south-west. A tablet had also been found, dated 229 BC, which describes a tower restored by Nebuchadnezzar, and some parts of this building were discovered in 1899. Excavations on the site of Babylon, from the mid-19th Century to the present, have uncovered much of the city of Nebuchadnezzar's reign. The city was surrounded by a massive double wall, and entrance to the inner city was through various large gateways. The most magnificent was the Ishtar Gate, the bricks of which were glazed and decorated with pictures of animals. Remains have also been found of temples dedicated to Ishtar and Marduk, and part of the palace throne room.

The site of the ancient city of Ur had revealed far older artefacts than any other site of the region. In the 1920s, the English archaeologist Sir Leonard Woolley discovered a royal cemetery dating back to 2500 BC, which contained the remains of gold and silver beakers, jewelry, weapons, and musical instruments.

The city of Mari is not mentioned in the Bible, but was one of the most important of the Mesopotamian city states. Excavations have revealed a huge palace there, dating from around 1775 BC, containing various treasures including over 20,000 cuneiform texts.

Egypt

The other main route for the advance of ideas and technology into Palestine was from Egypt. The trade routes from the Nile delta to the east followed the Mediterranean coast turning northward through

DAILY LIFE CAPTURED
This tablet, found in Diyala in present-day Iraq, depicts scenes of everyday life in Mesopotamia. It dates from around 2600–2500 BC. Pictographic tablets from the 4th Millennium BC provide evidence that writing originated in Mesopotamia.

Canaan, there is considerable archaeological evidence of Egyptian influence on Bible lands. The sites in Egypt are even more impressive than those of Mesopotamia, because what survived is not arbitrary and accidental. The Egyptians wanted their rulers to have luxury in the next world, so they stocked their tombs with the costliest artefacts possible, and they did so with the intention of preservation.

Archaeology in Egypt began when Napoleon invaded the country in 1798, and much of the best work has been carried out by French archaeologists, though it was the Englishman Howard Carter who discovered Tutankhamun's tomb in 1922. Tutankhamun died within a hundred years of Moses' lifetime, and from the extraordinary treasures of his tomb we can discover what it was like for Moses to grow up in an Egyptian palace. It also throws light on the construction of the tabernacle and the Ark of the Covenant, for elaborate tent-shrines and wooden chests were found in the tomb.

Another discovery relating to Old Testament accounts was that of the ruins of temples and palaces at Tanis, now San el-Hagar, in the Nile delta. The buildings dated from the 9th Century BC, but many of the blocks were inscribed with the name of Rameses II who lived 400 years earlier. These blocks are thought to have been transported from Qantir, 18 miles (29 km) to the south, where the remains of a city were discovered. The city is believed to be Pi-Ramesse, or the Raamses that the Israelites were forced to build by their Egyptian taskmasters (Exodus 1:11).

Canaan

Compared with the powerful empires to the east and southwest, the Israelites were a rough peasant people, with a less developed culture in the form of literature, art, or military or administrative skills. There are particular difficulties with some of the areas that conceal potentially valuable information. Damascus has been continuously occupied for thousands of years, and Jerusalem also dates back to ancient times. Unfortunately, because both are now huge, modern cities, major excavations are not usually possible.

Jericho is another ancient city, but it is uninhabited and so has been available for archaeological research. Work began in 1868, but it was not until the 1950s that significant research was carried out by the archeologist Kathleen Kenyon. She found that the remains of walls previously discovered and thought to be those destroyed by Joshua were, in fact, the ruins of buildings destroyed by an earthquake before 1500 BC. Pottery, weapons, and furniture of this period have also been found. Nothing had been found of the city that Joshua conquered, but ruins have been found nearby of the winter palace of Herod the Great, built in Jericho about 100 BC.

Such excavations that have been possible in Jerusalem have also yielded evidence of the many magnificent buildings erected by Herod the Great, particularly the temple, which was ruined in AD 70. However, probably the most interesting Herodian remains have been found in Masada, west of the Dead Sea. On this isolated rock, Herod built a huge fortress and two palaces. Israeli archaeologists made extraordinary discoveries at Masada in the 1960s. Reservoirs had been cut into the rock, with channels and aqueducts to supply water to the fortress. A strong double wall enclosed barracks, storerooms, and the two palaces, one built for administrative and official purposes, the other as a pleasure palace. Some of the most interesting discoveries were from a later period, when Masada was occupied by Jewish zealots who were using the fortress as a stronghold against the Romans in AD

66–73. The remains of a synagogue and ritual baths were found, as well as fragments of leather scrolls, some bearing biblical texts.

MORE OF EGYPT'S ENEMIES A Bedouin, a Hittite, a Nubian and a bearded Syrian have pride of place in the great temples of Rameses III.

ARCHAEOLOGY OF BIBLE TEXTS

In order to survive for very long periods of time, texts, and documents need to be written on stone or clay. These are slow to produce and extremely difficult to transport, so are characteristic of settled civilizations. The advanced societies surrounding the Palestine area left a great deal of writing behind. The library of Ashurbanipal at Nineveh, discovered in the 1850s, is an excellent source of information on Assyrian culture and contains, amongst other things, the *Epic of Gilgamesh*. This story is written on a clay tablet dating back to at least 1600 BC and tells the story of a great flood, with remarkable similarities to the Genesis story. Mari was another source of interesting clay tablets, giving an insight into political, military, religious, and social life in the region.

THE DEAD SEA SCROLLS

The Hebrew people did not dwell securely enough or for long enough anywhere to leave much writing in a durable form. Most biblical texts have come down to us as a result of repeated copying in a perishable medium such as leather or papyrus. This can give rise to doubts about the historical authenticity of the texts. The most important archaeological breakthrough in this field of research has

THE QUMRAN CAVES
The Dead Sea Scrolls were discovered iin several different sites here between 1947 and 1956.

been the discovery of the Dead Sea Scrolls.

The Qumran Caves

Qumran is the name of a wadi and a nearby ruin (Khirbet Qumran) just north-west of the Dead Sea. Early in 1947, a shepherd chanced upon a cave in the cliff face and discovered some jars containing bundles of old cloth and rolls of leather with writing on them. He returned a little later with friends and discovered more of the same.

The rolls went through many hands before they finally made their way to the American School of Oriental Research in Jerusalem, where an American scholar, John Trever, identified them as scrolls of Hebrew texts and realized that one of them was a copy of the Book of Isaiah, which appeared to be older than any known Hebrew manuscript.

The results of Trever's research were made public in April 1948, and in the following years archaeologists explored all the caves in the area. More scrolls were found, although these were mainly fragments, not as well preserved as they had not been kept in jars. Between 1951 and 1956, the archaeologists turned their attention to the Khirbet Qumran site and excavated a building there that appeared to have belonged to a community of people. The evidence suggested that they had occupied the site for two centuries up to AD 68, with a 30-year break between about AD 4 and 34.

The community seemed likely to have been a branch of the Jewish Essene sect; it was clear that this had been their property. Pottery found in the caves and the ruins were identical, and jars found in the ruins were similar to those that had contained the scrolls. Roman troops, marching through Palestine to suppress the Jewish revolt, would have reached the Dead Sea region in about AD 68. The Essene community at Qumran probably hid their scrolls at that point, and were either killed or fled from the area.

The Bible Scrolls

The manuscript that Trever identified as the Book of Isaiah was a roll of leather 24 inches (61 cm) long and ten inches (25 cm) high. It was made of 17 sheets sewn together end to end, and covered with 54 columns of Hebrew text. It has been confirmed that this scroll is around 1,000 years older than any existing Hebrew manuscript.

JEWISH DOCTRINE
Solomon reading the Torah, generally defined as God's instructions to Israel. The illustration is taken from a late 13th Century Hebrew Bible and Prayer Book.

Much can be derived about the Essenes' theology from the biblical commentaries. They thought of themselves as the righteous remnant of Israel and rejected the Hasmonean dynasty. They spoke of someone whom they called "The Teacher of Righteousness," but he appears to have been a leader and teacher of the sect rather than a Messiah figure. Members of the sect spent many hours in study of the law, and their interpretation of it was stricter than that of the Pharisees. Their interpretation of scripture was apocalyptic and they lived in expectation of the "end-time." They were expecting the last days to signal the end of the "epoch of wickedness" and awaited the coming of a Messiah of David's line who would be a warrior prince, leading the faithful of Israel to victory over the "sons of darkness." They also awaited a judgement and a general resurrection at the end-time.

Eventually fragments of every canonical book of the Hebrew Old Testament, except for the Book of Esther and some of the apocryphal books, were found in the caves. The manuscripts date from the period before AD 100. Most are in Hebrew, but some are in Aramaic. They include texts that the Masoretic scholars would have used and the text underlying the Septuagint. There are also texts similar to the Hebrew Pentatuech used by the Samaritans. The pieces are now all in the Israel Museum in Jerusalem and are still in the process of being studied and evaluated.

The Essenes

As well as the Bible texts found, the library in the Qumran caves included large numbers of texts that related to the life and beliefs of the community who lived there. Together with the remains of buildings and artifacts found in the ruins of Khirbet Qumran, they have enabled us to build up a picture of the "people of the scrolls" who lived there.

MANUAL OF DISCIPLINE
A detail from *Manual of Discipline*, one of the Dead Sea Scrolls. The work was found in the same cave as, among other pieces, the *War Scroll*, *Genesis Apocryphon* and *Thanksgiving Hymns*, and most importantly, the Book of Isaiah.

The non-biblical texts included Bible commentaries, books of rules for community life and regulations concerning worship. The evidence from these is close enough to what has been learned about the Essene sect from contemporary writers such as Josephus, Pliny and Philo, for most scholars to be convinced that the Qumran community were Essenes. This sect flourished during the period from about 100 BC to AD 100 and are of particular interest because of some similarities between their beliefs and practices and those of the early Christian Church.

Like other Essene communities, the people at Qumran lived a simple, rigorously disciplined and austere life. The Essenes believed in the practice of hospitality and communal ownership of property. There was a novitiate of two years before anyone could join the community; admission was preceded by a ritual ablution or purification in water; and solemn fellowship meals were held in secret.

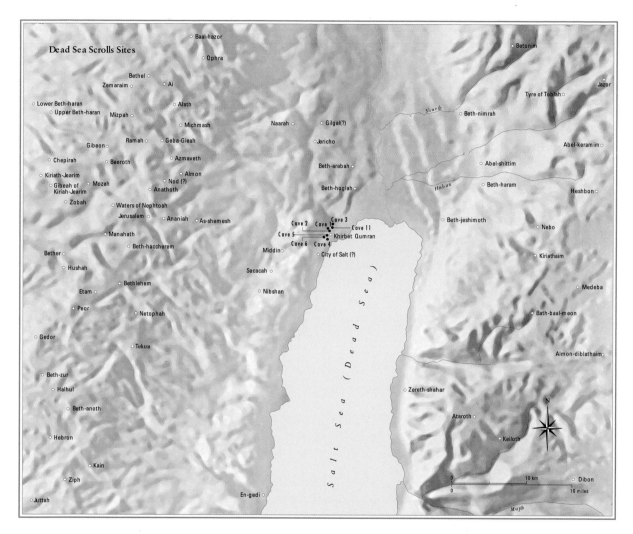

Dead Sea Scrolls Sites

Baal-hazor
Betonim
Ophra
Bethel
Zemaraim
Ai
Jazor
Lower Beth-haran
Alath
Tyre of Toblah
Upper Beth-haran
Mizpah
Beth-nimrah
Michmash
Naarah
Gilgal(?)
Abel-keramim
Ramah
Geba-Gieah
Gibeon
Jericho
Chepirah
Beeroth
Azmaveth
Abel-shittim
Kiriath-Jearim
Almon
Beth-arabah
Mozah
Nod (?)
Gibeah of
Kiriah-Jearim
Anathoth
Beth-haram
Heshbon
Zobah
Waters of Nephtoah
Beth-hoglah
Jerusalem
Ananiah
As-shemesh
Beth-jeshimoth
Nebo
Cave 2 Cave 3
Manahath
Cave 3
Cave 11
Beth-haccherem
Cave 5
Khirbet Qumran
Bether
Cave 6 Cave 4
Kiriathaim
Hushah
Middin
City of Salt (?)
Secacah
Medeba
Bethlehem
Etam
Nibshan
Peor
Netophah
Bath-baal-meon
Gedor
Tekoa
Almon-diblathaim
Beth-zur
Halhul
Zereth-shahar
Beth-anoth
Ataroth
Hebron
Keiloth
Kain
Ziph
Dibon
Juttah
En-gedi

Salt Sea (Dead Sea)

N

0   10 km
0   10 miles

Although there are some parallels to Christian rituals of baptism and communion here, there are also significant differences, and the Essene rituals did not have the sacramental significance of Christian ones.

WRITERS OF THE SCROLLS

The Essenes were located at the northern end of the Dead Sea. The monastic community was destroyed by the Romans because of its support of the revolt against Roman rule.

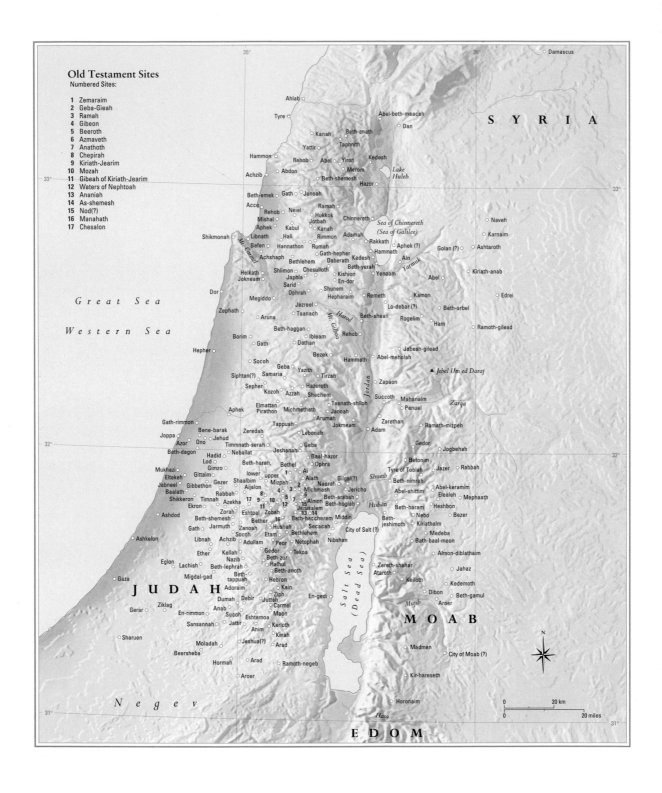

Old Testament Sites

Numbered Sites:

1 Zemaraim
2 Geba-Gieah
3 Ramah
4 Gibeon
5 Beeroth
6 Azmaveth
7 Anathoth
8 Chepirah
9 Kiriath-Jearim
10 Mozah
11 Gibeah of Kiriath-Jearim
12 Waters of Nephtoah
13 Ananiah
14 As-shemesh
15 Nod(?)
16 Manahath
17 Chesalon

SYRIA

Damascus

JUDAH

MOAB

EDOM

Great Sea

Western Sea

Negev

Sea of Chinnereth
(Sea of Galilee)

Lake
Huleh

Salt Sea
(Dead Sea)

Jebel Um ed Daraj

0   20 km
0   20 miles

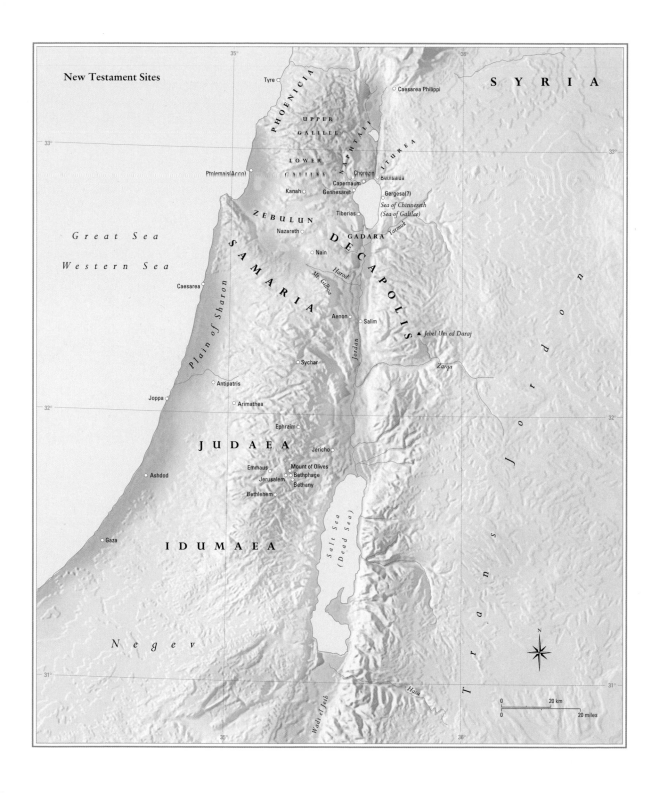

New Testament Sites

SYRIA

Tyre

Caesarea Philippi

PHOENICIA

UPPER
GALILEE

NAPHTALI

ITUREA

LOWER
GALILEE

Ptolemais(Acco)

Chorazin

Bethsaida

Capernaum

Gennesaret

Gergesa(?)

Kanah

Sea of Chinnereth
(Sea of Galilee)

ZEBULUN

Tiberias

Nazareth

GADARA

DECAPOLIS

Yarmuk

Nain

Great Sea

Mt. Gilboa

Harod

Western Sea

SAMARIA

Caesarea

Aenon

Salim

▲ Jebel Um ed Daraj

Plain of Sharon

Jordan

Zarqa

Sychar

Antipatris

Joppa

Arimathea

Ephraim

JUDAEA

Jericho

Emmaus

Mount of Olives

Ashdod

Jerusalem

Bethphage

Bethany

Bethlehem

Salt Sea
(Dead Sea)

Gaza

IDUMAEA

Transjordan

Negev

Wadi el Jeib

Hasa

N

0   20 km
0   20 miles

History of the Bible

WE ARE USED TO SPEAKING OF THE BIBLE AS A BOOK, BUT
IN FACT IT IS A COLLECTION OF BOOKS, OF DIFFERENT
AUTHORSHIP AND WRITTEN AT DIFFERENT TIMES, WHICH
HAVE BEEN SELECTED FROM A WIDER RANGE OF WRITINGS
TO MAKE UP THE BIBLE AS WE KNOW IT.

THE OLD TESTAMENT

The books of the Old Testament were written over centuries and some of them were added to or changed their form over many years. None of the original manuscripts have survived.

We use the word canon, meaning "a rule," to denote the list of books that are considered to be the authoritative collection. The Pentateuch, or Five Books of Moses (Genesis, Exodus, Leviticus, Numbers, and Deuteronomy), were already considered to be canonical by the time of Ezra and Nehemiah in the 5th Century BC. Recognition of the other books came at various times, but by the 2nd Century BC they were organized into the 24 books that make up the Hebrew Bible. These are the books that the first Christians would have recognized as authoritative, although the manuscripts still existed only as separate scrolls.

The earliest translation of the Hebrew scriptures was the Septuagint, a translation into Greek of all the Old Testament canonical books and some of those that are regarded by many as apocryphal. The Jewish translators (traditionally there were held to be 72 of them) started work on the Pentateuch in Alexandria in the first half of the 3rd Century BC. The other canonical books appear to have been translated by the end of the 2nd Century BC, and non-canonical books at various times down to the 1st Century AD. The Greek of the Septuagint was much influenced by the Hebrew original, and the accuracy is sometimes questionable, but the Septuagint was the basis for several subsequent

A NEW TESTAMENT SCENE
A detail from an engraving by
the German artist Albrecht
Dürer (1471–1528) illustrates
the Book of Revelation in one
of the earliest printed Bibles.

Baruch

This book is supposedly the work of Baruch, who was the scribe or secretary of the Prophet Jeremiah. It is, however, thought to be of composite authorship. It begins with an address by Baruch to the exiles in Babylon, with a prayer of confession, and prayers asking for forgiveness and salvation. The next section speaks in praise of wisdom, and the last chapters are a lament of Jerusalem for the captives, with a final assurance that they will be restored to their home.

Additions to Daniel

The additions to the Book of Daniel are derived from the Septuagint. The first addition comes in chapter three, and consists of the prayer of Azariah (Abednego) in the fiery furnace, in which he praises God's mercy and asks for deliverance; this is followed by the *Song of the Three Holy Children*, a hymn of praise uttered as they walk unharmed in the fire, with the refrain "praise and exalt Him above all for ever."

The story of Susanna follows from the end of the prophecies of Daniel. It tells of a beautiful and pious woman married to a Babylonian. Two elders of the people see her bathing and, when she rejects their advances, have her falsely accused of adultery. She is condemned to death but Daniel proves that the elders are lying. The people accept Susanna's innocence and put the elders to death. The last addition, the story of Bel and the Dragon, is written to mock idolatrous worship. In it Daniel proves to the King that neither the idol Bel nor a dragon are living gods.

Prayer of Manasses

In 2 Chronicles 13, the reign of Manasseh, son of Hezekiah, is described. He was a worshipper of Baal and other idols, and heavily involved in occult practices. He was captured by the Assyrians and in his affliction prayed to the God of his fathers for release. God heard him and Manasseh was released, subsequently restoring the worship of God to Judah. This book purports to be the prayer of Manasseh when in captivity. It is thought to be Jewish in origin, but was not known before the 3rd Century AD.

THE TOPOGRAPHY AND COMMUNICATIONS OF THE NEAR EAST
Along these ancient ways traveled ideas, spiritual and practical, as well as the commodities of everyday trade.

Topography of the Near East

——— International routes

1 and 2 Maccabees

These books are concerned with Jewish history between 175 and 134 BC and the heroic family of the Maccabees. It describes their struggles against the Syrian King, Antiochus Epiphanes, the Hasmonean Wars, and the line of priest-kings that they established. The first book was translated from a Hebrew work, in about 100 BC. The second book is said to be extracted from a work by Jason of Cyrene, of whom

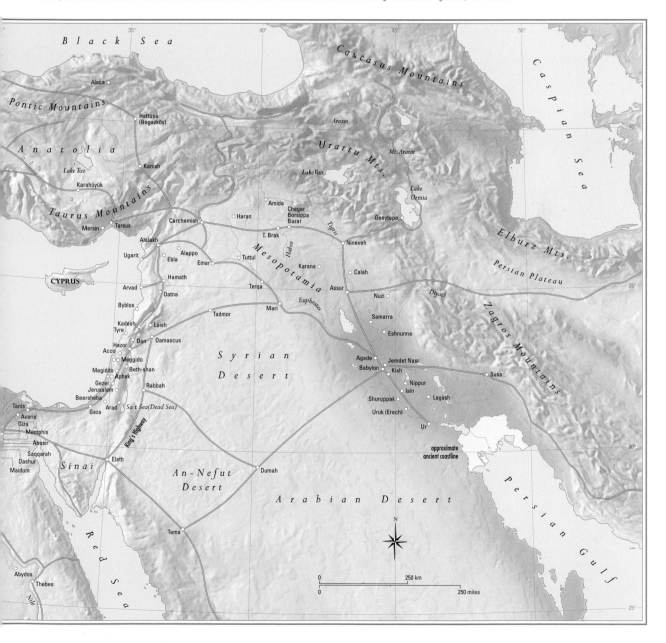

nothing else is known. It covers similar ground to the first, but there are various discrepancies, and the first is thought to be more accurate.

MANUSCRIPT BIBLES

The first attempts at translating parts of the Bible into English began in the 7th Century AD. These were not so much translations as poetical works of paraphrase, and no manuscripts have been found. The Venerable Bede is said to have translated the Gospel of John, but again we have no concrete evidence of the work.

One surviving work is that of the Lindisfarne Gospels, a beautifully ornamented manuscript, which was written in Latin in about AD 700, but with an English gloss or interlinear translation added in about AD 950. About 50 years after this, the West Saxon Gospels were produced. During the later Middle English period, various parts of the Bible were translated, but the most significant work was that associated with John Wycliffe (1320–84), a reformer whose aim was to make the scriptures accessible to the people. There were two versions undertaken in Wycliffe's name, parts of which were written by Wycliffe himself. Both were translations from the Latin Vulgate, but the English of the later version, made by John Purvey, one of Wycliffe's followers, is far more idiomatic and less archaic.

The Printed Bible

Although Bibles were being printed in Europe from the middle of the 15th Century, it was not until 1525 that the first Bible to be printed in English appeared. This was the Tyndale Bible, produced by William Tyndale, a scholar who, like Wycliffe, was determined to make the Bible more available to ordinary lay people. The first section of his Bible, the New Testament, was printed in Germany, partly in Cologne and partly in Worms. It was significant, not just as the first printed English Bible, but as the first to be translated from the Greek, rather than Latin. By 1534, Tyndale had produced a complete Pentateuch, the Book of Jonah and other selections from the Old Testament, translated from the Hebrew texts. In 1535, Tyndale was arrested for heresy and executed. His translation had been enormously influential, and much of his work is preserved in the English of the King James Version.

At the same time as Tyndale was working on his translation, a complete English Bible was being prepared by Miles Coverdale, whose work was published in 1535. Coverdale was ignorant of both Greek and Hebrew and his version was taken in parts from the Vulgate, from the German versions and from Tyndale. His was the first Bible in which non-canonical books were published under the separate heading of "Apocrypha."

In 1537, the English version known as Matthew's Bible appeared. Though it claimed to be "truly and purely" translated into English by Thomas Matthew, it was in fact the work of John Rogers, a friend and follower of Tyndale, and the Bible was not a new translation but a compilation of Tyndale's and Coverdale's work. Two years later, the Taverner Bible appeared, but this was no more than a revision of Matthew's Bible.

THE STORY OF DAVID AND BATHSHEBA
As Bible stories spread, their influence can be seen in folk art around the world. This 17th-Century Norwegian tapestry shows the crowned figure of King David and Bathsheba is probably the figure at the bottom.

Another very influential work appeared in 1539, the Great Bible, so called because of its large size. This was prepared by Miles Coverdale, commissioned by Thomas Cromwell, and was based on Matthew's Bible, drawing also from Coverdale's earlier work and Tyndale. This Bible was authorized by Archbishop Cranmer for distribution in all churches and to all people.

Under Mary Tudor, Protestants were persecuted and Bibles were taken from churches. Many Protestants fled from England, and a group of them who went to Geneva began to produce a Bible there. The Geneva Bible was mainly the work of William Whittingham, who based it on the Great Bible, but with attention paid to Hebrew scholarship.

This was the first Bible where the chapters were divided into verses. When Elizabeth I took over the throne in 1558, England became safe for Protestants again, but the work continued to be centered in Geneva. It appeared in 1560, with a dedication to Elizabeth, but did not receive official endorsement. Instead, the Archbishop of Canterbury, Matthew Parker, ordered a revision of the work, the Bishops' Bible, which appeared in 1568, with a revised version in 1572. This revised version was to be the basis for the King James Version.

Just as Protestants had fled to Europe in Mary's reign, Catholics fled in Elizabeth's reign. A group that had settled in France published a New Testament in Rheims in 1582 and an Old Testament in Douay in 1610. The Douay Version is mainly a translation from the Vulgate.

The Authorized or King James Version was commissioned by James I. Work started on it in 1604, and it was printed in 1611. The basis for the translation was the Bishops' Bible, but the translators consulted the Greek and Hebrew texts, and followed Tyndale, Matthew's, Coverdale or the Geneva versions when it seemed to them that these translations were more accurate. The first edition was marred by typographical errors; subsequent editions have corrected these and modernized spelling and punctuation. The King James Bible became the standard version for Protestants all over the English-speaking world. It is still much used today, and nearly all modern translations are indebted to it.

In 1870, work on a Revised Version of the King James was started, organized by the Church of England, but involved other denominations and American Bible scholars. The complete work was published in 1885 in England, with the American Standard Version published six years later.

Some 20th-Century versions that deserve mention include the Revised Standard Version of 1952, the Roman Catholic Jerusalem Bible of 1966, the New International Bible of 1978 and the best-selling and very popular modern version, the Good News Bible of 1976.

SPECIALLY NAMED EDITIONS

Some Bibles have been given special names because of a typographical error or peculiarity of vocabulary. Some of these are listed below:

Adulterous Bible: see Wicked Bible

Breeches Bible: Another name for the Geneva Bible. Genesis 3:7 says that Adam and Eve "sowed figgetree leaves together and made themselves breeches."

Bug Bible: Another name for the Coverdale Bible in which Psalm 91:5 reads, "Thou shalt not need to be afrayd for eny bugges by night."

Discharge Bible: An 1806 edition in which 1 Timothy 5:21 says, "I discharge thee ... that thou observe these things," instead of "I charge thee."

Ears to Ear Bible: An edition of 1810, where Matthew 13:43 reads, "Who hath ears to ear, let him hear."

Idle Shepherd: An 1809 edition in which the 'idol shepherd' of Zechariah 11:17 becomes "the idle shepherd."

Murderers' Bible: An 1801 edition where Jude 16 reads, "These are murderers..." instead of "murmurers."

Placemakers' Bible: The 1562 second edition of the Geneva Bible, where Matthew 5:9 reads, "Blessed are the placemakers."

Printers' Bible: An early 18th-Century edition where Psalm 119:161 says, "printers have persecuted me without a cause," instead of "princes."

Rebekah's Camels Bible: An 1823 edition that gives Genesis 24:61 as "Rebekah arose, and her camels," instead of "her damsels."

Standing Fishes Bible: An edition of 1806 where Ezekiel 47:10 has "And it shall come to pass that the fishes shall stand on it," instead of "fishers."

To Remain Bible: A Bible printed in Cambridge in 1805. A proofreader queried a comma; the editor pencilled in "to remain." As a result, Galatians 4:29 read, "he that was born after the flesh persecuted him that was born after the spirit to remain, even so it is now."

Treacle Bible: A name for the Bishops' Bible because of its use of "tryacle," for "balm," as in Jeremiah 8:22, "Is there no tryacle in Gilead?"

Unrighteous Bible: A Cambridge edition of 1653. In 1 Corinthians 6:9 the word "not" was omitted, leaving 'the unrighteous shall inherit the kingdom of God'; and Romans 6:13 read, "Neither yield ye your members as instruments of righteousness unto sin," instead of "unrighteousness."

Vinegar Bible: An Oxford edition printed in 1717 where the heading in Luke 20 reads, "Parable of the Vinegar," instead of "Vineyard".

Wicked Bible: Also called Adulterous Bible: An edition of 1632 in which the word "not" was omitted from the seventh commandment (Exodus 20:14).

Wife-hater Bible: An 1810 edition where Luke 14:26 says, "If any man come to me, and hates not his father ... and own wife also," instead of "his own life."

PATRIARCHS AND THEIR WORLD

GOD GAVE A SERIES OF COVENANTS TO A NOMAD NAMED ABRAHAM, HIS SON ISAAC AND GRANDSON JACOB. THESE AGREEMENTS ESTABLISHED HEBREW RIGHTS TO THE TERRITORY THEY LATER OCCUPIED. MEANWHILE, THE HEBREWS MIGRATED TO EGYPT. THEY TRAVELED UNDER THE PROTECTION OF JOSEPH, ONE OF JACOB'S SONS WHO HELD HIGH OFFICE THERE.

About 3000 BC, the Middle East witnessed the rise of a new culture based upon bronze. Soft and malleable copper no longer met the requirements of populations that were becoming increasingly urban. Harder metals were needed. The Bronze Age lasted until c. 1200 BC, and it is divided into three eras. The first period (3000–2100 BC) witnessed the civilizations of the Old Kingdom in Egypt, the Kingdom of Sargon of Akkad, and the Sumerian Empire in Mesopotamia. Following a blurred interim period, the Middle Bronze Age (2000–1600 BC) was integral to the flourishing of two great civilizations—the Middle Kingdom of Egypt (c. 2030–1640 BC) and a Mesopotamian culture under the rule of Hammurab (c. 19th and 18th Centuries BC). The Late Bronze Age (1600–1200 BC) saw large-scale international contact being developed between Egypt, Canaan, Assyria, the Hittites and Babylonia.

The key to the growth of urban settlements lay in the cultivation of cereal production made possible by extensive irrigation systems allowing wheat and barley to be grown extensively in the Tigris and Euphrates valleys in Mesopotamia. Permanent communities developed employing stone or mud brick as building materials. The oldest and most developed of these cities was Jericho (Tell es-Sultan) in the Jordan Valley. Although largely an agricultural settlement in its origins, Jericho evolved into a major regional center. Settlements spread with cultivation of once arid, semi-desert areas. As a result, many settlements appeared on the edge of the Mesopotamian riverine plain.

The importance of irrigation systems and of river systems was paramount, since the control of these meant richer agricultural yields and growth and domination over rival communities. For example, one of the major economic and strategic issues arising in Mesopotamia in the 2nd Millennium was the control of the Tigris and Euphrates and the struggle for water rights that ensued, which led to conflict between neighboring city states. Some methods would include damming the water above rival cities, to deprive them of water for irrigation, to be followed by the sudden release of the dam to create widespread flooding, as happened at Larsa (c. 1750 BC) under the Babylonian King, Hammurabi.

Once communities had moved beyond pure subsistence farming by the 4th Millennium BC, more people could engage in metalwork and building, along with other crafts such as pottery, ceramics, and jewelry. Stimulated by a parallel growth in commerce and transit trade between the communities of Greece, Mesopotamia, and Asia Minor came the rise of civilizations built upon the development of city states.

As Middle Eastern cities developed into state societies by the 3rd Millennium, they became administrative and manufacturing centers of urban civilization administered by rulers and literate élites. Earlier cities such as Jericho had been merely an agglomeration of populations; the new city states differed greatly, and demanded administration and a high degree of social and economic organisation. Such movements required the development of written languages, which allowed for greater sophistication in communication and a degree of centralized control in the hands of a ruling élite. These in turn managed the bureaucracies for the administrative functioning of societies and armies for external security. Increased literacy was crucial to the early civilizations for the development of law codes, tax records and accounts, such evidence providing historians with incredible details of these ancient societies. Hittite royal archives in the 2nd Millennium BC contained a wealth of historical information concerning government, religion, and mythology in Hittite society, and even a reference to a city known to us as Troy. In Mesopotamia and adjacent regions, cuneiform script was first utilized by the Sumerians, then by the Akkadians, Babylonians, Assyrians, and Hittites. Sumerian influence was so great that it lasted long after the disappearance of the Sumerian polity.

SAQQURA
The first pyramid ever built in Egypt as it might have looked on completion, part of King Djoser's sacred complex.

Archaeological excavations in Ur, Kish, Eridu, and other cities have unearthed clay tablets with cuneiform inscriptions that recorded commercial transactions and in a later period bore works of a religious, literary, and scientific nature. Historians have been provided with a wealth of material on Babylonian and Sumerian societies. The tale of a fruitless search for immortality by the Great King of Uruk, the *Epic of Gilgamesh,* recounts belief systems of Sumerian society in as well as emphasizing mankind's dependence upon the forces of nature and the great dangers of flooding. Similarly, the discovery of Hammurabi's law code, inscribed on a stele in the cuneiform script of Akkadian, the successor to Sumerian, tells us about the regulation of society.

In Mesopotamia in the 4th and 3rd Millennia BC, organized religions played a significant role in society, both in spreading belief systems and in the carrying out of administration from temples. Such activities probably included food distribution in times of poor harvests. The ziggurats in the temple of Uruk symbolized a transcendental link between heaven and earth in a society believing that kings came from heaven and laws were granted by the gods, who in their anthropomorphic forms generated security for the people and the fertility of their crops and livestock. The deities provided for different needs: Anu, the god of heaven; Enki, the god of water; and, Enlil, the god of the earth.

By the 2nd Millennium BC, the major cities were recording the arrival of non-local products such as gold, silver, precious stones, and wine together with raw materials essential for industrial and technological production (copper, tin, oil) as well as luxury items (textiles, precious objects, and furnishings). The interchange of luxury items carried by court officials, diplomats, and professionals, such as physicians, comprised part of international relations and the exchange of ideas. The major route followed, in and near Palestine, was named the Way of the Sea, and was the Philistine road from Egypt. Other routes were seaborne to the Philistine coastal cities and to the northern ports such as Joppa, Byblos, Tyre, and Ugarit. Sea trade from Africa and southern Arabia was augmented by caravans bringing gold and spices from Sheba through Tema to Dumah for Babylonia or westward to join the King's Highway through Midian, Edom and Moab into Palestine or northward to Rabbath-ammon and outward to Damascus. Lebanon contributed valuable wood, floated down the coast or dragged to streams for transit to eastern cities as tribute. In the north, tin from sources east of Mesopotamia was exchanged for copper, some tin reaching Canaan via Hazor from Mari.

Mesopotamia was one of the cradles of civilization with an agricultural economy reliant on irrigation and rich river alluvial soil, but subject to terribly destructive floods from the Tigris and Eurphrates rivers. About 3500 BC, from the north-east came the Sumerians, a non-Semitic people who pushed into the southwest part of Mesopotamia, establishing a number of wealthy city states, such as Babylon, Kish, Isin, Shurrupak, and Uruk. Around 2300 BC, a powerful wave of Semitic nomads surged into the region from the Syro-Arabian desert, the Zagros Mountains, and Persia,

The Ancient Near East in the Time
of the Patriarchs (2000–1550 BC)

- Old Assyrian kingdom
- Kingdom of Mari
- Old Babylonian kingdom
- Egypt
- Egyptian influence

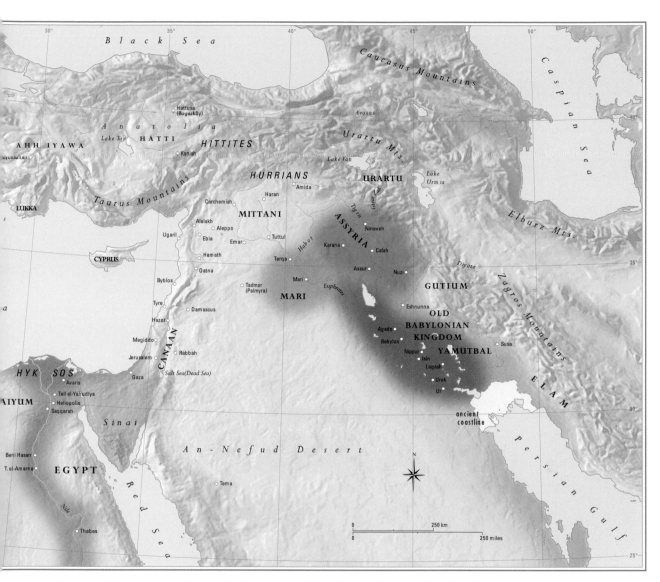

pounding the civilized areas, and laying the foundations of the Akkadian kingdom. The Akkadians were united by Sargon (c. 2334–2279 BC) who developed trade routes to the northeast, to Asia Minor in the west; Akkadian trade even reached the Indus valley. The Empire established by Sargon and his sons reached to the Persian Gulf, conquered Elam, Upper Mesopotamia, and Syria, ruling from sea to sea. The Akkadians fell to the Gutians, invaders from the Zagros Mountains again, but the Sumerians regained their power and their civilization enjoyed a renaissance, commenced by Utukhegal of Uruk who drove out the Guti. This Sumerian renewal witnessed a golden age of literature, Babylonian mathematics with evidence of squares and square roots, of cubes and cube roots, and the sums of squares and cubes required for the numerical evaluation of cubic equations

THE KING'S HIGHWAY
(far right)
Major routes between Egypt, in the west, connecting to the major states of Mesopotamia, passed through the bottleneck of Palestine. The Promised Land of the Hebrews proved to be of great interest to the superpowers of the Biblical period. Egyptians, Assyrians, Persians, and others all passed through this small but strategic area.

and exponential functions. The mud brick buildings have not survived, so the design of the Hanging Gardens of Babylon is an assumption.

Toward 2000 BC, Amorites and Semites from the Syro-Arabian desert settled in Mesopotamia leading to the dynasty of the Amorite, Sumuabum of Babylon. Under Hammurabi's leadership, Babylon defeated Mari, and established an empire of letters, including 20,000 inscribed clay tablets from Mari alone. However, Babylonian power declined in the face of Kassite invasions from the northeast, being followed by Hurrian invasions, and biblical Horites, drifting in from the Caucasus. Around 1500 BC, the Hurrians established the northern Mesopotamian Kingdom of the Mitanni, conquered by the Assyrians about 1300 BC. In turn, the Assyrians were pressed by the Arameans, but an Assyrian world empire emerged, its highest level of ascendancy being under Tiglath-pileser I.

Mesopotamian literature has left behind many texts. These are invaluable because they often reflect the conditions of the people and their belief systems. The Sumerians refer to their freshwater god, Enki, who fertilizes the goddess Ninhursag, the earth-mother. In his seed are found the origins of trees and the myth demonstrates the importance the Sumerians accorded to water for irrigation and for life in this "Paradise Myth." Another tale witnesses the conflict between pastoralism and an agricultural lifestyle. Instead of the violence between Cain and Abel in Genesis 4, the Sumerian myth is located in the realm of the gods, and the conflict between Dumuzi, god of shepherds, and Enkimdu, the farmer's god, ends with a happy reconciliation. Equally interesting is the survival of a flood story. The chief character, Ziusudra, like Noah, receives a heavenly message that the gods were planning to inundate the earth. In order to survive he is advised to build a boat. The myth ends thus:

"AFTER, FOR SEVEN DAYS (AND) SEVEN NIGHTS,

THE FLOOD HAD SWEPT OVER THE LAND,

(AND) THE HUGE BOAT HAD BEEN TOSSED ABOUT BY THE WINDSTORMS ON THE GREAT WATERS,

UTU [THE SUN GOD] CAME FORTH, WHO SHEDS LIGHT ON HEAVEN (AND) EARTH,

ZIUSUDRA OPENED A WINDOW OF THE HUGE BOAT,

THE HERO UTU BROUGHT HIS RAYS INTO THE GIANT BOAT,

ZIUSUDRA, THE KING,

PROSTRATED HIMSELF BEFORE UTU,

THE KING KILLS AN OX, SLAUGHTERS A SHEEP."

King Sargon was the subject of a myth reminiscent of Moses in the bulrushes, as written in Exodus 2:1–10

"SARGON, THE MIGHTY KING, KING OF AGADE, AM I.

MY MOTHER WAS A CHANGELING (?), MY FATHER I KNEW NOT.

THE BROTHER(S) OF MY FATHER LOVED THE HILLS.

MY CITY IS AZUPIRANU, WHICH IS SITUATED ON THE BANKS OF THE EUPHRATES.

MY CHANGELING MOTHER CONCEIVED ME, IN SECRET SHE BORE ME.

SHE SET ME IN A BASKET OF RUSHES, WITH BITUMEN SHE SEALED MY LID.

SHE CAST ME INTO THE RIVER WHICH ROSE NOT (OVER) ME.

THE RIVER BORE ME UP AND CARRIED ME TO AKKI, THE DRAWER OF WATER.

AKKI, THE DRAWER OF WATER LIFTED ME OUT AS HE DIPPED HIS E(W)ER.

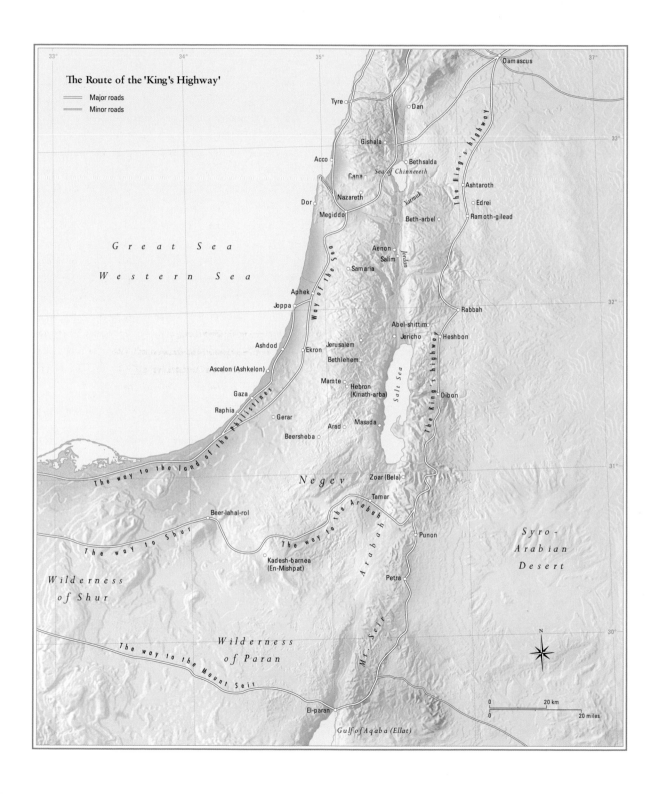

The Route of the 'King's Highway'

Major roads
Minor roads

Damascus

Tyre
Dan

Gishala
Bethsalda
Acco
Sea of Chinnereth
Cana
Ashtaroth
Nazareth
Edrei
Dor
Yarmuk
Ramoth-gilead
Megiddo
Beth-arbel

G r e a t   S e a

Aenon
Salim
W e s t e r n   S e a
Samaria
Jordan

Aphek
Joppa
Rabbah

Abel-shittim
Jericho
Heshbon
Ashdod
Jerusalem
Ekron
Bethlehem
Ascalon (Ashkelon)
Salt Sea
Mamte
Gaza
Hebron
(Kiriath-arba)
Dibon
Raphia
Gerar
Arad
Masada
Beersheba

N e g e v
Zoar (Bela)

Tamar
Beer-lahal-rol
S y r o -
A r a b i a n
Punon
D e s e r t
Kadesh-barnea
(En-Mishpat)
Petra

Wilderness
of Shur

W i l d e r n e s s
of Paran

N

El-paran
0   20 km
0   20 miles

Gulf of Aqaba (Ellat)

AKKI, THE DRAWER OF WATER, (TOOK ME) AS HIS SON (AND) REARED ME.

AKKI, THE DRAWER OF WATER, APPOINTED ME AS HIS GARDENER.

WHILE I WAS A GARDENER, ISHTAR (GODDESS OF LOVE) GRANTED ME (HER) LOVE…"

The *Epic of Gilgamesh* provides a story, too, echoing Ziusudra, predating Biblical Noah. Gilgamesh, on his journey searching for everlasting life, meets his ancestor Utnapishtim, who relates the event of a ruinous flood once sweeping the earth. The wise god Ea, counsels him to build a ship to escape the danger. The ancient man stated:

"WHEN THE SEVENTH DAY ARRIVED,

I SENT FORTH AND SET FREE A DOVE.

THE DOVE WENT FORTH, BUT CAME BACK;

SINCE NO RESTING-PLACE FOR IT WAS VISIBLE, SHE TURNED ROUND.

THEN I SENT FORTH AND SET FREE A SWALLOW.

THE SWALLOW WENT FORTH, BUT CAME BACK;

SINCE NO RESTING-PLACE FOR IT WAS VISIBLE, SHE TURNED ROUND.

THEN I SENT FORTH AND SET FREE A RAVEN.

THE RAVEN WENT FORTH AND, SEEING THAT THE WATERS HAD DIMINISHED,

HE EATS, CIRCLES, CAWS AND TURNS NOT ROUND.

THEN I LET OUT (ALL) TO THE FOUR WINDS AND OFFERED A SACRIFICE.

I POURED OUT A LIBATION ON THE TOP OF THE MOUNTAIN."

The question remains, are these themes borrowed directly by the Bible or were these tales a common tradition amongst Middle Eastern peoples who were dominated, nurtured, and occasionally killed by the elemental forces of fierce floods or, indeed, something other.

The Hittites are another people mentioned in the Bible, ancient Egyptian and Mesopotamian documents attesting that this people played an important part in the international politics of the day. The Bible is especially significant in showing the existence of Hittite inhabitants of Canaan, Biblical writers believing that the Hittites belong in north Canaan rather than Anatolia. Abraham is said to have bought a cave at Hebron from the "sons of Heth" (Genesis 23), and Esau married some Hittite girls (Genesis 26:34; 36:2). Uriah, one of David's soldiers, was an Hittite (2 Samuel 11:3). Solomon's wives included Hittite princesses (I Kings 11:1), and he traded with Hittite kings ((2 Chronicles 1:17). Finally, when the Arameans were besieging the city of Samaria, they fled believing rumors that Hittite forces were coming to help Israel (2 Kings 7:6). Where, then, did the Hittites fit into the ancient world?

The Hittites were an Indo-European people, probably originating beyond the Black Sea, and invading Anatolia in the 2nd Millennium BC. After defeating the indigenous population, the Hittites, under Labarna, conquered nearly all central Anatolia, founding his kingdom's (known as Hatti) capital at Hattusas (present-day Bogazköy). King Hattusilis (1650–1620 BC) extended Hittite power over northern Syria, his grandson defeating Aleppo and conquering Babylon (c. 1590 BC). The most powerful Hittite ruler was Suppiluliumas I (1380–1346 BC) who razed the capital city of the Mitanni and projected his power to Carchemish, which became a dependency along with Ugarit and Aleppo. The Assyrian vassals of the Mitanni shrugged off their overlords and built their own state with a capital at Ashur, but a Mitanni rump state survived as a buffer between rival empires. Hittite power

infiltrated the Aegean and trickled into Lebanon where conflict with Egypt broke out with a drawn battle at Kadesh. Further disputes were prevented by a treaty between Pharoah Rameses II and Mutuwallis of Hatti in 1275 BC, detailing a mutual defense agreement and a dynastic marriage. Soon after 1200 BC, the Hittite state collapsed under attack from migrating Sea Peoples, with Anatolia being overrun by Phrygians. However, many city states retained their Hittite identity, Carchemish in particular.

At the other end of the Fertile Crescent was Egypt, dependent for its agricultural survival upon the annual floods of the Nile fertilising the riverine field system. Egypt's contacts with the outside world were dictated by its natural boundaries. To the west and east, extensive deserts protected the Nile Valley. Southward, rocky, desert upland secured the border, and in its upper reaches the Nile was difficult to navigate owing to rapids. The northern frontier was defined by the Mediterranean, leaving the people to live safely along the fertile river banks and delta of the Nile. At first there were two kingdoms, Lower and Upper Egypt, but these were unified around 3000 BC. Pharoah Senusret III (1878–1843 BC) invaded Palestine along the Way of Horus to Gaza and beyond as far as Shechem. Egyptian artifacts from this period have been found at Bethsam, Megiddo, Gezer, Jericho, Lachish, and Sharuhen. Trade also flourished with Egyptian artifacts discovered at Byblos, Qatna, and Ugarit, with known trade routes extending to Anatolia, Cyprus and Crete. Despite later internal divisions and Lower Egypt falling under the domination of the Hyksos (usually translated as "rulers of foreign lands"), these Semitic-Asiatics were expelled about 1580 BC.

The Egyptians utilized the chariot, a weapon adopted from the Hyksos, to expand their power into Canaan and beyond. Pharoah Thutmose III (1479–1426 BC) decided to reaffirm Egyptian power in Palestine commenced by his grandfather, Thutmose I. He had attacked the Mitanni, erecting a stele on the banks of the Euphrates claiming it as his northern border. A monumental gate at Karnak lists place names from Byblos to Sumur, suggesting that this campaign might have been sea-borne. Thutmose III invaded Palestine 17 times. He firstly marched via Gaza to Joppa, engaged and defeated an alliance of city states at Aruna, and lay siege to Megiddo, taking it after seven months. He eventually reached the Euphrates, and erected another stele placed next to his grandfather's. Kadesh, the last remaining Hyksos city, was also defeated. After 1400 BC, Egyptian foreign policy became more peaceful during the Amarna period. Letters found at Amarna, addressed to Pharoahs Amenhotep III and IV, mention a large number of virtual city states, amongst others being Ashkelon, Hebron, Jerusalem, Gezer, Shechem, Megiddo, Acco, Damascus, Tyre, and Byblos.

The strip of land joining Egypt to the seats of power on the Fertile Crescent is Canaan or Palestine. Two major highways traversed the land. The Way of the Philistines and Way of the Sea advanced along the coastal plain joining Raphia and Gaza to Tyre before dividing with roads going north and to Damascus. The second route, the King's Highway, passed south from Damascus through the highlands east of Lake Galilee and the Dead Sea. The road splits into two: one road leads west along the Way of Arabah and the Way to Shur through Beth-lahel-roi to Egypt; the other continues south through Punon, Petra and the Gulf of Eilat (Aqaba). The early history of the Israelites places the Patriarchs and their history in this Canaanite locale and international environment. Canaanite city states peppered the Negev and Judaean mountains as far north as

Gishala, Bethsaida and Ashtaroth. Canaan is divided into roughly three parts: the long narrow strip along the Mediterranean Sea known as Phoenicia; Aram, the area of the Aramean city states, stretching from the Huran, south of Damascus to the last Hittite states near the Euphrates; and Mount Lebanon to the west. The land fought over by the Israelites includes the low hill country of the Shephelah and the hill lands, now known as the West Bank, but previously as the old kingdoms of Israel and Judah. Into this territory came the Israelites after their flight from Egypt under Moses, most probably in the reign of Rameses II.

BURIAL PLACE OF THE PATRIARCHS
This reconstruction illustrates the original Herodian construction at Machpelah. The cutaway section shows the original cave where Abraham and Sarah are buried. A mosque now occupies the site.

THE JOURNEYS OF ABRAHAM

"NEITHER SHALL THY NAME ANY MORE BE CALLED ABRAM, BUT THY NAME SHALL BE ABRAHAM; FOR A FATHER OF MANY NATIONS HAVE I MADE THEE. AND I WILL MAKE THEE EXCEEDING FRUITFUL, AND IT WILL MAKE NATIONS OF THEE, AND KINGS SHALL COME OUT OF THEE."   GENESIS 17:5–6

The Hebrews were latecomers to history. Across the Bible lands, civilizations and cultures had arisen and fallen for hundreds and thousands of years before Abraham was born. The ancestors of Israel's peoples were a mixture of many groups, although predominantly northern Semitic, perhaps Amorite or Aramean stock, who entered Palestine in the 2nd Millennium BC. These peoples sometimes found their way to Egypt during a time of low rainfall whilst pursuing a semi-nomadic lifestyle; they may have lived as virtual state slaves before rebelling and fleeing under Moses. Whatever the historical interpretation, many vicissitudes must have followed wandering clans and tribes. The stories of the Patriarchs possibly includes the type of adventures met while developing a particular religion, a normative Yahwehist Hebrew faith, bolstered by the unconditional support of God in a covenant that shaped Israelite national hopes. The biblical account of events and Abraham's life is rooted in traditions based on oral transmission rather than by historical records, so no true biography as we understand it can be written. The biblical story of Abraham encapsulates the tragedies, drama and dreams of a wandering people seeking somewhere as a stable home, but promised Canaan by their God.

Terah, a descendant of Shem, lived in the city of Ur of the Chaldees, where his sons were born—Abram, Nachor, and Aran. Terah, under divine inspiration, took Abram and his wife, Sarai (his half-sister), and Lot, son of the deceased Aran, traveling to Haran where he died. Then, at the call of God, Abram, Sarai, and Lot, and a party of people they had gathered in Haran, journeyed into Canaan to

DIVINE COVENANT
God's covenant with Abraham is illustrated by this excerpt from a 14th-Century French manuscript.

CREATION STORIES *(below)*
The opening chapters of the Book of Genesis were shaped by nomadic Hebrew herdsmen who preserved them in their oral traditions.

ABRAHAM'S JOURNEY
According to Jewish tradition, Abraham, the first Patriarch, left his home in Ur to migrate westward through the Fertile Crescent, eventually reaching Canaan. Though there is no scientific evidence to support the existence of Abraham as a person, archaeology confirms that Semitic shepherds lived a nomadic life at this time—probably seeking a suitable homeland in which to establish permanent settlements. Some settled in Canaan; others traveled east to Egypt or west to Mesopotamia.

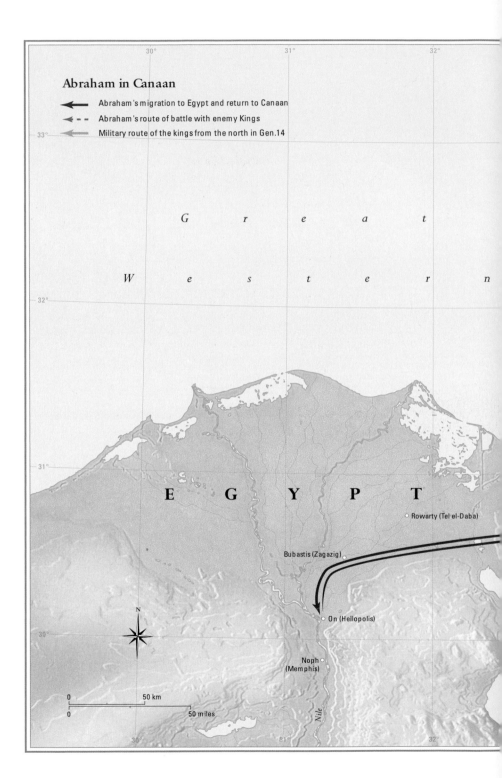

Abraham in Canaan

← Abraham's migration to Egypt and return to Canaan

◄ - - Abraham's route of battle with enemy Kings

← Military route of the kings from the north in Gen.14

G r e a t

W e s t e r n

E G Y P T

Rowarty (Tel el-Daba)

Bubastis (Zagazig)

On (Hellopolis)

Noph (Memphis)

Nile

0   50 km
0   50 miles

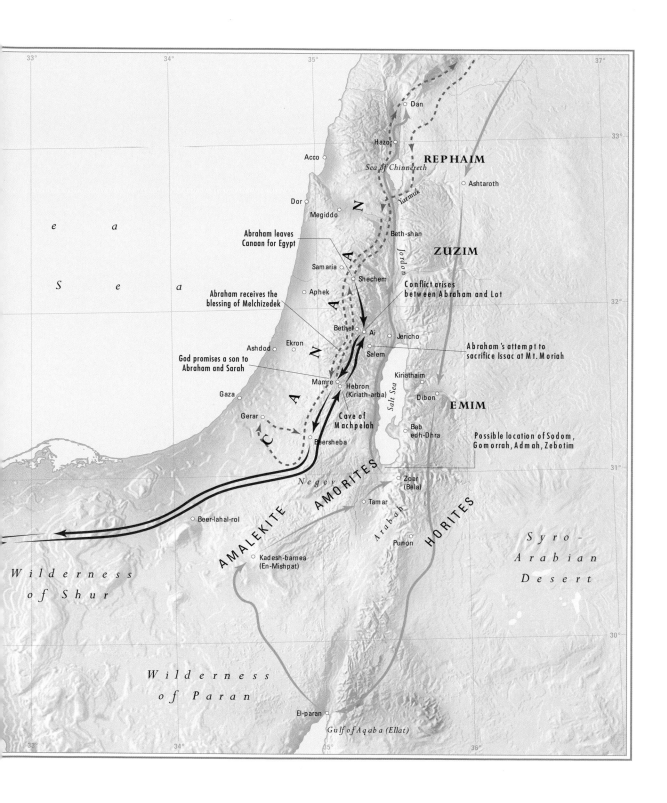

33°

34°

35°

36°

37°

33°

○ Dan

○ Hazor

REPHAIM

Acco ○

Sea of Chinnereth

○ Ashtaroth

Dor ○

Megiddo ○

Yarmuk

Beth-shan ○

ZUZIM

Abraham leaves
Canaan for Egypt

C
A
N
A
A
N

Samaria ○

Shechem ○

Conflict arises
between Abraham and Lot

32°

Aphek ○

Abraham receives the
blessing of Melchizedek

Bethel ○

Ai ○

Jericho ○

Ashdod ○

Ekron ○

Salem ○

Abraham's attempt to
sacrifice Issac at Mt. Moriah

God promises a son to
Abraham and Sarah

Mamre ○

Kiriathaim ○

Gaza ○

Hebron
(Kiriath-arba)

Dibon ○

EMIM

Gerar ○

Cave of
Machpelah

C
A
N

Beersheba ○

Bab
edh-Dhra ○

Possible location of Sodom,
Gomorrah, Admah, Zebotim

31°

Negev

Zoar
(Bela) ○

Beer-lahal-rol ○

AMALEKITE

AMORITES

Tamar ○

Arabah

HORITES

*Syro-
Arabian
Desert*

Kadesh-barnea
(En-Mishpat) ○

Punon ○

*Wilderness
of Shur*

30°

*Wilderness
of Paran*

El-paran ○

Gulf of Aqaba (Ellat)

33°

34°

35°

36°

Sea

e   *a*

S   *e*   *a*

Jordan

Salt Sea

EGYPTIAN TEMPLES
In deference to Sun, the principle god of Egypt, temple buildings were carefully orientated to ensure the rays of the rising sun shone into the innermost sanctuary.

Sichem and Beth-el where Abram built an altar. When a severe famine hit Canaan, Abram moved into Egypt. Fearing Sarai was so beautiful that he might be killed for her, he claimed she was his sister. Reports of her attractions reached the Pharoah who took her into his harem, but finding out the truth of her relationship with Abram, returned her untouched. He berated Abram for his lie and dismissed him from Egypt. Returning to Beth-el in Canaan and realising that their combined herds and flocks were too great for the land to sustain, which would lead to strife between their respective herdsmen, Abram and Lot agreed to part company. Lot chose to enter the plain of Jordan, while Abram stayed in Canaan. There, God told Abram that all the land around would be his, and his progeny would be numberless. Abram then moved his tents to Mamre in Hebron.

The political environment erupted when the kings of nearby Sodom and Gomorrah rebelled against their overlord, Chedorlaomer, King of Elam. The ensuing conflict that developed amongst nine northern kings saw the Elamite king victorious. Lot's community and flocks were seized while returning home. Hearing about his nephew's capture, Abram led 318 men in a surprise attack on Elam who had reached Dan. While journeying home with his victor's booty, Abram was met by Melchizedek, King of Salem and priest, who blessed him. Abram gave him tithes of his spoils retaining nothing for himself.

Meanwhile, Sarai who was childless, told Abram to take her handmaid, Hagar, as a concubine, a common practice in the circumstances, resulting in the birth of Ishmael. Thirteen years later, God appeared to Abram and promised him a son by Sarai saying his legacy would be a great nation. Symbolically, he changed Abram's name to Abraham and Sarai's to Sarah in a covenant, which also established the rite of circumcision.

While sitting in his tent at Mamre, Abraham was approached by God and two angels in human form and offered them hospitality. The promise of a son, Isaac, was renewed but when Sarah laughed at her child-bearing years being over, she was rebuked by the Lord. Abraham was informed about the impending destruction of Sodom and Gomorrah for the sin of wickedness. He pleaded with God to spare the cities. God agreed that he would do this if he could find ten righteous men there. The ten could not be found and God destroyed both cities. Lot and his two daughters were preserved from the destruction sheltering in a cave . They made him drunk, committed incest, and the children they bore were the eventual fathers of the Moabites and Ammonites.

Seeing the smoke of destruction over the destroyed cities, Abraham moved south to Gerar. Again fearing for his life, Abraham stated that Sarah was his sister. She was taken by the King of Gerar, Abimlech, but her status was revealed to him in a dream and she was returned untouched. The king chastized Abraham for his deception. The two men were reconciled and God, in return, cured all the barrenness in the king's household.

Sarah gave birth to Isaac and he was circumcised on the eighth day. Jealous of Ishmael, Sarah had him and Hagar, the Egyptian, ejected into the wilderness. God saved them from dying of thirst, promising Hagar that her son would be the progenitor of a nation. Islamic tradition cites Ishmael as the father of the Arabs.

Genesis refers to a dispute between Abraham and Abimlech over a well that ended with a treaty between them. Abraham dug a new well, naming it Beersheba. At Jehovah-jireh, Abraham next engaged in a trial of faith and God commanded him to sacrifice Isaac. Just as Abraham was going to strike his son, his hand was stayed by an angel and a ram was sacrificed instead, this act instructing that human sacrifice was to cease forthwith. At Kirjath-arba, Sarah, aged 127 died being buried in a cave in Machpelah, which Abraham had bought from Ephron the Hethite (Hittite).

Abraham's career continued when he found Rebekah, a wife for Isaac, from the city of Nachor where his brother, Nahor, resided. Thus, Isaac married into the clan left behind in Haran in Mesopotamia. Abraham married Keturah who bore him six sons. He finally died, aged 170, leaving all his possessions to Isaac, and was buried in the cave at Machpelah.

Isaac, Jacob, and Joseph

"AND IT CAME TO PASS THE SAME DAY, THAT ISAAC'S SERVANTS CAME, AND TOLD HIM CONCERNING THE WELL WHICH THEY HAD DIGGED, AND SAID UNTO HIM, WE HAVE FOUND WATER. 'AND HE CALLED IT SHE-BAH: THEREFORE THE NAME OF THE CITY IS BEER-SHEBA UNTO THIS DAY."

GENESIS 26:32–33

I
saac was a pastoral nomad, the son of Abraham and his wife, Sarah, and the heir of God's Covenant. As a youth, his father had offered him as a sacrifice. Certain that both Abraham and Isaac were totally obedient to His will, God accepted a ram as a substitute. Thus, the Hebrews rejected human sacrifice thereafter.

Isaac, or "laughter" in Hebrew, was born to Sarah in the desert between Gerar and Beersheba. Spending most of his life constantly seeking water for his flocks and occasional crop growing when suitable conditions prevailed, he replicated his father's lifestyle seldom moving 50 miles from his birthplace in the northern Negev. When his mother died, Isaac lived at Beer-lahai-roi, an oasis on the caravan trail to Egypt and the place where an angel consoled the pregnant Hagar when she fled the cruelty of Sarah, her mistress. Isaac met his wife Rebekah at Beer-lahai-roi and their twin sons, Esau and Jacob were born there.

The Negev provides a hard living, especially when springs and wells run dry. Flocks and people can die. In early Biblical times, Egypt was a fertile area that could prove a sanctuary from climatic disasters. When famine hit Gerar, Isaac considered a refuge in Egypt, but obeyed God's will by not going there. The Gerar region possesses abundant wells and lies between real desert and areas of permanent settlement. The region is not barren and irrigation systems can top up the six to ten inches (15–26 cm) of annual rainfall. Isaac re-opened Abraham's old wells, sowed crops and reaped a hundredfold in the same year. So wealthy and powerful did Isaac become that King Abimelech, feeling threatened, ordered him away. Isaac sought water in the Valley of Gerar, but disputed water rights with local herdsmen until

ISAAC, JACOB, AND JOSEPH
Isaac lived his life in the Negev Desert. However, his son, Jacob traveled through lands ranging from Haran, near the Euphrates River to the Nile delta of Egypt. Jacob's youngest and favorite son, Joseph, traveled north from his home to seek his brothers. In their jealousy they sold him into slavery and his enforced journey took him south into Egypt.

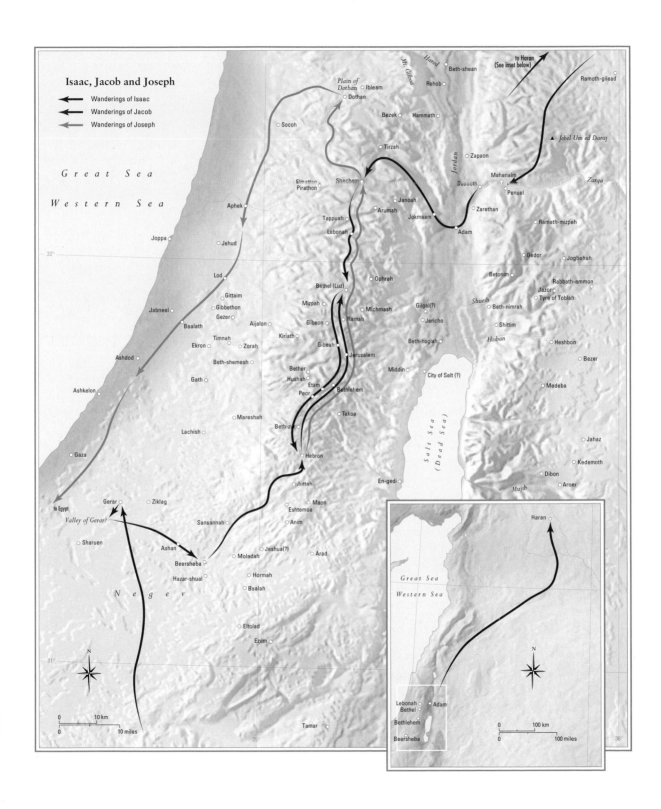

Isaac, Jacob and Joseph

→ Wanderings of Isaac
→ Wanderings of Jacob
→ Wanderings of Joseph

Great Sea

Western Sea

to Haran
(See inset below)

Harod

Beth-shean

Ramoth-gilead

Rehob

Plain of Dothan ○ Ibleam
○ Dothan

Bezek ○ Hammath

○ Socoh

○ Tirzah

Mt. Gilboa

○ Zapaon

▲ *Jebel Um ed Daraj*

Elmattan ○ Pirathon

Shechem

○ Janoah

Jordan

Mahanaim

Zarqa

Dusseth ○ Penuel

○ Arumah

Jokmeam

Zarethan

Tappuah ○

Lebonah ○

○ Ophrah

Adam ○

○ Ramath-mizpeh

Great Sea

Western Sea

Bethel (Luz)

○ Gedor

○ Jogbehah

Mizpah ○

Michmash

Gilgal(?)

Betonim ○

Rabbath-ammon

Jazor ○ Tyre of Toblah

○ Aphek

Gibeon ○

Ramah

Jericho

Shueib

Beth-nimrah

○ Joppa

○ Jehud

Kiriath ○

Gibeah ○

Jerusalem

Beth-hoglah

Hisban

○ Shittim

Heshbon

○ Lod

Gittaim ○

Gibbethon ○
Gezer ○

Aijalon ○

Bether ○
Hushah ○

Etam ○

Beth-zur ○

Middin ○

City of Salt (?)

○ Bezer

○ Jabneel

Timnah ○

Zorah ○

Peor ○

Bethlehem ○

○ Medeba

○ Baalath

Ekron ○

Beth-shemesh ○

○ Tekoa

○ Ashdod

Gath ○

Mareshah ○

Salt Sea (Dead Sea)

○ Jahaz

En-gedi ○

○ Kedemoth

○ Ashkelon

Lachish ○

Hebron ○

○ Dibon

○ Aroer

○ Gaza

Mujib

to Egypt

Gerar ○

○ Ziklag

○ Juttah

Gerar ○

Valley of Gerar?

Ashan ○

Sansannah ○

○ Maon

Eshtemoa ○

○ Anim

○ Sharuen

Beersheba ○

○ Moladah

Jeshua(?) ○

○ Arad

Hazar-shual ○

○ Hormah

○ Baalah

N e g e v

○ Eltolad

○ Ezem

○ Tamar

N

0   10 km

0   10 miles

Great Sea

Western Sea

Haran ○

N

Lebonah ○
Bethel ○ ○ Adam

Bethlehem ○

Beersheba ○

0   100 km

0   100 miles

he dug his own well, named Reheboth. Despite finding peace in that part of Gerar, Isaac obeyed God and went to the oasis of Beersheba.

Isaac's son, Jacob, was a quiet man unlike his older twin, Esau, who became a desert hunter. Esau hunted deer one day for Isaac, but when he returned exhausted and hungry, he sold his birthright to Jacob for some bread and a pot of lentils. At Beersheba, Rebekah helped Jacob, her favorite son, deceive her husband by placing the skins of goat kids upon his hands and neck so when the nearly blind Isaac touched him, he would mistake him for the hairier Esau. The fraud worked and Isaac gave his second son, Jacob, God's blessing. Having lost his blessing and birthright, Esau planned to kill his twin. Jacob promptly traveled northward to his mother's people, Aramaeans, in Paddan-aram near Haran, seeking safety and also a wife.

Jacob's likely route took him through the hill country via Hebron, Jerusalem, Shiloh and Shechem. A major event took place at Luz, called Bethel by Jacob. He dreamt he saw a ladder leading to God who told him that his family and descendents would be numerous (Genesis 28:10–22). The route from

"THY NAME SHALL BE CALLED NO MORE JACOB, BUT ISRAEL: FOR AS A PRINCE HAST THOU POWER WITH GOD AND WITH MEN, AND HAST PREVAILED ... AND JACOB CALLED THE NAME OF THE PLACE PENIEL: FOR I HAVE SEEN GOD FACE TO FACE AND MY LIFE IS PRESERVED." GENESIS 32:28, 30

Bethel went through Damascus and then north via Hamath and east via Carchemish or a southern road via Tadmor to Mari and Babylon. Paddan-aram is identified with Aram-Naharaim (Aram of the two rivers), the area between the River Khabur in the east and the great bend of the Euphrates to its west.

On Jacob's arrival at Haran, he met his cousin, Rachel, at a well where she was watering her father's flocks. She ran to her father, Laban, who welcomed Jacob. Laban offered Jacob work and pay, but Jacob requested Rachel in marriage and offered to serve Laban for seven years for the honor. At the wedding ceremony, Laban tricked Jacob into marrying Rachel's older sister, Leah. So Jacob worked for another seven years as a bride price for Rachel. He continued working for Laban, raised a family and became an extremely wealthy man. After residing with Laban for 20 years, Jacob decided to return to Isaac in Canaan fleeing with his family and livestock as Laban was away tending his flocks. Laban pursued Jacob, overtaking his party in the hills of Gilead. Disputes over the ownership of the flocks and herds took place, but Jacob and Laban were reconciled, making a peace covenant.

Jacob moved to Mahanaim, overshadowed by the limestone cliffs of the Jabbok Valley, sending peace messengers to Esau in Edom. Hearing that Esau was approaching with 400 men, Jacob divided his clan and goods into two, and placed them in different locations, presuming that one company would survive if his brother wanted a fight. Jacob also sent gifts to his brother and prayed for a reconciliation. That night, Jacob wrestled with a man until morning. The man said, "Thy name shall be called no more Jacob, but Israel: for as a prince hast thou power with God and with men, and hast prevailed ... And Jacob called the name of the place Peniel: for I have seen God face to face and my life is preserved." (Genesis 32:28, 30)

Jacob and Esau met, and the brothers made peace. Esau finally returned to Edom. Jacob reached Succoth in the Jordan Valley and built an house and shelters for his cattle. The heat was so intense and

THE MEETING OF JACOB AND RACHEL
This engraving by the 17th-century Italian artist Badalocchio depicts the meeting of Jacob with his cousin and future wife at the well.

draining that he crossed the Jordan into Canaan up the Wadi Farah to the town of Shalem in Shechem, buying land nearby and erecting an altar called El-elohe-Israel. Disaster befell Jacob's daughter, Dinah, who was raped by Shechem, son of the Hivite Prince Hamor. Her brothers Simeon and Levi took revenge by killing the prince, his son, the men of Shechem, seizing all livestock and the Shechem women and wrecking every house.

Jacob took his people to Bethel, where he built an altar. He retraced Abraham's route through the mountains. Rachel died giving birth to Benjamin near Bethlehem. Jacob was reunited with his father at Mamre near Hebron. When Isaac died, reputedly 180 years old, Esau and Jacob buried him in a cave. Esau returned to Edom where he allegedly founded the Edomites while Jacob personified the nation of Israel, his sons becoming the patriarchs of the 12 tribes of Israel: Reuben, Simeon, Levi, Judah, Issacher, and Zebulon (from Leah); Joseph and Benjamin (from Rachel); Gad and Asher (from Zilpah, Leah's handmaid); and, Dan and Naphtali (from Bilhah, Rachel's handmaid).

The story of Joseph, told in Genesis 37–50, probably took place some time between 1720 and 1500 BC, the time when the Hyksos dynasty ruled in Egypt. The Hyksos were Semitic in origin, but had adapted completely to Egyptian culture. There is evidence that many Semites of various tribes were taken as slaves to Egypt at that time, with and some reaching high office.

Joseph was the favorite son of his father Jacob. His father's favor and his own apparent arrogance earned him the enmity of his ten older half-brothers, who plotted to kill him. Finding him alone, they threw him into a well. Soon after, a group of merchants passed by on their way to Egypt, and they were happy to buy Joseph to sell as a slave there. The brothers covered up their crime by

smearing goat's blood on Joseph's coat so that his father would believe he had been killed by wild animals.

Joseph was sold to Potiphar, one of the Pharaoh's officials. Joseph was so efficient that he was promoted rapidly, and soon was running the whole household. All went well until the handsome young Hebrew caught the eye of Potiphar's wife, who set out to seduce him. Joseph constantly rebuffed her. Infuriated, she told her husband that his Hebrew servant had tried to rape her and Potiphar had Joseph imprisoned.

Joseph's abilities and intelligence again worked in his favor and he came to be entrusted with much of the prison's administration. When two of Pharaoh's officials, his chief butler and baker, were imprisoned, Joseph was assigned to look after them. Both had dreams that Joseph interpreted for them. He said that in three days

"COME, AND LET US SELL HIM TO THE ISH-MEE-LITES, AND LET NOT OUR HAND BE UPON HIM; FOR HE IS OUR BROTHER AND OUR FLESH. AND HIS BRETHEREN WERE CONTENT.

'THEN THERE PASSED BY MID-I-A-NITES MERCHANTMEN; AND THEY DREW AND LIFTED UP JOSEPH OUT OF THE PIT, AND SOLD JOSEPH TO THE ISH-MEE-LITES FOR TWENTY PIECES OF SILVER; AND THEY BROUGHT JOSEPH INTO EGYPT."

GENESIS 37:27–28

THE JUDEAN DESERT
Esau, brother of Jacob, became a hunter roaming the wilder parts of Judea and Edom, where he sought out his pray. Elder son of Isaac and the first-born of twins, Esau was entitled to the family birthright. However, he sold this to his brother, Jacob, in return for lentil stew. Jacob also tricked Esau out of his father's blessing. Esau hated his brother for this and wanted to kill him, but eventually the brothers were reconciled.

"AND JOSEPH SAID UNTO HIS BRETHREN, COME
NEAR TO ME, I PRAY YOU. AND THEY CAME NEAR,
AND HE SAID, I AM JOSEPH YOUR BROTHER,
WHOM YE SOLD INTO EGYPT."

"NOW THEREFORE BE NOT GRIEVED, NOR
ANGRY WITH YOUR SELVES, THAT YE SOLD ME
HITHER: FOR GOD DID SEND ME BEFORE YOU
TO PRESERVE LIFE.

'FOR THESE TWO YEARS HATH THE FAMINE BEEN
IN THE LAND: AND YET THERE ARE FIVE YEARS,
IN WHICH THERE SHALL NEITHER BE EARING
NOR HARVEST."   GENESIS 45:4–6

time the baker would be executed, but the butler would be pardoned. Joseph asked the butler to put in a good word for him with Pharaoh, but after his release the man forgot about Joseph.

Two years later Pharaoh himself had strange dreams that all his wise men were unable to interpret. At last the butler remembered the young man who had successfully interpreted his dream in prison. Joseph was sent for and was able to tell Pharaoh the meaning of his dreams. They signified that there would be seven years of good harvests, followed by seven years of famine. Joseph advised Pharoah to store food during the years of plenty to draw on in the years of famine. Pharaoh was so impressed by Joseph that he made him a governor over Egypt, in charge of organizing the storage of grain.

There were such bountiful harvests in the first seven years that Joseph was able to provide grain during the famine, not only for the Egyptians but for people from other countries that were also short of food. One such country was Canaan, and when Jacob heard that grain was obtainable in Egypt he sent his ten older sons there to buy some.

When his brothers appeared, Joseph knew them immediately, but they failed to recognize him. He did not acknowledge them, but accused them of being spies. He demanded that they prove their story that they were simply brothers from Canaan come to buy food, and that they should bring Benjamin, Jacob's youngest son and Joseph's only full brother, to Egypt. He forced them to leave one of their number, Simeon, as a hostage. Then Joseph loaded their packs with grain and money, and they returned to Canaan.

Jacob was reluctant to let his sons return to Egypt with Benjamin but when the famine continued, he had to let them go. Again Joseph pretended not to recognize them, and tricked them by planting a silver cup in Benjamin's pack and then accusing him of the theft, insisting that he must remain in Egypt as a slave. Judah pleaded for his young brother, telling Joseph it would break their father's heart to lose his youngest son. At last Joseph relented and revealed who he was. He forgave his brothers and loaded them with gifts. Eventually Jacob and all his sons settled in Egypt.

JACOB'S LADDER *(far right)*
This painting by the painter William Blake (1757–1828) shows the sleeping Jacob at Bethel dreaming of angels going up and down a ladder.

THE EXODUS

INCREASINGLY, THE HEBREWS WERE REGARDED AS ALIENS BY THE EGYPTIANS. AT SOME POINT DURING THE LONG REIGN OF RAMESES II, THEY ESCAPED TO CANAAN. THEY WERE LED BY MOSES, WHO HAD BEEN GIVEN A SACRED COVENANT NAMING THE HEBREWS AS GOD'S "CHOSEN PEOPLE." HEBREW LAW WAS AN EXPRESSION OF THE PEOPLE'S GRATITUDE THEREAFTER.

I n about 1285 BC an Egyptian army led by King Rameses II (1290–1224 BC) ran into a trap at Kadesh in northern Palestine, just north of what is now Lebanon. The front section of the army, led by Rameses, was cut off by Hittite charioteers who attacked the second section leaving the king and his section isolated. Only desperate fighting saved the situation.

Kadesh appears as a victory in Egyptian records, but the treaty that eventually followed left the Egyptian frontier in Palestine further south than it had ever been. Earlier in Rameses II's reign, the Egyptian capital had been moved to a site near the old Hyksos capital at Avaris, in the north-eastern part of the delta, as part of a vast, extensive building program. Thus, the Nile delta was once more the most important part of Egypt, and was vital to Egyptian security with mounting pressure from Libya to the west, and the uneasy peace with the Hittites.

These developments in Egyptian history have clear links with events described in the Bible. Therefore, it is assumed that it was during the reign of Rameses II that the Hebrews escaped from Egypt, as described in the Book of Exodus. When the Asiatic Hyksos rulers of Egypt were overthrown around 1550 BC, the descendants of the Hebrew nomadic shepherds who had settled near the delta found themselves under increasing suspicion as aliens. They would certainly have been chosen as one of many groups forced into labor gangs to build Rameses' new capital and frontier fortifications. In Exodus 1:11, it is described: "Accordingly they put slave-drivers over the Israelites to wear them down under

EGYPT *(far right)*
Egypt's empire and its area of influence reached from Irem in the south to the frontiers of Syria and the Hittite Empire in the north.

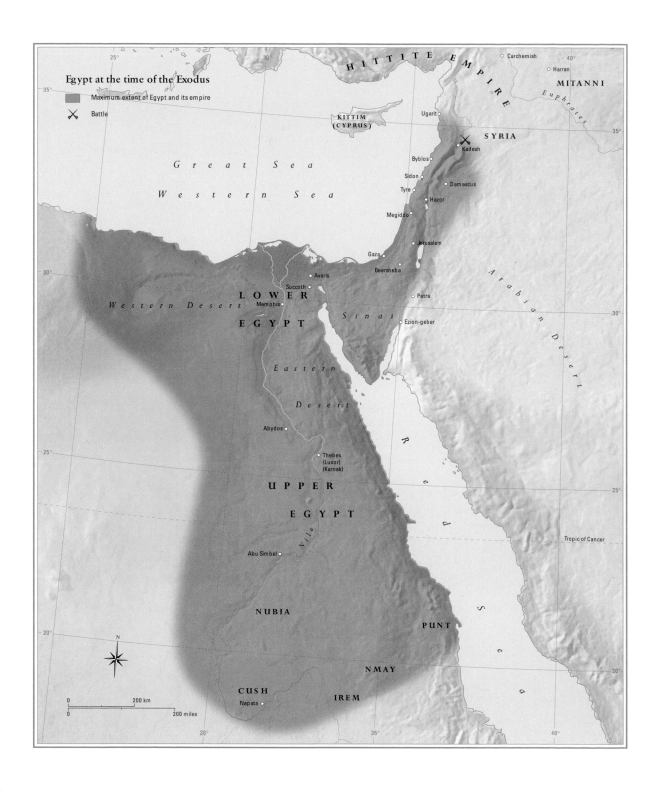

Egypt at the time of the Exodus

Maximum extent of Egypt and its empire

✗ Battle

HITTITE EMPIRE
MITANNI
Carchemish
Harran
Euphrates
KITTIM
(CYPRUS)
Ugarit
SYRIA
✗ Kadesh
Byblos
Sidon
Damascus
Tyre
Hazor
Megiddo
Jerusalem
Gaza
Beersheba
Avaris
Succoth
Petra
LOWER
Memphis
Western Desert
Sinai
EGYPT
Ezion-geber
Great Sea
Western Sea
Eastern
Desert
Abydos
Red
Thebes
(Luxor)
(Karnak)
UPPER
EGYPT
Arabian Desert
Nile
Tropic of Cancer
Abu Simbel
Sea
NUBIA
PUNT
N
NMAY
CUSH
IREM
Napata
0   200 km
0   200 miles

"AND THE CHILDREN OF ISRAEL WERE FRUITFUL,

AND INCREASED ABUNDANTLY, AND MULTIPLIED,

AND WAXED EXCEEDING MIGHTY; AND THE LAND

WAS FILLED WITH THEM.

NOW THERE AROSE UP A NEW KING OVER EGYPT,

WHICH KNEW NOT JOSEPH."   EXODUS 1:7–8

heavy loads. In this way, they built the store-cities of Pithom and Rameses for the Pharaoh."

The Hebrew leader, Moses, is presented as the adopted child of an Egyptian princess. He therefore had access to the royal court. But of equal importance are his contacts with the Midianites of the Sinai Desert, who gave him shelter and a wife when he first had to flee Egypt. The Midianites, who were descendants of Midean, son of Abraham, worshipped the same God as the Hebrews, and Moses returned to Egypt with the conviction that God had chosen him to lead his people to freedom.

The famous plagues described in Exodus 7–12 can all be seen as natural phenomena, but for both the Hebrews and the Egyptians they were contests between the Hebrew God and the Egyptian gods—of whom Rameses II was one. The broad background to the account in the Book of Exodus is entirely consistent with the situation in Egypt at the time. Religion was territorial, and neither the Egyptians nor the Hebrews would want a Hebrew religious festival to be held on Egyptian soil, so the Hebrews asked permission to go into the desert to celebrate. This was the request that the Egyptian king at first refused, and then granted after the series of devastating plagues.

The Hebrew escape from Egypt is described in the Book of Exodus 12—15. These chapters, and the subsequent ones that deal with the Covenant at Mount Sinai, must be the most heavily edited passages in the Old Testament, for the events they describe are as central to the Hebrew religion as the Crucifixion and Resurrection of Jesus are to Christianity. The account of the exodus and Covenant reached its present form in the Book of Exodus about seven centuries after the events occurred and some points are still disputed. But the final editors were able to refer to very old written sources and firm traditions were kept alive through their regular use in Hebrew worship.

The description of the escape starts with the Passover regulations in Exodus 12. This celebration was, and still is, the key to Hebrew worship and the festival to which the other major feast is linked. It was originally a protection rite for nomadic shepherds as they moved along the routes in search of pasture. The blood of a sacrificed lamb, symbolizing and containing the life-giving power of God, gave them protection against any evil forces and the meal then sealed the links between God and his people. The escape from Egypt gave this rite new meaning, as a commemoration of the Hebrew God's victory over the Egyptian gods and his covenant with his chosen people. All subsequent acts of deliverance throughout Hebrew history were then seen as consequences of his exodus and God's deliverance and were celebrated therefore as extensions of the Passover. When the Hebrews became farmers after the occupation of Canaan, the Canaanite harvest festivals were celebrated as manifestations of the same power of God that had brought the people safely out of Egypt.

The actual crossing out of Egypt pursued by Egyptian soldiers, depicted in Exodus 14, occurred at what the Hebrews called Yam Suph. When this was translated into Greek, about 1,000 years later, a

THE EXODUS *(far right)*
Most probably the Hebrews crossed the marshy region to the east of the Nile delta where Moses' 'parting of the waters' would have occurred. They then journeyed to the sacred mountain, and their experiences in the Sinai Peninsula became the foundation of the nation's religion and identity.

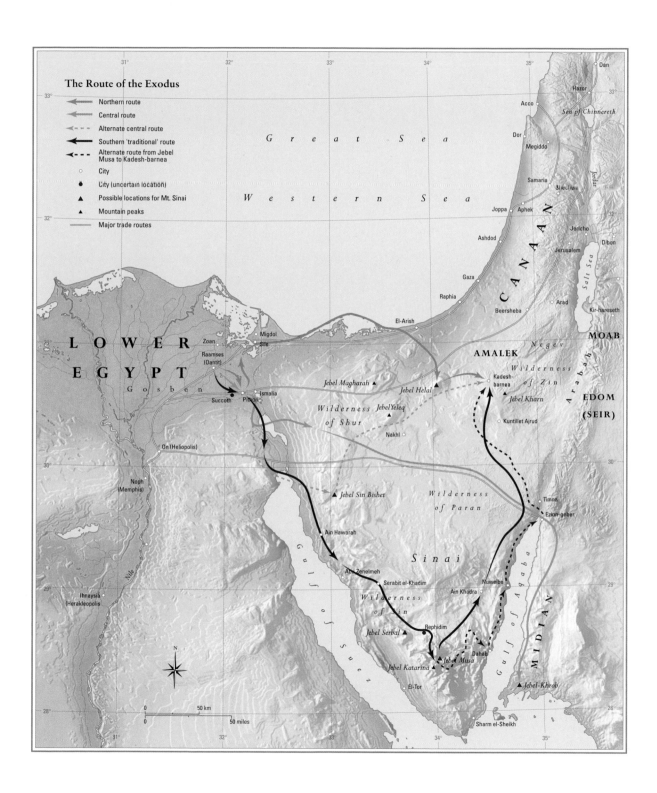

The Route of the Exodus

→ Northern route
→ Central route
-→ Alternate central route
← Southern 'traditional' route
-← Alternate route from Jebel
   Musa to Kadesh-barnea
○ City
● City (uncertain location)
▲ Possible locations for Mt. Sinai
▲ Mountain peaks
── Major trade routes

Dan
Hazor
Acco
Sea of Chinnereth
Dor
Megiddo
Samaria
Shechem
Jordan
Joppa
Aphek
Jericho
Ashdod
Jerusalem
Dibon
Gaza
Salt Sea
Raphia
Beersheba
Arad
Kir-hareseth
El-Arish
MOAB
Negev
AMALEK
Wilderness
of Zin
EDOM
(SEIR)
Kadesh-
barnea
Jebel Kharn
Migdol
Sile
Zoan
Arabah
Raamses
(Dantit)
Jebel Magharah ▲
Jebel Helal ▲
Kuntillet Ajrud
LOWER
EGYPT
Goshen
Ismalia
Jebel Yeleq
Succoth
Pithon
Wilderness
of Shur
Nakhl
On (Heliopolis)
Timna
Jebel Sin Bishet ▲
Wilderness
of Paran
Ezion-geber
Noph
(Memphis)
Ain Hawarah
Great Sea
Western Sea
Sinai
Ain Khadra
Nuweiba
Ihnaysia
(Herakleopolis)
Abu Zenelmeh
Serabit el-Khadim
Wilderness
of in
MIDIAN
Gulf of Aqaba
Gulf of Suez
Nile
Rephidim
Jebel Serbal ▲
Dahab
Jebel Katarina ▲
Jebel Musa ▲
Jebel-Khrob ▲
El-Tor
CANAAN
Sharm el-Sheikh

N

0   50 km
0   50 miles

RAMESES II c. 1290–1225 BC
Enormous statues of Egyptian
Pharaohs symbolized their power
and status of gods. Despite their
brief period of forced labor
under the Egyptians and their
dramatic exodus, it was here that
Hebrews looked for protection
from the powers of Assyria and
Babylon. This limestone statue of
Rameses II can be seen in
Memphis today.

phrase meaning "Red Sea" was used, implying that the Hebrews crossed the Gulf of Suez. However, the Hebrew should more properly be translated "Sea of Reeds," which also agrees with the place names given in the early part of the journey (Exodus 13:17–14:2). The "road to the land of the Philistines" (Palestine) left the north-east edge of the Nile delta, where the ancient Egyptian capital of Memphis was then located, and followed the coast into Canaan. Succoth, where the Hebrews first camped on their journey, was probably west of Lake Timsah (today's Suez Canal), while Migdol was a border fortress near the coast at Tell el-Heir. Pi-hahiroth (Exodus 14:9) faced Baal-zephon, where there was a temple for sailors on a narrow peninsula.

This route takes the Hebrew escape well north of the Gulf of Suez, into the marshy area near the Mediterranean coast. This fits both the Hebrew "Sea of Reeds" and the account of Egyptian chariot wheels being clogged, which comes from one of the earlier strands of the traditions woven together in Exodus 14. The crossing therefore probably occurred north of Lake Timsah. After this the Hebrews turned south, both to avoid Egyptian officials on the main routes into Palestine and to reach the wilderness areas grazed by the nomadic shepherd tribes. One of these tribes was the Midianites, to whom Moses had fled before returning to Egypt as the leader of his people.

Despite a wealth of information in the Books of Exodus, Leviticus, Numbers, and Deuteronomy, there can be no absolute certainty about the route the escaping Hebrews took from Egypt to the mountain of the Covenant and Canaan, nor how long the whole journey took. There are also some different views about the actual location of the mountain.

Some of the contradictory information becomes much clearer if it is accepted that the biblical accounts of the journey combine traditions about several waves of Hebrew penetration into Canaan, with at least two distinct journeys. One of these was opposed by kingdoms in the plains of Moab to the east of the Dead Sea, while an earlier journey was able to pass unhindered. In addition, there would have been Hebrews living in southern Canaan who had not gone to Egypt at the time of the entry of Joseph and his brothers.

Egyptian records lend support to such a view, for it appears that there were no organized kingdoms east of the Dead Sea in the 14th Century BC. But by the 13th Century BC, kingdoms had emerged in Edom and Moab, which would account for opposition to a Hebrew group during the latter part of the reign of Rameses II. In any event, there were fortified Canaanite cities across the south of Canaan that could prevent Hebrew groups of any size from penetrating past the region of Kadesh-barnea. Such groups would then have to cross eastward to take the traditional nomadic route, the King's Highway. There need be far less uncertainty about the location of the mountain itself. It is referred to variously as Mount Sinai, Mount Horeb, and Mount Paran, and all three names point to the granite mountains in the southern Sinai Peninsula.

The most important incident of the whole tradition need not be doubted, and would account for the mingling of all the traditions into one: the Covenant at the sacred mountain from which the Hebrews derived their national identity and their sense of religious unity. All Hebrews would have the strongest motives for associating their ancestors with this tradition and for seeing the Covenant as their entitlement to the land of Palestine. The events at Mount Sinai are cast in a form similar to treaties between so-called savior-kings and their subjects, whose relationships were based on a great victory or

"AND MOSES
WENT UP UNTO
GOD, AND THE
LORD CALLED
UNTO HIM
OUT OF THE
MOUNTAIN,
SAYING, THUS
SHALT THOU
SAY TO THE
HOUSE OF JACOB,
AND TELL
THE CHILDREN
OF ISRAEL;
YE HAVE SEEN
WHAT I DID
UNTO THE
EGYPTIANS, AND
HOW I BARE
YOU ON EAGLE'S
WINGS, AND
BROUGHT YOU
UNTO MYSELF."
EXODUS 19:3–4

deed that placed the subjects under an obligation to their king. The relationship between them was then specified by laws accepted by the people, backed by the power of the gods and by sanctions. The Hebrew Covenant was thus based on the escape from Egypt, the supreme manifestation of God's power and of His choice of the Hebrew people. Hebrew law then became the expression of the people's gratitude, and their obligations to God and to each other as God's chosen ones. All Hebrew law, whether it already existed or developed subsequently, was an expression of the Covenant and so was incorporated into the narrative.

The Ten Commandments (Exodus 20:1–17 and Deuteronomy 5:1–21) are in a class of their own. As direct, absolute commands from God to the Hebrews, rather than laws presented in the form of cases and precedents, the Ten Commandments have no known parallels in the ancient Near East and could well go back to Moses himself.

MOUNT SINAI *(far left)*
The mountain where the Covenant with God was revealed to Moses during the Exodus is believed to be either Mount Sinai, Mount Horeb, or Mount Paran, all granite mountains in the southern Sinai Peninsula.

"I AM THE LORD THY GOD WHICH HAVE BROUGHT THEE OUT OF THE LAND OF EGYPT, OUT OF THE HOUSE OF BONDAGE. THOU SHALT HAVE NO OTHER GODS BEFORE ME.
"THOU SHALT NOT MAKE UNTO THEE ANY GRAVEN IMAGE, OR ANY LIKENESS OF ANY THING THAT IS IN HEAVEN ABOVE, OR THAT IS IN THE EARTH BENEATH, OR THAT IS IN THE WATER UNDER THE EARTH.
"THOU SHALT NOT BOW DOWN THYSELF TO THEM, NOR SERVE THEM: FOR I THE LORD THY GOD AM A JEALOUS GOD, VISITING THE INIQUITY OF THE FATHERS UPON THE CHILDREN UNTO THE THIRD AND FOURTH GENERATION OF THEM THAT HATE ME; AND SHOWING MERCY UNTO THOUSANDS OF THEM THAT LOVE ME, AND KEEP MY COMMANDMENTS.
"THOU SHALT NOT TAKE THE NAME OF THE LORD THY GOD IN VAIN; FOR THE LORD WILL NOT HOLD HIM GUILTLESS THAT TAKETH HIS NAME IN VAIN.
"REMEMBER THE SABBATH DAY, TO KEEP IT HOLY. SIX DAYS SHALT THOU LABOR, AND DO ALL THY WORK. BUT THE SEVENTH DAY IS THE SABBATH OF THE LORD THY GOD: IN IT THOU SHALT NOT DO ANY WORK, THOU, NOR THY SON, NOR THY CATTLE, NOR THY STRANGER THAT IS WITHIN THY GATES. FOR IN SIX DAYS THE LORD MADE HEAVEN AND EARTH, THE SEA, AND ALL THAT IN THEM IS, AND RESTED THE SEVENTH DAY: WHEREFORE THE LORD BLESSED THE SABBATH DAY, AND HALLOWED IT.
"HONOR THY FATHER AND THY MOTHER: THAT THY DAYS MAY BE LONG UPON THE LAND THAT THE LORD THY GOD GIVETH THEE.
"THOU SHALT NOT KILL.
"THOU SHALT NOT COMMIT ADULTERY.
"THOU SHALT NOT STEAL.
"THOU SHALT NOT BEAR FALSE WITNESS AGAINST THY NEIGHBOR.
"THOU SHALT NOT COVET THY NEIGHBOR'S WIFE, NOR HIS MANSERVANT, NOR HIS MAIDSERVANT, NOR HIS OX, NOR HIS ASS, NOR ANY THING THAT IS THY NEIGHBOR'S."

INVASION AND CONQUEST

THE NEAR AND MIDDLE EAST WAS ENTERING A LONG PERIOD OF TURMOIL. THE POWERS THAT HAD PREVIOUSLY OCCUPIED CANAAN COLLAPSED OR WERE WRACKED BY CIVIL WARS. LOCAL PEOPLES AND MIGRANTS, SUCH AS THE PHILISTINES AND HEBREWS, STRUGGLED FOR CONTROL OF THE LAND OF CANAAN.

The most probable date for the Hebrew escape from Egypt, the Exodus, is the latter part of the reign of King Rameses II of Egypt (1290–1224 BC), which would mean that the Hebrews penetrated into Canaan from the east at the end of the 13th or beginning of the 12th Centuries BC. Canaan was soon to become known as "Land of the Philistines," and eventually, Palestine. This time marks the beginning of nearly three centuries of weakness and turmoil for the great powers, which normally considered Canaan an essential part of their defences and trading interests. It was certainly not a period of peace for the area, but the protagonists were local to Canaan, or migrants such as the Hebrews.

The geography of the area forced the international routes from Egypt to Mesopotamia and Asia Minor through the narrow land of Canaan, between the desert and the sea. Throughout its recorded history, Canaan was at the mercy of the dominant powers of the Near and Middle East; it was nearly always occupied by one of these powers, and served as a battleground between them. During most of the 2nd Millennium BC, Canaan had been under the control of Egypt. The Canaanite city states, always at war among themselves, had seen Egypt as a source of support against each other. But from the beginning of the 15th Century BC, the powers of Asia Minor and upper Mesopotamia had resisted Egyptian pressure and forced the Egyptians back from Carchemish in the north. The Battle of Kadesh (c. 1275 BC), between Egyptians and the Hittites of Asia Minor, left the northern limits of Egyptian control running from Damascus to the Phoenician coast. Egyptian-controlled territory would probably have been pushed back to the Nile delta itself if the Hittites had not themselves been

HEBREW SPIES *(far right)*
Moses sent one man from each of the 12 tribes of Israel on a spying mission into the land of Canaan to seek out a possible invasion routes and gather any useful information. They returned with tales of fortified cities and of the fierce people that lived in them. But the lure of the land was irresistible.

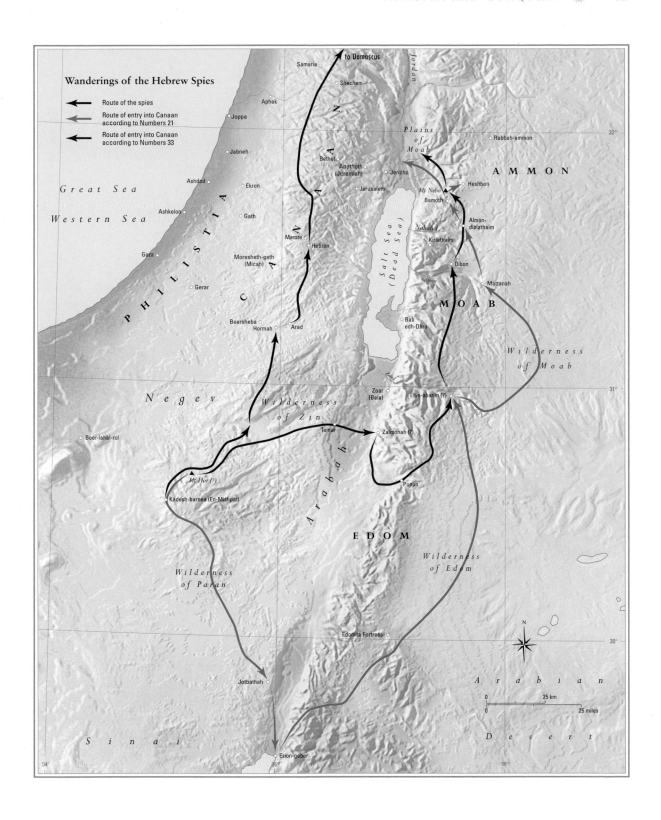

Wanderings of the Hebrew Spies

→ Route of the spies

→ Route of entry into Canaan according to Numbers 21

→ Route of entry into Canaan according to Numbers 33

to Damascus

Samaria

Shechem

Aphek

Joppa

Jabneh

Bethel

Anathoth (Jeremiah)

Ashdod

Ekron

Jerusalem

Great Sea

Western Sea

Ashkelon

Gath

Mamre

Hebron

Gaza

Moresheth-gath (Micah)

Gerar

Salt Sea (Dead Sea)

Beersheba

Hormah

Arad

Negev

Zoar (Bela)

Beer-lahal-rol

Wilderness of Zin

Tamar

Zalmonah (?)

Mt Hor (?)

Kadesh-barnea (En-Mishpat)

Punon

Wilderness of Paran

Arabah

EDOM

Wilderness of Edom

Edomite Fortress

Jotbathah

Sinai

Ezion-geber

Plains of Moab

Rabbah-ammon

AMMON

Heshbon

Mt Nebo

Bamoth

Almon-diblathaim

Nahaliel

Kiriathaim

Dibon

Mattanah

MOAB

Bab edh-Dhra

Iye-abarim (?)

Wilderness of Moab

C A N A A N

P H I L I S T I A

A r a b i a n

D e s e r t

N

0   25 km

0   25 miles

Jericho

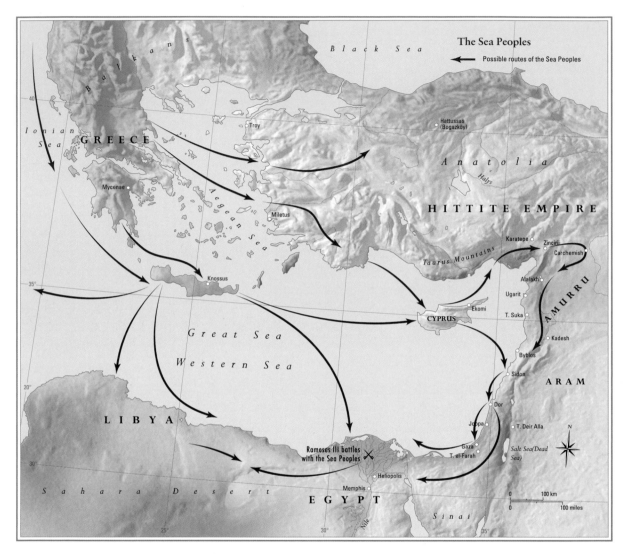

THE SEA PEOPLES
The movement of these peoples created a period of great instability. It was against this background that the Hebrews and the Philistines struggled to settle and control Canaan.

overwhelmed by migrants known as the Sea Peoples, who had probably been driven out of the Balkans and Greece.

Egypt might have gained full control of Canaan, but in turn had to fight off the Sea Peoples who attacked the delta region of Lower Egypt during the reign of Rameses II's successor, Merneptah (1224–1214 BC). Egypt repulsed the migrants from the delta, but could not prevent them gaining control of the coastal strip in southern Canaan, where they became known as the Philistines. They established themselves in five main cities: Gaza, Ashkelon, Ashdod, Gath, and Ekron, where they were technically subject people of the Egyptians. Their presence points to Egyptian weakness. Egypt was entering a period of internal disorders and economic problems. The priests grew enormously powerful on wealth that they built up through the temples and kept secure from the state. Gradually

Upper Egypt fell under the control of the priests of Thebes, while Lower Egypt was ruled by the kings from Tanis in the delta. Libya increased its pressure on Egypt from the west and Nubia gained its independence. Egypt would not be fully united and powerful again for several centuries.

In this period of turmoil the Hebrews arrived in Canaan. Joshua sent his spies to gather intelligence, to search out possible invasion routes in particular. Camped on the plains of Moab at Abel-shittim were the Hebrews, making their preparations for the invasion. The invasion epic, found in the books of Joshua and the Book of Judges, was probably based on the combined experience of many invading groups covering some decades, perhaps even centuries. There is no doubt, however, that the Hebrews had to fight to gain control of the land of Canaan—their "Promised Land."

At the moment Joshua launched the first invasion, the Hebrews crossed the River Jordan over a dry riverbed. The river had providencially experienced a blockage upstream, stemming the flow of water, at least while the army crossed.

Joshua selected Gilgal as his base, then set about extending Hebrew authority over the immediate area. This would form a secure centre of operations from which to launch his campaign against the local settlements and on into the central highlands. The first major city to be attacked, and one of the best-known battles of the Bible, is Jericho. For six days the Hebrews marched around the city. On the seventh day, priests blowing rams' horns continued to circle the city, and the walls eventually fell. The Hebrews entered and massacred its inhabitants, taking the treasure they found there for "the house of the Lord."

However, extensive archaeological work on the site of Jericho reveals no walled city from the period of the Hebrew conquest. There was a walled city, but its violent end came some 300 years earlier, possibly the result of local wars or invaders. Perhaps the Jericho stories were handed down and woven into the biblical epic when the Hebrew conquest stories began to take shape.

The Canaanites, the people facing this Hebrew assault, were predominantly farmers living in heavily fortified settlements from which they could work the fertile land within safe reach. Agriculture and defence were the two keys of their way of life and religion, but the rivalry between the many fortified towns meant they did not achieve political unity and were thus unable to offer, at least initially, a united front to stem Hebrew advance. The shifting patterns of alliances and leagues are similar to those of Greece during the classical period about 1,000 years later. It is possible that the Hyksos rulers of Egypt, from the mid-17th to mid-16th Century BC, were originally Canaanites, and that this was a brief period of political unity and power in an area stretching from Lower Egypt to the borders of Asia Minor.

Ai, a typical Canaanite settlement of some 1,000 people stood in the way of the Hebrew advance. Joshua launched a direct attack, but was repulsed with the loss of 36 men. He then formulated a plan that drew the defenders of Ai into the open to the north, while another force attacked from the west. Ai fell, the town was burned and the inhabitants slaughtered.

The case of Shechem presents an interesting insight into the Hebrew settlement of Canaan. The Shechemites were of mixed origin, their city commanded an important area of the hill country. Some of its people may have been part of the movement that had earlier brought Abraham to Canaan. These people may have had affinities with the Hebrews, and this might explain the gathering at the pass

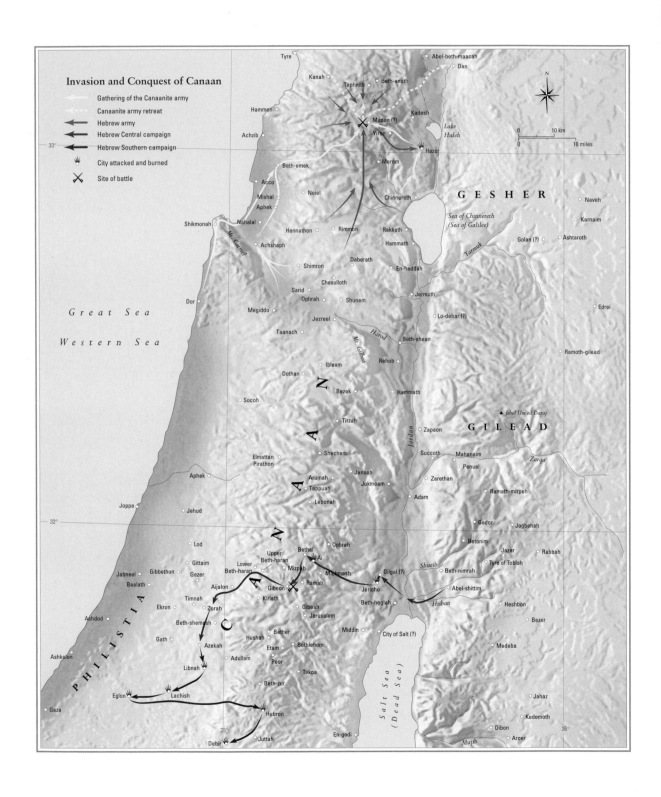

Invasion and Conquest of Canaan

→ Gathering of the Canaanite army
⇢ Canaanite army retreat
← Hebrew army
← Hebrew Central campaign
← Hebrew Southern campaign
⚜ City attacked and burned
⚔ Site of battle

N

0   10 km
0   10 miles

Tyre
Kanah
Taphnith   Beth-anath
Abel-beth-maacah   Dan
Hammon
Kadesh
Achzib   Madon (?)
Yiron   Lake
Hulch
Beth-emek   Merom
Hazor
Acco   Chinnereth   GESHER   Naveh
Mishal   Karnaim
Aphek   Sea of Chinnereth
Shikmonah   Nahalal   (Sea of Galilee)   Golan (?)   Ashtaroth
Hennathon   Rimmon   Rakkath
Achshaph   Hammath   Yarmuk
Shimron   Daberath
Chesulloth   En-haddah
Dor   Sarid   Ophrah   Shunem   Jermuth   Edrei
Megiddo   Jezreel   Lo-debar (?)
Taanach   Harod   Ramoth-gilead
Great Sea   Beth-shean
Western Sea   Ibleam   Rehob
Dothan   Hammath   Jebel Um ed Daraj
Socoh   Bezek   GILEAD
Tirzah   Zapaon
Elmattan   Shechem   Succoth   Mahanaim
Pirathon   Penuel   Zarqa
Aphek   Arumah   Janoah   Zarethan   Ramath-mizpeh
Tappuah   Jokmeam   Adam
Joppa   Lebonah
Jehud   Gedor   Jogbehah
Betonim
Lod   Bethel   Ophrah   Jazer   Rabbah
Upper   Ai   Gilgal (?)   Tyre of Toblah
Lower   Beth-haran   Mizpah   Shueib   Beth-nimrah
Jabneel   Gibbethon   Beth-haran   Michmash   Jericho   Abel-shittim
Baalath   Gezer   Ramah   Beth-hoglah   Heshbon
Aijalon   Gibeon   Hisban
Timnah   Kiriath   Bezer
Ekron   Zorah   Gibeah
Beth-shemesh   Jerusalem
Ashdod   Hushah   Middin   City of Salt (?)   Medeba
Gath   Bether
Azekah   Adullam   Etam   Bethlehem
Ashkelon   Libnah   Peor
Gaza   Eglon   Lachish   Beth-zur   Tekoa
Hebron   Salt Sea   Jahaz
Juttah   (Dead Sea)   Kedemoth
Debir   En-gedi   Dibon   Aroer
Mujib

PHILISTIA
CANAAN
Mt. Carmel
Mt. Gilboa
Jordan

between Mounts Gezarim and Ebal of "sojourner as well as homeborn" for the blessing of Israel. The Hebrews moved into and through this area by treaty with these indigenous people.

The control of the lands around the vital area of Gibeon was also by treaty. The people in this area called themselves Hivites, not Canaanites. The treaty, though created to deceive the Hebrews, was still honored. This agreement gave Joshua and his invading army access to the Shephelah, the low hills bordering Philistia.

The Canaanite city of Megiddo was on a fortified hill commanding the coastal road where it emerged into the Valley of Jezreel from a pass in the ridge of Mount Carmel, and branched into its northern and Mesopotamian routes. The city was repeatedly destroyed and rebuilt as each victor in turn took advantage of its strategic position. Excavations at the site have revealed some 20 layers of occupation. It was to receive its most impressive additions during the later reign of King Solomon (c. 970–931 BC), but it was also powerful and wealthy during the 13th Century BC. At that time it already possessed a great fortified palace to the east of the main gate, and a fortified temple. A hoard of carved ivory plaques, jewelry, god vessels, and precious beads point to the wealth in the city at the time. It was a feudal society, under the absolute authority of a king.

Most of the Canaanite cities were dependent on agriculture and water supplies within their fortifications. Therefore, they were almost all situated near the coastal plain, with a few scattered across to the edges of the Jordan Valley. The destruction of the coastal city of Ugarit by the Philistines about 1200 BC makes it possible to put a final date to the hundreds of written texts discovered on the site. They were in the form of clay tablets, which included religious and mythological material. From these, and from the excavations of Canaanite sanctuaries, it is possible to reconstruct something of the beliefs and practices of Canaanite religion without having to depend too closely on the hostile and critical descriptions contained in the Bible.

The next phase of the Hebrew assault on Canaan was toward the fertile hills and forests of Galilee to the north. The major city of the area was Hazor, with its moat and defensive walls, was the largest city in Canaan. Joshua gathered his forces in Upper and Lower Galilee in order to launch a surprise attack. He met the Canaanite army in the narrow defiles and forests at Merom where the Canaanite cavalry and chariots were of little value—there was simply no room to manoeuvre. Using the terrain to its advantage, the Hebrew army won a major victory, putting the Canaanites into shambolic retreat. The Hebrews cut off the Canaanite escape route to Hazor, leaving the them no option but to withdraw northward. Hazor was left undefended. The city suffered the same fate as cities to the south—its population was slaughtered ,and the city was razed to the ground. Extensive archaeological research conducted between 1920 and 1960 confirmed the city's destruction in the 13th Century BC.

The Old Testament shows that some of the language and symbolism of the Canaanite religion was also used by the new Hebrew settlers, particularly the name of the chief god, El, and some of the aspects of the Canaanite creation myths. El is called "El the Bull" in some of the Canaanite texts, while Baal has titles such as "Rider of the Clouds," with control over the storms and rain that water the soil for the crops. In the creation myths, Baal fights the death god and the god of the chaotic waters, and at one stage is himself killed. His sister forces the death god, Mot, to give Baal life for half of the year, and the water god is banished to the sea. Wherever the Hebrews have drawn from such

INVASION AND CONQUEST OF CANAAN
(far left)
The invasion of Canaan began by the crossing of the Jordan River. Fortunately the river was at a low level or almost dry. The army crossed with ease and began their campaign of conquest. Forming a base at Gilgal, Joshua attacked Jericho capturing the city. He then moved into the central highlands, but the city of Ai blocked his route. After an unsuccessful first attack he developed a plan that eventually captured the city. His campaign continued through the highlands and toward Philistia.

ideas, they have subordinated them to the unique savior-God of the escape from Egypt and the Covenant. However, the influence of the Canaanites can most be seen in the Hebrew sacrifices and festivals.

The Canaanites offered animals, crops, and incense as sacrifices, in which all or some of the offering was burnt, and as communion sacrifices with an associated sacred meal. The main Canaanite festivals were celebrations of the various stages of the harvest. They appear in Hebrew religious celebrations as the three major harvest festivals, known in English translations of the Bible as the festivals of Unleavened Bread, Pentecost (or Weeks) and Tabernacles. Whatever their origins, the Hebrews associated these festivals with the God of the Covenant, and so detached them from their Canaanite origins.

Everyday life for the great majority of people in the ancient world was almost totally concerned with survival. The essentials of life were food, which had to come from their crops and livestock, and protection, which came from being part of a social unit that could defend its members. For the nomadic pastoral peoples, such as the Hebrews during the earlier part of their history, clan, or tribe, provided protection. For all others, security depended on being a member of a territorial group, as small as a fortified town or as large as a country. Their security was only as sure as their ability to defend that territory. To be conquered by invaders meant slavery or death. Every detail of life— housing, family structures, religion, and even the selection of children for survival—evolved as a result of these basic concerns.

In the nomadic tribes the social structure reflected the natural authority and the basis of the family. Blood ties were all important. The family was polygamous (men had more than one wife), but the basic rights of members of the extended family were recognized and protected. Even slaves related to the family by blood had limited rights; other slaves had no rights. The flocks and herds were the common property of the group.

The social systems of agricultural settlements dependent on a particular territory were far more rigidly structured. A strict hierarchy of authority and subordination existed, with rule by an absolute monarch. Egypt does not even appear to have had codified laws. Mesopotamia regulated its social structures with a written code from at least the beginning of the 2nd Millennium BC. Houses were built of mud brick with flat roofs, which could be used for drying crops. They usually consisted of one room, with a raised sleeping platform on which a mat would be spread. For defensive reasons, at least in Canaan, the houses were clustered in positions that could be fortified and surrounded by heavy defensive walls. The main gate was usually approached by a ramp, set at an angle so that attackers had to expose their right, unshielded, sides to the defendants. Access to water during siege, either by storage or fortified spring, was important, as were safe storage facilities for harvested crops. The olive tree was much valued as a source of oil from the pressed fruits, for use in lamps, cooking, cosmetics, and in medicine. It was such a universal symbol of health, prosperity and security that the Hebrews eventually used it to show that authority had been conferred on a person by anointing them with olive oil. From this practice comes the word "messiah," literally meaning "the anointed one."

In monarchical systems, law was administered by the king or his delegates. For the patriarchal nomads, the father or grandfather acted as judges, considering cases in the presence of the whole

HEBREW SETTLEMENT OF CANAAN *(far right)*
The Hebrew settlement of Canaan probably took many years to complete. At first the Hebrews tended to occupy the marginal land that had not been brought under cultivation by the Canaanites and only later did they capture the cities. The Canaanites themselves were too disunited to be able to offer any coherent resistance. They would normally have appealed to Egypt for help, but she was beset by internal problems.

Hebrew Settlement of Canaan

- Early Hebrew settlements
- ✕ Battles
- • Conquered cities

Great Sea

Western Sea

Plain of Sharon

Shephelah

PHILISTIA

Negev

CANAAN

Salt Sea (Dead Sea)

Sea of Chinnereth

Lake Huleh

Jordan

Yarmuk

Jabbok

Arnon

Tyre
Laish (Leshem)
Achzib
Kedesh
Madon
Beth-shemesh
Hazor
Acco
Rehob
Kabul
Chinnereth
Aphek
Achshaph
Ashtaroth
Shimron
Jokneam
Dor
Megiddo
Jezreel
Remeth
Karnon
Edrei
Taanach
Beth-shan
Ham
Ramoth-gilead
Ibleam
Hepher
Socoh
Jabesh-gilead
Tirzah
Shechem
Zaphon
Succoth
Penuel
Tappuah
Adam
Joppa
Gilgal
Shiloh
Jazer
Jogbehah
Bethel
Ai
Shaalbim
Gezer
Aijalon
Gibeon
Jericho
Rabbah
Jerusalem (Jebus)
Abel-keramim
Ashdod
Ekron
Heshbon
Beth-shemesh
Bethlehem
Beth-jeshimoth
Gath?
Jarmuth
Medeba
Ashkelon
Adullam
Libnah
Gaza
Eglon
Lachish
Hebron
Debir
Dibon
Goshen
Aroer
Eshtemoa
Beer-sheba
Hormah
Arad?
Kir-hareseth

0   10 km
0   10 miles

N

family or tribal group. This practice continued after the Hebrews developed a monarchy, in the form of town elders sitting in judgement in the open area just inside the town gate. Just as there was no clear boundary between religion and the secular, so the law dealt with religious and secular offences in the same "court." Education was within the family group and related to the family's trade, unless the child was destined for one of the specialized administrative skills, such as scribe, priest, or royal official, when technical training would be given. Such professions were not usually distinct from each other, especially in the earlier period.

There were no extensive roads, as we would know them, until the Romans developed their system

HEBREW SANCTUARY
The Hebrews established a central sanctuary in the middle of Canaan for their mobile shrine, the Ark of the Covenant.

of paved roads wide enough to take wheeled vehicles. The donkey was the usual means of transport, used as a pack animal, although the camel came into use for crossing desert areas toward the end of the 2nd Millennium BC. It was a static world for most non-nomadic peoples who, by modern standards, had a very short life expectancy and harsh standards of living.

The Hazor temple, captured in Joshua's attack, has particular significance because its general architecture is similar to that of the Hebrew Temple in Jerusalem built by King Solomon in the 10th Century BC. In the court outside the temple building at Hazor were several smaller altars, and a drainage channel to carry away the blood from the sacrificed animals. At the Hebrew Temple, as at Hazor, the animal sacrifices took place outside the building, while incense was burned inside. Other Canaanite temples of this period, particularly at Shechem and Megiddo, had features similar to the Hazor temple.

For the Hebrews, as for other people of the time, sacred places were used for the worship of their own god even when they had associations with other gods. The Hebrews found no problems in using Canaanite sacred centres—but not for the worship of Canaanite gods.

THE RUINS OF GEZER
This Canaanite city was one of the last to fall into Hebrew hands.

The events of the conquest happened over a short or long period, with or without coalitions. The biblical narratives end with a list of conquered Canaanite cities, but it also mentions areas still to be taken, perhaps indicating the complex nature of the settlement process. As the Hebrews took over the land and were exposed to new styles of life, they transformed from wandering nomads to that of farmers living in fortified settlements. Farming and exposure to new religious practices that to some extent challenged their old beliefs. They had arrived in the Promised Land.

STRUGGLES OF THE JUDGES

ALTHOUGH VARIOUS TRIBES FOUGHT MANY BITTER WARS AGAINST THE CANAANITES AND OTHER COMMON ENEMIES, THERE WAS LITTLE CENTRAL HEBREW ORGANIZATION UNTIL SAUL WAS CHOSEN AS KING ABOUT 1030 BC. THE HEBREWS WERE CHALLENGING THE RULE OF THE PHILISTINES, WHO HAD CONQUERED MUCH OF CANAAN AND RENAMED IT PALESTINE.

The Book of Judges is organized around the deeds of 12 "judges" who, at various times, rallied groups of Hebrews to resist attack from Canaanites or from peoples beyond the borders of Canaan. They had a special charismatic gift for leadership in times of danger, rather than serving in the normal Hebrew authority structure, based on heads of families and tribes. Judges also tells the history of Israel from the death of the prophet and leader Joshua to the time just before the prophet Samuel. The book possesses considerable historical value as a source, the only biblical one, for ascertaining the events and social conditions of that period. Most historians consider Judges to be a composite work written between the 7th and 6th Centuries BC, the majority after 538 BC during the Babylonian captivity. Contained within the book are ancient fragments of Hebrew literature, such as the *Song of Deborah*.

The international historical setting of the Book of Judges is important to an understanding of how a loose tribal or clan confederacy formed and survived at this time. Had the Egyptian empire held firm, then Hebrew history could have taken a different direction. The Egyptian 20th Dynasty established itself in power under Set-nakht and his son Rameses III (c. 1183–1152 BC). This latter Pharaoh faced assaults by the Sea Peoples as well as by Libyan tribes. Among the Sea Peoples, Rameses listed the Pelasata (the Philistines), among others who he could not eject from his territories, being forced to allow the Philistines to settle, maybe as mercenaries to man garrisons, and give their name to Palestine. The Egyptian Empire never recovered from the alien incursions.

HEBREW SETTLEMENT AT THE BEGINNING OF THE PERIOD OF THE JUDGES
(far right)
God commanded Joshua to "allot the land of Israel for an inheritance," though much of Canaan remained to be conquered. The question of exact locations and borders of the tribes is one of the most difficult to resolve.

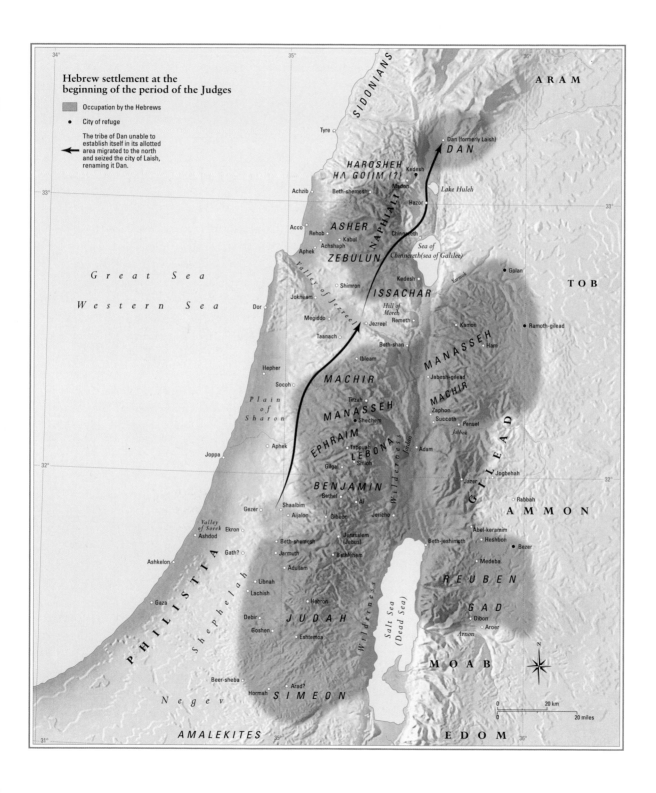

Hebrew settlement at the
beginning of the period of the Judges

Occupation by the Hebrews

• City of refuge

The tribe of Dan unable to
establish itself in its allotted
area migrated to the north
and seized the city of Laish,
renaming it Dan.

SIDONIANS

ARAM

Tyre

Dan (formerly Laish)
DAN

HAROSHEH
HA GOIIM (?)   Kedesh

Achzib   Beth-shemesh   Madon   Lake Huleh

Hazor

Acco   ASHER   Chinnereth

Rehob   Kabul

Aphek   Achshaph   Sea of
Chinnereth (sea of Galilee)

ZEBULUN

Golan   TOB

Kedesh

Shimron   ISSACHAR   Yarmuk

Jokneam   Hill of
Moreh

Dor   Megiddo   Jezreel   Remeth   Kamon   Ramoth-gilead

Great Sea   Taanach

Western Sea   Beth-shan   MANASSEH   Ham

Ibleam

Hepher   Jabesh-gilead   MACHIR

Socoh   MACHIR   Zaphon
Tirzah   Succoth

Plain   MANASSEH   Penuel
of   Shechem   Jabbok
Sharon   EPHRAIM

Aphek   LEBONA
Tappuah   Adam   GILEAD

Joppa   Gilgal   Shiloh

Jogbehah

Jazer

BENJAMIN   Rabbah
Bethel   Ai   AMMON

Gezer   Shaalbim
Aijalon   Gibeon   Jericho

Valley   Ekron   Abel-keramim
of Sorek   Jerusalem   Heshbon
Ashdod   (Jebus)   Beth-jeshimoth   Bezer

Ashkelon   Beth-shemesh   Bethlehem
Gath?   Jarmuth   Medeba

Adullam   REUBEN

Gaza   Libnah
Lachish   Hebron   GAD
Debir   Salt Sea   Dibon
Goshen   Eshtemoa   (Dead Sea)   Aroer
JUDAH   Arnon

PHILISTIA   MOAB

Beer-sheba   Arad?   N

Negev   Hormah   SIMEON

0   20 km

AMALEKITES   0   20 miles

EDOM

The remnants of Egypt's Asian holdings were up for grabs. The Hittite Empire had vanished. Assyria had weakened with the assassination of Tukulti-ninurta I (c. 1197 BC), and even the resurgence under Tiglath-pileser I (c. 1116–1078 BC), who had defeated Babylon, Armenia, Anatolia, and northern Phoenicia, did not last. The reason for the subsequent two centuries of Assyrian weakness lay in the increasing pressure of mainly Arameans who were pressuring all sectors of the Fertile Crescent during this period. Syria and Upper Mesopotamia became predominantly Aramean, seeing the creation of small city states such as Sham'al, Carchemish, Beth-eden, and Damascus. The international political scene was in a state of flux, which gave a nascent Israel freedom to develop without immediate threat.

Canaan, weakened without the defence of an imperial power, faced the Israelites who occupied the highlands of Palestine, the Sea Peoples nibbling away at the coastal plains, and the Arameans' pressure dominating the Syrian hinterland. Canaanite enclaves endured and the bulk of the population remained with their land. Elsewhere the Phoenicians recovered from attacks by the Sea Peoples and regenerated quickly, with Byblos and other cities becoming bustling trade centres.

The Book of Judges describes Israel's history as one of continuous if intermittent fighting, alongside peaceful periods and times of deep crisis. The Hebrews' territories were not a well-knit whole. The mountain areas were mainly in their hands, but Israelites could not move onto the plain lest they faced the chariots of the city states on the littoral. The coastal strip and the Plain of Jezreel (Esdaelon) were outside Israel's control. Any Israelites settling there intermarried with Canaanites or became subject to them. Some Canaanite enclaves existed in the mountains, including in Jerusalem.

Geographical features made an impact, too. The Galilean tribes were cut off from their kin by Canaanite lands in the Jezreel Valley. The Jordan rift valley separated eastern and western tribes and the highlands were so riven with valleys and broken terrain that communities tended to develop in some isolation developing their own customs, traditions, and interests, often with patriarchal traditions. Localisation militated against any common Hebrew unity. When danger threatened Israel, only those nearest to the issue reacted. Thus, the Book of Judges demonstrates the incredible disunity of the tribes, despite the spiritual power of the Covenant. Nevertheless, the latter did provide enough religious and political glue to hold the tribes together for two centuries.

Compared to their neighbor, the Hebrews were a poor, fairly socially homogenous group with no pretensions of developing an aristocracy. However, during the Judges period, camel caravans and links to seaborne trade allowed some tribes to develop a measure of prosperity. The judges entered this situation by criticising Israel for absorbing alien elements through its mass conversions. Theological chaos is strongly revealed in Judges. Although the Israelite league swore loyalty to Yahweh, pagan cults did not automatically die out. Some worshipped fertility cults as commensurate with an agricultural life and others accommodated their allegiance to Yahweh with worship of Baal.

The 12 judges emerging to deliver Israel are prresumably mentioned in chronological order, but precise dates are impossible to determine. No common characteristics can be assigned to the individuals. Gideon was motivated by a divine vocation, whereas Jephthah was a bandit who found Yahweh. He sacrificed his virgin daughter to fulfil a vow, an event that is described tragically and piteously:

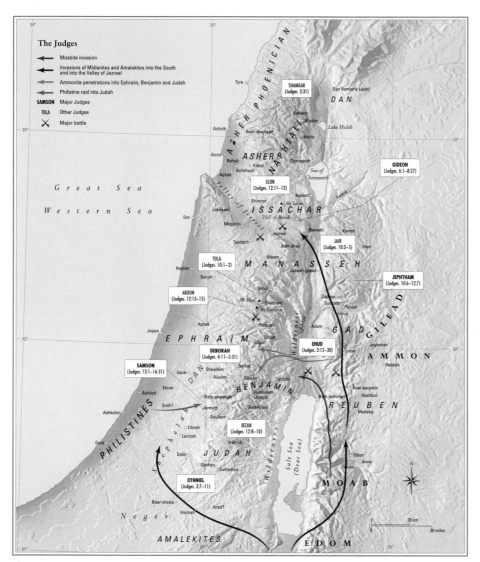

The Judges

- ← Moabite invasion
- ← Invasions of Midianites and Amalekites into the South and into the Valley of Jezreel
- ← Ammonite penetrations into Ephraim, Benjamin and Judah
- ← Philistine raid into Judah
- **SAMSON** Major Judges
- TOLA Other Judges
- ✕ Major battle

SHAMGAR
(Judges 3:31)

GIDEON
(Judges 6:1–8:27)

ELON
(Judges 12:11–12)

JAIR
(Judges 10:3–5)

TOLA
(Judges 10:1–2)

JEPHTHAM
(Judges 10:6–12:7)

ABDON
(Judges 12:13–15)

DEBORAH
(Judges 4:11–5:31)

EHUD
(Judges 3:12–30)

SAMSON
(Judges 13:1–16:31)

IBZAN
(Judges 12:8–10)

OTHNIEL
(Judges 3:7–11)

THE JUDGES

The Book of Judges begins with an account the various tribes to conquer their allotted territories, some successful and some total failures. In Judges 1, the recorded failures were more significant for the subsequent history of the region than the successes. Notably, Canaanites remained in several areas especially in the north and Israel also faced many invasions: from the Philistines in the west, and from the Moabites, Edomites and Amalekites in the south and east.

"And she said unto her father, Let this thing be done for me: let me alone two months, that I may go up and down upon the mountains, and bewail my virginity, I and my fellows. And he said, Go. And he sent her away for two months: and she went with her companions, and bewailed her virginity upon the mountains. And it came to pass at the end of two months, that she returned unto her father, who did with her according to his vow which he had vowed: and she knew no man. And it was a custom in Israel that the daughters of Israel went yearly to lament the daughter of Jephthah the Gileadite four days in a year" (Judges 1:27–40).

All judges had one thing in common: they were capable of firing up the tribes to fight. Othniel, the first judge to be mentioned (Judges 3:7–11), repulsed the invasion of Cushan-rishathaim of Aram-naharaim. Interpretations have variously portrayed this incursion of originating from Edom or the district of Qusanaruma in northern Syria (Aram).

Ehud's victory over Moab (Judges 3:12–30) occurred in the 12th Century BC. Moabite territory north of the River Arnon had been grabbed by Sihon the Amorite, from whom Israel seized the land, subsequently being occupied by the tribe of Reuben. Moab had regained this land and encroached into Benjaminite territory. Although the Moabites were repulsed, it is unknown whether they were ejected from Reubenite territory. Reuben was an early victim and was no longer an effective leader.

Shamgar (Judges 3:31) is an enigmatic figure. He was not even an Israelite, but existed before Deborah when the Sea Peoples were encroaching upon Hebrew territory. Reputedly, he was a city king of Beth-anath in Galilee who threw back the Philistines killing 600, saving both himself and Israel.

Deborah and Barak of Naphtali (Judges 4–5) are best placed historically about 1125 BC or a little before. Israel was almost cut in half by the Valley of Jezreel and Canaanite leagues dominating neighboring Israelite clans. Deborah and Barak rallied six tribes from Benjamin to Galilee that were aided by a rainstorm churning up the land, bogging down Canaanite chariots and allowing Israelite infantry to slaughter their crews. The victory did not make the Israelites masters of Jezreel, but for some considerable time they could travel and settle in it.

Gideon's career developed when Jezreel and the nearby highlands were attacked by camel-riding nomads from the desert—Midianites, Amalekites and Benê Qedem. This is the first recorded instance of domesticated camels. Annual raids occurred at harvest time generating an economic downturn and starvation. Gideon, a Manassite, rallied his tribe and his neighbors and drove the raiders from the land, his victories giving him immense authority. His people wanted him to assume a kingship, but he categorically refrained even though his son, Abimelech, established himself as king in Shechem for a short time before being killed. Such local kingship was not customary in Israel.

The tale of Jephthah depicts human sacrifice occurring in Israel despite its incompatibility, since the time of Isaac, with Yahwehism, and shows how easy civil war could happen. Samson's career (Judges 13–16) with its marital adventures accurately reflect the situation on the Philistine borders before open war erupted. It is possible that Samsonite-style raiding provoked the Philistines into more militant action against the Hebrews.

Judges demonstrates that the tribal league survived as a loose governmental form for a long time throughout a series of defensive wars. Possibly, the Israelites controlled less land by Samuel's time than at Joshua's death. The tribe of Reuben was virtually erased. Dan could not retain control of the central Shepheleh and moved north to seize land around Laish, north of the Sea of Galilee. All tribes were tormented by the Canaanite enclaves remaining in their midst.

**TRIBAL AREAS
ACCORDING TO JOSHUA**
(far right)
Some tribes possessed land east of the Jordan River, granted to them by Moses. To the west of the river, the land was allotted by Joshua, some areas to these same tribes. Not all tribes completed the conquest of their areas, but instead settled down alongside the Canaanite population.

Tribal Areas According to Joshua

Sidon

TYRE

ARAM

Damascus

Ahlab

Ijon

Tyre

Abel-beth-maacah

Kanah

Beth-anath

DAN

SYRIA

Taphnith

Hammon

Kadesh

Achnib

Yiron

Lake
Huleh

ASHER

Hazor

Beth-emek

Merom

Acco

Neiel

NAPHTALI

EAST
MANASSEH

Mishal

Chinnereth

Naveh

Aphek

Rimmon

Karnaim

Shikmonah

Nahalal

Sea of Chinnereth
(Sea of Galilee)

Golan (?)

Ashtaroth

Hennathon

Rakkath

Mt. Carmel

Achshaph

ZEBULUN

Hammath

Helkath

Chesulloth

Daberath

En-haddah

Yarmuk

Sarid

Kishelon

Dor

Megiddo

Ophra

En-dor

Shunem

Jermuth

Edrei

ISSACHAR

Jezreel

Lo-debar (?)

Taanach

Mt. Gilboa

Beth-shean

Harod

Ramoth-gilead

Great Sea

Dothan

Ibleam

Rehob

Jabesh-gilead

Western Sea

Bezek

Hammath

Habel-mehola

Socoh

WEST
MANASSEH

Jebel Um ed Daraj

Tirzah

Zapaon

AMMON

Elmattan

Shechem

Succoth

Mahanaim

Pirathon

Arumah

Janoah

Penuel

Zarqa

Aphek

Tappuah

Jokmeam

Zarethan

Ramath-mizpeh

Joppa

Lebonah

Adam

GAD

Gedor

Jehud

EPHRAIM

Ophra

Jogbehah

Lod

Bethel

Betonim

DAN

Gittaim

Shaalbim

Beth-haran

Gilgal(?)

Tyre of Toblah

Jazer

Rabbah

Jabneel

Gezer

Ramah

Jericho

Beth-nimrah

Gibbethon

Aijalon

Adummim

Shittim

Baalath

Kiriath

Kirian

Beth-hoglah

Hisban

Heshbon

Ekron

Timnah

Eshtoal

Jerusalem

BENJAMIN

Bezer

Zorah

Bether

Middin

Ashdod

Beth-shemesh

Hushah

City of Salt (?)

Medeba

Gath

Etam

Bethlehem

Ashkelon

Peor

Tekoa

REUBEN

Jahaz

Mareshah

Beth-zur

Salt Sea

Kedemoth

Lachish

(Dead Sea)

Dibon

Gaza

JUDAH

Hebron

Aroer

Mujib

Juttah

En-gedi

Gerar

Ziklag

Eshtemoa

Maon

Sharuen

Sansannah

Anim

MOAB

Ashan

Moladah

Jeshua(?)

Beersheba

Arad

Hazar-shual

Baalah

Hormah

Kir-hareseth

SIMEON

Eltolad

Ezem

Negev

Hasa

EDOM

N

Tamar

Arabah

0   20 km
0   20 miles

THE ARK CAPTURED

"AND THE PHILISTINES FOUGHT, AND ISRAEL WAS SMITTEN, AND THEY FLED EVERY MAN INTO HIS TENT: AND THERE WAS A VERY GREAT SLAUGHTER; FOR THERE FELL OF ISRAEL THIRTY THOUSAND FOOTMEN.

"AND THE ARK OF GOD WAS TAKEN; AND THE TWO SONS OF E-LI, HOPH-NI AND PHIN-E-HAS, WERE SLAIN."

1 SAMUEL 5:10–11

An understanding of what the Ark of the Covenant meant to the tribes of Israel is essential if the significance of its loss is analysed. The central shrine of the Israelite league of 12 tribes provided a cult with its sacred rites and occasions, and above all it contained Covenant law. The tent-shrine was a feature of desert origin, moveable, and is sometimes known as "the tent of meeting," where Yahweh, God, met His chosen people and made known His will. Sometimes, the shrine was regarded as

"the Tabernacle" where God tented amongst His people. "And let them make me a sanctuary; that I may dwell among them" (Exodus 25:8). This type of shrine was well-known with Ugaritic texts describing a portable shrine of El and the copper mines at Timna witnessed the uncovering of a Midianite tent-shrine. Descriptions of the shrine can be found in Exodus 25–31 and 35–40. Here, the ornate, resplendent Ark and Tabernacle are depicted in great detail as if the writer is attempting to project backward a later temple, legitimizing it with the past. Another, probably more realistic description can be found in the tent-shrine set up by David. "And they brought in the Ark of the Lord and set it in his place, in the midst of the tabernacle that David had pitched for it: and David offered burnt offerings and peace offerings before the Lord." (2 Samuel 7:17) This shrine was the successor to the league shrine captured by the Philistines. The portable tent-shrine is symbolic of the Israelites' origins in the desert with the heritage of a primitive desert belief system. Additionally, the shrine was the focal point for the tribal league and the core institution for the tribes. Accordingly, there had to be a central official shrine, which did not preclude worship at other places.

The Bible places the tribal center, after the conquest of Canaan at Shiloh, in the holdings of the tribe of Ephraim. Maybe this site had no associations for the tribes who had no vested interests in it. The tribal center might have been previously located elsewhere during the conquest. Gilgal was an important site (Joshua 4 and 5) both then and later. "And all the people went to Gilgal: and there they made Saul King before the Lord in Gilgal; and there they sacrificed sacrifices of peace offerings before the Lord; and there Saul and all the men of Israel rejoiced greatly" (1 Samuel 11:15). Some historians believe that the central shrine was first erected at Shechem, then at Bethel, before the final resting place at Shiloh. It seems likely that a regular rite of Covenant renewal took place during certain feasts at the shrine.

During Pharaoh Rameses III's reign, Egypt was assaulted by Libyans and the Sea Peoples. These tribes had been attacking the eastern Mediterranean coastline for many years. Probably originating in Balkans, these peoples destroyed the Hittite state in Anatolia and the Bronze Age states of Greece. Rameses III witnessed them moving southward by land and sea with their possessions, women, and children. No one knows what motivated this wave of people—were they marauders or dispossessed refugees? A naval attack was pushed back at the Nile delta and Rameses list some tribes: Shakarusha, Tjikar, Danuna, and the Pelesata (the Philistines). The Philistines and Tsikal were allowed to settle in Palestine, named after the Philistines, either as vassals or as mercenaries to man Egyptian garrison posts. Thus, the Philistines appeared in the region only a few years after the Israelite tribes. The Philistine migrants established themselves in the coastal area between the Shephelah and the sea, part of which is now the Gaza Strip. The Philistines captured five Canaanite cities: Gaza, Ashkelon, Ashdod, Gath, and Ekron. The last two could control the main route of the coastal road from Egypt to the north and to Mesopotamia. The other three were on the route to Joppa, the only sheltered harbor south of Acco. Under the Philistines, each city had its own king, but it was a closely-knit federation that appointed a single leader for warfare. They were technologically more advanced than the Canaanites or the Hebrews. With iron weapons, chariots, and good discipline, the Philistines soon extended their control into the Negev, the central mountains and the Valley of Jezreel. Neither the Canaanites nor the Hebrews were able to withstand them and they effectively ended Egyptian control of the area. Never particularly numerous, the Philistines were essentially a military aristocracy ruling a mainly Canaanite population. The Philistines also possessed the ability to act in concert, something at which Canaanite cities failed, as did the Israelite tribes.

The Hebrews may have been perceived as a threat to Philistine security or to the trade routes leading inland from the coast. Hence, they attempted to win control of all western Palestine. No one knows when the Philistines began their aggression. One imagines they sought to dominate the remaining coastal Canaanite city states and other Sea Peoples settling in the region. The tribes of Judah and Dan felt pressurized, the latter moving from their lands. Doubtless, border incidents, skirmishes, and guerrilla warfare were the norm as evidenced by the Samson stories.

Around 1050 BC, the Philistines attacked under the leadership of the King of Gath, their base being

THE ARK OF THE COVENANT
(far left)
A reconstruction of what the Ark of the Covenant may have looked like. At a battle fought near Ebenezer, the Philistines succeeded in capturing the Ark, but after suffering various unhappy events, including afflictions with tumors, the Philistine leadership decided to send the Ark out of their territory. The Hebrews happily received the Ark back, taking it to Kiriath-jearim where it remained for approximately 20 years until taken, by King David, to his new capital, Jerusalem.

"AND THEY LAID THE ARK OF THE LORD UPON THE CART, AND THE COFFER WITH THE MICE OF GOLD AND THE IMAGES OF THEIR EMERODS. "AND THE KINE TOOK THE STRAIGHT WAY TO THE WAY OF BETH-SHE-MESH, AND WENT ALONG THE HIGHWAY, LOWING AS THEY WENT, AND TURNED NOT ASIDE TO THE RIGHT HAND OR TO THE LEFT; AND THE LORDS OF THE PHILISTINES WENT AFTER THEM UNTO THE BORDER OF BETH-SHE-MESH. "AND THEY OF BETH-SHE-MESH WERE REAPING THEIR WHEAT HARVEST IN THE VALLEY: AND THEY LIFTED UP THEIR EYES, AND SAW THE ARK, AND REJOICED TO SEE IT."   I SAMUEL 7:11–13

Aphek, at the edge of the coastal plain. The Israelites were crushed at Ebenezer when 4,000 were killed. The Ark was brought from Shiloh, hoping God would bring victory. The Israelite army was destroyed, the Bible recording 30,000 dead. The Ark was captured, the priests in charge, Phinehas and Hophni, being killed. The Philistines then occupied the land, took Shiloh and destroyed the tent-shrine of the tribal league. Occupation garrisons were placed at key military points. The Philistines prevented the manufacture of weapons and retaining a monopoly of iron, took away any metal industry of the Israelites making them dependent on Philistine smiths for metallurgy. "Now there was no smith found throughout all the land of Israel: for the Philistines said, lest the Hebrews make themselves swords or spears. But all the Israelites went down to the Philistines, to sharpen every man his share, and his coulter, and his axe, and his mattock. Yet they had a file for the mattocks, and for the coulters, and for the forks, and for the axes, and to sharpen the goads. So it came to pass in the day of battle, that there was neither sword nor spear found in the hand of any of the people that were with Saul and Jonathan" (1 Samuel 13:19–22). Iron remained uncommon in Israel until the reign of King David.

The Philistine occupation was incomplete, but Philistia held much of the Negev, the central mountain range and the Valley of Jezreel. Control was probably not exercised over all Galilee and not in Transjordan. Even the garrisoned central mountains were impossible to police since the Israelites managed to arm themselves and develop resistance techniques. The Israelite league was without an army temporarily, its tent-shrine destroyed, and much of the priesthood killed. The situation looked hopeless.

The Philistines took the Ark to Ashdod, placing it in the temple of their god, Dagon. Later, their idol was found fallen on its face. Upon replacing the statue, next day it was found with its head and hands cut off. Ashdod and its environs then suffered a plague of emerods or haemorrhoids (1 Samuel 5:6). The Philistines then moved the Ark to Gath and then to Ekron, but the plague struck each place in turn. After seven months, the Philistines decided to return the Ark, accompanied by expensive gifts. The Ark arrived at Beth-shemesh. The Ark was then transported to Kiriath-jearim where it remained for 20 years, doubtless under watchful Philistine eyes. However, the old Hebrew tribal league was smashed forever; a monarchy was about to be established.

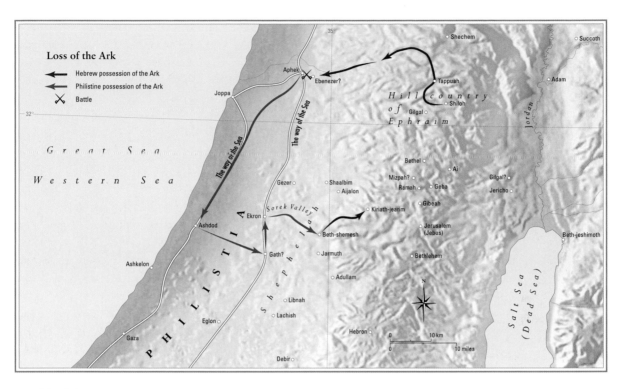

Loss of the Ark

→ Hebrew possession of the Ark

→ Philistine possession of the Ark

✗ Battle

LOSS OF THE ARK

The Philistines attacked the Hebrews near Aphek and defeated them. The Hebrews withdrew to rally their forces and counter-attack. This time they took the Ark of the Covenant into battle. They were defeated again, still worse the Ark was lost.

MESSAGE FROM THE PAST

At the time of the Ark man's presence in the Negev – the arid region that forms much of southern Israel – is revealed by the Hebrew writing still visible on rocks in the area.

SAMUEL

SAMUEL IS REPRESENTED IN THE BIBLE AS BOTH A JUDGE AND
PROPHET, FAMED FOR HIS ROLE IN INSTIGATING A JEWISH
MONARCHY. HIS CHILDLESS MOTHER, HANNAH, HAD PRAYED TO
GOD FOR A CHILD, AND IN DUE COURSE, SAMUEL WAS BORN.

Eternally grateful, Hannah dedicated Samuel to the service of the chief religious sanctuary of Shiloh. After he was weaned, he left his birthplace of Rameh, and was placed in the care of Eli, the Shiloh priest.

Samuel was born into a world when border strife with the Philistines intensified. United under the King of Gath, the Philistines crushed the Jews at Ebenezer, capturing the Ark of the Covenant. Eli's sons were killed in the battle and the Shiloh shrine was destroyed.

When Eli died, Samuel inherited the spiritual leadership of the Hebrews. Samuel was convinced that his people could only be free and secure if their faith was strong. Accordingly, he called the Hebrews to Mizpah where they confessed their sins, Samuel praying to the Lord on their behalf. The Philistines learned of the Hebrews congregating and attacked Mizpah: "...But the Lord thundered with a great thunder on that day upon the Philistines, and discomfited them; and they were smitten before Israel" (1 Samuel 7:10). Despite their rout, the Philistines were soon back in force at Geba, in a strong position dominating the main eastern approach through the Saddle of Benjamin into the Judaean hills. Eventually the Hebrews pushed them out with extreme difficulty.

Border warfare continued unabated with the hills and the Shephelah foothills as a battleground. Nevertheless, the times were peaceful enough for Samuel to conduct an annual ministry circuit from his home at Rameh to Mizpah, Bethel, Naraan, Gilgal, and Geba. Whilst visiting these communities, Samuel dispensed judgement in disputes and dispensed justice. As Samuel aged, his sons were considered unworthy to succeed him. The future looked uncertain with no respected spiritual leader available. The Hebrew elders thought that only a centralized government, with power held in the hands of a strong

"THEN E-LI CALLED SAMUEL, AND SAID, SAMUEL, MY SON. AND HE ANSWERED, HERE AM I.

"AND HE SAID, WHAT IS THE THING THAT THE LORD HATH SAID UNTO THEE? I PRAY THEE HIDE IT NOT FROM ME: GOD DO SO TO THEE, AND MORE ALSO, IF THOU HIDE ANY THING FROM ME OF ALL THE THINGS THAT HE SAID UNTO THEE.

"AND SAMUEL TOLD HIM EVERY WHIT, AND HID NOTHING FROM HIM. AND HE SAID, IT IS THE LORD: LET HIM DO WHAT SEEMETH HIM GOOD.

"AND SAMUEL GREW AND THE LORD WAS WITH HIM, AND DID LET NONE OF HIS WORDS FALL TO THE GROUND.

"AND ALL ISRAEL FROM DAN EVEN TO BEER-SHEBA KNEW THAT SAMUEL WAS ESTABLISHED TO BE A PROPHET OF THE LORD."   1 SAMUEL 3:16–20

THE CALLING OF SAMUEL
An illustration of the much-loved story of the calling of Samuel. The child Samuel is shown with the priest Eli in this scene from the John Brown Bible.

leader, could respond quickly and decisively against the Philistines. Their means of survival was a request to Samuel to anoint a king to govern them as did other monarchies elsewhere. Samuel argued against the notion, claiming that royal power could be abused, but the elders ignored his pleas. Ultimately, the Bible states that the Lord commanded Samuel to heed the Hebrews' wishes and find a king. Samuel's choice fell upon Saul of Gibeah, a known warrior fully capable of leading men. He possessed few supporters and, therefore, no power base for abuse, and would therefore be constrained in his actions. Saul of the tribe of Benjamin was anointed and installed as king. Samuel retired from his leadership, but surfaced again when he rejected Saul for religious failures and later still when he anointed David as King in secrecy.

Saul, First King of Israel

SAUL IS REMEMBERED AS THE FIRST KING OF ISRAEL (C. 1021–1000 BC), CHOSEN BY THE JUDGE SAMUEL AND BY PUBLIC DEMAND FOR A LEADER.

S aul would govern like the judges, but his major function was to defend Israel against its many enemies, the Philistines in particular. The intensification of Philistine pressure to expand its power base while constraining any Israelite growth was the main catalyst for bringing Saul to power.

Accordingly to one folktale, Saul sought out the local seer as he searched for his father's donkeys in a neighboring village. That man was the prophet Samuel, who promptly anointed him as king. Another version of events sees Samuel summoning the tribes of Israel at Mizpah in order to choose and publically select a king by lot. Saul was the reluctant choice. He returned to Gibeah in Benjamin to his wealthy father, Kish. All Israel hoped he would unite the tribes, a loose confederation the unity of which was dependent upon their religious faith and Covenant with God. These bonds were renewed at intervals in ceremonies at the central shrine of Shiloh. Now, Saul had to fight better-armed and organized Philistines with their iron weapons and chariots. However, his first test of resolve and leadership was not against this strong enemy, but against the Ammonites.

The Ammonite leader Nahash besieged the Israelite town of Jabesh-gilead, across the Jordan in the north. Nahash demanded the right eye of every townsman as a condition for making peace. "On this condition I will make a treaty with you, that I gouge out all your right eyes, and thus put disgrace upon all Israel" (1 Samuel 11:2). The Jabeshites sent out messengers seeking help. At Gibeah, Saul responded by summoning the men of Israel to Bezek, on the way from Shechem to Beth-shan. He led his forces at night across the Jordan through the Wadi Yabis to a valley below Jabesh-gilead. A three-

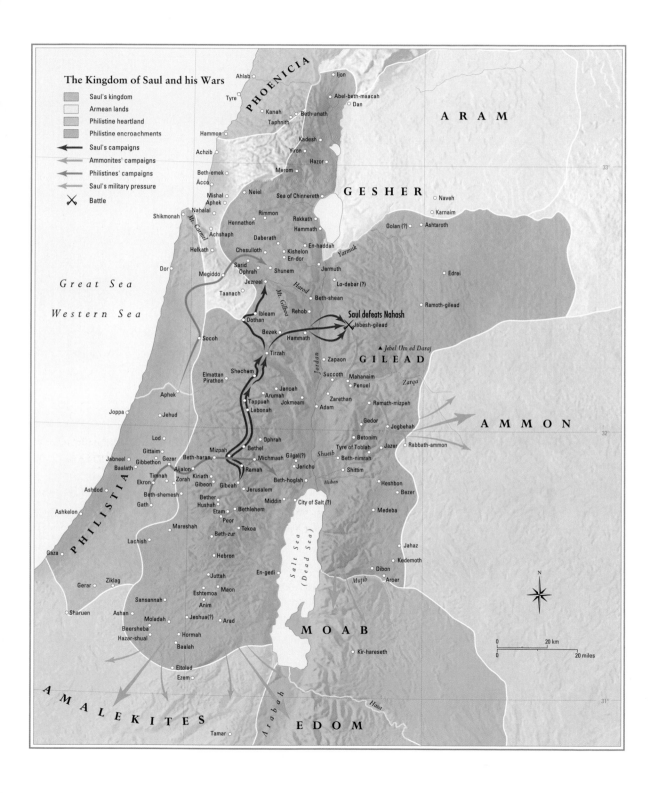

The Kingdom of Saul and his Wars

Saul's kingdom
Armean lands
Philistine heartland
Philistine encroachments
Saul's campaigns
Ammonites' campaigns
Philistines' campaigns
Saul's military pressure
Battle

PHOENICIA

ARAM

GESHER

Great Sea

Western Sea

GILEAD

Saul defeats Nahash
Jabesh-gilead

AMMON

PHILISTIA

Salt Sea
(Dead Sea)

MOAB

AMALEKITES

EDOM

pronged dawn attack caught the Ammonites unawares and they were hunted down and killed—it was a total victory. Saul's reputation as a military leader was made and he was re-acclaimed as King at Gilgal.

To the west, barely 15 miles (25.5 km) away at Geba, Philistine forces sat astride the strategically important pass that lead into the Israelite hill territory. With the tribes united, probably for the first time, Saul caught the Philistines with their guard down. He took Gibeah, which controlled the southern end of a strategic crossing of a steep valley that separated the settlement from Michmash. Saul collected 3,000 men, taking 2,000 with him, leaving the remainder under his son Jonathan at Gibeah.

The headstrong Jonathan launched a surprise attack on Geba, defeating its garrison. Saul broadcast news of the victory in order to rally more Hebrews to his command. However, the Philistines collected together their garrisons and outposts into a large concentration of infantry and charioteers. "And the Philistines gathered themselves together to fight with Israel, thirty thousand chariots, and six thousand horsemen, and people as the sand which is on the sea shore in multitude: and they came up and pitched in Michmash, eastward from Beth-aven" (1 Samuel 13:5).

Saul's terrified army disintegrated, forcing him to retreat to Gilgal. Deserters hid in caves and secret places throughout the region. An impatient Saul waited for Samuel to make God a burnt sacrifice; the judge was delayed and Saul made the offering himself, breaking religious practice and protocol. Saul had to face an angry Samuel. Saul had presumed too much; Samuel claimed Saul's kingdom would fail and God would seek a man after his own heart as king. Samuel then abandoned Saul for Gibeah.

Despite this bad beginning to the campaign, Saul took his remaining 600 men, moving to Gibeah and avoiding three large companies of raiders leaving Michmash. Jonathan and his armor-bearer, carried out their own raid, destroying a Philistine outpost of 20 men on a rocky crag. The Philistines panicked, and Saul threw his entire force at the enemy camp, causing confusion and slaughter. As the Philistines fled, Israelite deserters emerged from hiding and joined the hunt of the routed Philistines westward to Beth-horon and past Aijalen to Philistia stopping at the border. This victory ensured the security of the highlands, the core of Saul's kingdom.

Saul then waged war against all surrounding enemies: Moab, Ammon, Edom, Zobah, and the Philistines. Samuel returned to Saul, and said God demanded the destruction of the Amalekites who had been harsh toward the Hebrews when they first entered the Promised Land. Saul captured the Amalekite king, Agag, and and killed his followers, but despite being ordered to destroy every living thing, the best of the flocks and oxen were sent to Gilgal. Samuel denounced Saul for not destroying all as the Lord required, saying again that God rejected him as king. The judge was adamant, ignoring Saul's repentance, and himself hacked Agag to death with a sword. Saul established a victory monument at Carmel, southeast of Hebron, possibly to demonstrate his claim to political power in the region.

Although Saul was victorious in many campaigns, he remained a military figure changing the nation's customary institutions. The sole royal official seems to have been Abner, Saul's cousin and a military commander. The court was austere, being a simple country fortress at Gibeah. Meanwhile,

SAUL ENCOURAGES DAVID
In this medieval illustration,
King Saul is shown top left
encouraging his favorite and
future rival, David, to attack
the Philistine giant Goliath.

minor skirmishes occurred regularly, and it was in one such that a future king, David, distinguished himself as a brave warrior achieving notice.

The Struggle for Power

DAVID IS A HERO IN ISRAEL'S HISTORY—HIS LEGEND SURROUNDED BY MYTH AS MUCH AS HISTORICAL EVENTS. HE CAME TO SAUL'S NOTICE, THANKS TO HIS WARRIOR SKILLS AND HIS ABILITY TO SOOTHE, WITH MUSIC, THE BOUTS OF MELANCHOLY FROM WHICH SAUL SUFFERED .

STRUGGLE FOR POWER
(far right)
Saul clashed with Samuel. Perhaps Saul's new form of government was too great a change, particularly while Samuel was still a powerful force, and he did not command the loyalty of the southern Hebrew tribes. David had served in Saul's court and had already acquired a powerful military reputation with a band of followers. However because of Saul's jealousy he fled to Philistia serving the king of Gath as a mercenary.

"And it came to pass, when the evil spirit from God was upon Saul, that David took a harp, and played with his hand: so Saul was refreshed, and was well, and the evil spirit departed from him" (1 Samuel 17:23).

The other version of events in 1 Samuel 17:32–51 suggests that David was first noticed when he faced Goliath, the huge Philistine. Border warfare was renewed, the Philistines again attempting to acquire the Shephelah. They were concentrating their forces between Socoh and Azekah, intending to attack the Judaean highlands. Saul placed the Israelite army in a blocking position in the Valley of Elah. Both contender's positions were strong and military stalemate was reached. An old tradition maintained that single combat between champions could resolve the situation. Goliath represented the Philistines, but was knocked down by a sling stone cast by David who then seized Goliath's sword and beheaded him. The Philistines then fled to the cities of Gath and Ekron. David was now a hero, and entered the king's service, immediately befriending Jonathan, Saul's son. David became a renowned military leader killing 200 Philistines winning Michal, Saul's daughter, in marriage. Saul became jealous of David's success. "And the women answered one another as they played, and said Saul hath slain his thousands, and David his ten thousands. And Saul was very wroth, and the saying displeased him; and he said, They have ascribed unto David ten thousands, and to me they have ascribed by thousands: and what can he have more but the kingdom?" (1 Samuel 18:7–8)

Saul grew to hate David and even threw his spear at him while he was playing his harp. Michal warned her husband that Saul was plotting his murder, and he ran from Gibeah, leaving a mannequin

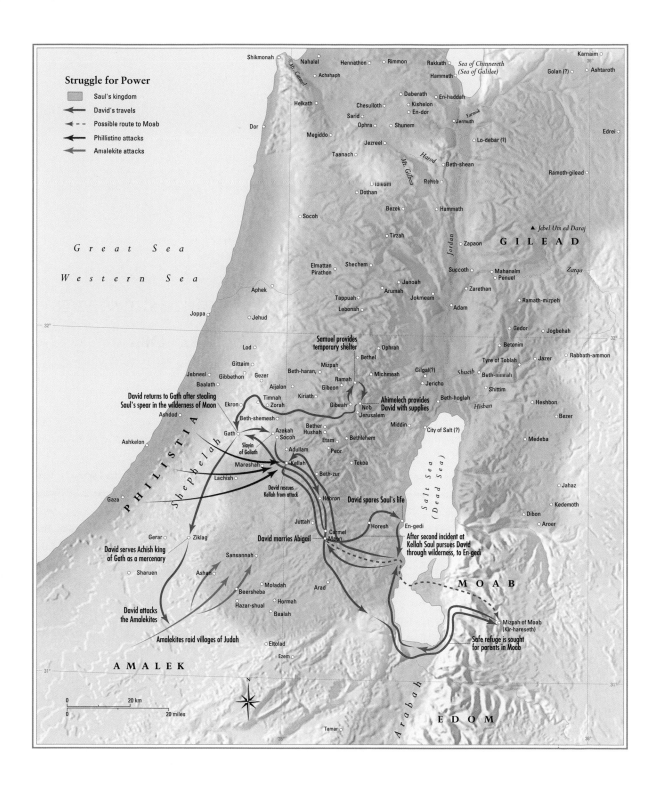

Struggle for Power

Saul's kingdom
David's travels
Possible route to Moab
Phillistine attacks
Amalekite attacks

Great Sea

Western Sea

Samuel provides temporary shelter

Ahimelech provides David with supplies

David returns to Gath after stealing Saul's spear in the wilderness of Maon

Slaying of Goliath

David rescues Kellah from attack

David spares Saul's life

David marries Abigail

After second incident at Kellah Saul pursues David through wilderness, to En-gedi

David serves Achish king of Gath as a mercenary

David attacks the Amalekites

Amalekites raid villages of Judah

Safe refuge is sought for parents in Moab

Mizpah of Moab (Kir-hareseth)

PHILISTIA

Shephelah

AMALEK

MOAB

EDOM

GILEAD

Salt Sea (Dead Sea)

Arabah

Sea of Chinnereth (Sea of Galilee)

Jordan

▲ Jebel Um ed Daraj

0   20 km
0   20 miles

DAVID SLAYS GOLIATH
Although David had a long and eventful reign as King of Israel and Judah, he is still most popularly remembered as the slayer of the Philistine warrior Goliath. This painting by Philippe le Bel de Breviare shows David with Saul and Goliath.

in his bed. David traveled to Rameh to win the support of Samuel, the judge who had anointed him as Israel's future king. Saul's agents, sent to seize David vanished; Saul himself went to Rameh, but was possessed by frenzied religious dancing and collapsed. David sought Jonathan's intercession, but was again warned about Saul's hostility; without a unarmed escort, he fled to Nob and persuaded the shrine's chief priest that he was Saul's agent, leaving with food and Goliath's sword, originally left there as tribute.

David then traveled to Philistia in search of sanctuary. He reached Gath, being quizzed by King Achish as to the motives of this notorious Philistine killer. To ensure survival, David feigned madness and was dismissed, walking ten miles (17 km) through the Shephelah to Adullam in no-man's land between Philistia and Saul. There, he encamped in inhospitable terrain, but with a water supply and a cave system for hiding places. At first, he was joined by his brothers and clan members, then by the discontented, the disaffected, and the indebted until he formed a renegade band of 400 men. David took his parents to the sanctuary of the Moabite king, while he moved from Adullam to the Forest of Hereth.

Learning that Philistines were attacking Keilah, an independent town, David assaulted and dispersed the besiegers, but the ungrateful population planned to betray David and his men to Saul. Consequently, David fled Saul's forces to Horesh and the Wilderness of Ziph. The inhabitants of this

DAVID'S RISE TO POWER
(far right)
As David, in the service of the Philistines, fights the Amalekites in the south, his employers march against King Saul and meet him in battle at Mount Gilboa. They destroy the Israelite army. The wounded Saul commits suicide rather than be captured. On hearing the news, David holds a wake for the dead king then sets about taking the reigns of power.

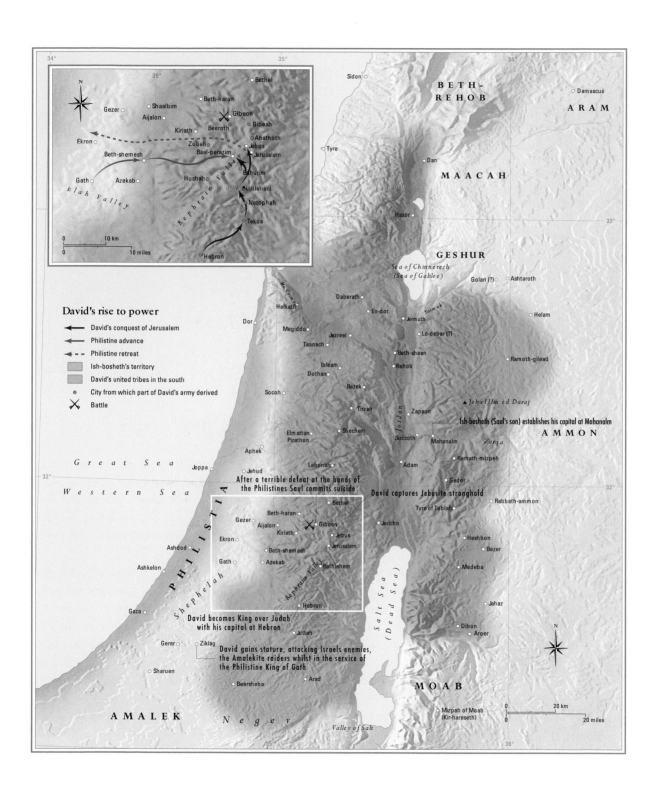

Inset map:

34°   35°   35°

N

Bethel

Gezer   Shaalbim   Beth-haran

Aijalon   Gibeon

Kiriath   Beeroth   Gibeah

Ekron   Anathoth

Zobah   Jebus

Beth-shemesh   Baal-perazim   Jerusalem

Bahurim

Gath   Azekab   Hushah

Elah Valley   Bethlehem

Rephraim Valley   Netophah

Tekoa

Hebron

0   10 km

0   10 miles

Main map:

Sidon   BETH-REHOB   Damascus   ARAM

Tyre   MAACAH   Dan

Hazor

GESHUR

Sea of Chinnereth (Sea of Galilee)   Golan (?)   Ashtaroth

Daberath   Helam

Helkath   En-dor   Jermuth

Dor   Megiddo   Jezreel   Lo-debar (?)

Taanach   Beth-shean   Ramoth-gilead

Ibleam   Rehob

Dothan   Bezek

Socoh   Tirzah   Zapoan

▲ *Jebel Um ed Daraj*

Elmattan   Shechem   Ish-bosheth (Saul's son) establishes his capital at Mahanaim

Pirathon   Succoth   Mahanaim   *Zarqa*   AMMON

Aphek   Adam

Lebonah   Ramath-mizpeh

Great Sea   Joppa   Jehud

Western Sea   After a terrible defeat at the hands of the Philistines Saul commits suicide   Gedor

Bethel   David captures Jebusite stronghold   Tyre of Tobiah   Rabbath-ammon

David's rise to power

→ David's conquest of Jerusalem

← Philistine advance

⇠ - - Philistine retreat

▨ Ish-bosheth's territory

▨ David's united tribes in the south

• City from which part of David's army derived

✕ Battle

Beth-haran   Gibeon   Jericho   Heshbon

Gezer   Kiriath   Jebus   Bezer

Aijalon   Jerusalem

Ekron   Beth-shemesh   Bethlehem   Medeba

PHILISTIA   Gath   Azekab   *Rephraim Valley*   *Salt Sea (Dead Sea)*

Ashdod   Jahaz

Ashkelon   Hebron   Dibon   Aroer   N

Shephelah   David becomes King over Judah with his capital at Hebron

Gaza   Juttah

Gerar   Ziklag   David gains stature, attacking Israels enemies, the Amalekite raiders whilst in the service of the Philistine King of Gath

Sharuen   Arad   MOAB

Beersheba

AMALEK   *Negev*   Mizpah of Moab (Kir-hareseth)

Valley of Salt   0   20 km

0   20 miles

Jordan

COOLING WATERS
Since biblical times the desert oases have drawn man to these fertile, cool areas, such as David Fall in En Gedi, now a National Reserve Oasis near the Dead Sea.

barren plateau informed Saul, and pursued by 3,000 men, David moved south to the Wilderness of Maon. Had the Philistines not raided the north—forcing Saul to give up his campaign against David—then the latter would probably have been captured. As it happened, David reached the Dead Sea at En-gedi.

The Bible states that, having dealt with the Philistines, Saul again chased David. Saul even entered a cave where David was hiding, but David refrained from killing him, instead surreptitiously cutting away a piece of Saul's clothing. Afterward, David shouted to Saul, showing him the portion of his robe, making Saul realize that he been at David's mercy. Immediately remorseful, Saul returned to Ramah and David went to his Adullam stronghold.

After Samuel died, David moved from the environs of Rameh and returned to the Wilderness of Maon, and at nearby Carmel, met his future wife Abigail. The Ziphites again betrayed David's presence to Saul. David and a companion crept into the king's camp at night, David refusing to let his comrade slay Saul. "As the Lord liveth, the Lord shall smite him: or his day shall come to die; or he shall descend into battle, and perish. The Lord forbid that I should stretch forth mine hand against the Lord's anointed: but I pray thee, take now the spear that is at his bolster, and the cruse of water, and let us go" (1 Samuel 26:10–11). Again, David demonstrated his actions, showing the spear and water bottle as evidence. As before, Saul retreated.

David still felt insecure and marched with his company of 600 proven soldiers to seek sanctuary at Gath. Saul now left the chase, knowing he could not enter Philistia. Achish gave David the Philistine town of Ziklag, in the Negev, to rule as his vassal. He wanted David to assault the Israelites in the Judaean foothills, but, instead, David raided into the Negev against the Amalekites, the Geshurites and the Gezrites. These victims were all killed and their livestock seized. David persuaded Achish that he had attacked southern Judea against the Jerahmeelites and Kenites. In reality, he was undermining Israel's southern enemies. Sixteen months were spent with the Philistines, but David eventually faced the problem when his host mustered a large army at Aphek in preparation for a final battle against Israel. The issue was removed from David when Achish sent his company back to Ziklag because he felt that David might betray him in battle. On his return to Ziklag, David found the town burnt and his men's families and possessions taken by vengeful Amalekites. David organized a quick pursuit of the camel-borne raiders beyond the Beser into the Negev. The raiders were found feasting. The men were killed, and the families, including David's two wives, were returned safely along with the loot of the Amalek raid into Philistia. David demanded that the booty should be shared equally amongst the elders of southern Judah, a shrewd move winning the potential support for a future move on the kingship.

The Philistines moved from Aphek into the Jezreel Valley, making their camp at Shunem under Mount Moreh. Saul's forces were at Mount Gilboa in the south, maybe near the mountain's springs. Saul was terrified of the sheer size of the Philistine army, and he could not receive an answer to his prayers about the battle's outcome. Anxious, he journeyed to the witch of Endor begging her to speak to Samuel's spirit. Samuel's ghost prophesied: "Because thou obeyest not the voice of the Lord, nor

THE OASIS OF EN-GEDI
Having fled Saul's forces, David moved south through the wilderness of Maon, finally resting near the shore of the Dead Sea at the oasis of En-gedi.

executest his fierce wrath upon Amalek, therefore hath the Lord done this thing unto thee this day. Moreover, the Lord will deliver Israel with thee into the hands of the Philistine's: and to morrow shalt thou and thy sons be with me: the Lord also shall deliver the host of Israel into the hand of the Philistines" (1 Samuel 28:18–19).

The Israelites were vastly outnumbered, and even if the terrain rendered Philistine chariots unusable, they were still severely disadvantaged. The Philistines stormed the Hebrew ranks and neither Saul nor Jonathan's bravery could deny the overwhelming enemy victory. Saul's forces were utterly overrun, fleeing up the sides of Mount Gilboa where they were hunted down in a savage pursuit. Here, three of Saul's sons fell: Jonathan, Abinadab, and Malchishua. Saul was wounded by an arrow, and commited suicide by falling on his sword, lest the Philistines capture him. The captured Israelite royals were beheaded and their weapons placed as an offering in the temple of Ashtaroth at Beth-shan. Saul's head was given to the temple of Dagon. The royal Israelite corpses were hung from the city's walls. News of their mutilation and fate of the bodies spread far and wide. Men from Jabesh-gilead, remembering how Saul had saved them earlier, secretly removed the bodies and ritually burnt them, burying the bones under a tree at Jabesh.

The Israelites had now lost the area bordering the Jezreel valley, abandoning their cities as refugees. News of the defeat reached David three days later. He and his men held a wake for Saul, his sons and the Israelites who had fallen in battle. David's emotional state produced the well-known lament:

"THE BEAUTY OF ISRAEL IS SLAIN UPON THY HIGH PLACES:

HOW ARE THE MIGHTY FALLEN! ... SAUL AND JONATHAN

WERE LOVELY AND PLEASANT IN THEIR LIVES AND IN THEIR DEATH

NOT DIVIDED: THEY WERE SWIFTER THAN EAGLES,

THEY WERE STRONGER THAN LIONS ... HOW ARE THE

MIGHTY FALLEN, AND THE WEAPONS OF WAR PERISHED!"

2 SAMUEL 1–19, 23 AND 27

Saul was the tragic hero, deranged in his slaughter of 85 priests and their families at Nob for helping David, but his military prowess prevented the complete occupation of his kingdom by the Philistines. David was able to take the remnants and work as a new deliverer of Israel from the hands of its triumphant enemies.

ANCIENT MEGALITHS
Looking from the foothills of southern Judea across the coastal plains of Philistia. It was through this terrain that the Hebrews fought long and costly campaigns against the Philistines.

KING DAVID

FACED WITH A DIVISIVE POLITICAL SITUATION AFTER SAUL'S DEATH, DAVID UNITED RIVAL HEBREW TRIBES, SECURED THEIR LOYALTY BY PROVIDING A NEUTRAL CAPITAL—JERUSALEM— AND SUBDUED THEIR VARIOUS ENEMIES.

The main sources of information about Kings David and Solomon were heavily edited by the historians of the southern Hebrew Kingdom of Judah. Jerusalem was the chief city of Judah, the city that David had captured and made his first effective capital of the united Hebrew people. The sources are therefore suspect and may underrate Saul and the northern Hebrews in order to emphasize the glories of David and Solomon. But unattractive aspects, such as David's murder of his officer, Uriah (2 Samuel 11), are included to show that the accounts are not mere propaganda. However biased they may be, 1 and 2 Samuel present a convincing picture of David as an outstanding personality.

After he had been made king, Saul exercised loose control over the central highlands from Judah to the edge of Mount Carmel, the area east of the River Jordan, the Valley of Jezreel and Galilee. The centers of his power lay in Benjamin country, just north of Jerusalem (which was still in Canaanite hands), and Bethlehem, just south of Jerusalem. The recognition by Samuel of the young David as future leader of the country (1 Samuel 16) is consistent with the role of Samuel as a seer, but the account has been written with hindsight. David was born in Bethlehem, the most northerly town in Judah. He joined Saul's court as other young Hebrews from various tribal areas would have done, and became a successful officer and a favorite of Saul's. There must be doubts about David's killing of Goliath at an engagement with Philistine forces on the edge of the Shephelah between Socoh and Azekah (1 Samuel 17), for, in a brief summary of David's clashes with Philistines, the killing of Goliath is attributed to one of his soldiers (2 Samuel 21:19).

David's marriage to one of Saul's daughters is told within the context of Saul"s mounting jealousy of David, whose popular reputation as a warrior had now surpassed Saul's own (1 Samuel 18). This would

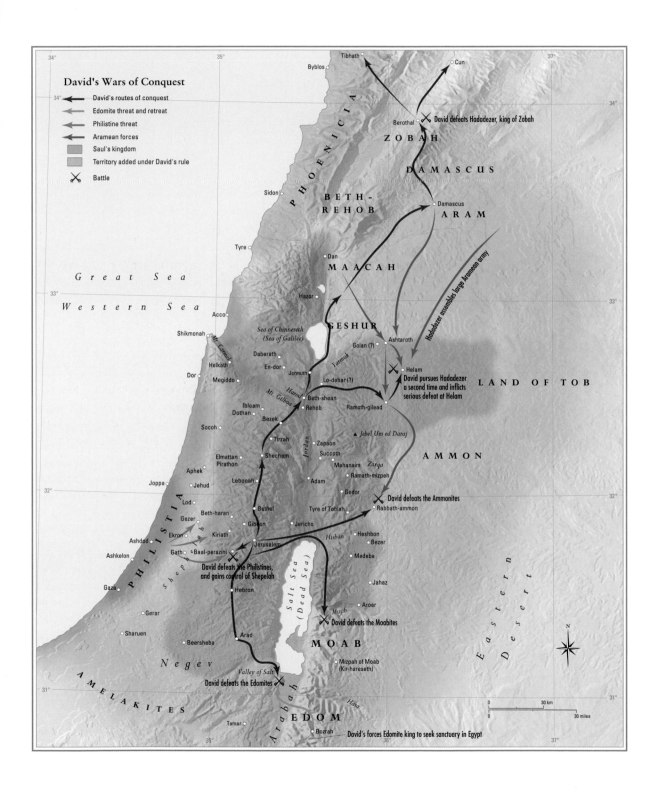

David's Wars of Conquest

➤ David's routes of conquest
➤ Edomite threat and retreat
➤ Philistine threat
➤ Aramean forces
▨ Saul's kingdom
▨ Territory added under David's rule
✗ Battle

Tibhath
Byblos
Cun
Berothai
✗ David defeats Hadadezer, king of Zobah
ZOBAH
DAMASCUS
PHOENICIA
Sidon
BETH-REHOB
Damascus
ARAM
Tyre
Dan
MAACAH
Hazor
Hadadezer assembles large Aramean army
Great Sea
Western Sea
Acco
Sea of Chinnereth (Sea of Galilee)
GESHUR
Golan (?)
Ashtaroth
Shikmonah
Mt. Carmel
Daberath
En-dor
Jermuth
Golan (?)
Yarmuk
✗ Helam
Dor
Helkath
Megiddo
Lo-debar (?)
David pursues Hadadezer a second time and inflicts serious defeat at Helam
LAND OF TOB
Harod
Beth-shean
Ibleam
Mt. Gilboa
Rehob
Ramoth-gilead
▲ *Jebel Um ed Daraj*
Dothan
Bezek
Socoh
Tirzah
Zapaon
Succoth
AMMON
Elmattan
Pirathon
Shechem
Mahanaim
Zarqa
Ramath-mizpeh
Aphek
Jehud
Lebonah
Adam
Joppa
Gedor
✗ David defeats the Ammonites
Lod
Bethel
Tyre of Tobiah
Rabbath-ammon
Beth-haran
Jericho
Heshbon
Gezer
Shephelah
Kiriath
Ekron
Ashdod
Gibeon
Jerusalem
Hisban
Bezer
Gath
Baal-perazini
Medeba
Ashkelon
✗ David defeats the Philistines, and gains control of Shepelah
Salt Sea (Dead Sea)
Jahaz
Gaza
Hebron
Mujib
Aroer
Gerar
✗ David defeats the Moabites
Eastern Desert
Sharuen
Arad
Beersheba
MOAB
Negev
Mizpah of Moab (Kir-hareseth)
N
Valley of Salt
✗ David defeats the Edomites
AMELAKITES
Arabah
Hasa
0   30 km
0   30 miles
Tamar
EDOM
Bozrah
David's forces Edomite king to seek sanctuary in Egypt

have been dangerous at any time in the turbulent history of Hebrew kings, including David's own reign, and so the marriage should be seen as a way of securing David's loyalty to Saul. Shortly afterward, Saul attempted to kill David because he was a threat to his authority. This is still a period when the leader's authority rested on his pre-eminence in battle, as it had for the judges, and Saul could not afford to have his own reputation surpassed by one of his court.

The subsequent actions of David, after his flight from King Saul, all show the political skill which he would eventually use to unite the various Hebrew groups and factions. He was helped by the members of the sacred city of Nob, near Jerusalem, where the priests of the central sanctuary had fled when Shiloh was captured and destroyed by the Philistines after the Battle of Aphek. David welcomed the survivor, Ahimelek, when Saul had Nob's priests executed. During this period David lived as an outlaw in the Judaean hills and in caves along the shores of the Dead Sea. He gathered around him the men who would become the nucleus of his own court. Eventually, he and his group became mercenaries in the service of the Philistines, following a long Hebrew tradition of service as mercenary soldiers. Even during this time, his sense of political realities kept him from antagonising any Hebrews whose support he would need if he were to unite the people. Saul died at the Battle of Gilboa (c. 1010). David and his men had been left behind because of their previous service under Saul. Thus, no Hebrew group could claim that David had fought against them.

King Saul's reign ended in disaster. He lost the support of Samuel and of the traditional Hebrew religion and, eventually, was defeated by the Philistines he had successfully resisted during his reign. Despite his reputation as a failed king, Saul did, for most of his reign, force the Philistines to relinquish control over the whole of the central highlands from Judah to the Valley of Jezreel. Saul's reign should be seen as an essential interlude of monarchical experiment between the ineffectiveness of the judges and the successful monarchy founded by King David.

David heard the news of Saul's defeat and death while he was at Ziklag, deep in the southern part of Judah, and immediately set about securing his own succession and acceptance by all the Hebrew tribes. He faced a delicate political situation, and his first steps were to dissociate himself from any involvement with the death of King Saul at the hands of the Philistines. David composed a lament; its beauty is in the tradition of David as poet and musician who wrote at least some of the psalms. The lament demonstrated to Saul's supporters that David mourned his death. David also executed the messenger who said that he had killed King Saul, at Saul's own request, when it was obvious that the Battle of Gilboa was lost. We know that Saul took his own life (1 Samuel 31:4; 2 Samuel 1:5–16). As he was about to become king himself, David had every reason to enforce respect for the person of the king.

It is clear that the Hebrew tribes constituted two distinct groups at this time — a southern group consisting mainly of Judah and Simeon, to which David belonged, and the northern tribes of the central highlands, Galilee and the Jordan area. The land between them, which included Jerusalem, may not yet have been under Hebrew control, and in any case the northern tribes had not looked for help from the southern tribes during the period of the judges. It is even probable that the southern Hebrews had not been amongst the Hebrews who escaped from Egypt.

The southern Hebrews anointed David King at the ancient southern sanctuary of Hebron, and at

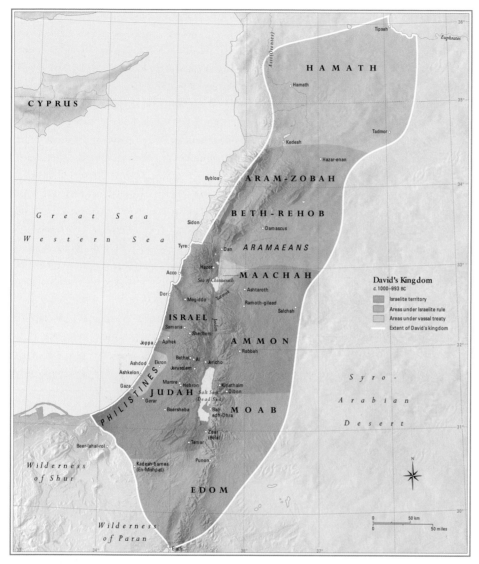

Having established an empire that extended many miles beyond his core territory, David had tested Palestine's ability to hold on to such varied and disparate possessions.

first there was open war between the southern and northern Hebrew tribes. Saul had been succeeded by his son Ishbaal (Ishbosheth), but he offended his senior army commander, Abner, who then negotiated with David to transfer his loyalties and those of the northern tribes. Fortunately for David, Abner was murdered by David's own senior army officer, Joab. David could dissociate himself from the murder and give Abner a solemn funeral to show his disapproval of the deed. King Ishbaal was now the only remaining obstacle, and he was assassinated by two of his own officers who were then foolish enough to take Ishbaal's head to David. Once more David could demonstrate his disapproval of murdering kings by having the assassins executed. David's way was clear, and his reign over the united Hebrew tribes dates from his acceptance as king by the northern group of Hebrews, whose leaders went to Hebron to anoint him, as the southern group had already done.

David secured his hold over the united Hebrew people by providing them with a capital that had no political or religious associations for any of the Hebrew tribes—Jerusalem. The small Canaanite city was on a narrow ridge that fell away each side at a steep angle and flattened out at the northern end to form a gentle hill. The Gihon spring at the foot of the eastern slopes of the ridge provided a dependable water supply and was protected by the city's defensive walls and a water shaft. Sitting as it was between two Hebrew groups, Jerusalem, had never been in Hebrew hands before David's soldiers captured it. Both groups could accept it without loss of face, and David sealed its new significance for his people by fetching the sacred Ark of the Covenant from the borders of Philistine territory and installing it in its tent at the northern end of the city.

Once he had secured the loyalty of all the Hebrew tribes, David turned to their various enemies— the remaining Canaanite cities, the Philistines, the small kingdoms east of the Jordan Valley and the nomadic groups who attempted to settle in what was now Hebrew territory. Although the Philistines retained their foothold in the southern coastal area with its five cities, David took control of the cities of the Shephelah and of the coastal plain north of the Philistines. The Philistines were only able to survive as subservient to the Hebrews. King David's successor, Solomon, inherited the areas traversed by the coastal road as Hebrew territory, and David also imposed his rule over the areas through which the eastern route passed, the King's Highway. He thus controlled both of the great international routes through Palestine, as well as the land area from Damascus to the Egyptian frontier, and from the Mediterranean Sea to the Syrian desert.

ENTRANCE TO DAVID'S CITADEL
In David's time Jerusalem lay to the south of the present-day "old city." Traditionally, this is supposed to be the entrance to David's Citadel although its authenticity is extremely doubtful. Despite this, it is a popular tourist attraction in modern Jerusalem.

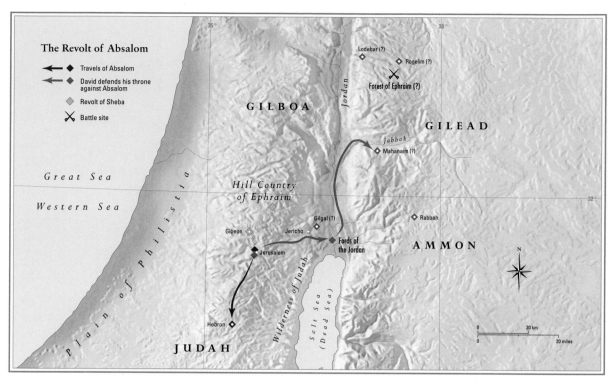

The Revolt of Absalom

➤◆ Travels of Absalom

➤◆ David defends his throne against Absalom

◇ Revolt of Sheba

⚔ Battle site

Lodebar (?)

Rogelim (?)

Forest of Ephraim (?)

GILBOA

Jordan

GILEAD

Jabbok

Mahanaim (?)

Great Sea

Western Sea

Hill Country of Ephraim

Gilgal (?)

Rabbah

Gibeon

Jericho

Fords of the Jordan

AMMON

Jerusalem

Plain of Philistia

Wilderness of Judah

Salt Sea (Dead Sea)

Hebron

JUDAH

N

0   20 km
0   20 miles

King David's political success was confirmed and secured by a major act of religious symbolism. David planned to build a temple to house the Ark of the Covenant (2 Samuel 7) and his successor did so. The prophet Nathan had told David that his descendants were to be the "house" of God's Covenant with the Hebrew people. The Hebrew monarchy itself was to be the sign of the Covenant and its guardian, so the Davidic succession became a form of divine right that should have provided the people with a secure and just administration. This idea of kingly responsibility was very important. For instance, when David had one of his officers murdered, so that he could take the officer's wife without scandal, Nathan rebuked him. This would have been normal behavior, perhaps, for a Canaanite king who owned his subjects in the name of the god Baal, but a Hebrew king must administer Hebrew Covenant law and be bound by it himself. The king was to be the guardian of the Covenant. David's reign (c. 1070 BC) included a major rebellion (c. 980 BC), led by one of his sons, Absalom. However, David regained control and was able to nominate his son Solomon as his successor just before his death.

THE REVOLT OF ABSALOM

Toward the end of his reign, the aging King David became increasingly remote from daily life. Taking advantage of this, David's third son, Absalom, raised a revolt. King David regained control and nominated his son Solomon as his successor before his death.

Solomon's Rule and Empire

SOLOMON CONSOLIDATED DAVID'S ADMINISTRATIVE SYSTEM
AND EXTENDED HIS INFLUENCE THROUGH TRADE LINKS,
REACHING FROM EGYPT IN THE WEST TO MESOPOTAMIA IN
THE EAST, AND TO OPHIR AND SHEBA IN THE SOUTH.

SOLOMON'S EMPIRE
(far right)
Solomon, the second son of
King David and Bathsheba,
had been anointed before
David's death. On his
accession, Solomon ruthlessly
removed any potential rivals,
ensuring an unthreatened
transfer of power.

The triumph of Solomon in the succession struggle marked the eclipse of the older, conservative religious traditions, and the ascendancy of the new way of life introduced by the conquest of Canaan. The Hebrews had become a predominantly settled, agricultural people, rather than nomadic shepherds. The priest of David's court, Abiathar, who had survived the slaughter of the old Hebrew priest-guardians of the Ark of the Covenant by King Saul, backed the losing side and was banished by Solomon to Anathoth. Zadok, a priest who first appeared after the capture of Jerusalem, became the most prominent religious figure in Solomon's court. It is reasonable to assume that Zadok was the priest of Jerusalem in its Canaanite days, before its capture by King David, and that his prominence under King Solomon marks a distinct movement toward the Canaanite expression of religious beliefs.

If religious symbolism does not alter with the changing needs of the people, it fossilises and becomes irrelevant. From the time of Solomon onward, a tension can be detected among the Hebrews. Some of them remained loyal to the old religion of the nomadic shepherds, while others expressed the essentials of the Covenant religion in ways that reflected the Hebrews' needs in their new economic, social, and political situation. The Hebrew Temple in Jerusalem, built by King Solomon, became the visible sign that the nomadic religion of the Hebrews who had fled from Egypt was being expressed in new forms.

The new temple was more than a permanent home for the Ark of the Covenant. It asserted that the Hebrew people had taken over the Canaanite way of life, with its fortified settlements, its agricultural economy, and its monarchical form of government. Not only was the Temple

Period of the Judges

Occupation by the Israelites

Great Sea
Western Sea

SOLOMONS EMPIRE

N

0   100 km
0   100 miles

Solomon's Empire

Maximum extent of Solomon's kingdom (inset above)

Traditional tribal boundaries divided into twelve provinces with a governor for each province

Damascus

ARAM

PHOENICIA

Tyre

Dan

CABUL GALILEE

Kedesh

Achzib

Madon

ASHER

Hazor

Lake Huleh

Acco

IX

VIII

NAPHTALI

GESHUR

Chinnereth

BEALOTH
ZEBULUN

Sea of
Chinnereth

Jo. ISSACHAR

Shimron

Yarmuk

Jokneam

X

Dor

IV

Megiddo

Jezreel

Ramoth-gilead

Taanach

V

ARGOB

Arubboth

Beth-shan

VI

Abel-meholah

Socoh

III

HEPHER

I

Tirzah

Jordan

Succoth

Mahanaim

Shechem

Jabbok

EPHRAIM

Zarethan
Adam

VII

Joppa

GILEAD

Jazer

Jogbehah

32°

Bethel

XI

Rabbah

II

Shaalbim

BENJAMIN

Gezer

Aijalon

Gibeon

Anathoth

AMMON

Beth-shemesh

Jerusalem
(Jebus)

Abel-keramim

Gath?

Jarmuth

Heshbon

Beth-jeshimoth

Libnah

Adullam

Medeba

Gaza

Lachish

GAD

PHILISTIA

Shephelah

Hebron

Salt Sea (Dead Sea)

XII

JUDAH

Wilderness

Dibon

Arnon

Aroer

N

Beer-sheba

MOAB

Negev

0   20 km
0   20 miles

EDOM

the shrine of the Ark, it was also the royal chapel administered by priests appointed by the king. At about this time a separate class of priests emerged to serve the Temple.

The plan of Solomon's Temple is similar to that of other temples in Canaanite areas, particularly the temple destroyed by the Hebrews at Hazor. The temple itself was a comparatively small building—at most some 120–150 feet (35–40 metres) long by 45–60 feet (15–20 metres) wide—as it was not designed to accommodate worshippers. It stood in the great court, which also contained the royal palace, and had its own inner court to which there was direct access from the palace. The Temple was entered though a porch between two ceremonial pillars, the symbol of God's greatness. It then opened out into the Hekal or main hall. This communicated with the Debir, the innermost shrine, which was raised higher than the rest of the building and housed the Ark of the Covenant.

The main hall contained an altar for burning incense, the table for the "bread of the presence"—which originally may have been a food-offering to God—and 10 lampstands. Themain focus for worship was the bronze altar of whole burnt offerings, a great raised hearth about 30 feet (10 metres) square and 15 feet (5 metres) high, which stood before the Temple porch and on which the main sacrifices were offered. Near it was a bronze basin some 15 feet (5 metres) in diameter and 8 feet (2.5 metres) high, with 10 wheeled basins for carrying water.

Solomon employed Phoenician architects and workmen for the Temple, sent by King Hiram of Tyre, who also supplied the cedarwood with which it was panelled. It is no longer possible to say precisely where the Temple was situated in relation to modern Jerusalem, for the Babylonians destroyed it in 587 BC, and its replacement, a temple built by King Herod the Great, was destroyed by the Romans in AD 70. It probably stood where the spectacular Muslim Dome of the Rock today protects a rocky outcrop with sacred associations.

The Temple and the royal palace were only a small part of the vast program of building undertaken by Solomon for which he used forced labor, a normal practice of the time. A number of Palestinian cities have remains of massive fortifications constructed during Solomon's reign. These included recessed stone gateways designed to provide several lines of defence, and walls of great thickness with hollow chambers built between the inner and outer surfaces that give access to the water supply. The latter, which have been found at Megiddo, are now thought to date from the period immediately after Solomon.

Solomon consolidated the centralized administrative system begun by King David, from which came the first reliable Hebrew written records. He also took advantage of Palestine's central position in order to develop existing trading connections both by land and by sea, with caravan routes into the Arabian Desert and a merchant fleet in the Red Sea. He also developed the Hebrew copper industry from ore deposits in the Jordan Valley and the area south of the Dead Sea. King Solomon's administrative ability is the foundation of his reputation for "wisdom," which created a golden age for the Hebrew people. His achievements required large-scale organization of labor, and his success owes much to his understanding of divisive tendencies in Hebrew society, with its traditions of tribal loyalties. Solomon managed to maintain a form of national unity, but it collapsed with his death in about 931 BC.

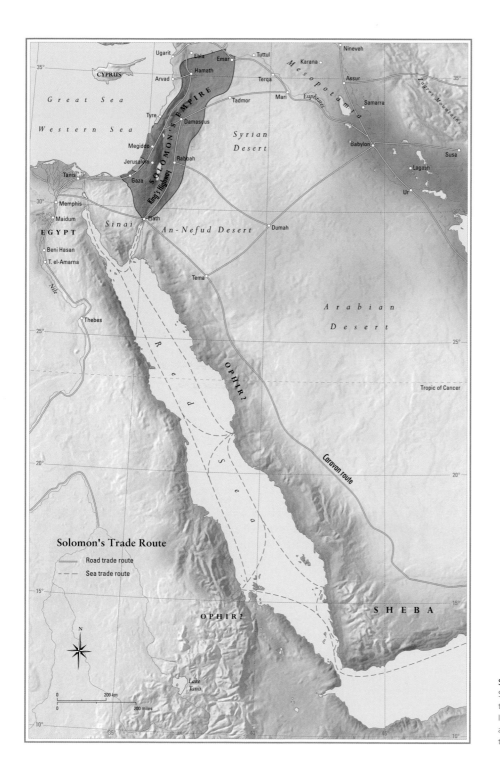

CYPRUS

Great Sea

Western Sea

Ugarit
Ebla
Emar
Tuttul
Nineveh
Karana
Hamath
Arvad
Terqa
Assur
Mesopotamia
Tadmor
Mari
Euphrates
Samarra
Zagros Mountains
Tyre
Damascus
Babylon
Megiddo
Jerusalem
Rabbah
Lagash
Susa
Gaza
Tanis
Ur

SOLOMON'S EMPIRE

King's Highway

Syrian Desert

Memphis
Maidum
Elath
Sinai
An-Nefud Desert
Dumah

EGYPT

Beni Hasan
T. el-Amarna

Tema

Nile

Arabian Desert

Thebes

Tropic of Cancer

R
e
d

OPHIR?

Caravan route

S
e
a

Solomon's Trade Route

———— Road trade route

– – – – Sea trade route

OPHIR?

SHEBA

N

0   200 km
0   200 miles

Lake Tana

35°   40°   45°

35°
30°
25°
20°
15°
10°

SOLOMON'S TRADE ROUTES
Solomon's Empire was effectively
the nerve centre of a network of
long-established trading routes
and therefore ideally situated to
take advantage of them.

DAVID AND SOLOMON'S CITY

JERUSALEM IS THE HOLY CITY FOR JEWS AS THE SITE OF
SOLOMON'S TEMPLE, AND FOR CHRISTIANS AS THE SCENE
OF CHRIST'S TRIAL, CRUCIFIXION, AND RESURRECTION.

Inhabited for over 4,000 years, Jerusalem has been under the rule of many different nations and has often been attacked, destroyed, and rebuilt. It is now a city full of contrast and variety, where modern buildings tower over the old Arab and Jewish quarters that evoke the city's rich biblical past.

The first written reference to Jerusalem is in a text dating back to 2500 BC. There is some evidence of prehistoric settlement, but little is known of the city's early history before the 14th Century BC, when Jerusalem was apparently under Egyptian rule. There is no mention of Jerusalem under that name, in the first five books of the Bible. However, it is believed that Salem, which was ruled by King Melchizedek and is mentioned in Genesis 14:18, is identical to Jerusalem.

At the time when the Israelites entered the land of Canaan in about 1210 BC, Jerusalem was in the hands of a Semitic people called the Jebusites. Their settlement was south of what was to become the Temple platform and ran down to the Pool of Siloam. Although Joshua and his army defeated the Jebusites and their allies in battle, the city remained under Jebusite rule (Joshua 15:63) and it was left to David to capture Jerusalem in about 1000 BC (2 Samuel 5). Under the Jebusites, the city was already known as "Zion"—a word whose meaning is obscure, but which has remained synonymous with Israel—and now it also acquired the title "City of David."

The city became the Israelite capital, where the holy Ark of the Covenant at last found a home. David had the city's fortifications improved and new buildings erected but it was his son, Solomon, who built the first Temple in Jerusalem. He spared no expense, employing the finest materials and the most expert craftsmen to build and decorate a place fit to house the Ark of the Covenant, which was kept in the inner

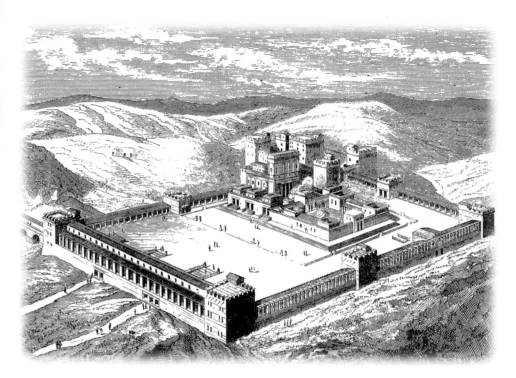

SOLOMON'S TEMPLE
A reconstruction of Solomon's
Temple in Jerusalem. The
construction of the building
is described in Kings 6–7 and
Chronicles 3–4.

sanctuary, the "holy of holies" (1 Kings 5–8). Once the Temple was complete, the city became a religious centre where people gathered to celebrate festivals and holy days, and it soon began to acquire symbolic significance as a holy city. The Psalms are full of references to the city, with such memorable exhortations as "Pray for the peace of Jerusalem" (Psalm 122:6) and "If I forget thee, O Jerusalem, let my right hand forget her cunning" (Psalm 137:5).

A City Besieged

After Solomon's death in around 930 BC the kingdom was divided into two, the northern kingdom of Israel and the southern kingdom of Judah. As the capital of the smaller southern kingdom, Jerusalem declined in importance to some extent. The city was now frequently under attack—by the Egyptians in 922, the Philistines in 850, the northern kingdom in 786, and the Assyrians in 701 —and, more than once, the palaces and Temple were sacked and looted. In 586, Jerusalem was besieged and captured by the Babylonians, under their King Nebuchadezzar; the entire city and the Temple were destroyed, and the people were taken into captivity in Babylon (2 Kings 25).

In 538 BC, Cyrus II of Persia overcame Babylon and allowed the exiles to return to Jerusalem. The Temple was rebuilt (Ezra 1–5) and later, under Nehemiah, the city walls were restored (Nehemiah 3–6). Two centuries later, the city came under the rule of Alexander the Great, and subsequently Ptolemy, and then it fell to the Syrians in 198 BC. The Temple was desecrated again, but after a Jewish revolt under Judas Maccabeus it was re-dedicated in 165 BC.

Roman Rule and the Early Church

Jerusalem remained under Jewish rule until it was taken by Pompey in 63 BC. However, Roman influence was countered by the power of the Herodian dynasty; Herod the Great repaired the ravages of the various plundering armies and began the work of rebuilding the Temple on a grand scale, one among many of his ambitious building projects. Under Herod, Jerusalem became great again, but his successors were less competent and Jerusalem became part of a minor Roman province under the rule of a procurator. So it was when Jesus was exercising his ministry, and it was the procurator, Pontius Pilate, who sentenced him to death (Matthew 27). The city was the scene of Jesus' trial, crucifixion and Resurrection. Jerusalem became the first centre for the early Church (Acts 1–7) until Christians there began to be persecuted; most of them then scattered into other regions to spread the Gospel (Acts 8:1). The city was now a symbol of God's glory for Christians as well as Jews, and in the last book of the Bible, John describes his vision of Heaven as "the Holy City, new Jerusalem" (Revelation 21:2).

CITY OF DAVID

David conquered Jerusalem, taking it from the Jebusites. He made it his new capital, established on the border between Judah and Benjamin, probably hoping to end inter-tribal rivalry.

City of David

— Present wall of Old City

— Site of the City of David

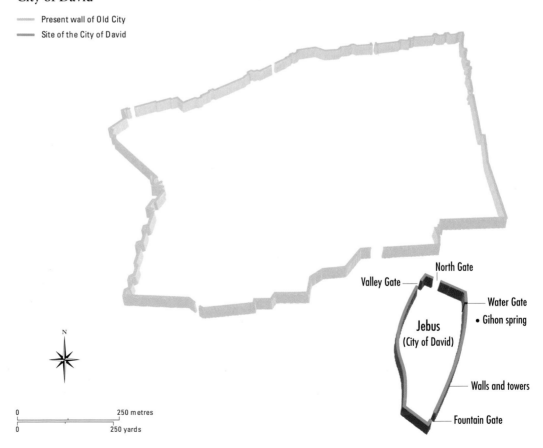

North Gate

Valley Gate

Water Gate

• Gihon spring

Jebus
(City of David)

Walls and towers

Fountain Gate

N

0   250 metres

0   250 yards

In AD 66, the Jews rebelled against their Roman rulers, and four years later Roman forces under Titus besieged and destroyed the city. There was never to be another temple in Jerusalem, but the Emperor Hadrian built a new city, Aelia Capitolina, on the site in 130. The layout of this city, on a typical Roman grid plan but smaller than before, is the basis for the modern city centre.

After Constantine became Emperor of the Roman Empire in AD 324 and made Christianity legal, churches and shrines were built and Jerusalem began its 'golden age' as a Christian city

Three Faiths

In AD 638, Jerusalem came under Muslim rule. The great mosque, the Dome of the Rock, was built on the Temple Mount in AD 691. For some centuries the Muslim rulers were tolerant of the Jews and Christians who lived and worshipped in the city, as well as the many pilgrims who visited it from all parts of Europe. However, in 1071, the Muslims destroyed the Christian shrines and cut

JERUSALEM FROM SOLOMON TO HEZEKIAH
The building of a Temple to house the Ark of the Covenant was completed by Solomon. He also created an impressive palace complex. These new buildings may have remained unwalled until the reign of Hezekiah.

Jerusalem from Solomon to Hezekiah

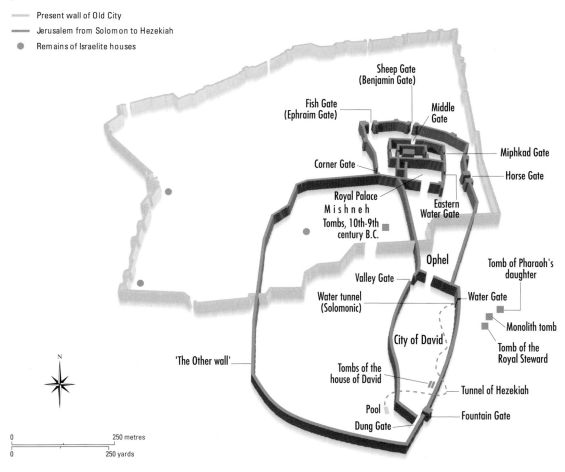

off the pilgrim routes. The European powers, with whom the Muslim rule of the Holy City had long been a sore point, decided to invade. In 1099 the Christian army of the First Crusade captured Jerusalem and established a state there; new churches were built and mosques were converted into churches. But forces led by Saladin, the Egyptian ruler, regained Jerusalem in 1187,and it was re-established as a Muslim city.

Egyptian rule ended in 1517 when Jerusalem was taken by the Turks. For 400 years after that, the city was part of the Ottoman Empire, slowly declining in importance. It was primarily a Muslim city, but Jews and Christians lived there and practiced their religions; Christian pilgrimages continued and Jewish immigration increased, particularly during the 19th Century. In 1917, following the defeat of the Turks in World War I, Jerusalem came under the British mandate.

Jerusalem in the 20th Century

British rule in Jerusalem lasted from its capture in 1917 until 1948, by which time the Zionists and Arabs were fighting each other and both fighting the British. Eventually, the city was split between Israel and Jordan. After the Six Day War, in 1967, Israeli troops won control of the whole city, but it remains an area of disputed claims. Although the state of Israel regards it as her capital city, it is not internationally recognized as such, and many international organizations and foreign embassies are sited in Tel Aviv rather than Jerusalem. The Israelis have expanded the city and erected many modern buildings, including government offices, cultural institutions, and extensive housing projects.

The Old City has been preserved intact. Although it is now only a small district of Jerusalem, it is by far the most interesting part of the city for both tourists and pilgrims. Divided roughly into Jewish, Muslim, Christian, and Armenian quarters, the Old City is essentially Oriental in character with narrow streets and bustling bazaars and markets. Dominated by the Dome of the Rock and the adjacent al-Aqsa mosque, it is also crowded with churches and ancient synagogues and Jewish study houses. The focus of Jewish pilgrimage is the Western Wall (or Wailing Wall), all that remains of Herod's Temple, where Jews pray and lament the destruction of Solomon's Temple. Christian holy places include the Church of the Holy Sepulchre, believed to be the site of Christ's crucifixion and burial—especially since modern research has established that the church is situated outside the perimeters of the original city walls.

The fact that Jerusalem has been continuously inhabited since the 2nd Century BC makes archaeological work difficult. Excavations began there in the 19th Century and have continued to the present day, particularly since 1967, with most of the work concentrated on the Temple Mount area. Extensive research into ancient documents has helped to reveal many clues to the structure and history of the Holy City over the vicissitudes of the last 4,000 years.

ANCIENT JERUSALEM
A view from the Mount of Olives shows the magnificent Dome of the Rock, which dominates the clustered buildings of the Old City of Jerusalem, including the Church of the Holy Sepulchre.

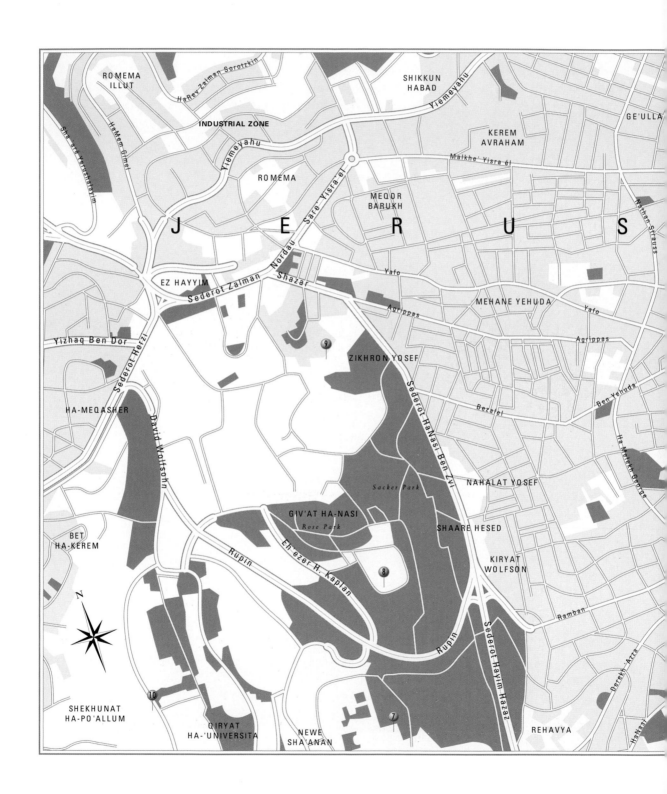

ROMEMA ILLUT

HaRav Zalman Sorotzkin

SHIKKUN HABAD

Yiemeyahu

GE'ULLA

INDUSTRIAL ZONE

Sha'are Yerushalayim

HaMem Gimel

Yiemeyahu

KEREM AVRAHAM

ROMEMA

Nordau

Sare Yisra el

Malkhe' Yisra él

MEQOR BARUKH

Nathan-Strauss

J E R U S

EZ HAYYIM

Shazar

Yafo

Sederot Zalman

Agrippas

MEHANE YEHUDA

Yafo

Yizhaq Ben Dor

9

Agrippas

Sederot Herzl

ZIKHRON YOSEF

Ben-Yehuda

HA-MEQASHER

Bezalel

Sederot HaNasi Ben Zvi

Ha-Melekh George

David Wolfsohn

Sacker Park

NAHALAT YOSEF

GIV'AT HA-NASI

Rose Park

SHAARE HESED

BET HA-KEREM

Rupin

Eh'ezer H. Kaplan

8

KIRYAT WOLFSON

Ramban

Rupin

N

Sederot Hayim Hazaz

Derekh 'Azza

10

HaNasi

SHEKHUNAT HA-PO'ALLUM

QIRYAT HA-'UNIVERSITA

NEWE SHA'ANAN

7

REHAVYA

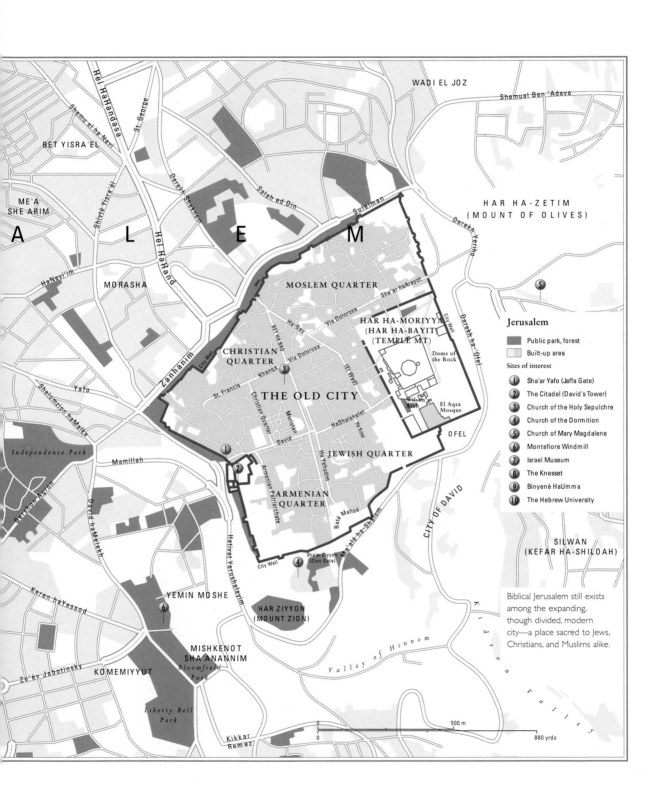

BET YISRA'EL

ME'A
SHE'ARIM

A L E M

MORASHA

WADI EL JOZ

Shemuel Ben 'Adaya

HAR HA-ZETIM
(MOUNT OF OLIVES)

Suleiman

MOSLEM QUARTER

Sha'ar haArayot

HAR HA-MORIYYA
(HAR HA-BAYIT)
(TEMPLE MT)

CHRISTIAN
QUARTER

Via Dolorosa

Dome of
the Rock

Wilson
Arch

El Aqsa
Mosque

THE OLD CITY

St. Francis

OFEL

JEWISH QUARTER

Independence Park

ARMENIAN
QUARTER

Armenian Patriarchate

Baté Mahse

CITY OF DAVID

Mamilla

SILWAN
(KEFAR HA-SHILOAH)

Sha'ar Ziyyon
(Zion Gate)

City Wall

YEMIN MOSHE

HAR ZIYYON
(MOUNT ZION)

Valley of Hinnom

Kidron Valley

MISHKENOT
SHA'ANANNIM

Bloomfield
Park

KOMEMIYYUT

Liberty Bell
Park

Kikkar
Remez

Jerusalem

- Public park, forest
- Built-up area

Sites of interest

1. Sha'ar Yafo (Jaffa Gate)
2. The Citadel (David's Tower)
3. Church of the Holy Sepulchre
4. Church of the Dormition
5. Church of Mary Magdalene
6. Montefiore Windmill
7. Israel Museum
8. The Knesset
9. Binyené HaUmma
10. The Hebrew University

Biblical Jerusalem still exists
among the expanding,
though divided, modern
city—a place sacred to Jews,
Christians, and Muslims alike.

500 m
0
0
880 yrds

THE NATION DIVIDED

SHORTLY AFTER SOLOMON'S DEATH, DIFFERENCES BETWEEN THE NORTHERN TRIBES—WHO WERE ANGRY AT BEING ECONOMICALLY EXPLOITED AND UNEASY ABOUT RELIGIOUS CHANGES—AND THE SOUTHERNERS CULMINATED IN THE KINGDOM'S COLLAPSE. THE OLD TESTAMENT WAS WRITTEN DURING THE CENTURIES OF CIVIL STRIFE, INVASION, AND EXILE THAT FOLLOWED.

K ings David and Solomon proved to be the only kings to reign over a union of the various Hebrew tribal groups—traditionally 12 in number—settled in Palestine. At the death of Solomon in about 931 BC, the united kingdom split into two factions, consisting of the northern and southern groups of tribes, along the old demarcation line through the center of Palestine. The split led to two separate Hebrew kingdoms. The southern one, Judah, with Jerusalem as its capital, was ruled by descendants of David until it was destroyed by the Babylonians in 587 BC. The northern group formed the kingdom of Israel, ruled by a series of dynasties with, eventually, Samaria as its capital. It survived until 721 BC when it was destroyed by the Assyrians.

The precarious unity of the Hebrew peoples had lasted little more than 70 years, from the choice of David as king by the two main groups of Hebrews, to the death of Solomon. Unity was only maintained by the outstanding abilities of these two kings. Shortly after the death of Solomon, Egypt reasserted her control over Palestine, but the Egyptians did not cause the split. The main causes were economic and religious, which amplified all the tensions that already existed between the two Hebrew groups.

The economic problems can be understood from the scale of King Solomon's building activities and the splendor of his court. Archaeology has confirmed the building program while, even allowing for possible exaggeration in the biblical accounts, it can be assumed that his court was resplendent. Both the taxation and the forced labor required for this building were sources of anger, and there is

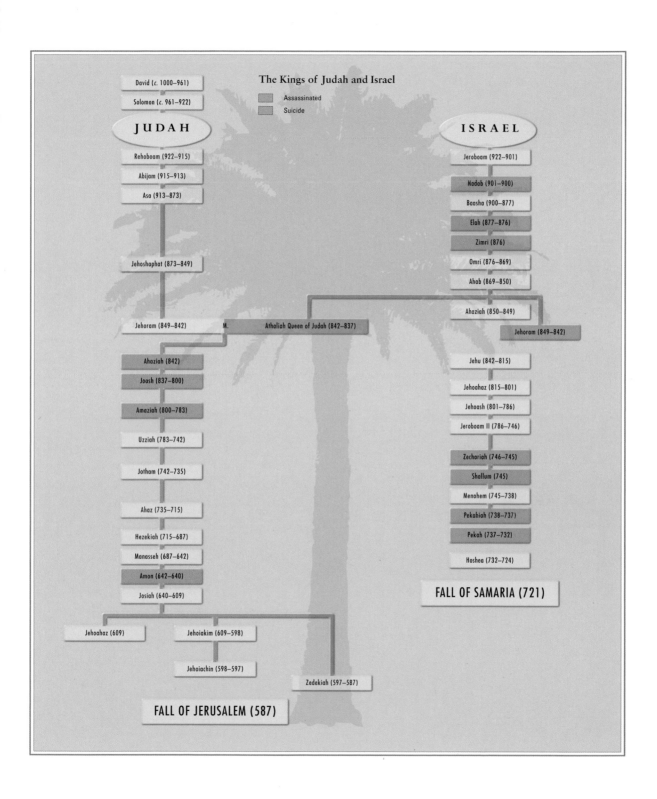

The Kings of Judah and Israel

Assassinated

Suicide

JUDAH

David (*c.* 1000–961)

Solomon (*c.* 961–922)

Rehoboam (922–915)

Abijam (915–913)

Asa (913–873)

Jehoshaphat (873–849)

Jehoram (849–842)   M.   Athaliah Queen of Judah (842–837)

Ahaziah (842)

Joash (837–800)

Amaziah (800–783)

Uzziah (783–742)

Jotham (742–735)

Ahaz (735–715)

Hezekiah (715–687)

Manasseh (687–642)

Amon (642–640)

Josiah (640–609)

Jehoahaz (609)   Jehoiakim (609–598)

Jehoiachin (598–597)

Zedekiah (597–587)

FALL OF JERUSALEM (587)

ISRAEL

Jeroboam (922–901)

Nadab (901–900)

Baasha (900–877)

Elah (877–876)

Zimri (876)

Omri (876–869)

Ahab (869–850)

Ahaziah (850–849)

Jehoram (849–842)

Jehu (842–815)

Jehoahaz (815–801)

Jehoash (801–786)

Jeroboam II (786–746)

Zechariah (746–745)

Shallum (745)

Menahem (745–738)

Pekahiah (738–737)

Pekah (737–732)

Hoshea (732–724)

FALL OF SAMARIA (721)

evidence in the Bible that at least part of the taxation fell more heavily on the northern group of Hebrews. A list of Solomon's administrators, given in the First Book of Kings (4:7–19), shows that the territory north of Jerusalem, from the coast to the eastern side of the Jordan Valley and the Dead Sea, was divided into 12 districts. Eight of the districts consisted of Hebrew tribal areas, while the four districts along the western coast, from the Philistine border to Mount Carmel, consisted of former Canaanite cities occupied by the Hebrews late in the settlement period. Between them, these 12 northern districts were made responsible for the expenses of Solomon's court, each district covering the cost of one month of the year. There is no mention of the southern Hebrew areas, occupied by David's tribe of Judah and by Simeon. Undoubtedly the northern Hebrews were far more prosperous and numerous than the southern ones, but this evidence of inequality of taxation provides at least one good reason for their subsequent split.

"AND THE KING ANSWERED THE PEOPLE ROUGHLY, AND FORSOOK THE OLD MEN'S COUNCIL THAT THEY GAVE HIM;

"AND SPAKE TO THEM AFTER THE COUNCIL OF THE YOUNG MEN, SAYING, MY FATHER MADE YOUR YOKE HEAVY, AND I WILL ADD TO YOUR YOKE: MY FATHER ALSO CHASTISED YOU WITH WHIPS, BUT I WILL CHASTISE YOU WITH SCORPIONS.

"WHEREFORE THE KING HARKENED NOT UNTO THE PEOPLE; FOR THE CAUSE WAS FROM THE LORD, THAT HE MIGHT PERFORM HIS SAYING, WHICH THE LORD SPAKE BY A-HI-JAH THE SHI-LO-NITE UNTO JER-O-BOAM THE SON OF NEBAT."   1 KINGS 12:13–15

To economic differences must be added differences in religious traditions. When David made his capital, Jerusalem, the religious center for the Hebrew people, and Solomon built the Temple for the Ark of the Covenant, they made it possible for the old Hebrew religion to serve the new needs of the Hebrew people as they changed from nomadic shepherds to settled farmers. But many Hebrews remained loyal to the old nomadic symbolism of the Hebrew religion, associated with such ancient sanctuaries at Bethel, Shiloh and Shechem. The new Temple in Jerusalem could easily by seen as a departure from tradition, especially as the traditional priestly organization of the old tribal confederation had been eclipsed by the new line of priests. The rebellion of the northern group, late in the 10th Century BC, was led, eventually, by one of Solomon's own senior officials, Jeroboam, who was in charge of the forced labor levies drawn from the northern Hebrew areas.

The biblical accounts of the Hebrew monarchy were edited into their present form after the destruction of the northern Hebrew kingdom, Israel, by the Assyrians in 721 BC. So this occurred at a time when only the southern kingdom, Judah, remained. It is therefore reasonable to beware of a certain bias in favour of the southern kingdom and so of the Davidic dynasty, reigning from Jerusalem, and the religion of the Temple. This is borne out by the historical books themselves, which select incidents to be included for their religious significance and their effects on the

THE KINGDOMS OF ISRAEL AND JUDAH *(far right)*
After Solomon was buried in Jerusalem, the nation split in two. Jeroboam became King of Israel while Solomon's son, Rehoboam, became King of Judah.

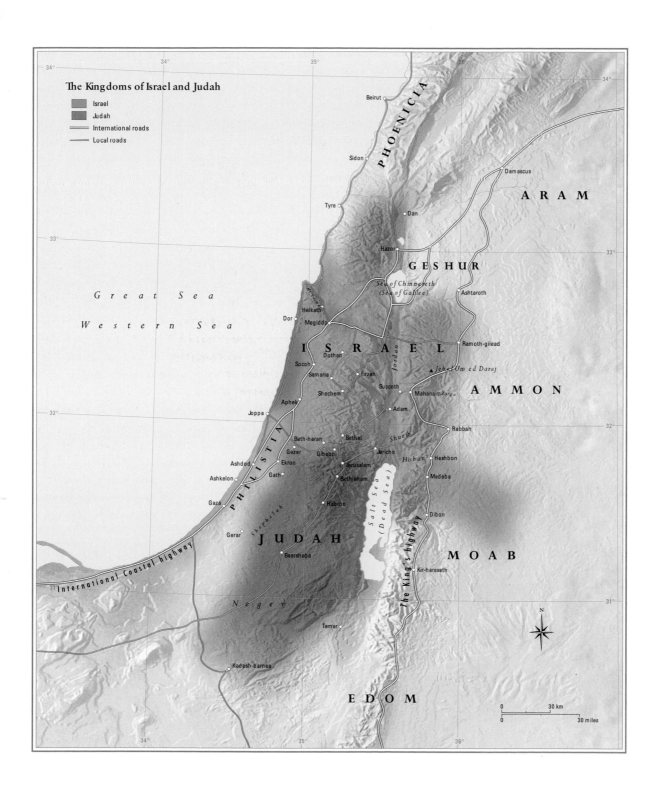

The Kingdoms of Israel and Judah

- Israel
- Judah
- International roads
- Local roads

PHOENICIA

Beirut

Sidon

Tyre

Dan

Hazor

GESHUR

Damascus

ARAM

Sea of Chinnereth
(Sea of Galilee)

Ashtaroth

Great Sea

Western Sea

Dor

Helkath

Megiddo

Ramoth-gilead

ISRAEL

Dothan

Socoh

Samaria

Tirzah

Shechem

Succoth

Jebel Um ed Daraj

Mahanaim

Zarqa

AMMON

Aphek

Adam

Joppa

Jordan

PHILISTIA

Beth-haran

Bethel

Gezer

Gibeon

Jericho

Shueib

Rabbah

Ashdod

Ekron

Jerusalem

Hisban

Heshbon

Ashkelon

Gath

Bethlehem

Medeba

Gaza

Salt Sea
(Dead Sea)

Dibon

Hebron

Sheriah

JUDAH

Gerar

MOAB

Beersheba

Kir-hareseth

The King's highway

International Coastal highway

Negev

N

Tamar

Kadesh-barnea

EDOM

0   30 km
0   30 miles

survival of the kingdom of Judah. The reader is told that the rest of the information; that which applies to the northern kingdom, Israel, is available in other records, long since lost (2 Kings 8:23; 10:34).

The leader of the split between the two Hebrew groups, Jeroboam, was an important official in King Solomon's administration. He had rebelled during Solomon's lifetime and fled to Egypt. When Solomon's successor, Rehoboam, refused concessions to a delegation of northern Hebrews and threatened to increase their burden, they made Jeroboam king of the northern tribes and fortified Shechem and Penuel. King Rehoboam of Judah assembled an army to put down the rebellion, but prophetic advice dissuaded him from attacking the northerners. It is possible that the prophets, as distinct from the royal priests, sympathized with the northern desire to curb the power of the Jerusalem kings and the Temple priests. In any case, the northern group was by far the stronger of the two, and in the many years of brutal civil warfare between the two Hebrew kingdoms, the northern kingdom became dominant.

> "WHEREUPON THE KING TOOK COUNSEL, AND MADE TWO CALVES OF GOLD, AND SAID UNTO THEM, IT IS TOO MUCH FOR YOU TO GO UP TO JERUSALEM: BEHOLD THY GODS, O ISRAEL, WHICH BROUGHT THEE UP OUT OF THE LAND OF EGYPT.
>
> "AND HE SET THE ONE IN BETH-EL AND THE OTHER PUT HE IN DAN."
> 1 KINGS 12:28–29

The split was sealed by the northern emphasis on the importance of two sanctuaries, Bethel, near the southern frontier with the Kingdom of Judah, and Dan in the far north of the Kingdom of Israel (1 Kings 12:26–33). The one at Bethel, in particular, would provide a center for northern Hebrews inclined to look to Jerusalem. Each of them contained a religious image in the form of a golden bull, a traditional symbol for the Hebrew god, Yahweh, but one which could easily be seen as a representation of the Canaanite god, Baal. The traditional Canaanite fertility religion was to be the main danger for the Hebrew people, both northerners and southerners, for the rest of the period of the monarchy. It is only natural, therefore, that the biblical histories roundly condemn these two sanctuaries of the northern Hebrew kingdom.

However, the internal struggles between the two Hebrew kingdoms was not the only factor to led them to lose control of Palestine. A few years after King Solomon died in about 931 BC, Shishak (Shoshenq I), the first King of the 22nd Dynasty, re-established Egyptian control of Palestine by a military campaign, which took him as far as the Phoenician cities and revived Egypt's trading relationships with Byblos, north of Damascus. Egypt thus once more had command of the coastal road to the north and to Mesopotamia. In the course of the campaign, Shishak took Jerusalem and stripped the royal palace and the Temple of its treasures. Egyptian supremacy in the region was comparatively short lived, for the 22nd Dynasty collapsed in civil war late in the 8th Century BC. By then the Hebrew kingdoms were too weakened by their mutual enmity to take advantage of Egyptian weakness. Moreover, the Assyrians had begun their great expansion, and would soon be the dominant power of both the Near and Middle East.

DOMINANT FORCE
This antique fresco is a
depiction of an Assyrian
warrior in full battle regalia,
with deadly bow and arrows,
sword and protective armor.
The Assyrians destroyed the
northern Hebrew kingdom
of Israel in 721BC, sweeping
on to take control of the
entire region.

EGYPT INVADES

SHISHAK BECAME PHARAOH DURING SOLOMON'S REIGN.
RELATIONS WERE AMICABLE, BUT THE SOLOMONIC STATE FORMED
A POWERFUL CARRIER, CONTROLLING TRADE ROUTES AND
CURTAILING EGYPT'S INFLUENCE AND TERRITORIAL AMBITIONS.

The dissolution of Solomon's united monarchy into Israel and Judah and the subsequent war between Rehoboam and Jereboam presented Shishak with a superb opportunity to exploit this weakness.

An Egyptian invasion is mentioned in the Bible (1 Kings 14 and 2 Chronicles 12) where the Pharaoh Shishak, capturing 15 Judaean fortresses, appropriated the gold from Solomon's Temple in return for sparing Jerusalem. The Bible claims that the Egyptian host comprised 1,200 chariots and 60,000 cavalry, suggesting that the invasion was no mere large-scale raid but a serious attempt to destroy the two Jewish successor states. Shishak had an account of his campaign inscribed in the Temple of Amon at Karnak. The carvings list over 150 places captured, demonstrating that communities were attacked in Judah, Israel, Transjordan, and in the Negev. Archaeological evidence is rich and supports the Egyptian account of the invasion. Fire marks can still be seen on gates and walls, and destroyed shops and houses show the results of Egyptian attacks. The path of destruction blazed across Judah and Israel 3,000 years ago provides the story for historians. The temple carvings also show the god Amon holding ropes attached to captured kings while other captives kneel before him.

Advancing through the plains of Philistia, the Egyptians marched to Gaza and there split their forces. One detachment attacked Sharuhen in the Negev; and places listed at Karnak include Beersheba, Arad-rabbah, Arad-jerachmeel, Ramat Matred, and Ezion-geber. Evidence of destruction at Beersheba and Etzion-geber could readily be attributed to Shishak. The Egyptians intended to weaken Judah's hold in the Negev and its influence over Edom, and also open up the trade routes to Arabia. The inventory at Karnak lists 70 place names in the Negev.

The Egyptians' northern force marched to Ashdod and Ekron where a two-pronged attack was

SHISHAK'S PALESTINIAN CAMPAIGN *(far right)*
Five years into Rehoboam's reign over Judah, the Pharaoh Shishak invaded the Hebrew kingdoms around 925 BC.

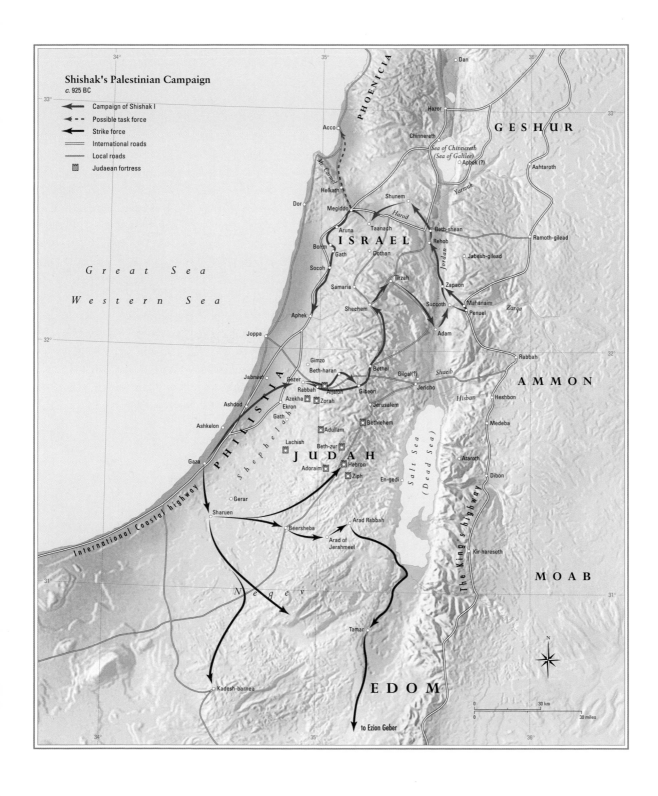

Shishak's Palestinian Campaign
c. 925 BC

→ Campaign of Shishak I
- - ← Possible task force
← Strike force
═══ International roads
─── Local roads
▢ Judaean fortress

PHOENICIA

GESHUR

ISRAEL

AMMON

MOAB

EDOM

JUDAH

PHILISTIA

Great Sea

Western Sea

Salt Sea (Dead Sea)

Sea of Chinnereth (Sea of Galilee)

Dan
Hazor
Chinnereth
Acco
Ashtaroth
Aphek (?)
Mt. Carmel
Helkath
Dor
Shunem
Megiddo
Beth-shean
Ramoth-gilead
Aruna
Taanach
Rehob
Borim
Gath
Dothan
Jabesh-gilead
Socoh
Tirzah
Zapaon
Samaria
Mahanaim
Aphek
Shechem
Succoth
Penuel
Adam
Joppa
Rabbah
Gimzo
Beth-haran
Bethel
Gilgal(?)
Jabneel
Gezer
Rabbah
Aijalon
Gibeon
Jericho
Ashdod
Azekha
Zorah
Jerusalem
Heshbon
Ekron
Gath
Medeba
Adullam
Bethlehem
Ashkelon
Lachish
Beth-zur
Ataroth
Gaza
Adoraim
Hebron
Dibon
Ziph
En-gedi
Kir-hareseth
Gerar
Sharuen
Arad Rabbah
Beersheba
Arad of Jerahmeel
Tamar
Kadesh-barnea
to Ezion Geber

Harod
Jordan
Yarmuk
Zarqa
Shueib
Hisban
Shephelah
Negev
International Coastal highway
The King's highway

N

0   30 km
0   30 miles

launched into Judah. One element of Shishak's army went north, turning eastward along the Way of Beth-horon, through upper Beth-horon, while a second element tore into the central hill country eight miles south along the Way of Beth-shenesh through Kiriath-jearim. The two forces met at Gibeon, six miles from Jerusalem. According to the Bible, this is where Rehoboam came to ransom Jerusalem with the temple's gold.

The Egyptian army traveled the central ridge route to enter the kingdom of Israel. No large, fortified cities existed to form a defensive chain. In fact, there was no defensive perimeter for Israel. Judah had not been considered a severe danger, Jereboam having been a political exile in Egypt, and it was thought that such an Egyptian invasion would be unlikely because Shishak was wrongly regarded as an ally. The powerful invasion force was unstoppable and Davidic and Solomonic fortifications offered little resistance to Egyptian military technology. Solomon's military engineers had favored casement walls where a double wall was connected by cross walls, thereby hampering battering rams. These and three chambered gates as uncovered by archaeologists at Gezer, Hazor, and Megiddo were inadequate. Passing and probably destroying Shechem, the Egyptians attacked and damaged the new capital of Israel at Tirzah. The Wadi Farah provided a route to the fords at Adam on the Jordan. The river was crossed. The Egyptians marched north to Succoth and through the Jabbok valley to Mahanaim and

"AND IT CAME TO PASS IN THE FIFTH YEAR OF KING RE-HO-BO-AM,

THAT SHI-SHAK KING OF EGYPT CAME UP AGAINST JERUSALEM:

"AND HE TOOK AWAY THE TREASURES OF THE HOUSE OF THE LORD,

AND THE TREASURES OF THE KING'S HOUSE; HE EVEN TOOK AWAY

ALL: AND HE TOOK AWAY ALL THE SHIELDS OF GOLD WHICH

SOLOMON HAD MADE.

"AND KING RE-HO-BO-AM MADE IN THEIR STEAD BRASEN SHIELDS,

AND COMMITTED THEM UNTO THE HANDS OF THE CHIEF OF THE

GUARD, WHICH KEPT THE DOOR OF THE KING'S HOUSE."

1 KINGS 14:25–27

EGYPTIAN ARMY ON THE MARCH
These wooden carvings were taken from an Egyptian tomb of 1800 BC. The campaign of Shishak is closely associated with Rehoboam of Judah, in whose reign Shishak captured 15 Judaean fortresses and plundered all the gold of Solomon's Temple at Jerusalem as a price for sparing the city.

Penuel, the latter being a royal city of Israel. Possibly, Shishak wanted to destroy Israelite power across the Jordan.

Shishak then retraced his route down the Jabbok Valley and moved north, destroying Zaphon before re-crossing the Jordan and following the Jezreel Valley at Beth-shan. The cities of Rehob, Beth-shan and Shunem were captured. The southern edge of the Great Plain saw Taanach destroyed and torched. Five miles away, Solomon's great city of Megiddo was attacked and burnt and then rebuilt as an Egyptian outpost guarding the Way of the Sea trail as it passed the Carmel Mountain ridge. A fragment of a stele commemorating Shishak's victory there provides evidence of Egyptian occupation.

The main campaign over, Shishak turned toward Egypt and followed the Way of the Sea, capturing towns along the route. Amongst those captured are listed Aruna, Borim, Gath, Yaham, and Socoh. In this fashion the Pharaoh controlled trade routes not just in the northern valleys but the Plain of Sharon and the coast all the way back to Philistia. The return itinerary is incomplete because the Karnak inscription breaks off here.

Shishak had now devastated Judah and Israel, but was forced to quell insurrections at home. Even though Shishak had not managed to rebuild Egypt's old Asian empire of Thutmose III, he ensured that there was no longer a strong power potentially threatening his northern border.

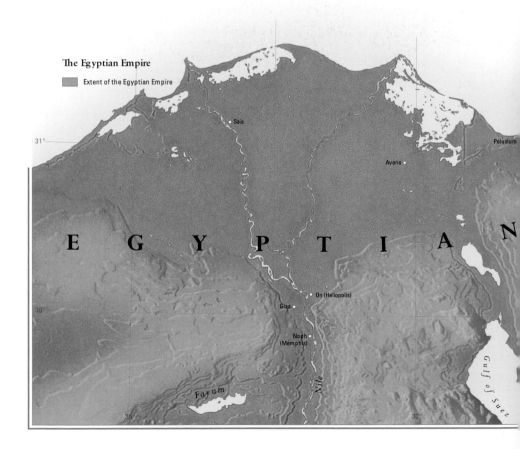

The Egyptian Empire

Extent of the Egyptian Empire

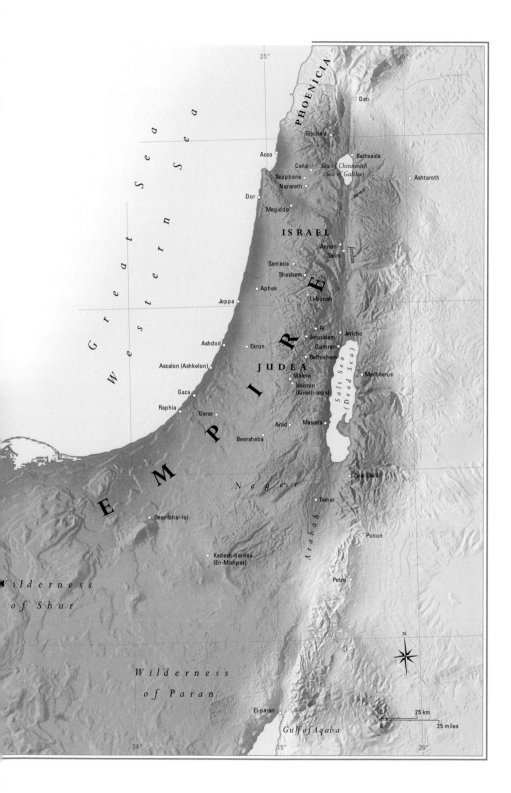

THE EGYPTIAN EMPIRE
The empire continued to seek
to control Palestine, creating
defence in depth for its
eastern border and to control
valuable trade routes.

WARS OF ISRAEL AND JUDAH

BY 877 BC, IN THE KINGDOM OF ISRAEL, THE SYRIANS HAD LAID WASTE TO PARTS OF UPPER GALILEE WHILE MOST OF THE LANDS OF BENJAMIN, ON THE SOUTHERN BORDER, WERE IN THE HANDS OF THE KINGDOM OF JUDAH.

Baasha of Israel left his son Elah to reign after him but Elah was murdered by Zimri, a charioteer commander, who annihilated Baasha's family. Elsewhere, the Israelite army was combating Philistines near Gibbethon. The troops proclaimed their leader, Omri, as king and he marched on Zimri's Tirzah. The city fell and Zimri immolated himself in the citadel of the palace there.

Omri not only founded a dynasty, but also introduced political and religious change to Israel. Judah became a junior power whilst Omri attempted to revive the Solomonic state, especially seeking peace and trade expansion with his neighbors. He made a political alliance with the Phoenicians, his crown prince, Ahab, marrying Jezebel of Tyre and Sidon. Omri also moved his capital west from Tirzah, building Samaria on land bought from Shemer, and using Phoenician architects.

Ahab succeeded his father in 869 BC, continuing his father's policies. However, his palace at Samaria was hidden from the city by a wall, shutting away the ruler from the very people who anointed the king from their midst. The House of Omri appeared to be moving even further away from its roots. The introduction of the Baal cult by Jezebel was of great concern to the people too. Substantial rebuilding took place at Megiddo and Hazor, the former becoming a base for Israel's chariot force, as evidenced by its large stable block. The latter became a strong fortress, covering its old acropolis and packing the old casement walls in order to strengthen them. The water supply was miraculous being at a depth of 100 feet, reached by 80 steps in a tunnel 15 feet high and up to 16.5 feet wide.

THE MIDDLE EAST *(far right)*
The minor states of the Levantine coast continued a series of wars. Meanwhile, larger states east and west consolidated and grew in power.

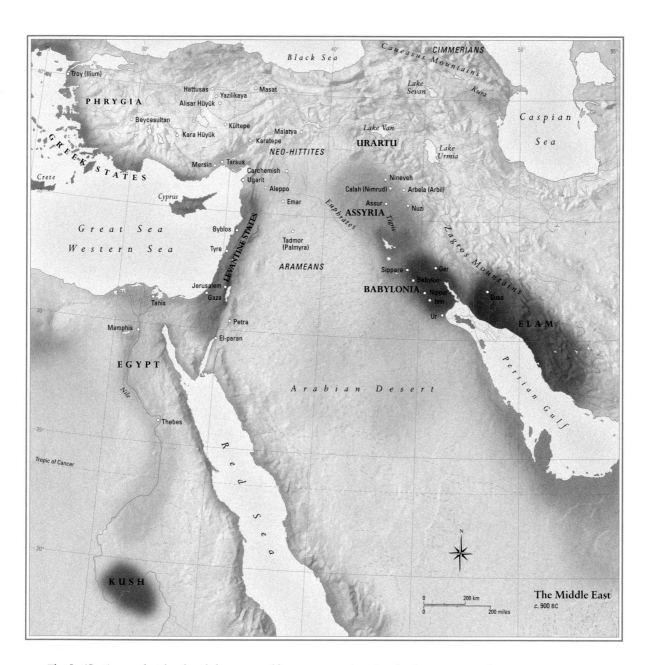

The Middle East
c. 900 BC

The fortifications undertaken by Ahab were possibly a response to invasions by the Aramaeans of Syrian Damascus. A conflict between Ben-hadad of Damascus and Ahab is poorly recorded but he besieged Samaria, being soundly defeated by Ahab. The following year, the Aramaeans returned, but Ahab blocked them before they crossed the Jordan. Each side sought to control Aphek, an important strategic locale east of the Sea of Chinnereth, where a key route leads up to the plateau of Bashan

THE OMERIDE DYNASTY
(far right)
Omri introduced religious and political change, seeking peace and trade with his neighbors. However, after his death, the dynasty drifted away from its Hebrew roots, laying the foundations for future difficulties.

and the road to Damascus. After a week's stalemate, the smaller Israelite force attacked, forcing the Syrians to retreat to Aphek where Ben-hadad surrendered. The defeated king handed back some Israelite cities and allowed Israelite traders into Damascus: in return, he was freed. Amongst Ahab's Transjordanian interests were the retention of Gilead and the control of Ammon and Moab. Ammon, however, kept its independence, but Moab's King Mesha became a temporary vassal placing Israelites in Moabite territory north of the River Arnon.

Elsewhere, Judah, under King Asa and his son Jehoshaphat, regained control of Edom along with lands lost in Shishak's military promenade and rebuilt Ezion-geber. A merchant fleet was based in the Gulf of Aqabah. New settlements were probably built west of Beersheba, and the Wilderness of Judah was occupied with settlements such as the City of Salt, with agriculture being tried out in harsh conditions to its west.

External forces now threatened the two Jewish kingdoms. In 859 BC, Shalmaneser III succeeded to the Assyrian throne. He projected his strength across the Euphrates into northern Syria right up to the Mediterranean. To meet this threat, Syria and Israel allied, fighting the Assyrians at the battle of Qarqar, with Ahab contributing 2,000 chariots. Each side suffered great losses with the Assyrians claiming victory, but their progress was stopped for four years. In this interval, Ahab attacked Syria again, intending to strengthen his strategic position in the borderlands, in alliance with Jehoshaphat of Judah. Israelite Gilead was a well-watered, forested area of uplands. Bashan's basalt and limestone plateaus were Syrian. The natural division between the two is the limestone plateau south of the River Yarmuk to the foothills of Gilead. The enemies confronted each other in battle at the strategic point of Ramoth-gilead. Ahab was wounded, but stayed on the battlefield lest his absence weaken the morale of his troops. When the combined Jewish forces withdrew, Ahab's dead body was taken to Samaria for burial. Ahaziah succeeded Ahab but died in an accident two years later, the throne then passing to his brother, Jehoram, in 849 BC.

"AND KING JE-HOR-AM WENT OUT OF SA-MAR-IA THE SAME TIME, AND NUMBERED ALL ISRAEL.

"AND HE WENT AND SENT TO JE-HOSH-A-PHAT THE KING OF JUDAH, SAYING, THE KING OF MOAB HATH REBELLED AGAINST ME: WILT THOU GO WITH ME AGAINST MOAB TO BATTLE? AND HE SAID, I WILL GO UP: I AM AS THOU ART, MY PEOPLE AS THEY PEOPLE, AND MY HORSES AS THY HORSES.

"AND HE SAID, WHICH WAY SHALL WE GO UP? AND HE ANSWERED, THE WAY THOUGH THE WILDERNESS OF E-DOM.

"SO THE KING OF ISRAEL WENT, AND THE KING OF JUDAH, AND THE KING OF E-DOM: AND THEY FETCHED A COMPASS OF SEVEN DAYS' JOURNEY: AND THERE WAS NO WATER FOR THE HOST, AND FOR THE CATTLE THAT FOLLOWED THEM." 2 KINGS 3:6–9

During these recent events, Mesha of Moab rebelled, his victories being inscribed on a stele at Dibon, the Moabite Stone. According to 2 Kings, Jehoram marched south, being joined

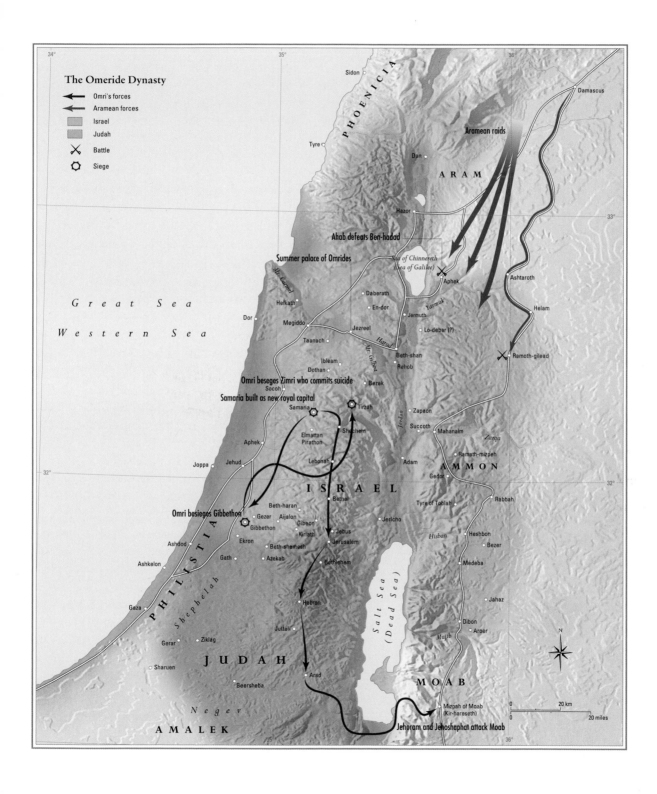

The Omeride Dynasty

→ Omri's forces
→ Aramean forces
▢ Israel
▢ Judah
✕ Battle
⬡ Siege

Sidon

PHOENICIA

Damascus

Tyre

Dan

ARAM

Aramean raids

Hazor

Ahab defeats Ben-hadad

Summer palace of Omrides

Sea of Chinnereth (Sea of Galilee)

Aphek

Ashtaroth

Daberath

En-dor

Jermuth

Yarmuk

Helam

Helkath

Megiddo

Jezreel

Lo-debar (?)

Dor

Harod

Taanach

Ibleam

Beth-shan

Rehob

Ramoth-gilead

Great Sea

Western Sea

Dothan

Mt. Gilboa

Socoh

Bezek

Omri beseges Zimri who commits suicide

Samaria built as new royal capital

Samaria

Tirzah

Zapaon

Jordan

Succoth

Mahanaim

Zarqa

Shechem

Elmattan Pirathon

Lebonah

Adam

AMMON

Ramath-mizpeh

Aphek

Gedor

Joppa

Jehud

ISRAEL

Bethel

Tyre of Tobiah

Rabbah

Omri besieges Gibbethon

Beth-haran

Gezer

Aijalon

Gibeon

Jericho

Hisban

Heshbon

Gibbethon

Kiriath

Jebus

Bezer

Ashdod

Ekron

Beth-shemesh

Jerusalem

Ashkelon

Gath

Azekab

Bethlehem

Medeba

PHILISTIA

Shephelah

Gaza

Hebron

Salt Sea (Dead Sea)

Jahaz

Jutteli

Dibon

Aroer

Mujib

N

Gerar

Ziklag

JUDAH

Arad

Sharuen

Beersheba

Mizpah of Moab (Kir-hareseth)

0   20 km

0   20 miles

Negev

MOAB

AMALEK

Jehoram and Jehoshaphat attack Moab

THE DISTRICTS OF JUDAH UNDER KING JOSIAH
(far right)
The hills and valleys of Judah acted as a defence against the assaults of the Mesha's short-lived coalition.

by Jehoshaphat and vassal Edomite forces. Passing Arad and using the Way of Edom, they arrived at Zoar where Elisha prophesied water for the thirsty soldiers and the wadis were filled. The army then moved along the Dead Sea to outflank Moab's southern defences. A battle near Horonim saw Mesha retreat along the King's Highway to Kir-hareseth. Apparently, Mesha sacrificed his son on the battlements, which caused the Israelite-led allies to lift the siege. However, the Moabite Stone records the devastation done to Israel: old Israelite communities like Ataroth and the fortress of Jahz were taken; indeed, the tableland around Medeba, Heshbon and the western scarplands to the Plains of Moab were lost.

Judah was also Mesha's target. Together with Ammonites and Edomites, the Moabites crossed the Dead Sea and took En-gedi. They traversed the Wilderness of Judah, coming to the Wilderness of Tekoa where the Judahites stopped them. The enemy coalition collapsed, with the Moabites and Ammonites turning on the Edomites. Judah was again hit hard when rebellious Edomites stopped and turned back Jehoshaphat's son, Jehoram of Judah, near Zoar. Thus, the Edomites regained the copper mines of the Arabah and Ezion-geber. Then Libnah, in the Shephelah, rebelled. Elsewhere, Jehoram of Israel re-entered the fray against Syria. Wounded, he went to Jezreel, his summer palace, where he was joined by his nephew, Ahazariah, who had become King of Judah. Now, enter Elisha and Jehu.

DESERT FORTRESS
Situated atop an isolated cliff at the western end of the Judean Desert stands majestic Masada, Hebrew for "fortress". The cliff overlooks the Dead Sea, where a coalition of Ammonites, Edomites and Moabites crossed and captured En-Gedi.

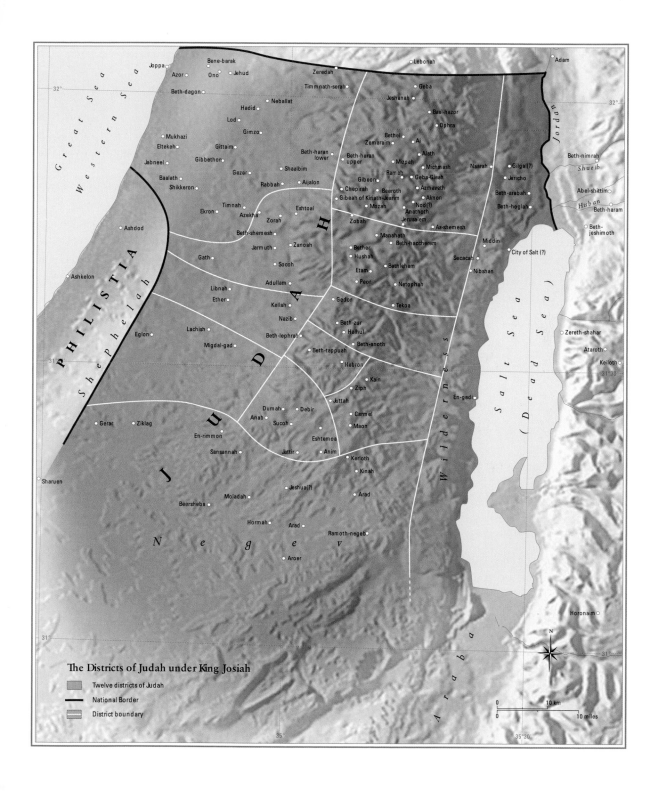

The Districts of Judah under King Josiah

Twelve districts of Judah
National Border
District boundary

THE PROPHET ELIJAH

ELIJAH, OR ELIAS, IS THE MOST POPULAR HEBREW PROPHET,
LIVING IN A PERIOD OF GREAT RELIGIOUS AND SOCIAL CHANGE,
AND LEADING A BITTER CONFLICT AGAINST THE IDOLATROUS
WORSHIP OF THE PHOENICIAN FERTILITY GOD BAAL.

The Elijah stories in 1 and 2 Kings are snapshots of the prophet's life and adventures, but no precise chronology of events is possible. What does stand out is that he was a man of the desert, dressed in skins and leather, sleeping rough, and popping in and out of state affairs like a ghost.

The historical background for Elijah is clear. In 869 BC, Ahab succeeded his father Omri as King of Israel, continuing the sound policy of friendship and trade with neighbors, especially Phoenicia whose builders were traditionally welcomed in Israel. Ahab married Jezebel, daughter of Ethbaal, King of Tyre and Sidon. She was unhappy with the Solomonic tradition of each foreign wife having a temple to her deity in the capital. She wanted to confront the entire God tradition and introduce the worship of Baal as a better alternative. Accordingly, she brought in several hundred priests of Baal and Asherah, giving them official status at court. People who resisted this cult could be killed, and Israelite places of worship were attacked and altars to the God of Israel destroyed.

Enter Elijah of Tishbe from Transjordan. He confronted Ahab and Jezebel and in the new capital of Samaria prophesied that a famine would savage Israel as God punished Israel for praying to false gods. Obeying God, Elijah left the court and crossed the Jordan. He then journeyed to Zarephath in Phoenicia where he performed miracles, staying with a poor widow whose store cupboard would never be empty while the drought prevailed.

In the drought's third year, Ahab sought Elijah and condemned him for Israel's troubles. Elijah immediately replied, accusing Ahab of breaking the commandments and following Baal, stating that this was the real cause of the country's woes. He challenged the king to summon the Baal and

THE PROPHET ELIJAH
In 1 Kings 17:1–6, the story is told of how the Prophet Elijah, hiding from King Ahab, was fed on bread and meat brought to him by ravens every morning
and evening. The engraving is by the Dutch artist Pieter Jansz Saenredam (1587–1665), after Abraham Bloemart (1564–1651).

Asherah priests to a religious duel on Mount Carmel. Ahab did as he was told and two altars were set up, one for each of the contending faiths. The priests of Baal prayed to their god to send fire to burn the dismembered bull on their altar. Despite pleading and self-mutilation, nothing happened. Elijah soaked his altar with water and God consumed it with fire. Elijah then commanded the false priests to be captured and led down to the Kishon brook where they were killed. The rains came and Israel was saved.

Meanwhile, Elijah fled Jezebel's wrath, travelling southward to Beersheba. Later, he confronted Ahab since Jezebel had instigated the murder of Naboth because she coveted his vineyard. After Ahab died in battle at Ramoth-gilead, Elijah went on his last journey with his young follower, Elisha, recruited at Abel-meholah. They walked to Gilgal, Bethel and Jericho, and crossed the Jordan. There, a flaming chariot drawn by horses of fire took, or translated, Elijah in a whirlwind to heaven. Afterward, Elisha took up Elijah's work in confronting and condemning Baal.

of Baal, but there were disastrous consequences.

Despite founding a dynasty that lasted for nearly 100 years, Jehu commenced a period of utmost weakness during which Israel nearly lost its independence. He saved Israel from a likely amalgamation into the pagan world, but left the country stunned. Ahab's alliance system, so useful in restoring Israel to a position of strength, was destroyed. The murder of Jezebel, her Tyrian retainers, the slaughter of the priests of Baal, and the insult to the god by destroying his place of worship, meant that the friendly relations with Tyre in Phoenicia were ended. The alliance with Judah could not survive after the killing of King Ahaziah along with many of his family and court. Thus, Israel lost the main source of her material wealth and her only dependable ally.

Internally, Jehu had maimed Israel. The slaughter of the entire court and most of officialdom caused feelings of horror. "So Jehu slew all that remained of the house of Ahab in Jezreel, and all his great men, and his kinfolks, and his priests, until he left him none remaining" (2 Kings 10:11). The paralysis that overcame the state lasted for years. Memories of the bloodbath and its excesses brought blood guilt to the house of Jehu thereafter. One hundred years later, the prophet Hosea remarked upon the events: "And the Lord said unto him, Call his name Jezreel; for yet a little while, and I will avenge the blood of Jezreel upon the house of Jehu, and will cause to cease the kingdom of the house of Israel" (Hosea 1:4). Jehu failed to address the ills of the country. Amos alluded to the social and economic divisions between classes, while Hosea and Kings pointed to the continuation of native pagan rites.

Militarily, Israel had been weakened, and was unable to resist Assyrian power as it surged south along the Phoenician coast. Jehu paid tribute to Assyria. After Shalmaneser III's forces returned north to face the hostile kingdom of Urartu, Hazael of Damascus attacked and Israel lost all of Transjordan south to the lands of Moab on the River Arnon. His son, Jehoahaz (815–802), faced worse problems. Defeated, he was allowed to keep a bodyguard of only ten chariots and 50 cavalry plus a police force of 10,000 infantry. "For the king of Syria had destroyed them, and had made them like the dust by threshing" (2 Kings 13:7). How had Israel fallen? Ahab had taken 2,000 chariots to the Battle of Qarqar. Now, Israel had all her Transjordan territory, the Valley of Jezreel, the coast, and Galilee under Aramean control, essentially reducing the state to a dependency of Damascus. So weak was Israel that Amos describes how its neighbors raided whenever they wanted.

Queen Mother Athaliah, Ahab's daughter, seized the throne of Judah ruling in Jerusalem from 842–837 BC. She killed all the seed royal she could find and continued to worship Baal (2 Kings 11:1–3). Elsewhere, an infant son of Ahaziah, Joash, was saved and hidden by his aunt, the wife of Jehoiada, the chief priest, being kept in the Temple precinct so the Davidic line could continue in Judah. When the child was aged seven years, Jehoiada plotted with officers of the royal guard. Joash was brought into the Temple proper and crowned. Athaliah cried treason, but the guard seized and executed her immediately. The temple of Baal was demolished and the new king was welcomed by his people. Elisha outlived Jehu but, during the reign of his grandson, Jehoash (801–786 BC), fell ill and died.

ELISHA CURES NAAMAN
(far right)
The captain of the Syrian army, Naaman, suffered from leprosy but was healed when the Prophet Elisha made him wash seven times in the River Jordan. The illustration comes from the 1816 edition of the John Brown Bible.

NAAMAN CURED OF HIS LEPROSY

TRIBUTE TO ASSYRIA

THE YEAR 842 BC SAW THE END OF THE HOUSE OF OMRI AND
THE WEAKENING OF ISRAEL AND JUDAH BY RELIGIOUS UNREST.
THERE WAS ALSO INTERMITTENT WARFARE WITH SYRIA AND
TRANSJORDAN. AMMON, MOAB AND EDOM WERE NOW
INDEPENDENT AGAIN, AND PARTS OF THE NEGEV WERE LOST.

Jehu's usurpation in Israel ended the alliance system that the Omrides had constructed with Phoenicia and Judah. Jehu's purges severely damaged Israel, as archaeological evidence suggests, with a reduction in the standard of living. Simultaneously, Hazael (842–806 BC) ofDamascus was expanding his power, and pressuring Israelite Gilead to such an extent that Jehu approached the Assyrian King Shalmaneser III for aid.

Assyria had been looming on the horizon for some time. Ashurnasirpal II handed to his successor a well-organized, highly compact state. Shalmaneser was ambitious, seeking to annex conquered peoples, to integrate them into the empire, and to exact annual tribute from a series of vassals. Annual campaigns were launched, especially toward the west. In 858 BC, Shalmaneser III met a coalition of Aramaean kings (Sam'al, Hattina, Carchemish and Bît Adini) at Lutibu. The Assyrian claimed victory although he did not break the allies. In campaigns of 857–854 BC, he captured and annexed Bît Adini, but was stopped at Qarqar, on the Orontes, in 854 BC, by an alliance of Irkhuleni of Hammath, Ben-hadad of Damascus, and Ahab of Israel. His western campaigns continued in 849, 846 and 842 BC. The Syrians and their allies were always beaten, but the Assyrians were prevented from moving further south because enemies from the mountains, especially the Caucasus, on the northern border of the state, were raiding. A clay fragment from the period records Shalmaneser III's views:

"In the eighteenth year of my rule, I crossed the Euphrates for the sixteenth time. Hazael of Damascus put his trust upon his numerous army and called up troops in great number, making the mountain Senir, a mountain facing the Lebanon, to his fortress. I fought with him and inflicted a

ANNUAL CAMPAIGNS
Campaigns were launched by the Assyrians planning to expand their empire and exact tribute from conquered peoples. This might involve the ruthless destruction of anyone who got in their way. Here Assyrian cavalry dispose of nomads who have been raiding the frontier.

THE ASSYRIAN EMPIRE

The Assyrian Empire expanded toward Palestine, down the coastal road to Egypt and along the King's Highway on the eastern edge of the Jordan Valley. The Assyrians were not yet ready to occupy the region, but the Palestinian kingdoms began to feel the pressure of Assyrian power. King Jehu of Israel, the northern Hebrew kingdom, bought off the Assyrian King Shalmaneser III with ingots of silver and gold, and vessels made of gold, but gained only a temporary respite for his people.

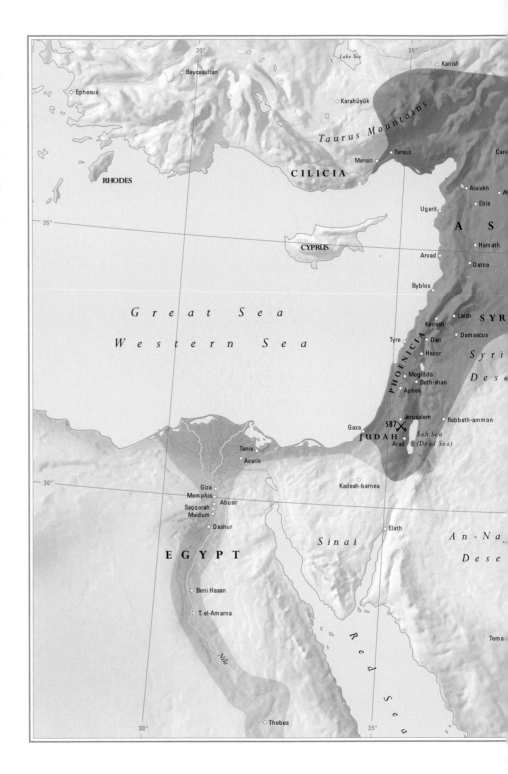

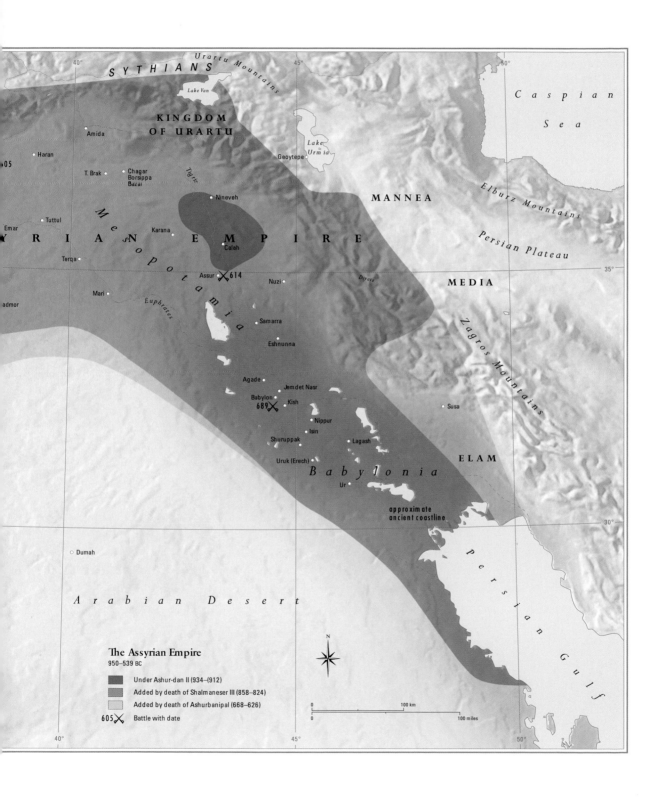

S Y T H I A N S

Urartu Mountains

Lake Van

KINGDOM
OF URARTU

Amida

Haran

T. Brak

Chagar
Borsippa
Bazai

Tigris

Nineveh

Karana

Calah

Assur ✗ 614

Nuzi

Geoytepe

Lake
Urmia

*Caspian
Sea*

MANNEA

Elburz Mountains

Persian Plateau

MEDIA

Diyala

05

Emar

Tuttul

Terqa

A S S Y R I A N   E M P I R E

Mesopotamia

admor

Mari

Euphrates

Samarra

Eshnunna

Agade

Jemdet Nasr

Babylon ✗ 689   Kish

Nippur

Isin

Shuruppak

Lagash

Uruk (Erech)

Babylonia

Ur

Zagros Mountains

Susa

ELAM

approximate
ancient coastline

35°

Persian Gulf

30°

Dumah

A r a b i a n   D e s e r t

N

The Assyrian Empire
950–539 BC

Under Ashur-dan II (934–(912)

Added by death of Shalmaneser III (858–824)

Added by death of Ashurbanipal (668–626)

605 ✗ Battle with date

0   100 km

0   100 miles

40°   45°   50°

defeat upon him, killing 16,000 of his experienced soldiers. I took from him 1,121 chariots, 470 riding horses as well as his camp. He disappeared to save his life (but) I followed him and besieged him in Damascus, his royal residence. There I cut down the gardens outside the city, and departed. I marched as far as the mountains of Hauran, destroying, tearing down and burning innumerable towns, carrying booty away from them that was beyond counting."

While the Assyrians' attention was elsewhere, Hazael of Damascus attacked Gilead, which generated Jehu's response. Shalmaneser's records showed he assaulted Damascus, but failed to breach its walls. He received tribute from Tyre, Sidon and Jehu, son of Omri. The Black Obelisk of Shalmaneser has scenes inscribed showing kings bringing tribute. One panel shows Jehu on his hands and knees making obeisance to the Assyrian king. The inscription states: "The tribute of Jehu, son of Omri. Silver, gold, a golden bowl, a golden vase, golden cups, golden buckets, tin, a staff for the royal hand, puruhati-fruits." How low had Israel sunk in ten years. Historians have pondered where the submission took place: at Hazor, Libnath, or Mount Carmel. Some historians claim that the site was at the Dog River near contemporary Beirut.

Israel, Damascus and the other Aramaean states were saved from more suffering because one of Shalmaneser's sons led a revolt allied to subject mountain peoples beyond the upper Tigris. Not wasting time, Hazael dispatched his armies not just into Gilead but all the way down the King's Highway to Aroer. In 2 Kings 10:33, it says Hazael was victorious "From Jordan eastward, all the land of Gilead, the Gadites, and the Reubenites, and the Manassites, from Aroer, which is by the river Arnon, even Gilead and Bashan." Hazael's next thrust was across the Jordan in a drive toward the sea. Battles occurred and Jehu's son, Jehoahaz, had his forces severely trounced with heavy losses. Hazael then marched down the coast along the Way of the Sea to capture Gath. Now, the Syrians could cross the Shephelah and, through defiles and wadis, attack Judah.

When the Omridite usurper, Queen Athaliah, was executed, Ahaziah's only surviving son, Joash, was put on the throne, aged seven. When Hazael marched on Jerusalem, Joash sent him a tribute of Temple treasure. Joash was assassinated by a Moabite and an Ammonite and was succeeded by his son, Amaziah, in 800 BC.

With a new Assyrian threat to Damascus, Amaziah took the opportunity to regain Edom. The Jewish army defeated the Edomites in the Valley of Salt and marched rapidly into Edom to capture Sela, thus gaining the rich copper deposits in the region. However, Amaziah might have taken another road into Edom via the waters of Tamar and to Sela via Punon. If so, the King of Judah acquired a trade route as well as copper.

Amaziah used his successes to demand of Jehoash, the Israelite King, (Jehu's grandson) that his daughter be wed to his son. However, a contentious issue between the two kings was the behavior of Israelite mercenaries whom Amaziah had hired for his Edom campaign, but sent back before his victory in the Valley of Salt. Deprived of the spoils of war, these men attacked and looted cities of Judah, and matters became very heated, causing war to break out.

The Israelites moved from Samaria by the Way of the Sea to attack Judah from the west. The clash took place at Beth-shemesh where Amaziah was taken prisoner. With no king and no army to defend it, Jerusalem fell and the victorious Israelites pulled down much of its northern wall

while looting the rest of the city and the Temple. They retreated, taking hostages, but they later released Amaziah.

The victories of Jehoash continued elsewhere. Persuaded by the declining Elisha, war was waged upon Damascus and the strategic point of Aphek was captured. Hence, the Aramaean jumping-off point into Israel became an Israelite springboard into Syria, one used by his son, Jeroboam II, who eventually took Damascus.

Judah's luck deteriorated further. Amaziah attempted to rule from a ruined capital, but time did not lead to repair and recovery. Morale declined and a plot was hatched against Amaziah. He sought sanctuary in the fortress city of Lachish near the Philistine border. The assassins followed him and murdered him. His body was taken to Jerusalem for burial by his 16-year-old son, Uzziah, who took the throne in 783 BC. This young man was to change the declining state of Judah and lead it to power simultaneously with the resurgence of Israel under Jeroboam II.

ASSYRIAN ENGINEERS
The outer walls of a captured city are expertly demolished, flames are already burning down the city's inner defences and gate.

CRAFTS AND INDUSTRIES

HUMAN SETTLEMENTS, WITH DEGREES OF DIFFERENTIATED LABOUR PATTERNS, HAVE BEEN ABLE TO DEVELOP NEW TECHNIQUES OF FOOD PRODUCTION, METAL WORKING AND POTTERY CREATION. IN ADDITION, THE DISCOVERIES OF NEW WAYS OF MAKING CLOTH AND THE INTRODUCTION OF NEW CROPS INTO THE AGRICULTURAL SYSTEM.

In the Neolithic and Chalcolithic Ages, pottery making was a domestic activity, probably carried out by women. However, by the the Early or Middle Bronze Age, professional male potters produced goods for the domestic and international commercial market. One of the oldest and most widely practised of crafts, pottery was created to store, prepare, and cook food. Commercially, vessels could transport oil and wine; the Classical amphora was a development of the Canaanite commercial jar. In the metallurgical industry, pottery was essential for crucibles.

In biblical times, pottery was made from clay containing a large amount of iron, which when fired in a well-enclosed kiln produced a reddish color to the finished product. Clay was dug from the ground, then puddled in water to eliminate all air, as documented in Isaiah 41:25, 'as the potter treadeth clay'. The clay was tempered by the addition of finely chopped straw or crushed stone or pottery to add plasticity and to prevent cracking during the drying process. The clay was formed into the requisite shape by using a wheel, press mould or built up by coils of clay. Decoration might be added by using a slip, painting, incising or by adding appliqué-work. This last form of decoration was known in Egypt, but never utilized in Palestine. The potter's wheel was used in Mesopotamia from at least 3500 BC. 'Then I went down to the potter's house, and, behold, he wrought a work on the wheels.' (Jeremiah 18:3). Palestine adopted this technique completely in about 2000 BC. Early pottery was possibly baked in the open, as in the Neolithic societies of sub-

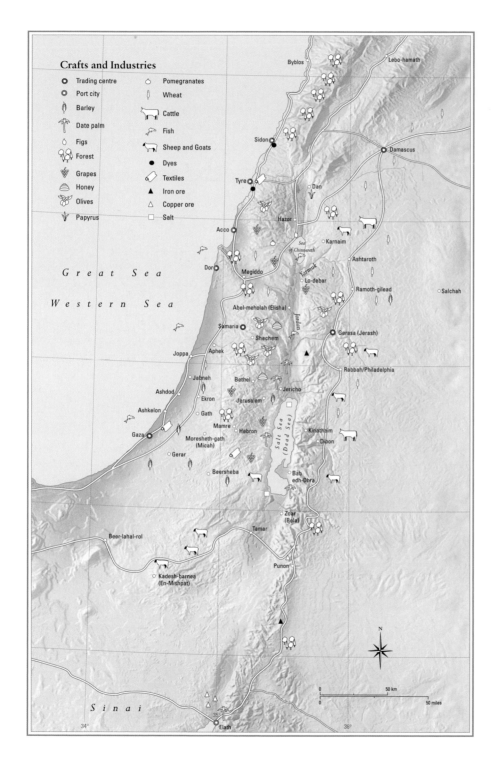

Crafts and Industries

- ◉ Trading centre
- ◉ Port city
- ♊ Barley
- 🌴 Date palm
- ◊ Figs
- 🌳 Forest
- 🍇 Grapes
- 🍯 Honey
- 🫒 Olives
- ↓ Papyrus
- ◠ Pomegranates
- ♊ Wheat
- 🐄 Cattle
- 🐟 Fish
- 🐑 Sheep and Goats
- ● Dyes
- ◇ Textiles
- ▲ Iron ore
- △ Copper ore
- ▢ Salt

THE ECONOMY OF THE HOLY LAND

The economy remained largely agricultural in the Bible lands. The main centres for production and trade in commodities and where mineral resources were exploited are detailed here. Trade was limited during this period due to limited water supplies, harsh terrain and basic transportation facilities and infrastructure.

Saharan Africa or the Americas, but the Early Bronze Age witnessed the adoption of the closed kiln, enabling greater fuel-efficiency, mass production, and product control.

By the Late Bronze Age, little jugs, known as bil-bils, were imported into Canaan. Some were used to hold opium; the jug's shape being similar to that of an upturned poppy head. In the same period, gracefully decorated Mycenean vessels, known as 'stirrup jars' were imported into Canaan, possibly containing perfumed oils. Jars of Egyptian design, dating from the 12th Century BC in Transjordan, were found in storerooms on the archaeological site at Tell es-Sa'idiyeh, and might have been used to store and transport wine.

Metalworking probably started with gold, moving on to copper. Both were worked cold, but by 4000 BC were smelted and cast. Southern Sinai was Egypt's copper source. Canaan, Egypt, and the Israelites, especially in the kingdom of Judah, constantly competed for control of the southern part of the Wadi Arabah and the north-eastern Sinai, demonstrating the significance of this raw material in ancient times.

The processing of copper ore commences with small pieces of ore being placed in a furnace on a bed of charcoal. Such furnaces were normally circular being basin-shaped to catch the molten metal, resulting in a pudding-shaped ingot. Bellows were used to provide a draft forceful enough to achieve smelting temperature. The ingot would require much hammering and re-smelting to drive out all impurities. Only then could the metal be used for tools and ornaments. Iron ingots could not be made in antiquity because the requisite temperatures could not be achieved. Later periods saw blacksmiths, organized in hereditary guilds, living and working together. Philistine superiority over the early Israelites lay in the latter's use of bronze rather than iron weapons.

Palestine does not possess the best climatic conditions to preserve ancient cloth. However, a cave in Nahal Hemar, near the Dead Sea, was found to contain cloth dating from around 7000 BC. Fibers used were generally linen, wool, and later on, cotton. Cloth was dyed in blue, purple, indigo and scarlet. 'And thou shalt make the robe of the ephod all of blue' (Exodus 38:31). Owing to the differing lengths and characteristics of the fibers used, specialized spinners developed techniques to handle them. Egyptian linen was renowned for its softness and pliability, being light and comfortable to wear. 'And Pharaoh took off his ring from his hand, and put it upon Joseph's hand, and arrayed him in vestures of fine linen' (Genesis 41:42). The linen was also hard wearing and could even be used for sail-making. 'Fine linen with broidered work from Egypt was that which thou spreadest forth to be thy sail: blue and purple from the isles of Elishah was that which covered thee' (Ezekiel 27:7). Linen was exported from inland western Syria, from Ebla and from Tyre. From the Early Bronze Age, flax was woven in Palestine, Galilee being well known for producing high grade flax. Retting out—soaking the woody portion of the flax—was often achieved by laying it out on house roofs so decomposition could be achieved by dew fall. 'But she had brought them up to the roof of the house, and hid them with the stalks of flax, which she had laid in order upon the roof' (Joshua 2:6).

Three types of loom were used in the ancient Middle East. The Egyptians had their own type of vertical loom, as documented by Herodotus. Here, the warp beam was at the top and the cloth beam at the bottom, the weft being downwards. The Greek loom was formed the other way round with the warps weighted at the bottom and the weft hammered upwards. Nomads utilised a portable

LOCALLY-MADE URN IN THE GREEK STYLE

The Greeks never achieved lasting political control over the region, but Greek art, drama, poetry, architecture, philosophy and political theory had enormous influence.

horizontal loom. Weaving was carried out by either sex, but most professional weavers were men. Loom weights were often made of unbaked clay and the spinning process twisted fibres in a continuous thread using a type of 'fly-wheel' or 'spindle whorl'.

Wine making was another craft and industry in the Middle East, using not just grapes, but dates and pomegranates as well, with the additional flavour of spices sometimes used. Wine was regularly used in daily life and was a pleasurable drink, especially old wine. It was also regarded as a medicine, applied internally or externally. 'Drink no longer water, but use a little wine for thy stomach's sake and thine often infirmities' (I Timothy 5:23). Also, '... And went to him, and bound up his wounds, pouring in oil and wine, and set him on his own beast, and brought him to an inn, and took care of him' (Luke 10:34). Grape harvesting was a social occasion, as was grape treading. Mechanical presses were used, as was squeezing grapes in folds of cloth. Fermentation started in a vat where the juice had been collected and then continued after transfer into skins or jars.

COINAGE
A shekel dating from the time of the first Jewish revolt against Rome.

ISRAELITE POTTERY
This collection of pots was found during excavation at Jaffa. Pottery is considered valuable evidence to archaeologists, as it provides proof of ancient settlements.

THE SPREAD OF WRITING

BOTH THE SUMERIANS AND THE EGYPTIANS APPEAR TO HAVE DEVELOPED SIMILAR WRITING METHODS AROUND 3000 BC. THE FIRST SCRIPTS EMPLOYED PICTORIAL SYMBOLS BOTH TO DEPICT OBJECTS AND REPRESENT SOUNDS. THEY WERE GRADUALLY REFINED INTO SYSTEMS OF PHONIC SYMBOLS.

Pre-Alphabet Scripts

In ancient civilisations, centralised economies needed to track how goods were collected and dispersed. A record system was required, and the earliest written records often listed the contents of storehouses, and eventually administrative matters. The earliest scripts were pictographic, which means that symbols were used for individual concepts and words.

The Egyptian forms of pictographs are hieroglyphs. Found mainly on walls, pillars and rock faces, but also on wood and ivory, these sacred scratchings have been uncovered in ancient Egyptian holy sites. Its use extended into the Early Dynastic period (c. 3100–2900 BC) and papyrus forms have been found from the period c. 2600–2500 BC. The script developed two cursive hand-written forms: hieratic was utilised by priests for religious purposes, and demotic, an adaptation of the hieratic, for everyday usage. By 1900 BC, Crete had developed a hieroglyphic script, maybe under Egyptian influence, or perhaps a parallel development. Later, Crete developed its script into two linear scripts, Linear A and B. Linear B (c. 1400–1200 BC) has been translated and represents Mycenaean Greek. Cyprus developed two indigenous scripts written on clay (c. 1500–1200 BC) and a syllabary (c. 750–300 BC), based on an earlier script, being used on monuments both in Greek and an unknown language. The Hittites had their own version of hieroglyphs, but in Luvian; they also used a version of cuneiform.

Writing in Mesopotamia developed cuneiform in the southern part of the Euphrates and Tigris river basin. Sumerian cuneiform probably originated in pictographs (as in Uruk), but grew in wedge- shaped strokes or impressions (from the Latin *cuneus*, or wedge). Finds at Ebla show that cuneiform was adapted to write a non-Sumerian language. The Akkadians (c. 2400–2250 BC) used Sumerian cuneiform even when

Babylonian and Assyrian replaced Sumerian as the Mesopotamian spoken language. After 2000 BC, Akkadian cuneiform became a vehicle for international communication, being borrowed by the Elamites (2250–350 BC), the Hurrians (by c. 1300 BC), the Hittites (1650–1200 BC) and the Urartians (c. 1000–585 BC). The spread of cuneiform may be associated with Assyrian merchants travelling throughout Asia Minor establishing colonies along trade routes. Trade stimulated the spread of various writing systems. These eventually became simplified into alphabets in the area known as Greater Canaan, comprising Palestine, western Syria and Lebanon, the area being not just a cockpit of war and imperial expansion, but vital for cultural and linguistic exchanges. The coastal regions, especially in the north, hosted many natural harbours making them transit points and intermediaries between neighbouring great powers.

The Ugarit cuneiform alphabet is believed to have originated in the port of Minet el-Beida, on the Mediterranean coast of northern Syria, south of modern Latakia. Excavated by archaeologists in 1929, its temple offered up a collection of books that co-existed with several private libraries. Texts were written on clay tablets. Among the texts were the *Legend of Keret*, the *Aghat Epic* (or *Legend of Danl*, the *Myth of Baal-Aliyan* and the *Death of Baal*), revealing an Old Canaanite mythology. It now seems that the patriarchal tales in the Old Testament were partially based on written documents of Canaanite provenance. Several of the Psalms were adopted from Ugaritic sources; the flood story nearly mirror images Ugaritic literature, which, apart from lists, is composed completely in the poetic metre that Biblical poetry follows in form and function.

The cosmopolitan nature of the city is obvious when viewing the usage of seven different scripts:

Egyptian and Hittite hieroglyphic, and Cypro-Minoan, Sumerian, Akkadian, Hurrian and Ugaritic cuneiform. The Ugarit alphabet comprised signs, with three vowels; shorter alphabets with 25 or 22 signs were in use by 13th-Century BC traders. The letters followed the same order as the later Hebrew alphabet and the system was known elsewhere, evidenced by an inscription from Beth-shemesh (Tel Bet Shemesh, Israel) and symbols on a copper dagger from near Mount Tabor.

Other simplified writing systems have been discovered on rocks in the Sinai peninsula. A miniature sphinx, about six inches (c. 15 cms) high, was found at Serabit el-Khadim in Sinai, with various symbols on its side, probably an attempt at an alphabet. The rock carvings are adjacent to copper mines exploited by Egypt. It is possible that Semitic slave mine-workers attempted a simplified script based on Egyptian hieroglyphs. Another Sinatic script has been found at an Egyptian turquoise mine (c. 1500 BC) that has links with the proto-Canaanite alphabet. Other linear-alphabetic scripts have been found at Lachish, Shechem, Gezer, Megiddo, and near Beth-shan, deriving from the same period. The al-Amarna letters

	OX	HOUSE	WATER
EGYPTIAN HIEROGLYPHICS c. 3000 BC			
CANAANITE c. 2000 BC			
PHOENICIAN c. 1000 BC			
HEBREW c. 700 BC			
OLD GREEK c. 650 BC			
ARAMAIC c. 350 BC			
FORMAL HEBREW c. 150 BC			
FORMAL GREEK c. 450 BC			
ROMAN c. 550 BC			

EYE	HEAD	PAPYRUS	
			Egyptian writing did not develop far from the use of pictorial symbols.
			Canaanite writing shows its pictorial origins, but in fact symbolizes basic sounds.
			The 22 basic symbols of the Canaanite system became the standard for the region.
			The Hebrews adopted the Canaanite alphabet in a modified form.
			The Canaanite origins can still be seen in archaic Greek script.
			Aramaic was the main language of the Persian Empire, and displaced Hebrew in Palestine.
			Classical Hebreew was written in a 'square' form of the common script of the region.
			The Greek alphabet allocated vowel sounds to some of the letters, and added more symbols.
			The Romans gained their alphabet from the Etruscans and Greek colonists.

THE DEVELOPMENT OF ALPHABETS

The first scripts were pictograms, pictorial representations of objects in the natural world, stylized and given a fixed form. They probably continued to be used in this primary sense, but their value for communication lay in the sounds they represented. Originally the sound would be the name of the object that the sign depicted and the sign could then be used for other words containing that sound. Ancient Egyptians used about 100 phonograms, signs expressing sounds, but 24 of them expressed only one sound and were used like an alphabet. The Canaanite scribes invented the first alphabet, from which all Western systems of writing were derived.

written from various Canaanite city states to the Egyptian Pharaoh demonstrate that Canaanites were used to writing, and that their script was internationally regarded and used.

Bible Languages

Linear alphabets were invented about 1100 BC, evidenced in particular by carvings on a large coffin, found in 1923 at Byblos. Other texts have been found at the site, including the epitaph for Ahiram, the King of Phoenicia. These writings involve the period of David and Solomon, and it is during this time that court historians wrote documents later amalgamated into the Bible. Theoretically, anyone could now learn to read and write. Linear alphabets simplified the number of letters: 30 in Ugarit and fewer in Hebrew and Greek. More people could use writing in everyday life, whatever the size of a community. However, professional scribes only became redundant with the development of printing.

Such alphabets had another universal advantage. Instead of being tied to a specific language like hieroglyphic or cuneiform scripts, these alphabets' symbols could ultimately be used for any spoken language. The existence of the Phoenician trading network in the eastern Mediterranean meant alphabets spread, especially among the Greeks, Aramaeans and Hebrews. Interestingly, the Hebrews adopted the language and script of the Canaanites, a more sophisticated culture than their own semi-nomadic society. Passages in Deuteronomy (26:5) and Isaiah (19:18) point to this, as does the non-biblical Farmer's Calendar from Gezer and the 620 BC potsherd uncovered at Yabne-Yam in 1960. An article in the *New York Times*, 13 November 1999, 'Discovery of Egyptian Inscriptions Indicated an Earlier Date for Origin of the Alphabet,' claims that the earliest known alphabet may now date from 1900–1800 BC. Limestone inscriptions at Wadi el-Hol near the Valley of the Kings in Egypt appear to be the work of Semitic peoples. The sacred texts of the Jews were written in this Canaanite script until the 6th-Century BC exile following the Assyrian and Babylonian conquests.

Exiles traveled to Egypt, Syria and into the Tigris and Euphrates cities of Mesopotamia. However, before this cataclysm, writings were often on leather and papyrus, but these materials have obviously rotted away leaving just engraved evidence.

The second language of the Bible is Aramaic, as documented in the Books of Ezra and Daniel. Kings 1 and 2 provide a wealth of information about 9th- and 8th-Century BC events. The Aramaeans had moved from the Syro-Arabian desert nomadic life, developing city states such as Damascus and adopting the Phoenician alphabet. This is seen in a number of inscriptions. These city states were swept away by their Assyrian political masters, but the language lived on and spread through the civilized lands of the Fertile Crescent from Persia to Egypt. The Jewish élites of Jerusalem represented Hebrews to the Assyrian king, thus: 'Then said Eliakim the son of Hilkiah, and Shebna, and Joah unto Rab-shakeh, Speak, I pray thee, to thy servants in the Syrian language for we understand it: and talk not with us in the Jews' language in the ears of the people that are on the wall' (2 Kings 18:26).

Persian domination (c. 540–330 BC) witnessed Aramaic as the language of diplomacy. Aramaic texts in the Old Testament (Ezra) originate in this period, as do papyri from a Jewish community from Elephantine Island (Yeb) in the Nile near Aswan. A Hebrew garrison was stationed there to protect the southern frontier of Egypt. The island apparently housed a Jewish sanctuary, destroyed in 410 BC at the instigation of some Egyptian priests. An Aramaic papyrus addresses the governor of Judah, Bagoas, and complains about the razing of the Jewish temple. The Book of Daniel uses both Hebrew and Aramaic. It seems likely that the common people lost their Hebrew to Aramaic leaving the older tongue as an élite religious language. Thus, Christianity was revealed in Aramaic and the early Christians spoke, wrote and thought in this language. Its supremacy led to the Jews ending their use of the Canaanite script and using instead the Aramaic square-shaped letters, the Jewish Bible still being printed using this style of characters.

The third biblical language is Greek. This became the international language after Alexander the Great established his empire, with Hellenisation taking place in the successor states. The Greeks had already assimilated the Phoenician alphabet by 800 BC, evidenced by the shape of many ancient Greek letters. The Diaspora Jews, ignorant of Hebrew, for example, were compelled to translate their texts into Greek for common consumption. Some sacred books were written in Greek, exemplified by the Book of Wisdom. The Early Christian Church, existing among Aramaic-speaking peoples, was forced to translate its teachings into common Greek, *koine*. Only now could the Christian message travel around the Roman Empire, where Greek was now the *lingua franca* of its time. For example, the Letter of James was written in sophisticated Greek, while experts consider the Four Gospels to have been written in Greek but using some Aramaic sources. The influence of Hellenism penetrates further: the word Sanhedrin is merely a Greek-loan word, *sunhedrion* (a sit-together).

HEBREW SCROLL
Most ancient writings or documents of reasonable length were in the form of scrolls.

AN EGYPTIAN PAPYRUS
Flowing from right to left, this Egyptian text captures the teachings of the writer Ani.

Renaissance of the Kingdoms

FOR A PERIOD IN THE 8TH CENTURY BC, JUDAH AND ISRAEL ENJOYED RELATIVE PEACE. THEIR ENEMIES WERE IN DISARRAY – SYRIA HAD BEEN OVERWHELMED BY ASSYRIA, WHO IN TURN WERE IN TURMOIL FOR NEARLY HALF A CENTURY.

The fate of Judah and Israel improved in the second decade of the 8th Century BC. Egypt was unimportant militarily, its sole international venture being Pharaoh Osorkon (c. 860–830 BC) sending soldiers to fight Assyrian King Shalmaneser III with Syro-Palestinian allies at Qarqar. Shalmaneser's son, Shamshiadad (824–812 BC), had only crushed a revolt with Babylonian aid. He was succeeded by Adadnirari III (811–784 BC) who came to the throne as a minor. He re-imposed tribute on some western states, but was being pushed territorially by Urartu. Nevertheless, he managed to capture Damascus in c. 806 BC, taking valuable tribute. Syria recovered from the mauling, but engaged in a bitter and unsuccessful rivalry with Hamath, evidenced from a contemporary stele of Zakir, King of Hamath. Syria was in no position to maintain a hold on Israel. His death led to internal weakness in Assyria. With both major power centres in decline, if only momentarily, Judah and Israel managed to prosper. Two energetic monarchs came to power to exploit the situation. Jeroboam II, son of Jehoash of Israel, ruled from Samaria (786–746 BC). Uzziah (or Azariah) followed his father, Amaziah, as King of Judah ruling from Jerusalem (783–742 BC). The two monarchs brought Israel and Judah to new heights of prosperity and power not known since the times of David and Solomon.

The fortunes of Judah changed under Uzziah. Energetic and thoughtful, Uzziah wanted to rebuild Judah in an efficient and coherent fashion to rival aspects of the Solomonic state. Firstly, he dug new wells and cisterns to support large flocks and herds, allowing agriculture to develop in a systematic fashion. Soil types were tested to establish the best crops per region: grain in the valleys and on the plains and vineyards on the hillsides. He continued Solomon's

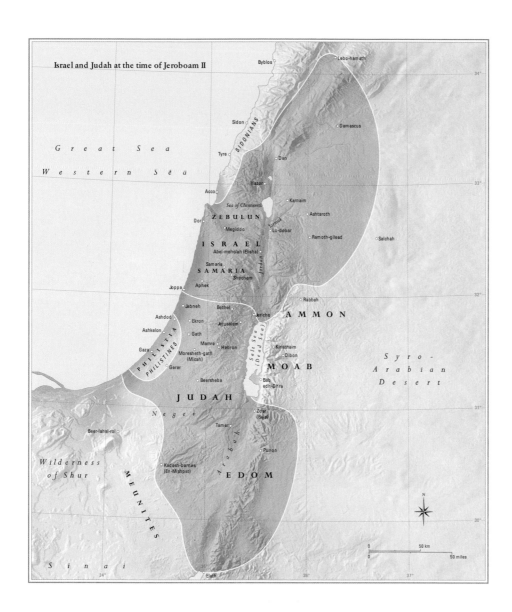

Israel and Judah at the time of Jeroboam II

ISRAEL AND JUDAH AT THE TIME OF JEROBOAM II AND UZZIAH

Two brilliant kings, Jeroboam II of Israel and Uzziah of Judah, succeeded in extending their respective domains bringing 40 years of stability.

scheme, as had Jehoshaphat , for establishing military-agricultural settlements in the Negev in order to secure and police trade routes in that desolate region. Thus, much Arabian traffic came under his remit. Fortifications were built to a standard military design with casement walls and a minimum of eight towers: these guarded crossroads and strategic points. Agricultural villages were created at many of these forts, but the sites were primarily military, farming secondary. These towers could be found at Beer-sheba, Hormah and Arad. Other towers existed: '...Also he built towers in the desert, and digged many wells' (2 Chronicles 26:10). Archaeologists have found many of these, but not all.

'ALSO HE BUILT TOWERS IN THE DESERT, AND DIGGED MANY WELLS: FOR HE HAD MUCH CATTLE, BOTH IN THE LOW COUNTRY, AND IN THE PLAINS: HUSBANDMEN ALSO, AND VINE DRESSERS IN THE MOUNTAINS, AND IN CARMEL: FOR HIS LOVED HUSBANDRY.

'MOREOVER UZ-ZI-AH HAD AN HOST OF FIGHTING MEN, THAT WENT OUT TO WAR BY BANDS, ACCORDING TO THE NUMBER OF THEIR ACCOUNT BY THE HAND OF JE-I-EL THE SCRIBE AND MA-A-SEI-AH THE RULER, UNDER THE HAND OF HAN-A-NI-AH, ONE OF THE KING'S CAPTAINS.

'THE WHOLE NUMBER OF THE CHIEF OF THE FATHERS OF THE MIGHTY MEN OF VALOUR WERE TWO THOUSAND AND SIX HUNDRED.

'AND UNDER THEIR HAND WAS AN ARMY, THREE HUNDRED THOUSAND AND SEVEN THOUSAND AND FIVE HUNDRED, THAT MADE WAR WITH MIGHTY POWER, TO HELP THE KING AGAINST THE ENEMY.'

2 CHRONICLES 26:10–13

Uzziah improved Jerusalem's fortifications by building towers at the corner and valley gates, and at the turning of the wall. He had built wooden structures on the city walls to protect his soldiers and constructed war machines to fire arrows and throw great stones or rocks. The Bible claims his armed forces reached 307,500 soldiers, armed with spears, bows, and slings with helmets, shields, and scale armour jackets. Included in his forces was an élite strike force, the 'mighty men of valour', which traced its origins to King David's personal guard.

Uzziah engaged in offensive actions against his neighbours (2 Chronicles 26: 6–8). He waged war on Edom, re-capturing territory all the way to Ezion-geber, which was rebuilt as a major fortified port and became an important town on the caravan route between Damascus and Egypt. He consolidated Judah's position along the trade routes by combating the north-western Arabian tribes. These were based in Gurbaal and the Meunites in the Edomite desert, and who could have threatened Judah's control over the southern portion of the King's Highway. The northern stretches of that highway were held by the Ammonites, who paid him tribute. His desire for a port on the Mediterranean coast led him to secure the Shephelah and invade Philistia. He constructed a fort at Azekah and destroyed the defenses of Gath, Ashdod, and Jabneh. Gath and Jabneh were digested by Judah as were some of Ashdod's lands. He eventually captured Joppa, thereby ensuring that all the dangerous western approaches to Judah were under his control. Cities were built among the Philistine population and inhabited by his people. His reputation spread far and wide, for he had restored the southern part of Solomon's united kingdom to Judah's rule.

In the northern kingdom of Israel, Jeroboam II restored his people's fortunes and laid conditions for a great increase in prosperity. The king intended to attack Damascus using Aphek as his base. He probably marched to Lodebar, winning victories along the way. After controlling the plateau in that area, which is a route into the Bashan-Gilead region, he captured Ramoth-gilead. Evidence suggests that he next assaulted Karnaim, which lies on a road running northwards to Damascus. Holding both Aphek and Ramoth-gilead, Jeroboam could have attacked Karnaim from both west and south simultaneously. His onslaught tore through Aram, into Damascus and northwards to Lebo-hamath, thereby reaching the furthest extent north of David's and Solomon's domain. Thus, Jeroboam was probably able to impose his authority on both Damascus and Hamath. 'Now the rest of the acts of Jeroboam, and all that he did, and his might, how he warred, and how he recovered Damascus, and Hamath, which belonged to Judah, for Israel, are they not written in the Book of the Chronicles of the Kings of Israel?' (2 Kings 14:28) Despite the obscure nature of the verse, one might assume that Israel annexed Aramean lands in Transjordan north of the Yarmuk River. In southern Transjordan, Israel's border reached a point along the Dead Sea ('Sea of Arabah'). However, this point is called the 'Brook of Arabah' in Amos 6:14, the 'river of the wilderness'. So, it is uncertain whether Jeroboam constrained the Moabites or totally conquered them. If the Brook of the Arabah is identical with 'the Brook of the Willows' in Isaiah 15:7, that is the Wadi el-Hesa (Zered) at the southern end of the Dead Sea, then complete conquest had been achieved. Whatever the case, the Moabites and Ammonites had been pushed out of Israelite territory and their ambitions checked.

Israel had now regained its rich Gilead lands and tribute from conquered peoples, a sound basis for economic prosperity and the conspicuous consumption it engenders. The population expanded until towns could no longer contain them. Archaeological evidence at Megiddo, an important administrative centre, uncovered many public buildings and quality stone houses. Excavators

THE HILL OF SAMARIA
Its easily defensible position probably influenced Omri in his decision to build a city here. For about 150 years this city served as the capital of Israel until destroyed by the Assyrians in 721 BC.

there found a wonderful seal bearing the image of a roaring lion with these words inscribed, 'Shema, servant of Jeroboam'. Shema had probably been the governor of the region, and this was his official seal. Evidence of wealth has been found in Samaria in the form of *ostraca*, pottery fragments. These provide evidence for notations of produce found in Samaria received at the royal warehouse, goods described as 'aged wine' or 'purified oil'. When the jars of liquid were delivered, they were recorded on a potsherd and then entered in a ledger.

At Hazor, archaeologists have uncovered examples of some of the finest Israelite houses, dating to Jeroboam's reign. On top of the ruins of Ahab's storehouse there are shops, workshops, and houses, built during Israel's 8th Century BC renaissance. All were of a good architectural standard, with skilled workmanship being used. One house had a courtyard measuring 30 x 26 feet (9 x 8 meters). Some houses had two storeys and were so well built that the stairs remain in place after 2,700 years. The household goods evidence a degree of wealth. High-grade pottery was used as were bowls and millstones made out of native basalt. One find was an ivory cosmetic spoon, its handle exquisitely carved in an inverted palmette design, common in the Middle East at that time. The back of the bowl is carved in the shape of a woman's head, with two doves entangled in her hair. Superior ivory objects have been found, but only in the royal palaces. Scenes of luxurious living can also be seen in ivory carvings.

About 760 BC, an earthquake damaged Hazor, allowing for the building of fine, new houses on the site. The scale of material well-being provides evidence for the wealth of Israel at the time. New types of fortification have also been found. Buildings near the edge of the Hazor mound were demolished to enable strengthening of the city wall with offsets and insets to provide stations for flanking fire against any onslaught. A stout rectangular tower measuring 33 x 23 feet (10 x 7 meters) was added to the north-western corner of the mound. Presumably, such fortifications were designed as a defence against a resurgent Assyria.

For some, despite war and earthquakes, life was good, but growing disparities between the wealthy and the poor was too much for the prophet, Amos of Tekoa. He objected to the display of wealth, describing the excesses and saying that these people would be punished: 'Ye that put away the evil day, and cause the seat of violence to come near; That lie upon beds of ivory, and stretch themselves upon their couches, and eat the lambs out of the flock, and calves out of the midst of the stall; That chant to the sound of the viol, and invent to themselves instruments of musick, like David; That drink wine in bowls, and anoint themselves with the chief ointments' (Amos 6:3–6).

The poorer people were ignored by the state; society was characterized by injustice. Small farmers were squeezed by money lenders and hammered by drought and crop failure leading to foreclosure, eviction or bond service. The wealthy bought land holdings from the poor, falsified weights and measures and other means of sharp practice. Israel's society had changed. The old unified social structure of the tribal league had dissolved. The advent of monarchy with its subsequent hierarchical power structure, together with the growth of commerce, created classes, destroyed tribal links and broke down traditional society.

Also, the absorption of many Canaanites, not integrated into the tribal system, generated a group of people with no obligation to or understanding of the Covenant. Ancestral strengths were departing.

The Samaria *ostraca* show as many names compounded with Baal as with Yahweh, although some examples of Baal (Lord) might be names for Yahweh. Argument says that many Israelites must have worshipped Baal and that native pagan deities had not been destroyed by Jehu, just Tyrian Baal. Amos and Hosea claim that even the state religion had absorbed pagan rites, and pagan rituals of sacrifice were put in place to secure the status quo by appeasing God. What is strange is that the prophetic orders, so strong against the House of Omri, had no rebukes against the current situation, presumably sated by Jehu's purge. The state cult had become perverted. Priests and monarchy alike thought that God's favourable attitude towards Israel had been secured for all time, forgetting that it was conditional upon keeping the covenantal obligations. Elaborate rituals were not enough, as the prophetic protests of Amos and Hosea pointed out.

Hosea described the Covenant bond as wedlock. Yahweh, as Israel's 'husband' expected Israel to be a faithful 'wife'. However, in worshipping other gods, Israel had committed 'adultery' and therefore faced 'divorce', a form of national ruin. Hosea attacked the Baal cult, claiming that Israel was morally rotten and totally impenitent. Like Amos, he saw Israel as being under the Covenant curse and thus faced destruction as a state and nation. 'Woe unto them! For they have fled from me: destruction unto them! Because they have transgressed against me: though I have redeemed them, yet they have spoken lies against me' (Hosea 7:13). And, 'My God will cast them away, because they did not harken unto him: and they shall be wanderers among the nations' (Hosea 9:17). Hosea ultimately believed that Yahweh's infinite love would forgive a penitent Israel, but only after an inevitable disaster broke the nation.

Amos inveighed against the decline in morals, about exploitation, drunkenness, injustice, and forgotten faith and prophesied that God's judgement would strike Israel. Another prophet, Hosea, wailed about the condition of religion and suggested that the ills of society would be punished when Assyria would invade again: '...An east wind shall come up from the wilderness, and his spring shall become dry, and his fountain shall be dried up: he shall spoil the treasure of all pleasant vessels. Samaria shall become desolate; for she hath rebelled against God; they shall fall by the sword: their infants shall be dashed in pieces, and their women with child shall be ripped up' (Hosea 14:15–16).

CHAOS

THE PROSPERITY AND WELL-BEING OF ISRAEL WAS SHATTERED
WHEN JEROBOAM DIED IN 746 BC. HIS SON ZECHARIAH LASTED
SIX MONTHS, RULING FROM FROM SAMARIA, WHEN HE WAS
MURDERED BY AN ASSASSIN AT IBLEAM.

The killer, Shallum, held the throne for a month when he was killed by Menahem, son of Gadi, of Tirzah, His brutality became legendary when his troops butchered pregnant women at the sack of Tappuah and destroyed the surrounding communities because the people refused him as king. Israel had now been seriously weakened and would soon face the might of a resurgent Assyria.

Meanwhile, Assyria changed its old policy of regarding the Euphrates as its western border, with trans-Euphrates states being vassals. Policy modification occurred because Assyria's northern rival, Urartu, had expanded westwards and forged an anti-Assyrian coalition. This alliance of north Syrian statelets from Melid to Arpad was a threat to Assyrian trade routes. In 745 BC, Tiglath-pileser III (the biblical Pul) acquired the Assyrian throne and, using his administrative and military skills, sought to expand the empire. A campaign settled the mountaineers, followed by an attack in 743 BC on the Urartian coalition in the west. The Urartian forces were defeated and Arpad, the major seat of resistance taken by siege in 740 BC, when it became the capital of an Assyrian province. Tiglath-Pileser next marched on Unqi at the northern end of the Orontes; Kullania, its capital, fell in 738 BC, its name being given to a new Assyrian province. Advances southwards resulted in the creation of the provinces of Simirra and Khatarikka, and the payment of tribute by various rulers including Rezin of Damascus, Menahem of Israel, and the Kings of Tyre (Hiram), Gubla, and Hamath. Assyria wanted to develop provincial government right up to the Mediterranean. The style of the new Assyrian policies was much harsher than before. These new campaigns did not merely exist to gain plunder, slaves, tribute and the security of trade routes; now, conquered lands were to be incorporated into the

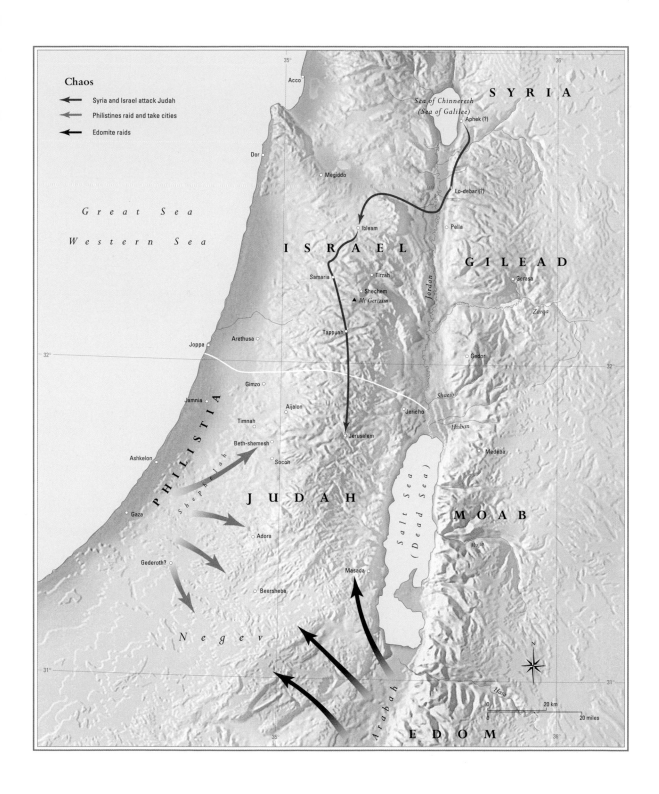

Chaos

→ Syria and Israel attack Judah

→ Philistines raid and take cities

→ Edomite raids

SYRIA

Sea of Chinnereth
(Sea of Galilee)

Aphek (?)

Acco

Dor

Megiddo

Lo-debar (?)

Ibleam

Pella

GILEAD

ISRAEL

Samaria

Tirzah

Gerasa

Shechem

▲ *Mt Gerizim*

Jordan

Zarqa

Great Sea

Western Sea

Tappuah

Gedor

Joppa

Arethusa

Shueib

Gimzo

Jericho

Hisban

Jamnia

Aijalon

Jerusalem

Medeba

Timnah

Beth-shemesh

Socoh

Ashkelon

Shephelah

JUDAH

Salt Sea
(Dead Sea)

MOAB

Gaza

Adora

Mujib

Gederoth?

Masada

Beersheba

N e g e v

Hasa

0   20 km
0   20 miles

Arabah

EDOM

'AND PUL THE KING OF ASSYRIA CAME AGAINST THE LAND: AND MENAHEM GAVE PUL A THOUSANDS TALENTS OF SILVER, THAT HIS HAND MIGHT BE WITH HIM TO CONFIRM THE KINGDOM IN HIS HAND. AND THEN MENAHEM EXACTED THE MONEY OF ISRAEL, EVEN OF ALL THE MIGHTY MEN OF WEALTH, OF EACH MAN FIFTY SHEKELS OF SILVER, TO GIVE TO THE KING OF ASSYRIA. SO THE KING OF ASSYRIA TURNED BACK, AND STAYED NOT THERE IN THE LAND.' 2 KINGS 15:19–20

Assyrian empire, as provinces and enemy leadership groups were deported deep into the empire as depopulated areas were settled with peoples from elsewhere in the empire. The coalition of minor countries also included 'Azriau from Iuda', Uzziah of Judah, the leper king, whose son, Jotham, served as regent. The tribute paid by Menahem was huge and weighed heavily upon the population of Israel.

Although the tribute won Menahem a breathing space of a further seven years for his kingship, his hold was weakened owing to building resentment over taxation, his method of achieving the kingship, and his bowing to Assyria. His son, Pekahiah, barely ascended the throne when he was murdered by Pekah, a captain, in a military coup by Gileadites.

Elsewhere, Tiglath-pileser confronted Urartian influences: in 739 BC in Ullubu (the Dohuk-Zakho region of north Iraq), in 737 BC in the Median area of northeast Iran, and in 735 BC they marched on Urartu itself. In 734 BC, Tiglath-pileser again turned westwards extending Assyrian control into Philistia, taking Gaza and reaching the Brook of Egypt (Wadi el-Arish). He crushed the nomadic tribes and appointed an Arab tribal chief as his warden in Sinai. Relationships were also built with other Arab rulers in northern Arabia and eastern Transjordan. Now, Pekah of Israel and Rezin of Damascus allied themselves in another anti-Assyrian coalition. It included Tyre, Askelon, and some tribes of north Arabia and Transjordan, and sough to persuade Jotham of Judah to join them. He refused, and his son Ahaz, ascending the throne in 735 BC, also refused.

The Israelite and Damascus confederates planned to invade Judah, depose Ahaz, and replace him with someone more amenable, the unidentified 'son of Tabeel'. However, Rezin dispatched his troops through Transjordan right down the King's Highway to acquire Ezion-geber. However, these territorial acquisitions were short-lived.

Rezin also sent forces to join Pekah in an attack upon Israel, it being probable that the Aphek-Lodebar route was used. The combined armies crossed the border and besieged Jerusalem, acquiring booty and prisoners along the way. These captives were later freed when the prophet Oded claimed their capture was a transgression against God, and Israel had sinned enough already. Possibly, Oded was the mouthpiece of opposition growing against Pekah. Ahaz thought an appeal for help to the Assyrian king would be a good idea, but the prophet Isaiah persuaded him otherwise. Reliance on God would see Judah through these difficult times.

However, the Israelite-Damascus armies pushed against Jerusalem and, simultaneously, Judah's old enemies took the opportunity for revenge. Edom recovered its freedom and grabbed the entire mineral-rich Arabah all the way to Ezion-geber; raids were also launched into the Negev. On the coast, the Philistines recovered lands lost to Uzziah, also acquiring the cities of Beth-shemesh, Socoh, Timnah, Aijalon and Gimzo.

The two invasion routes into Judah, the Ways of Beth-horon and Beth-shemesh, were open—leaving Ahaz and Judah insecure. Additionally, the Philistines seized Gederoth and commenced raids into the Negev, destroying Uzziah's system of agricultural-military communities.

'SO AHAZ SENT MESSENGERS TO TIGLATH-PILESER KING OF ASSYRIA, SAYING, I AM THY SERVANT AND THY SON: COME UP, AND SAVE ME OUT OF THE HAND OF THE KING OF SYRIA, AND OUT OF THE HAND OF THE KING OF ISRAEL, WHICH RISE UP AGAINST ME. AND AHAZ TOOK THE SILVER AND GOLD THAT WAS FOUND IN THE HOUSE OF THE LORD, AND IN THE TREASURES OF THE KING'S HOUSE, AND SENT IT FOR A PRESENT TO THE KING OF ASSYRIA.'

2 KINGS 16:7–8

DEPORTATIONS *(far left)*
This bas-relief, from the palace of Tiglath-pileser at Calah, shows the deportation of the inhabitants of a conquered city. According to the inscription, this is Ashtaroth, east of the Sea of Galilee.

WAYS OF WAR

FROM EARLIEST TIMES, SMALL BANDS OF PEOPLE COMPETED FOR
RESOURCES. THE FIRST CONFRONTATIONS WERE PROBABLY
DISPLAYS OF THREAT RATHER THAN ACTUAL COMBAT, BUT AS
MORE SETTLED SOCIETIES BEGAN TO APPEAR, THE NEED TO
DEFEND, AND PERHAPS TO EXPAND, BECAME MORE EVIDENT.

After the end of the last Ice Age, 12,000 years ago, the ice retreated, glaciers melted, sea levels rose and climates warmed. The era called the Mesolithic by archaeologists had arrived, with signs of increasing population and social complexity with, in places, increasingly permanent settlements and the first evidence of organized warfare. Examples include Offnet Cave in Germany, with 34 skulls all showing damage made by stone axes, and Jebel Sahaba in Upper Egypt, with the remains of 59 people all killed by arrows.

Some 10,000 years ago in the hills of Palestine, the Anatolian plateau and in the foothills of the Zagros Mountains, in eastern Iraq, numbers of mudbrick villages and their associated plots of wheat, barley and other crops, together with herds of goats and sheep began to appear. Within 2,000 years, settlements like these were spreading along the Mediterranean coast.

Warfare between these settled groups and passing nomads could be settled by ritualized threat with few casualties, but should this fail then bloody hand-to-hand combat ensued with higher casualty rates usually among males only. Clans and tribes could also effect raids upon their enemies, extremely bloody affairs aimed at killing as many of the enemy as possible regardless of sex or age. Entire tribes or clans could be wiped out in protracted primitive wars. Compared to modern societies where losses can be heavy, but total loss is almost unknown.

During the millennia that followed, with the continued spread of agriculture and settlement, the human population continued to multiply driving the growth of new levels of social

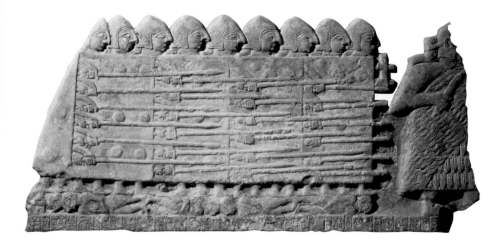

SOLDIERS OF LAGASH
This detail from the Stele of the Vultures (c. 2450 BC) shows men of Lagash, protected by helmets of metal or leather, advancing with an overlapping arrangement of shields and spears.

complexity including a formal political authority capable of strategic planning. It has been suggested that the evolution to this higher political authority required two things: irrigation and warfare, and internal management and external defense. These two requirements inevitably seemed to work together.

As settled populations grew, they controlled their surrounding hinterlands and complex defenses soon appeared. Jericho, near the Dead Sea, has the oldest fortifications in the world: stone walls 6 feet (2 meters) thick, towers 12 feet (4 meters) high defending a community perhaps 2,000-strong. Fortified cities like Jericho became common around the Middle East and through the historical mist appear two cities about which we have some information—Lagash and Umma. These two cities were repeatedly in conflict over a section of irrigated land. Lagash recorded its claims on a series of inscriptions; according to these, despite arbitration, Umma invaded and seized the disputed area. In the two battles that followed, Lagash was victorious.

Cities like these struggled with each other for power. However, this pattern was broken sometime after 2400 BC. The new imperial visionary was Lugalzagesi, King of Umma. After settling scores with the old enemy, Lagash, he went on to expand his rule over the cities of the Euphrates and the Tigris rivers, possibly extending his rule to the Mediterranean coast. Others looked on and learned, and this new escalation in warfare was adopted and developed by Sargon of Akkad, who put an end to the glory of Lugalzagesi.

Equipment carried into battle falls into two categories: shock and missile. The original shock weapon was the prehistoric club that, through time, was 'refined' with sharpened edges: the Stone Age prototype of the sword. The first missile weapon was the rock that could be hurled at the enemy. The velocity of the missile was much improved by the development of the simple leather sling, a well-chosen stone could be delivered on target at a greater range and greater force then the human arm alone could achieve. From these two basic concepts, weapons continued to develop: the javelin for throwing, the pike for thrusting. The bow and arrow and its high rate of fire, developed in the late Stone Age, was a valuable asset for the fighting man.

The Battle of Megiddo
1457 BC

Phase 1

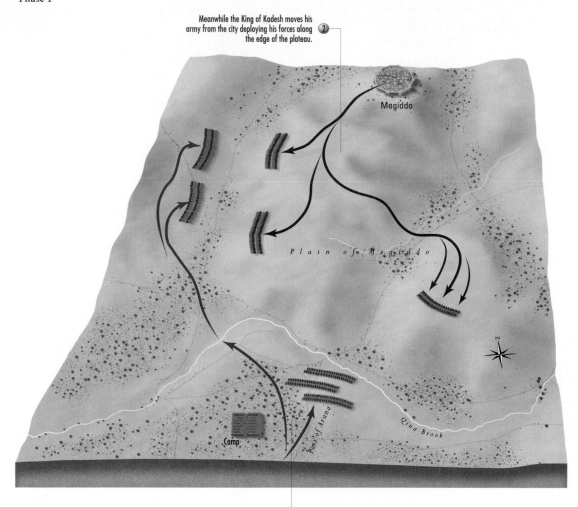

Meanwhile the King of Kadesh moves his
army from the city deploying his forces along
the edge of the plateau.

Megiddo

Plain of Megiddo

N

Pass of Aruna

Qina Brook

Camp

Thutmose, marching through the Pass of Aruna, camps
by the brook. The next day he deploys his chariot
formations along the low hills around the plain of
Megiddo, leaving his infantry to guard the camp.

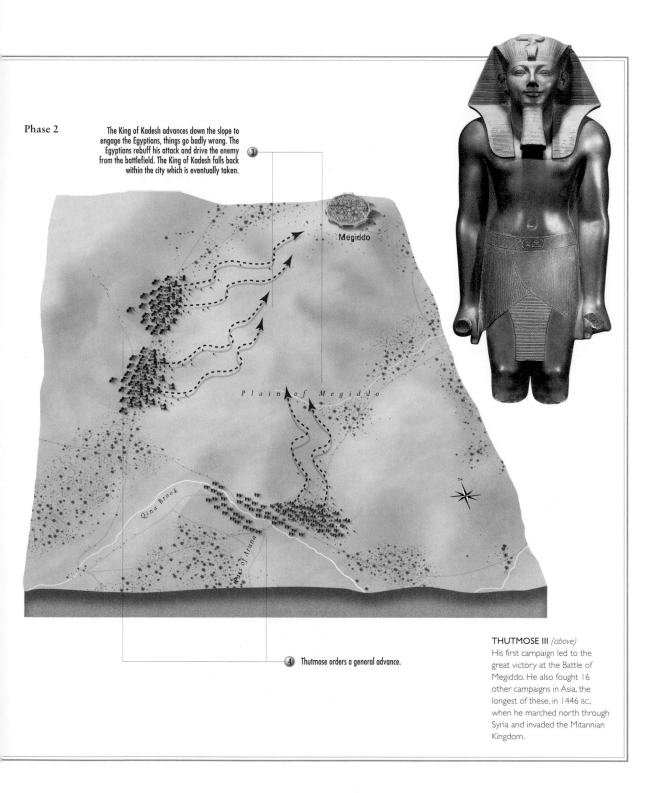

Phase 2

The King of Kadesh advances down the slope to engage the Egyptians, things go badly wrong. The Egyptians rebuff his attack and drive the enemy from the battlefield. The King of Kadesh falls back within the city which is eventually taken.

③

Megiddo

Plain of Megiddo

Qina Brook

Pass of Aruna

④ Thutmose orders a general advance.

THUTMOSE III *(above)*
His first campaign led to the great victory at the Battle of Megiddo. He also fought 16 other campaigns in Asia, the longest of these, in 1446 BC, when he marched north through Syria and invaded the Mitannian Kingdom.

The Egyptian corps of Amon
and Re advance west of Kadesh.

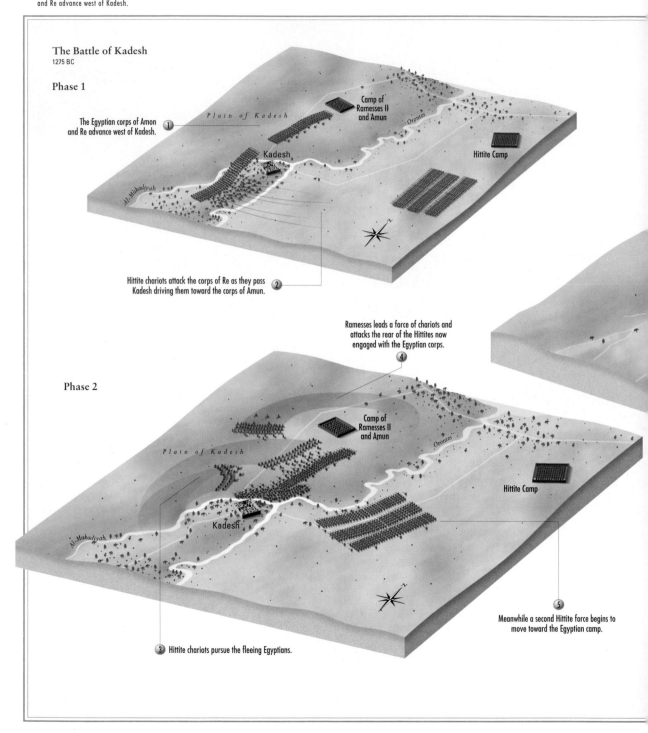

The Battle of Kadesh
1275 BC

Phase 1

The Egyptian corps of Amon
and Re advance west of Kadesh. ①

Plain of Kadesh

Camp of
Ramesses II
and Amun

Orontes

Kadesh

Hittite Camp

Al-Mukadiyah

Hittite chariots attack the corps of Re as they pass
Kadesh driving them toward the corps of Amun. ②

Ramesses leads a force of chariots and
attacks the rear of the Hittites now
engaged with the Egyptian corps. ④

Phase 2

Plain of Kadesh

Camp of
Ramesses II
and Amun

Orontes

Hittite Camp

Al-Mukadiyah

Kadesh

③ Hittite chariots pursue the fleeing Egyptians.

⑤
Meanwhile a second Hittite force begins to
move toward the Egyptian camp.

Phase 3

The Ne`Arin arrive from Amurru providing the
Egyptian force with support on the left flank. The
Hittite attack which gradually loses coheasion and falls
back accross the Orontes.

9

Lake of Homs

Camp of
Ramesses II
and Amun

Orontes

Plain of Kaḍesh

Hittite Camp

Kaḍesh

ukadiya

Orontes

N

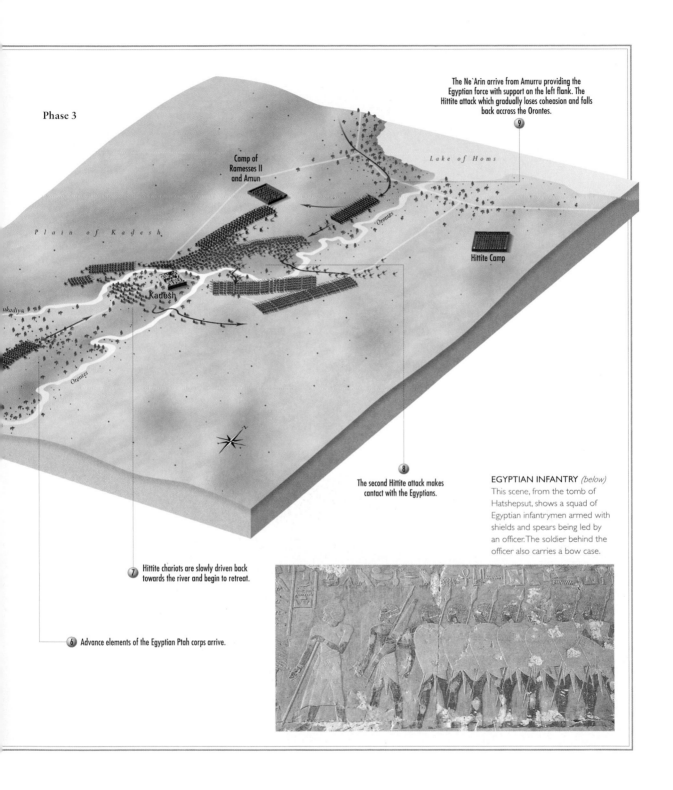

8 The second Hittite attack makes
contact with the Egyptians.

EGYPTIAN INFANTRY *(below)*
This scene, from the tomb of
Hatshepsut, shows a squad of
Egyptian infantrymen armed with
shields and spears being led by
an officer. The soldier behind the
officer also carries a bow case.

7 Hittite chariots are slowly driven back
towards the river and begin to retreat.

6 Advance elements of the Egyptian Ptah corps arrive.

Sometime around 2000 BC, metallurgy had developed, and this honed the effectiveness of these weapons and thus evolved the sword, which appeared on the blood-spattered battlefield, probably introduced by the Assyrians.

Alongside offensive weapons developed the defensive: wicker, leather or wooden shields, leather and quilted cloth armour. With metallurgy came breastplates, helmets and other forms of body armour. Thus equipped, men marched to meet their enemies intent on conquest or defense. The tactics they deployed consisted of large masses of infantry utilizing little protection other than a simple shield and carrying a spear to thrust at a similarly armed enemy. This mass usually came from the poorest group in society, around which a noble or professional warrior élite could operate. There would also be troops who would be armed with slings and bows who could deliver their missiles. Alongside the infantry what might be called chariots appeared, slow and unmanoeuvrable at first, but in time became the striking force of many enemies, that is until cavalry began to take this role.

The sole objective of these early armies was to find a suitable place of battle and overwhelm the enemy before they could do the same. Objectives became greater than defeating the next door city, battles turned into campaigns as geographical horizons widened. Military opportunities advanced. The men who made up such armies had little training, except the military élites, and went into battle motivated by fear of their commanders and also by the prospect of booty.

PARTHIAN EMPIRE

The Roman Empire contested its eastern boundary with the Parthian Empire for some 400 years. For most of this time Parthia was the largest organized state on the frontier of the Roman Empire. Rome invaded Parthia in AD 113, but, this success was shortlived, and the occupation ended in AD 117. In AD 226 Parthia was annexed to Sassanid Persia.

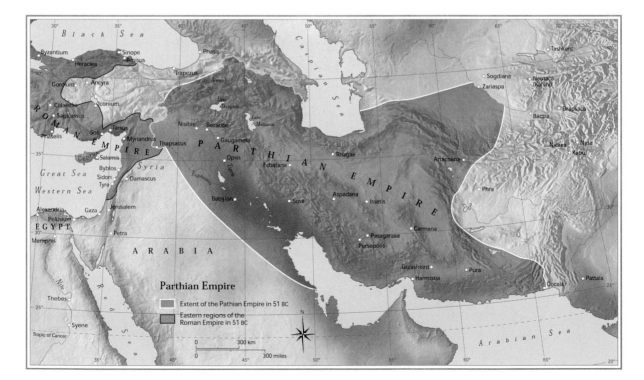

Parthian Empire

Extent of the Pathian Empire in 51 BC

Eastern regions of the Roman Empire in 51 BC

0   300 km
0   300 miles

When armies met on the battlefield the mass, usually spearmen, stayed together in groups. The élite in their chariots, or on horseback, on the flanks or in front with groups of archers or slingers, forming a forward skirmish line. The archers and slingers maintained a harassing fire until the chariots or cavalry sensed the right moment to charge. The skirmishes then moved to the flanks and rear through the massed infantry who were, by now, moving forward. Occasionally the initial charge would drive the enemy terror-stricken from the battlefield, but more usually the opposing forces would converge and hand-to-hand butchery would begin, ending only when one side sensed defeat. This communicated itself quickly through the ranks of troops, usually only a small proportion of the defeated army escaped.

THE EMPEROR VALERIAN
In this carved relief from Nagshe Rostam, Valerian is depicted cowering in front of the Persian king after his defeat and capture at Edessa in AD 268. The Romans have to both cope with controlling their eastern possessions and protect them from external threats, such as the powerful and militarily successful Sassanid Dynasty of Persia.

The territory that was occupied by the Hebrew people—the 'Promised Land'—seems to have been a dangerous place to call home. Straddling the major communication routes between Egypt, based on the Nile, and other great powers based on the Euphrates and the Tigris rivers, the Hebrews had to fight to gain this land. They fought their neighbouring peoples and fought petty wars and vendettas against each other.

Apart from relatively brief periods the Hebrew states were part of, or controlled by, larger powers—imperial Egyptians, the utter militarism of Assyria, exile at the hands of the Babylonians, return and restoration under the Persians, Macedonians, Syrians and, finally, as far as our story covers, the Romans.

The Jews rose up twice against Rome, the greatest military power of its age. The first revolt in AD 67–70 initially surprisingly successful, was soon overwhelmed and saw the destruction of Jerusalem with great loss of life and enslavement for many. The second revolt more successful than the first, the Jews developed guerrilla tactics—hit and run—to keep the Roman army guessing rather than allowing themselves to be trapped in fortresses where Roman siege skills made their defeat inevitable. In the year of AD 131, the revolutionaries established their own government in Jerusalem declaring 'Year One of the Redemption of Israel'. Inevitably, Roman power eventually defeated the revolt and a terrible price was paid by the Jews—those who did not, or could not, flee the land were killed or enslaved, the Jewish religion was proscribed and Jerusalem was Romanized, resettled by non-Jews and a temple to Jupiter was built on the site of the Holy of Holies. The name Judah was changed to the province of Syria-Palestine. The surviving Jews joined Jewish communities abroad and became people without a homeland—this would remain their fate until the establishment of the modern state of Israel in 1948. Such was the cost of living in the ways of war.

THE ROMAN EMPIRE AD **214**

The Roman Empire stood almost at its peak in extent and power at this point; its army occupying bases from northern Britain to the trading cities of Syria, from the forests of Germany to the deserts of north Africa. The Roman army protected this vast frontier with most of its forces along the European border, but also concentrated some of its best units in Palestine and Syria, protecting the rich grain lands of Egypt and Asia Minor. The army alone needed 100,000 tons of grain per year to feed its troops.

The Roman Empire
AD 214

▨ Roman Empire

▨ Client state

▨ Disputed territory in
northern Britain

◣ Legionary bases
in 214 AD

— Frontier of the
Roman Empire

I A

Gemina

I Aduitrix

duitrix

annonia
ferior

ia

VII Claudia

Moesia
Superior

Dacia

V Macedonia

XIII Gemina

Danube

XI Claudia

I Italica

Moesia
Inferior

Thrace

BOSPORAN
KINGDOM

Pontus Euxinus

Black Sea

ARMENIA

Mare Caspium

Caspian Sea

Byzantium

Philippi

Macedonia

Athens

Achaea

Bithynia and Pontus

Zela

Galatia

Asia

Ephesus

Lycia

Cappadocia

XV Apollinaris

XII Fulminata

III Parthica

Cilicia

Antioch
XVI Flavia

IV Scythica

Syria
Coele

PARTHIAN
EMPIRE

I Parthia

rum

Creta

Cyprus

G   r   e   a   t

W   e   s   t   e   r   n   S   e   a

S   e   a

Cyrene

Alexandria

Cyrenaica

II Traiana

Aegyptus

III Gallia

Syria
Phoenicia

VI Ferrata

X Fretensis

Syria
Palestina

Jerusalem

III Cyrenaica

Nabataea

Nile

Sinus
Arabicus

A   r   a   b   i   a   n

D   e   s   e   r   t

THE DESTRUCTION OF ISRAEL AND JUDAH

AFTER SEVERAL CENTURIES OF RUTHLESS DOMINATION
OVER MESOPOTAMIA, ASSYRIA FORGED THROUGH SYRIA
AND PALESTINE IN THE 8TH CENTURY BC, GOING ON TO
CONQUER THE ENTIRE FERTILE CRESCENT.

Tiglath-pileser of Assyria decided to enhance his domains in the west by destroying Damascene independence. However, he realized that it could not be achieved in one campaign. Egypt had always to be taken into account as a potential enemy and a rival empire. Pekah of Israel's alliance with Rezin of Damascus put his kingdom at risk, but not immediately—the Assyrian armies wanted to move through Israel rather than conquer it. Tiglath-pileser mounted three campaigns to achieve his ends: in 734, 733, and 732 BC.

In 734 BC, Assyrian forces began their march along the Way of the Sea towards the Brook of Egypt, the traditional northern border of Egypt. The army moved past Tyre and Acco, traveling inland through the first pass in the Carmel range rather than traversing the route cramped by the Carmel promontory where it meets the sea. The force entered the mountains at Jokneam emerging east of Dor and then rejoined the Way of the Sea rather than moving inland where the problems of inland fortresses would need to be dealt with. Along the route, Gezer was torched and the old Solomonic gate finally destroyed. Evidence of this destruction can be found at the Assyrian king's palace at Nimrud. Tiglath-pileser then captured Gaza and established forces along the Brook of Egypt to prevent any Egyptian raids northwards. In fact, a weakened Egypt could never mount more than brief spoiling attacks to retake Gaza and preferred to encourage other states to rebel in order to divert Assyrian forces.

In 733 BC, the Assyrians re-entered the fray targeting Israel directly, possibly intending to capture the Galilee and Gilead thereby isolating Syria in the west and south. Assyrian troops passed Mount Hermon descending into the rift valley guarded by the fortresses at Ijon and Abel-beth-maacah, both

being quickly captured. The army then moved to confront Hazor, a massive fortress on a 130-foot (39 meter) high mound. The citadel was stormed, the destruction being so massive that only foundations below floor level were left with few archaeological remains to find. The final incineration left a three foot thick layer of ash.

At Hazor, the Assyrians divided their army into three detachments. The first was dispatched through Upper Galilee by Kadesh to Janoah, both places being destroyed, and then reaching the coast at Acco. This force did pass between Carmel and the sea on its way to Dor, where history loses track of its itinerary. The second and third detachments moved south to Chinnereth on the Sea of Galilee. Splitting here, one unit moved south and east through Pehel to Jabesh-gilead with a smaller sub-strike force moving on to Mahanaim while the Assyrians moved throughout Gilead. The final detachment moved out of the rift valley at Adamah and marched westwards through the central area of Lower Galilee, smashing the towns of Rumah, Kahah, Jotbah and Hannathon, then taking a valley route south to the Great Plain to confront Megiddo.

MODEL OF MEGIDDO

Excavations at Megiddo have exposed the great walls and gateway built by King Solomon to strengthen Palestine after the Hebrews captured it. Solomon's numerous building projects depended on heavy taxation and forced labour, which were particularly resented by the Hebrews of the northern parts of the kingdom.

The Megiddo fortress controlled a major pass (Wadi Aria) through the Carmel range and was one of the most important cities in Israel, being an administrative and military base. Megiddo was now besieged by the formidable Assyrian siege train, possibly being reinforced by troops who had crossed Upper Galilee. Archaeologists suspect that Megiddo was flattened, because the subsequent Assyrian rebuild followed an entirely different plan, the fortress becoming the administrative capital of the new province of Magiddu. The entire northern part of the kingdom of Israel was appropriated by the growing Assyrian Empire.

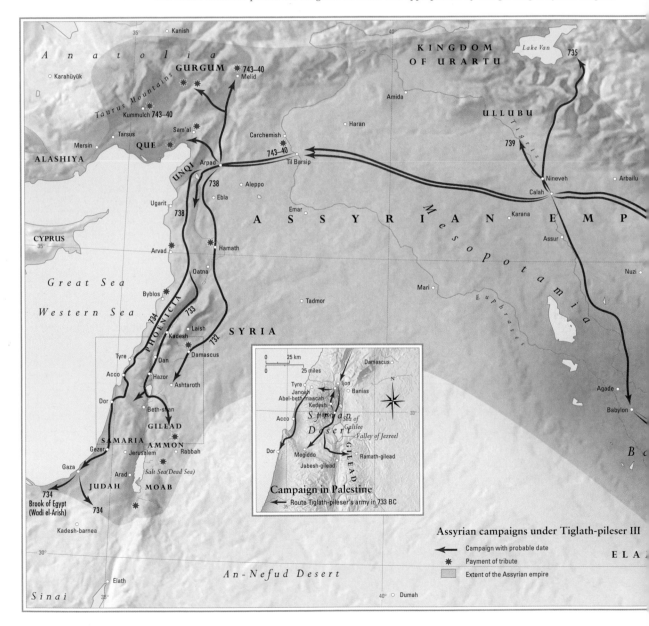

Campaign in Palestine
← Route Tiglath-pileser's army in 733 BC

Assyrian campaigns under Tiglath-pileser III
← Campaign with probable date
✻ Payment of tribute
▨ Extent of the Assyrian empire

Simultaneously, from the coast south of Mount Carmel to a border at the Kanah Brook became part of the province of Dor.

In Israel, events moved on. Pekah was deposed by Hoshea who became the last King of Israel. Tiglath-pileser's records state that the

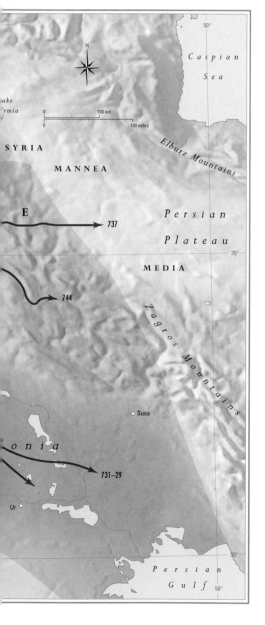

SEASONAL CAMPAIGNS *(left)*
The Assyrians had launched a series of seasonal campaigns, the major policy change was to incorporate conquered territories within the Empire rather than arranging a series of dependences.

ASSYRIAN INFANTRY *(above)*
This detail, from the relief at the palace of Ashurbanipal at Nineveh, shows Assyrian infantry equipped with spears attacking Elamites, who are largely archers.

'IN THE DAYS OF PE-KAH KING OF ISRAEL CAME TIG-LATH-PI-LE-SER KING OF ASSYRIA, AND TOOK I-JON, AND A-BEL-BETH-MA-A-CHAH, AND JA-NO-AH, AND KE-DEA SH, AND HA-ZOR, AND GILEAD, AND GALILEE, ALL THE LAND OF NAPH-TA-LI, AND CARRIED THEM CAPTIVE TO ASSYRIA.' 2 KINGS 15:29

ISRAEL IS DEFEATED

The campaigns of 721–720 BC involved the final destruction of Israel as a nation.

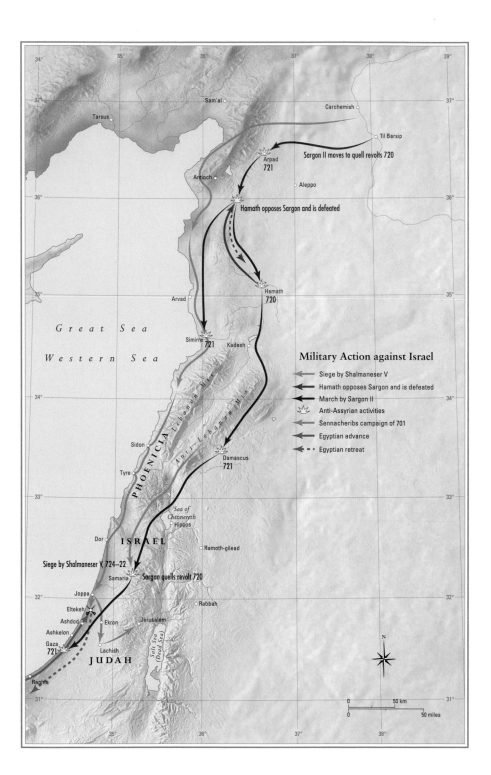

Carchemish

Sam'al

Tarsus

Til Barsip

Arpad
721

Sargon II moves to quell revolts 720

Antioch

Aleppo

Hamath opposes Sargon and is defeated

Hamath
720

Great Sea

Western Sea

Arvad

Simirra
721

Kadesh

Military Action against Israel

⟶ Siege by Shalmaneser V
⟶ Hamath opposes Sargon and is defeated
⟶ March by Sargon II
✳ Anti-Assyrian activities
⟶ Sennacheribs campaign of 701
⟶ Egyptian advance
⟵- - - Egyptian retreat

Sidon

PHOENICIA

Lebanon Mts.

Anti-Lebanon Mts.

Damascus
721

Tyre

Sea of Chinnereth
Hippos

Dor

ISRAEL

Ramoth-gilead

Siege by Shalmaneser V, 724–22

Samaria

Sargon quells revolt 720

Joppa

Rabbah

Eltekeh

Ashdod

Ekron

Jerusalem

Ashkelon

Gaza
721

Lachish

Salt Sea (Dead Sea)

JUDAH

Raphia

N

0   50 km
0   50 miles

coup was Assyrian-aided. This, a rump state of Israel, now existed with precarious independence. Gilead was lost as was territory west of the Jordan. Now halved, resources were severely reduced and annual tribute had to be culled from the remnant of the country. Surrounded on three sides by Assyria, Israel was indefensible apart from Samaria. The country was now wide open to attack.

In 732 BC, Tiglath-pileser captured Damascus and moved south to control Bashan. Huge numbers of people were then deported into Assyria. Syria was divided into the Assyrian provinces of Damascus, Karnaim and Hauran Ammon. Edom and Moab remained under loose Assyrian control paying tribute, but gained Assyrian protection from nomadic raids from east and south. Ahaz of Judah was summoned to the King in order to abase himself. He was foolish enough to place a copy of a foreign altar in the temple moving the altar to God into a less significant position; thus was Ahaz subservient and also transgressed God's will.

Tiglath-pileser III died in 727 BC being succeeded by Shalmaneser V. Hoshea chose this moment to rebel, being assured of help from the Egyptian Pharaoh. The Assyrians moved swiftly, Hosea being taken prisoner and Samaria invested. Shalmaneser died during the siege, and was replaced by Sargon II. The siege lasted three years, resulting in the kingdom of Israel ceasing to exist. Sargon claims to have moved 27,290 inhabitants into Assyria, with Jews being placed near Goran, the Nineveh-Halah region, and in Media. The Israel rump state was combined with Dor to create the province of Samaria. New people were moved in from Babylonia, merging with the remaining poor Israelites and adopting their faith to

DEPORTATIONS TO AND FROM ISRAEL

Assyrian policy involved the movement of conquered peoples. In the case of Israel, people were moved in as well as moved out to far provinces of the Empire.

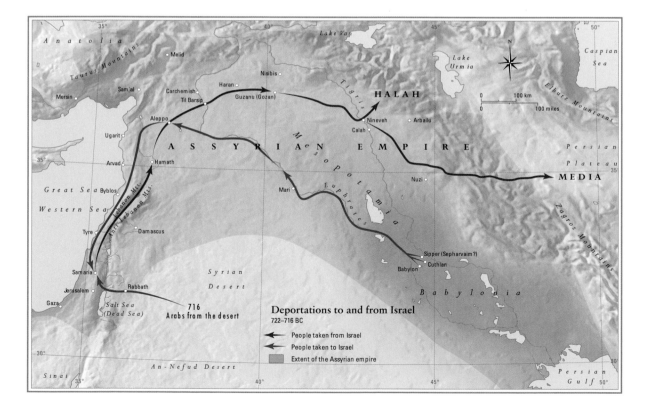

Deportations to and from Israel
722–716 BC

◄—— People taken from Israel
◄—— People taken to Israel
▨ Extent of the Assyrian empire

716
Arabs from the desert

create a new Samaritan identity.

Sargon claims that revolts broke out in Hamath, Damascus, Samaria and Gaza in 720 BC, possibly inspired by Hamath but were quickly defeated as was an Egyptian army seeking to recapture Gaza. Sargon moved south and destroyed Raphia, torching it, and moving its 9,000 or so inhabitants into Assyria. A later rebellion occurred at Ashdod, encouraged by Egypt and aided by Judah, Edom and Moab, with the latter three rapidly withdrawing their support. Ashdod fell and became a province; Gath, Ekron, Gibbethon and Azekah also fell leaving the Assyrians controlling the Way to Beth-shemesh. Judah's survival now hung by a thread.

After Sargon II destroyed Israel, the Assyrian monarch confronted an insurrection in Babylon led by Merodach-baladan. The conflict lasted 12 years, Sargon being compelled to withdraw troops from Samaria and its environs to suppress the Babylonian rebellion. Consequently, revolts occurred in the newly conquered territories along the Mediterranean coast. Hezekiah of Judah joined in these uprisings (713–12 BC), in an attempt to overturn his father's pro-Assyrian policies. Sargon suppressed all these challenges, and left his empire intact to pass on to his son Sennacherib in 704 BC.

Whilst the new Assyrian King spent time upgrading his capital at Nineveh, Egypt was re-united under the 25th (Ethiopian) Dynasty. As far as Egypt was concerned, any state in Palestine that gained independence would provide a valuable bastion against potential Assyrian invasion. Hence, Judah and the Phoenician cities were important foreign policy targets. Likewise, the states of Palestine could now look to Egypt for support against Assyria. Hezekiah took advantage of this foreign policy situation and refused tribute, whilst preparing his realm for an expected attack by the Assyrians.

War preparations included designating four cities as military depots. Jerusalem, Socoh Lachish and Ziph were consequently strengthened for this role. One remnant of Hezekiah's preparations was the water tunnel dug under the city from the Gihon Spring in the Kidron Valley to ensure a water supply whilst under siege. This tunnel stretches 1,750 feet (533 meters), chiseled out of solid rock. The width varies from three to 11 feet (0.9 to 3.3 meters) and in height from four to 16 feet (1.2 to 4.8 meters), and to this day pours water into the Pool of Siloam. Springs which might support the enemy were dammed or polluted. Defense works elsewhere are unrecorded but the hills of the Shephelah and those of Samaria would provide natural obstacles to an invader as would the compact mountain range, the heartland of Judah.

However, there were weaknesses in Judah's defences. The Shephelah is riven by a series of defiles, especially the Way of Beth-shemesh, which provides a broad road to Jerusalem. Evidently, Hezekiah concentrated his defences here, giving Sennacherib a hard time handling them. Presumably, he used Reheboam's old line of fortifications as the basis. Sennacherib claimed that he torched 46 cities and walled forts in Judah, thereby providing evidence that Hezekiah had indeed turned Judah into a hedgehog of fortifications. Hezekiah made other preparations. He standardized military equipment, collected huge supplies of spears and shields and re-armed his soldiers. Edom was raided to secure the southern frontiers.

Hezekiah utilized religious reform as a means of stiffening Judah's resolve. All the Assyrian gods brought in by his father were repudiated, and religious values re-introduced to revive nationalism. The Prophet Isaiah supported Hezekiah. Some of the social abuses and economic exploitation were ameliorated, allowing a measure of prosperity to return to Judah resulting in the doubling or trebling of Jerusalem's population. The king attempted to involve Samaria and Galilee in his adventures but they refused.

Hezekiah sought support elsewhere even receiving ambassadors from Babylon's resurgent Merodach-baladan. A sizable anti-Assyrian coalition was built with the King of Tyre as a ringleader. King Sidqa of Ashkelon joined as did Ekron, which sent its King, Padi, a captive to Jerusalem since he remained loyal to Sennacherib. Ashdod and Gaza did not commit themselves. Pharaoh Shabako signed a treaty with Judah despite the fury of Isaiah who claimed that Egypt was a paper tiger. Ammon, Moab and Edom might have been implicated in the rebellion. If so, they offered no resistance to Sennacherib.

The year 702 BC witnessed the end of the Babylonian revolt, leaving Sennacherib free to combat the enemy coalition. In 701, massive Assyrian forces marched down the Mediterranean coast in an assault on Phoenicia. Luli, King of Tyre fled to Cyprus while Tyre and its inland town of Uzu were utterly devastated. This great port, despite being rebuilt, lost its commercial importance to the Greeks and some of its own colonies, such as Carthage. Byblos, Arvad, Ashdod, Moab, Edom and Ammon swiftly sent tribute to Sennacherib. Only Ashkelon, Ekron and Judah continued to hold out, watching the Assyrian advance down the Way of the Sea. Ashkelon's dependency, Joppa, fell quickly, leaving the Assyrians to turn on Ekron. An Egyptian army, strengthened by bowmen, chariots and cavalry, marching to relieve Ekron, collided with the Assyrians at Eltekeh. The Egyptians suffered a defeat, Eltekeh was destroyed. However the Egyptians retreated unharassed by the Assyrians, who wanted to finish off the coalition. Sennacherib then took other Philistine cities at leisure, such as Timnah and Ekron.

Judah was the next target. One Assyrian force traversed the Way of Beth-horon intending to strike Jerusalem from the north. This force fought its way through Bethel, Aiath, Michmash, Geba, Anathoth and Nob. One unit took Ramah, thereby isolating the lynchpin of Hezekiah's northern defences. Sennacherib then surrounded Jerusalem with earthworks so no one could enter or leave the city. While the King of Judah was locked up like 'a bird in a cage' as Sennacherib stated, the other Assyrian army assaulted the fortified cities of the Shephelah, storming them in turn after taking the key defence of Lachish. The histories of Sennacherib write about earthworks, tunnels, breaches and sappers in the siege. Archaeology shows fire was used as an offensive weapon. A huge pit has been found containing the remains of some 1,500 bodies, covered with pig bones and other Assyrian debris. 'Your country is desolate, your cities are burned with fire: your land, strangers devour it in your presence, and it is desolate, as overthrown by strangers. And the daughter of Zion (Jerusalem) is left as a cottage in a vineyard, as a lodge in a garden of cucumbers, as a besieged city' (Isaiah 1:7–8). The populations of 46 cities were executed or deported.

Hezekiah's position was untenable. Judah was being systematically consumed, some of Judah's troops deserted; even Isaiah told Hezekiah to sue for terms. The king sent some of the Temple's gold and silver to Sennacherib and negotiations were opened. However, military operations continued with Moresheth-gath and Mareshah falling. Plague affected the Assyrian besiegers of Jerusalem. 'And it came to pass that night, that the angel of the Lord went out, and smote in the camp of the Assyrians an hundred fourscore and five

ASSYRIAN PROVINCES UNDER TIGLATH-PILESER III

After Tiglath-pileser had gained control of the region from Syria to the Egyptian border, he set about re-ordering the area. These areas would be ruled either as provinces or via nominee vassals, as happened with what was left of Israel where Pekah was deposed and replace with Tiglath-pileser's nominee, Hoshea.

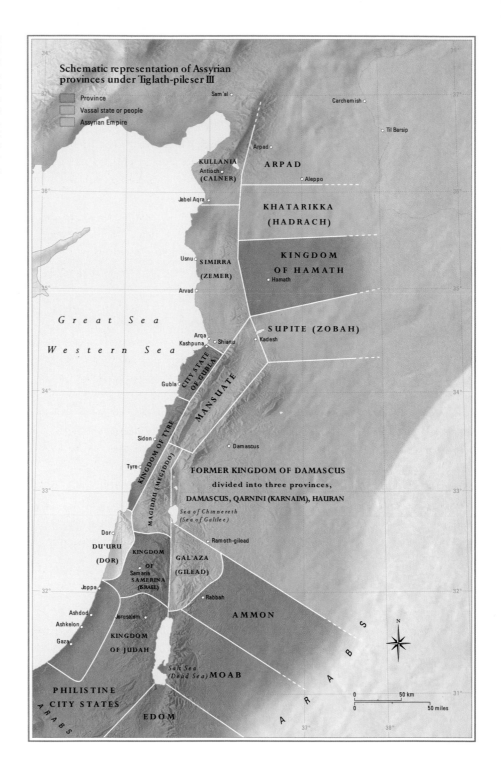

Schematic representation of Assyrian provinces under Tiglath-pileser III

Province
Vassal state or people
Assyrian Empire

Sam'al
Carchemish
Til Barsip
Arpad
ARPAD
KULLANIA
Antioch
(CALNER)
Aleppo
Jabel Aqra
KHATARIKKA
(HADRACH)
Usnu
SIMIRRA
(ZEMER)
KINGDOM
OF HAMATH
Hamath
Arvad
Great Sea
Western Sea
Arqa
Kashpuna
Shianu
SUPITE (ZOBAH)
Kadesh
CITY STATE
OF GUBLA
Gubla
MANSUATE
Sidon
Damascus
KINGDOM OF TYRE
Tyre
FORMER KINGDOM OF DAMASCUS
divided into three provinces,
DAMASCUS, QARNINI (KARNAIM), HAURAN
Sea of Chinnereth
(Sea of Galilee)
MAGIDDU (MEGIDDO)
Dor
Ramoth-gilead
DU'URU
(DOR)
KINGDOM
OF
Samaria
SAMERINA
(ISRAEL)
GAL'AZA
(GILEAD)
Joppa
Rabbah
Ashdod
Ashkelon
Jerusalem
AMMON
Gaza
KINGDOM
OF JUDAH
A R A B S
N
Salt Sea
(Dead Sea) MOAB
PHILISTINE
CITY STATES
A R A B S
EDOM
0   50 km
0   50 miles

thousand: and when they arose early in the morning, behold, they were all dead corpses' (2 Kings 19:35). The 5th-Century BC Greek historian Herodotus writes of a plague of mice, possibly a reference to plague carrying rats. The Assyrians departed.

The punishment meted out to Judah was immense. The King of Ekron was returned and some territory divided between Sennacherib, Ashdod and Gaza. Sennacherib listed the tribute as containing 'Thirty talents of gold, eight hundred talents of silver, precious stones, antimony, large cuts of red stone, couches (inlaid) with ivory, chairs (inlaid) with ivory, elephant hides, ebony wood, boxwood [and] all kinds of valuable treasures, his (Hezekiah's) daughters, concubines, male and female musicians.' Sennacherib also boasted of driving 200,000 people from their homes while seizing their horses, mules, donkeys, camels and big and small cattle. Judah was devastated.

In 687 BC, Hezekiah died and his son Manasseh succeeded him, reigning for 45 years. Being a realist, he abandoned resistance and abased himself before Assyria. He paid tribute to Sennacherib, placed Assyrian god images in Jerusalem and as a loyal vassal, provided troops for Assyrian expansion into Egypt. Here, the 25th Dynasty was destroyed with only Prince Neco of Sais of the Egyptian princes being spared.

Manasseh remained loyal to Assyria throughout his reign, on one occasion giving materials for King Asshurbanapal's building projects. Judah's religious establishment suffered a return to policies of Ahaz. The reformers were repudiated while pagan practices, both native and foreign, flourished. Astral deities were worshipped as if they were members of Yahweh's court and social injustice returned. 'Moreover Manasseh shed innocent blood very much, till he had filled Jerusalem from one end to another; beside his sin wherewith he made Judah to sin, in doing that which was evil in the sight of the Lord' (2 Kings 21:16). Resentment against his rule grew; Kings calling him the worst king ever to sit on David's throne. In foreign policy terms, Manasseh had no choice, nor did his son, Amon, who followed his father's policies until he was murdered in 640 BC, being succeeded by his eight-year-old son, Josiah.

Externally, Judah saw Assyria's power weaken. Egypt broke away, establishing the 26th (Saite) Dynasty, Babylonia rebelled, while Medes, in the north, pressured the country. Interestingly, the Egyptian Pharaoh feared a new Mede-Babylonian power growing and gave help to a struggling Assyria in order to create a buffer. However, by 609 BC Assyria was finished, leaving Palestine in a power vacuum after Assyrian forces were withdrawn to defend core Assyria.

When Josiah reached 20 years of age in 620, Judah became free by default, the kingdom enjoying a burst of energy and glory unseen since Uzziah. Josiah pushed for sweeping religious reforms supported by the prophet Zephaniah who was outraged by the religious practices under Manasseh. The Temple was repaired and purified, while a consistent purge of foreign cults and practices took place. Assyrian cult images went as did a variety of solar and astral cults of Mesopotamian origin. Native pagan rites, introduced by Manasseh, were ended and their personnel, such as eunuch priests and prostitutes of both sexes, executed. As Josiah took control of northern lands, reforms were extended into Samaria, the rival temple at Bethel being desecrated, destroyed and its priesthood killed. According to 2 Chronicles 34:6, reforms were extended into northern Galilee. The execution of idolatrous priests was legitimized by a law in Deuteronomy pronouncing idolatry a capital crime. The attack on Assyrian cults can also be seen as

EXILE TO BABYLONIA

THE REGION OF BABYLONIA LAY NEAR THE SOUTH-EASTERN END OF MESOPOTAMIA, AND TOOK ITS NAME FROM THE PRINCIPAL CITY, BABYLON, ON THE RIVER EUPHRATES.

T he Babylonians figure prominently in the Old Testament, and 'Babylon' became an instantly recognizable symbol of any great oppressive power for both Jews and Christians. However, their actual period of domination after they had defeated the Assyrians only lasted some 80 years. They were overthrown by the Persians in 539 BC.

The Old Babylonian Empire had collapsed under pressure from the Kassites in the middle of the 2nd Millennium BC, ending a period of power and splendour, of which the law code of Hammurabi from the 18th Century BC is ample evidence. The Babylonians were rebellious subjects of the Assyrians for five centuries, repeatedly brought to heel and at one time ruled directly by Assyrian kings. As with most of the nations of the Near and Middle East, they were a mixture of peoples, and, during the main part of the Assyrian ascendancy, the dominant Babylonian group were Aramaean nomads from the Syrian Desert who invaded Babylonia during the early part of the 1st Millennium BC and merged with the Chaldeans of southern Babylonia. One of these Aramaen Chaldean chiefs seized power in 721 BC and opposed Sargon II of Assyria. That attempt at Babylonian independence failed, but another Aramaean descendant, Nabopolassar, successfully rebelled in 626 BC and began the war that was to end some 20 years later with the Babylonians in control of the Assyrian Empire.

The destruction of Assyria was assisted by incursions of wild, disorganized mounted tribesmen through the eastern mountains, who fanned out through Mesopotamia and the Near East as far as the Egyptian frontier. These hordes were part of the Scythian migration, which has left its mark on

Hebrew and Christian writings as the armies of Gog and Magog (Ezekiel 38–39; Revelation 20:8). Their tombs have yielded delightful gold, silver and bronze figures of wild animals and mounted horsemen. They settled nowhere, but their threat, combined with the Babylonian rebellion, forced the Assyrians to withdraw their troops from Palestine. This gave the Hebrews one of their brief periods of freedom from foreign control which lasted from 625 to 609 BC, before first the Egyptians and then the Babylonians once more took over Palestine.

The Babylonians, under King Nabopolassar, destroyed the Assyrian capital Nineveh in 612 BC. His successor, Nebuchadnezzar (605–562 BC) defeated the Egyptian King Necho II (609–594 BC) of the 26th Dynasty, far up the River Euphrates at Carchemish, now known as Cerabulus, on the border of modern-day Syria and Turkey. At first the Babylonians did little to interfere with the only remaining Hebrew kingdom, Judah, and allowed King Jehoiakim (609–598 BC) to continue to rule the country from its capital, Jerusalem. However, the Hebrews intrigued to get the Egyptians to free them from Babylonian rule, but this failed and in 598 BC the Babylonians captured Jerusalem after a siege that had lasted for three months.

The king and his leading officials were deported to Babylon where they were allowed to live in some comfort at Babylonian state expense, and another descendant of King David, Zedekiah (597–587 BC), was placed on the throne of Judah. The intrigues with Egypt continued, and in 589 BC the Babylonians again attacked Jerusalem. This time they besieged it for more than two years. There was a brief respite when an Egyptian army tried to relieve the city, but the Babylonians finally destroyed it in 587 BC. The king and people were deported to Babylonia where the Hebrew monarchy ended. The territory was lost to Hebrew control from the 48 years of the exile until the Babylonians, in their turn, were overthrown by the Persians in 539 BC.

Babylonian religion, like that of the Assyrians, was the common religion of Mesopotamia. It included temple-towers, a vast pantheon of gods, divination and belief in a multitude of demons.

RUINS OF JERUSALEM
The ruins of the older part of Jerusalem have been excavated and confirm the deliberate destruction of the city in 587 BC.

THE BABYLONIAN EMPIRE
The Babylonians turned their attention to the Fertile Crescent' after vanquishing the Assyrians in Mesopotamia. At the same time King Josiah was introducing his religious reforms, destroying the shrines of foreign religions and giving new life to the old Hebrew laws of the Covenant. Under Nebuchadnezzar, the invaders were a much stronger and more unified force; they captured important towns including Jerusalem, which they took in 598 BC and then destroyed almost ten years later.

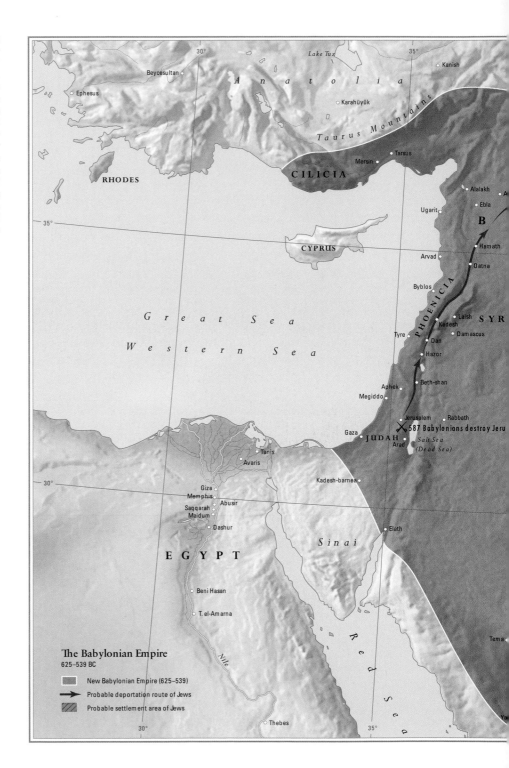

The Babylonian Empire
625–539 BC

- New Babylonian Empire (625–539)
- → Probable deportation route of Jews
- Probable settlement area of Jews

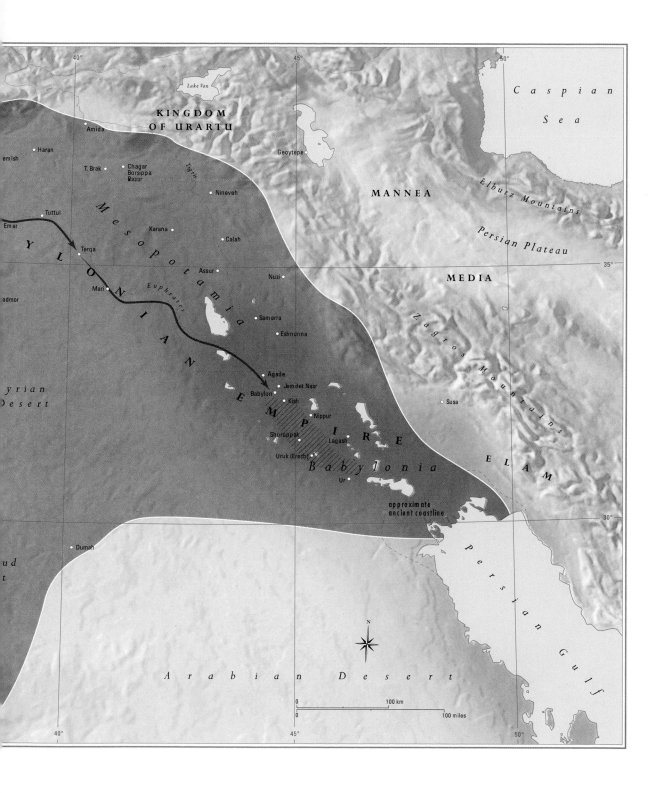

Lake Van

KINGDOM
OF URARTU

C a s p i a n
S e a

Amida

Haran

emish

T. Brak

Chagar
Bazar

Borsippa

Geoytepe

MANNEA

Elburz Mountains

Nineveh

M e s o p o t a m i a

Tigris

Tuttul

Emar

Karana

Calah

Persian Plateau

B
Y
L
O
N
I
A
N

Terqa

Mari

Assur

Nuzi

MEDIA

admor

Euphrates

Samarra

Eshnunna

Z a g r o s   M o u n t a i n s

yrian
Desert

E

M

Agade

Jemdet Nasr

Babylon

Kish

P

Nippur

I

Shuruppak

Lagash

R

Susa

E

Uruk (Erech)

B a b y l o n i a

Ur

ELAM

approximate
ancient coastline

Dumah

ud

P e r s i a n   G u l f

t

N

A r a b i a n   D e s e r t

0   100 km
0   100 miles

BABYLON

THE ONCE GREAT CITY OF BABYLON, WHERE JEWS WERE
HELD CAPTIVE FOR DECADES, BECAME A SYMBOL OF POWER,
MATERIALISM AND CRUELTY.

T he city was capital of the ancient land of Babylonia in southern Mesopotamia. It was situated on the River Euphrates 50 miles (80 km) south of Baghdad, just north of what is now the modern Iraqi town of al-Hillah.

The Tower of Babel

The name Babylon is a Greek form of the Hebrew name Babel, itself derived from a Sumerian name meaning 'Gate of God'. Genesis 10:10 describes the founding of the city of Babel by Nimrod, a descendant of Ham, son of Noah. Genesis 11:1–9 describes the building of the city and its famous tower 'whose top may reach unto heaven', and how God punished the people's arrogance by creating a confusion of different languages.

Although Babel and Babylon are probably one and the same, there is not sufficient written or archaeological evidence to establish that Babel was on the same site as Babylon and, though many have attempted to locate the ruins of the original Tower of Babel, no one has succeeded. It is now thought that the legend of the tower refers to a ziggurat built in the 18th Century BC.

The Growth of Babylon

Although there is some evidence of occupation from prehistoric times, Babylon was not established as a city until the 23rd Century BC. It was at first a provincial capital ruled by the kings of the city of Ur, but in the late 19th Century BC the Amorite King Sumuabum established a kingdom there. Babylon was enlarged and improved by his successors, particularly Hammurapi, sometimes called

CENTRAL BABYLON
A reconstruction of Nebuchadnezzar's great city, showing a ziggurat and temples, with the River Euphrates flowing through the middle of the city.

Palace of Nebuchadnezzar

Ishtar Gate

Euphrates

Ziggurat
(Known as the Tower of Babel)

Holy Gate

N

Temple of Marduk

Hammurabi (1792–1750 BC) who enlarged his territory to include many of the neighbouring cities, creating a kingdom of Babylonia that stretched over southern Mesopotamia and into Assyria, with Babylon as its capital. It was under his rule that the first ziggurat, the Tower of Babel, was built. Hammurapi is best known for his Code of Laws—not so much a code as a set of legal judgements on 282 different cases that was inscribed on a stone stela placed in the temple of the god Marduk. Large fragments of this stela were discovered in 1902 by Jean Vincent Scheil in Susa and it now stands in the Louvre in Paris. The judgements cover economic and family law as well as criminal cases, and are in some way similar to the Hebrew Mosaic Law.

Under the Amorite dynasty Babylon flourished but it fell to the Hittites in 1595 BC and then came under control of the Kassites, who established a dynasty that dominated the region for over 400 years, although frequently under foreign attack, particularly from the Assyrians and the Elamites. In 1158 BC Babylon was sacked by the Elamites, but soon Elam was conquered by Nebuchadnezzar I, who established a new dynasty in Babylon. This was a time of cultural and literary development when the ancient Babylonian *Epic of Gilgamesh* was rewritten in its finest version.

For several centuries Babylon was a focus of conflict between Assyrian forces and Aramean and Chaldean tribespeople. Assyrian kings dominated from the 9th to the later 7th Centuries BC, and it is with reference to that period that the city if first unequivocally mentioned in the Bible. Hezekiah the King of Judah (716–687 BC) was visited by emissaries from the King of Babylon when he was ill. When he admitted to the prophet Isaiah that he had let these men see the full extent of his wealth, Isaiah prophesied that all the royal treasures would, one day, be carried off to Babylon (2 Kings 20:12–18). In 689 BC, after a period of nationalist uprisings and unrest in Babylon, the Assyrian King Sennacherib ordered that the city be destroyed. His son Esarhaddon rebuilt it, but the city was badly damaged by fire in 648 BC during a war between the Assyrian King Ashurbanipal and his brother who ruled over Babylon.

Pride and Fall

The decline of the Assyrian Empire enabled a Chaldean leader, Nabopolassar, to take control of Babylon in 626 BC. He founded a dynasty that began to restore the damaged city. Under his successor, Nebuchadnezzar II (the Nebuchadnezzar of the Bible) who ruled from 605 to 562 BC. Babylon became a great imperial power and the city was splendidly rebuilt, fortified and extended so that it became the largest city the world had ever seen. The River Euphrates flowed through the middle of the city, though it has since changed its course westwards.

Nebuchadnezzar built or restored palaces and temples, the Processional Way, the Ishtar Gate and the ziggurat that was known as the Temple of Babel. If the famous Hanging Gardens, one of the Seven Wonders of the World, ever existed, they were built at this time. They may have been a series of terraces covered in trees and plants. Nebuchadnezzar's army conquered Jerusalem, destroyed and plundered the Temple, and took the people of Judah back to Babylon as captives (2 Kings 25:1–21). The overweening pride and arrogance of King Nebuchadnezzar is described in the first four chapters of the Book of Daniel.

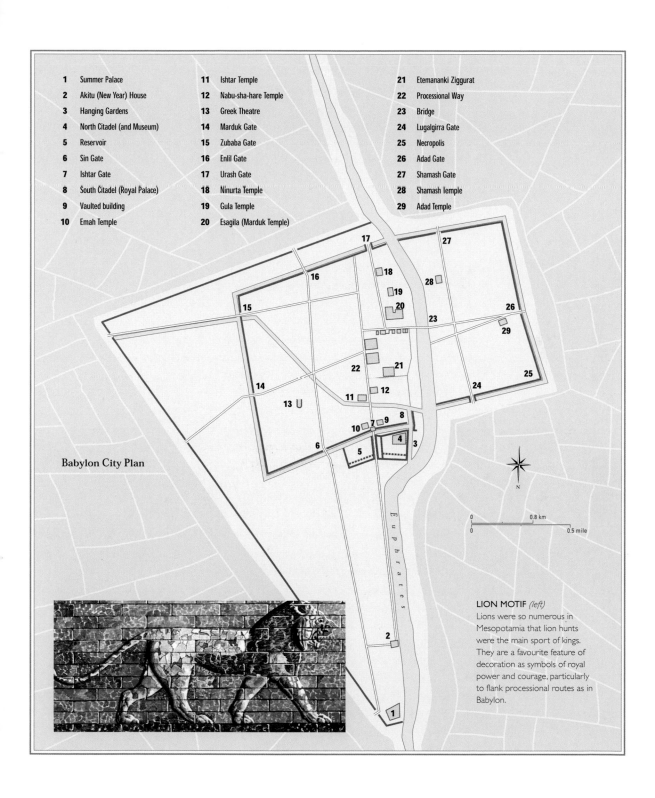

Babylon City Plan

1   Summer Palace
2   Akitu (New Year) House
3   Hanging Gardens
4   North Citadel (and Museum)
5   Reservoir
6   Sin Gate
7   Ishtar Gate
8   South Citadel (Royal Palace)
9   Vaulted building
10 Emah Temple

11 Ishtar Temple
12 Nabu-sha-hare Temple
13 Greek Theatre
14 Marduk Gate
15 Zubaba Gate
16 Enlil Gate
17 Urash Gate
18 Ninurta Temple
19 Gula Temple
20 Esagila (Marduk Temple)

21 Etemananki Ziggurat
22 Processional Way
23 Bridge
24 Lugalgirra Gate
25 Necropolis
26 Adad Gate
27 Shamash Gate
28 Shamash Temple
29 Adad Temple

LION MOTIF *(left)*
Lions were so numerous in Mesopotamia that lion hunts were the main sport of kings. They are a favourite feature of decoration as symbols of royal power and courage, particularly to flank processional routes as in Babylon.

The despair of the Jewish exiles in Babylon and the prediction of the city's fall are conveyed in several Bible passages, particularly Psalm 137 ('By the rivers of Babylon, there we sat down, yea we wept, when we remembered Zion'); Isaiah 13–14, 21 ('Babylon is fallen, is fallen', 21:9); and Jeremiah 50–51 ('How is Babylon became a desolation among the nations', 50:23). Daniel 5 describes the death of Nebuchadnezzar's son and successor, Belshazzar, when the city was sacked by the Persians under Cyrus in 539 BC. Darius the Mede (Daniel 5:31–6:1–28) was possibly a governor appointed by Cyrus.

Babylon remained under Persian rule for 200 years, diminished in importance, but still retaining some of its splendor until the city was destroyed by Xerxes I when he suppressed a rebellion in 482. In 331 BC, Alexander the Great conquered Babylon; he had ambitions to rebuild the city and make it his capital, he died there in 323 BC, before he had time to implement his plans. A new city of Seleucia was built on the Tigris and much of Babylon's population moved there in 275 BC. After this Babylon rapidly declined, eventually falling into ruins.

The New Testament mentions Babylon only in reference to the exile of the Jews (Matthew 1:17; Acts 7:43) or as a symbol for Rome which had taken over the role as the great but corrupt oppressor of the people of Israel (Revelation 17:5).

The Ruins

Travellers and explorers have been drawn to Babylon for centuries, but serious archaeological research did not start until the mid-19th Century. Much of the more recent work was carried out by German teams, but in the last few decades the task has been taken over by the Iraqis. Almost all that has been discovered on the site relates to the great city built by King Nebuchadnezzar II. The change in the course of the Euphrates and a rise in the water-table, combined with the fact that Nebuchadnezzar rebuilt the city so thoroughly, means that very little from before his time has been found or is likely to be.

Many inscriptions in cuneiform writing, then in general use in Mesopotamia, have been found which describe the city. There is also an account by the Greek historian, Herodotus, who visited Babylon in about 460 BC. These made it possible to attempt a reconstruction of Babylon in its prime. There was a vast double wall on both sides of the Euphrates with eight gates, at least one of which, the Ishtar Gate, was faced with glazed bricks depicting bulls and dragons. From the Ishtar Gate ran the

THE ISHTAR GATE
On the northern wall of the city is the main entrance into Babylon, the Ishtar Gate. The gate itself was covered with blue enamelled brick reliefs of bulls and dragons.

Processional Way—a wide paved road flanked with walls decorated with glazed and gilded bricks showing lions and dragons—which led to the Temple of Marduk and the adjacent Tower to Babel ziggurat, which reached to 300 feet (90 meters) high. There were four other temples, and west of the Ishtar Gate stood two palace complexes. The German archaeologist, Koldewey, who excavated the site from 1899 to 1917, found vaults in one of the palaces that he identified as the foundations of the Hanging Gardens.

The present site consists of several mounds that cover the remains of Nebuchadnezzar's summer palace, the Ishtar Gate and a further palace complex, the temple of Marduk and the ziggurat, and a residential area. A reconstruction has been made of the Ishtar Gate and other works of reconstruction and restoration are being carried out by the Iraqis.

BABYLON

The city of Babylon, seen from the north, as it may have looked at the time of Hammurabi. The Processional Way led from the Ishtar Gate to the central area where the zigarrat and the Temple of Marduk stood.

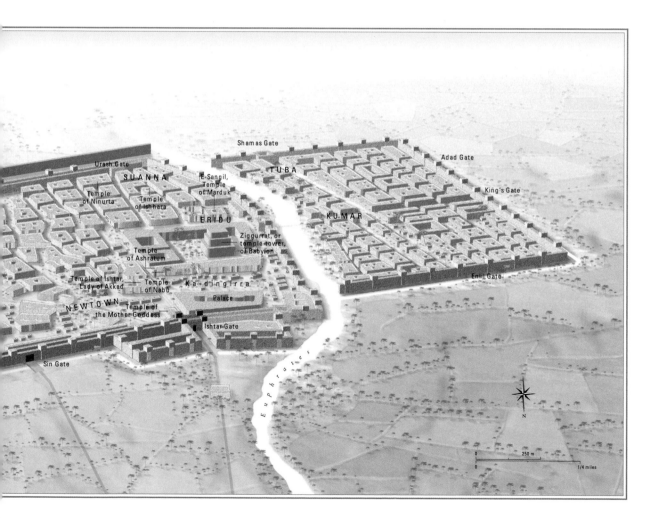

The Rise of Persia

AFTER A BLOODLESS VICTORY OVER THE BABYLONIANS IN 539 BC,
THE PERSIAN KING, CYRUS, WENT ON TO BUILD UP A STRONG,
TOLERANT EMPIRE, WHICH EXTENDED AS FAR SOUTH AS EGYPT.
THE PERSIANS EMPLOYED UNUSUAL MILITARY TACTICS, AND
REMAINED THE DOMINANT POWER IN THE NEAR AND MIDDLE
EAST FOR MORE THAN 200 YEARS.

In 539 BC, King Cyrus of Persia (555–529 BC) received the surrender of Babylon without having to fight. This was the climax of the campaign in which the Persian armies had swept across the eastern frontiers of the Babylonian Empire from the Indian Ocean to the Black Sea, and then struck southwards into the heart of Mesopotamia. Tension between King Nabonidus of Babylon (556–539 BC) and the Babylonian priests of the chief god, Marduk, lay behind Cyrus's bloodless victory. Nabonidus had tried to replace the worship of Marduk with the worship of the moon god, Sin, and the Babylonian priests had moved against him.

It was wise of the priests of Babylon to welcome the Persian victor, for Persian rule proved to be remarkably sympathetic and tolerant. Subject races of the Persian Empire had to give military and other kinds of service, but they were treated as equals by the Persian troops and they reached high rank in both the army and the civil service. The exiled Hebrews in Babylonia were only one of many exiled national groups that received compassionate treatment at the hands of Cyrus. Such peoples were offered the opportunity of returning to their native lands together with the treasures looted from them by the Babylonians, and were provided with support from the Persian treasury to rebuild their cities and temples. There was certainly taxation and tribute exacted from all parts of the empire, but it was used to benefit the provinces. Although King Cyrus remained faithful to his own gods, it is not surprising that the Hebrews saw the hand of their own God in his victories (Isaiah 44–45).

COURT DIGNITARIES
Persian official art, like this frieze on the palace staircase at Persepolis, avoided the Assyrian celebration of barbarity. The Persian Empire achieved a stability that united the various states of the Middle East, ruling their vast empire by using local élites and using Aramaic as the language of administration.

THE PERSIAN EMPIRE
(overleaf)
Cyrus extended the frontiers of the Persian Empire westwards through Mesopotamia and Asia Minor during the 6th Century BC, an expansion given greater impetus still and consolidated by his successors, Cambyses II and Darius I. The Persians were defeated decisively by the Greeks at Marathon in 490 BC, although their Empire survived for some 200 years.

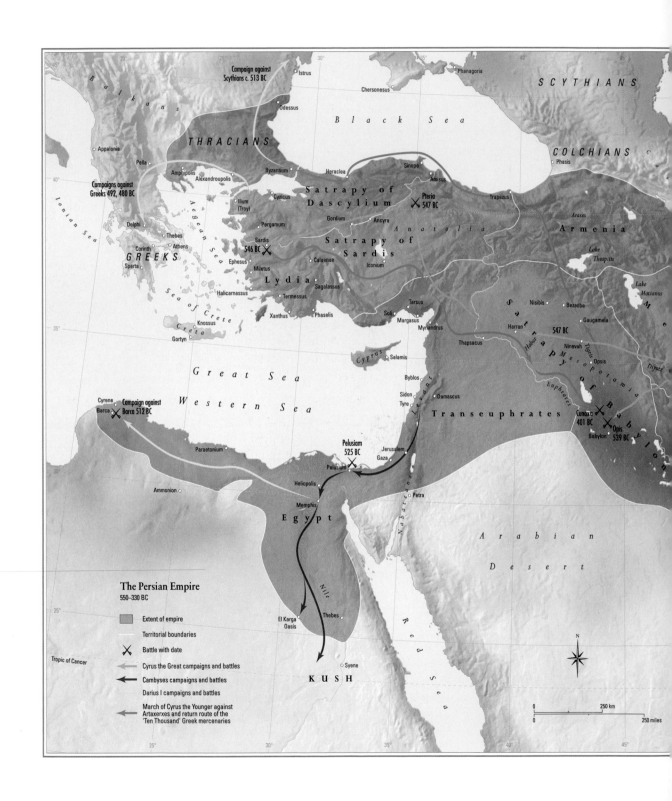

SCYTHIANS

Campaign against
Scythians c. 513 BC

Istrus

Phanagoria

Chersonesus

Black Sea

COLCHIANS

Odessus

Appalonia

THRACIANS

Phasis

Pella

Byzantium

Heraclea

Sinope

Amisus

Amphipolis

Alexandroupolis

Trapezus

Campaigns against
Greeks 492, 480 BC

Ilium
(Troy)

Cyzicus

Satrapy of
Dascylium

Pteria
547 BC

Araxes

Armenia

Pergamum

Gordium

Ancyra

A n a t o l i a

Delphi

Thebes

Sardis

Satrapy of

Lake
Thospitis

Corinth

Athens

546 BC

Sardis

Sparta

Ephesus

Calaenae

Iconium

Lake
Matianus

Miletus

Lydia

Sagalassus

Nisibis

Bezabde

Gaugamela

Halicarnassus

Termessus

Tarsus

Harran

547 BC

Ninevah

Xanthus

Phaselis

Soli

Margasus

Thapsacus

Opsis

Diyala

Knossus

Myriandrus

Mesopotamia

Creta

Gortyn

Cyprus

Salamis

Euphrates

Great Sea

Byblos

Babylon

Western Sea

Sidon

Damascus

Tyre

Transeuphrates

Cunaxa
401 BC

Opis

Cyrene

Campaign against
Barca 512 BC

Babylon

539 BC

Barca

Paraetonium

Pelusiam
525 BC

Jerusalem

Gaza

Pelusium

Ammonion

Heliopolis

Petra

A r a b i a n

Memphis

D e s e r t

Egypt

The Persian Empire
550–330 BC

Extent of empire

Territorial boundaries

Battle with date

El Karga
Oasis

Nile

Thebes

Red Sea

Tropic of Cancer

Cyrus the Great campaigns and battles

Cambyses campaigns and battles

Darius I campaigns and battles

Syene

March of Cyrus the Younger against
Artaxerxes and return route of the
'Ten Thousand' Greek mercenaries

KUSH

N

0   250 km

0   250 miles

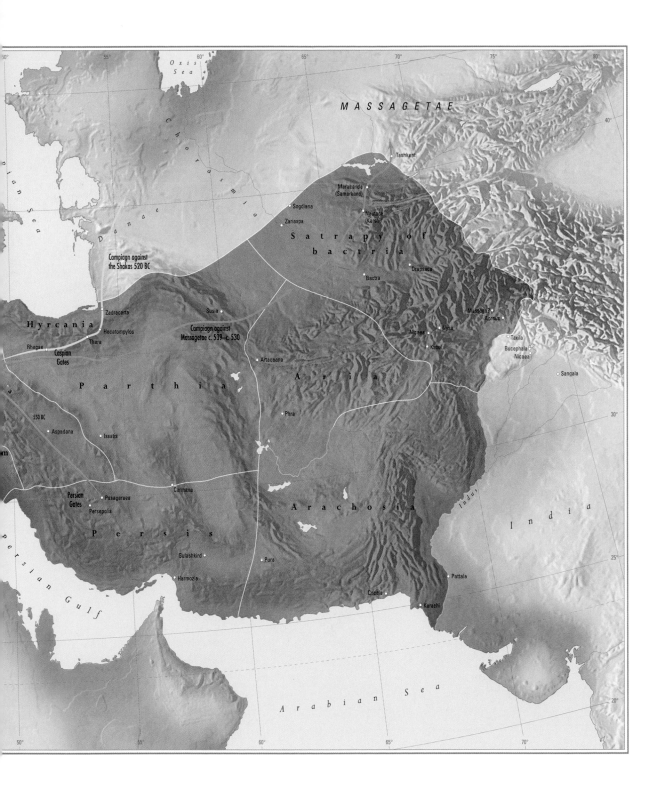

Oxis Sea

Caspian Sea

MASSAGETAE

Tashkent

Chorasmia

Maracanda
(Samarkand)

Sogdiana

Nautaca
(Karshi)

Danae

Zariaspa

S a t r a p y   o f
b a c t r i a

Drapsaca

Bactra

Campiagn against
the Shakas 520 BC

Massaga?

Aornus

Zadracarta

Susia

Nicaea

Nysa

HYRCANIA

Hecatompylos

Campiagn against
Massagetae c. 539–c. 530

Taxila

Thara

Artacoana

Kabul

Bucephala

Rhagae

A r i a

Nicaea

Caspian
Gates

Sangala

P a r t h i a

Phra

550 BC

Aspadana

Issatis

I n d i a

Carmana

Persian
Gates

Pasagaraea

A r a c h o s i a

Indus

Persepolis

P e r s i s

Gulashkird

Pura

Harmozia

Cocala

Pattala

Persian Gulf

Karachi

A r a b i a n   S e a

'THAT CONFIRMETH THE WORD OF HIS SERVANT,
AND PERFORMETH THE COUNSEL OF HIS
MESSENGERS; THAT SAITH TO JERUSALEM, THOU
SHALT BE INHABITED; AND TO THE CITIES OF JUDAH,
YE SHALL BE BUILT, AND I WILL RAISE UP THE
DECAYED PLACES THEREOF:
'THAT SAITH TO THE DEEP, BE DRY, AND I WILL DRY
UP THY RIVERS:
'THAT SAITH OF CYRUS, HE IS MY SHEPHERD, AND
SHALL PERFORM ALL MY PLEASURE: EVEN SAYING TO
JERUSALEM, THOU SHALT BE BUILT; AND TO THE
TEMPLE, THY FOUNDATION SHALL BE LAID.'
'THUS SAITH THE LORD TO HIS ANOINTED, TO
CYRUS, WHOSE RIGHT HAND I HAVE HOLDEN, TO
SUBDUE NATIONS BEFORE HIM; AND I WILL LOOSE
THE LOINS OF KINGS, TO OPEN BEFORE HIM THE
TWO LEAVED GATES; AND THE GATES SHALL NOT BE
SHUT.'   ISAIAH 44:26–28; 45:1

The army was the key to Cyrus's rise to greatness. The tactics which brought this success depended on fighting at a distance and overwhelming the enemy with a hail of arrows while cavalry harassed the ranks. It was mobile warfare at a time when armies usually confronted each other in ranks, and the Persian bowmen fought with little personal protection so that they were free to move swiftly and fire repeatedly. Hand-to-hand fighting had to be avoided at all costs. When the Greeks did at last manage to make a Persian army stand and fight at close quarters at Marathon in 490 BC, the Persians were overwhelmed. The Athenians trapped the Persians against their ships in a narrow position, by giving them no chance to manoeuvre, and they were slaughtered in close fighting with the hoplites, the Greek infantry.

From his capital, Ecbatana, King Cyrus laid the foundations of an empire which was to last for more than 200 years, until it fell to Alexander the Great in 331 BC. Cyrus was succeeded by Cambyses II (529–522 BC) who extended Persian rule into Egypt, His successor, Darius I (522–486 BC), moved the capital to Persepolis after a year of disorders following the succession. By then the Empire stretched from the north-west of the Indus Valley to Asia Minor, and included all of Mesopotamia, Palestine and Egypt, where the Persian emperors constituted the 27th Dynasty. Control of Egypt was never easy, however, particularly after the Persian defeat by the Greeks at Marathon in 490 BC, and the Persians lost control of Egypt for 60 years during the 28th, 29th and 30th Dynasties (400–343 BC) only to regain it for a mere 10 years before Alexander took over.

The Persian Empire was organized in provinces controlled by satraps who were relatively independent of the central government, despite a system of separate military commands and a courier system unsurpassed in the ancient world until the Romans. Aramaic—a Semitic language— was adopted as the official language and became the common tongue of the Persian Empire.

The main religion of Persia at the height of its power was Zoroastrianism, which was a monotheism introduced by the prophet Zoroaster. Its god was Ahura Mazda, creator and lawgiver. In this religion, the world was viewed as a battleground between equal forces of good and evil.

PERSEPOLIS
The great Persian ceremonial city founded by Darius I (522–486 BC). This gateway was built by his son, Xerxes (486–465 BC).

RETURN FROM EXILE

BY THE 6TH CENTURY BC, THE MIDDLE EAST WAS ENTERING A NEW STAGE OF UPHEAVAL. IN THE CLASH BETWEEN DECAYING AND NEW EMPIRES, THE DREAM OF THE EXILED SURVIVORS OF JUDAH TO RETURN TO JERUSALEM WAS TO BE FULFILLED.

Nabonidus, the final King of Babylon, fell foul of his priests by introducing new religious practises thus causing him to move his royal residence to Tema, an oasis to the south in the Arabian Desert while Belshazzar, his son, deputized for him.

Persia, a vassal state of the Median Empire to the east of Babylon, rebelled under the leadership of Cyrus in 562 BC, capturing Ectabana the capital and acquiring the Median Empire in one stroke. Neighboring states thought that Cyrus would now attack Babylon, considering its proximity to Persia. But Cyrus adopted an indirect approach. Feeling that Babylonia's strength was all bluff with no substance, he pursued a different course. He looked toward Asia Minor, which had been politically weak since the fall of the Hittite Empire. However, by the 6th Century BC, the powerful state of Lydia, ruled by Croesus, had been created. He was legendary for his wealth, much of it based upon his conquest of Ionia. Croesus formed an alliance with Nabonidus, while Egypt and Sparta promised to send troops. Invading Cappadocia, he fought an inconclusive battle at Pteria and retreated to build his alliance. Cyrus crossed the Halys (546 BC), surprised Croesus and stormed the Lydian capital at Sardis. This western thrust meant an ultimate confrontation between western and eastern civilisations during the time of Alexander the Great. Cyrus then turned east, subduing the regions now known as Pakistan and Afghanistan. With his frontiers secure, Cyrus turned on Babylonia and in a decisive battle at Opis (539 BC) on the Tigris River, broke the Babylonian army. Babylon fell without opposition, but was not sacked. Cyrus ordered that people and their property be respected. When Cyrus reached the city, he was welcomed and acclaimed as the deliverer from the oppression of the unpopular Nabonidus.

Cyrus was a tolerant and enlightened king who eschewed the brutality of Assyria and Babylon

THE PROPHET EZRA
The Prophet had been commanded by Artaxerxes I to restore Jewish law. His most important contribution was the codification of the first four books of the Bible. These, together with Deuteronomy, make up the Jewish Torah. Ezra arrived in Jerusalem with presents from the king for the Temple and its priests. He was distraught when he saw the lamentable state into which his religion had fallen.

with their deportation of captured populations. Cyrus also tolerated the beliefs, practices, and institutions of all the constituent subject peoples under his rule, thereby unifying these peoples into a great and powerful empire. The famous Cylinder of Cyrus shows that the king gave exiled peoples the chance of returning to countries of their birth. This policy did not mean that nations could regain their independence; Cyrus exerted firmer control over his territories compared with the Assyrians and Babylonians, the Empire being divided into 20 satrapies, each of which comprised a number of provinces.

Jewish exiles in Persia received an edict (538 BC) allowing them to return to Judah; an Aramaic text of one of Cyrus' decrees states:

"IN THE FIRST YEAR OF CYRUS THE KING THE SAME CYRUS THE KING MADE A DECREE CONCERNING THE HOUSE OF GOD AT JERUSALEM, LET THE HOUSE BE BUILDED, THE PLACE WHERE THEY OFFERED SACRIFICES AND LET THE FOUNDATIONS THEREOF BE STRONGLY LAID; THE HEIGHT THEREOF THREESCORE CUBITS, AND THE BREADTH THEREOF THREESCORE CUBITS; WITH THREE ROWS OF GREAT STONES, AND A ROW OF NEW TIMBER: AND LET THE EXPENSES BE GIVEN OUT OF THE KING'S HOUSE: AND ALSO LET THE GOLDEN AND SILVER VESSELS OF THE HOUSE OF GOD, WHICH NEBUCHADNEZZAR TOOK FORTH OUT OF THE TEMPLE WHICH IS AT JERUSALEM, AND BROUGHT UNTO BABYLON, BE RESTORED, AND BROUGHT AGAIN UNTO THE TEMPLE WHICH IS AT JERUSALEM, EVERY ONE TO HIS PLACE, AND PLACE THEM IN THE HOUSE OF GOD."
EZRA 6: 3–5

An enthusiastic group of exiles, led by Sheshbazzar, traveled to Judah, from the Nippur region in Babylonia. On arrival in Palestine, they found Judah to be an impoverished, backward place with a poor economy. Jerusalem lay in ruins, witness to the savagery of the Babylonian attack some 50 years before. On the hilltops lived a few poor Jews left behind at the time of the exile; now, the owners of the land, they resented the incomers as did the Edomites, forced from their lands to make room for Arab tribes who were now living in some districts. The Samaritans claimed authority over Jerusalem resenting the exiles, especially since the returning exiles would not let them help rebuild the city because they considered the Samaritans to be religiously unclean. Crop failure led to food shortages, which left the returned exiles weak and unable to rebuild the city.

New energy arrived with a second wave of Babylonian Jews coming to Jerusalem led by Zerubbabel, nephew to Sheshbazzar, and Jeshua, who eventually became High Priest. The Jews settled in area of the Judaean hill country measuring about 40 miles (64 kilometres) east to west and 30 miles (48 kilometres) north to south. In the east, they reached into the Jordan valley around Jericho, while in the west they encroached on to the coastal plain at Lod and Ono. In the north, they pushed beyond Bethel and in the south they occupied the strategic site of Beth-zur, but were cut off from Hebron, which was occupied by Edomites. Insecurity faced the population until Jerusalem could be re-fortified. Zerubbabel became the civil governor, and all were inspired by the arrival of two

STAR OF DAVID CARVING
The Star of David, here shown
carved as part of the decoration
of the synagogue at Capernaum,
became a symbol of the new
Jewish nation after the exile in
Babylon. By that time the
Hebrew kings had been replaced
by the rule of the priests of the
Temple in Jerusalem, but King
David remained the ideal Jewish
leader. He had given his people
victory over their enemies and
made Jerusalem the central
symbol of Hebrew solidarity. The
interlocking star became an
expression of hope in God, who
would restore the glories of King
David's time and give the Jews as
great a leader.

prophets, Haggai and Zechariah.

Opposition to the Jews emanated from Tattenai, the Governor of Abarnahara—of which Judah (Yehud) was part—he wanted to know who authorised the build. Cyrus' decree was produced and Tattenai was told to allow building to continue with finance from the royal revenues. In 515 BC, the Temple was re-consecrated; it was no longer the focus of a nation, but the center of a religious community. The rebuilding had unified the people, but once finished, unity collapsed. Religious life deteriorated, mixed marriages were contracted and trade tended to foster assimilation. Existence in the hills was hazardous and agricultural conditions harsh. The poor condition of the Jews of Yehud was heard of by Nehemiah in Susa, cupbearer to the King of Persia. He requested that he be allowed to travel to Jerusalem and rebuild its fortifications. His wish being granted, and he was made governor of the province.

RESETTLEMENT AND RECONSTRUCTION

THE 5TH CENTURY BC WITNESSED A REORGANIZATION OF
THE JEWISH COMMUNITY IN YEHUD — ITS STATUS WAS
CLARIFIED, ITS RELIGIOUS AND PHYSICAL IDENTITY PRESERVED,
AND RE-ESTABLISHMENT OF THE LAW THAT CONTINUES TODAY .

These achievements were implemented by Nehemiah and Ezra; the former won the political status and administrative reforms for the Jewish community, while the latter reorganized and reaffirmed the purity of its spiritual life.

Yehud's importance to the Persian kings lay in its position athwart lines of communication to Egypt where chronic unrest and the revolt of Megabyzus threatened the military road and its supply bases. A quiescent Palestine would prevent unrest spreading, hence the need to end the Samaritans' high-handed treatment of Jews; therefore, Nehemiah was loyal to his king's interests as well as his co-religionists.

The political environment in Palestine was changing in other ways, particularly in the expansion of international trade, notably with Greece. Phoenicia held the coast from Acco to Gaza, and its ports hosted colonies of Greek merchants. Dor was a prime example. Evidence of imports of Attic pottery have been found at Acco, Gaza, and Ashdod. Gaza, now a royal Persian fortress, was becoming a trade outlet for Arabs who had sifted from north Arabia into Edom, the Negev, and southern Syria to establish themselves as an important commercial people—the Nabateans. Dispossessed Edomites were pushed into Yehud, settling in the desert south of Beersheba and Hebron, and later became known as Idumeans. The Transjordan was ruled by Tobiah, Governor of Ammon, with family connections to the High Priest in Jerusalem, while Samaria, under Governor Sanballat, resented the fact that Yehud had been shorn from the province of Samaria and given to Nehemiah when he arrived. When Nehemiah entered Yehud, he found a demoralized and divided Jewish people with competing interests, all thinking they were the true heirs of Judaism.

On inspecting the city walls, Nehemiah decided that work must commence immediately on rebuilding them. Labor was levied from all Yehud, and the wall was divided into sections with a group responsible for each. Obstacles to the build came from Tobiah, Sanballat, Ashdod, and Geshem, the Arab ruling the desert peoples. The first two men even used a fifth column of their friends and relations in Jerusalem to slow down the build. Eventually, Arabs, Ammonites, and Asdodites terrorized Jewish villages, and the historian, Josephus, claims many Jews were killed. Nehemiah divided his building crews into two—one group being armed with spears, shields, bows, and mail coats, standing to arms in shifts, while the other groups worked with swords at their waists. Jews from the countryside were also drawn into Jerusalem, both for their own safety and to secure the city. The walls went up in 52 days, but the works of wall reinforcement, and finishing the battlement, gates, and revetments required another two years and four months. Nehemiah's task was achieved. After 12 years, he returned to Susa but gained re-appointment as governor of Yehud.

Nehemiah's second term of office was characterized by uncoordinated religious reforms; finding adequate funds for the Temple and its priests by the rigorous collection of tithes; enforcing Sabbath observance; opposing mixed marriages, to the extent of physically assaulting offenders. To stop the conduct of business on the Sabbath, he ordered the city gates closed on that day, and when he found markets being set up outside the walls, he threatened the traders with arrest. Finding children of mixed

Jerusalem as rebuilt by Nehemiah

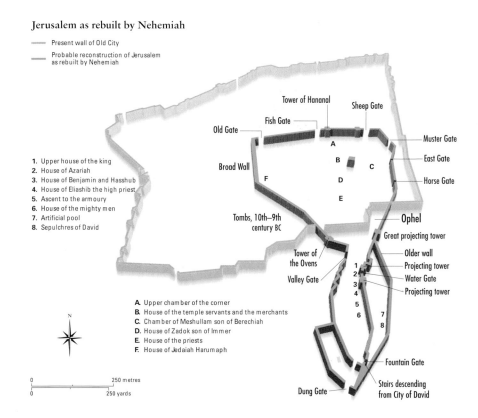

marriages who could not speak Hebrew, he became enraged. When he found that a grandson of the High Priest Eliashib had married the daughter of the Samaritan Sanballat, he forced him into exile. "And one of the sons of Joida, the son of Eliashib the High Priest, was son in law to Sanballat the Horonite: therefore I chased him from the country" (Nehemiah 13:28). Nehemiah's actions were purely ad hoc in his attempt to advocate religious purity. What was required was a systematic religious policy, and in this he failed. However, Nehemiah saved the Jewish community, bringing an honest administration, ensuring the running of the Temple, and providing political status and security, no mean feat considering the opposition he faced.

The requisite religious policies were provided by a priest named Ezra, a man who had secured royal authority over Jewish religious affairs in the satrapy of Abar-nahara. He rode across the desert without military escort, bringing financial contributions from Babylonian Jews, treasure from the king, and the law, which had to be taught and enforced. This religious sheriff had the right to compel all those who claimed loyalty to the Temple cult (those who called themselves Jews) to order their affairs in accordance with the Law brought by Ezra. This "Royal Secretary for the Law of the God in Heaven" and his deputies used the Feast of the Tabernacles to read out the Law in public and explained it in more than one language.

Abuses continued, Ezra being particularly insensed by mixed marriages by which "Jewishness" could be lost, or Jews not bred. He made a public confession of the people's sins before the Temple, hoping that the people themselves would acknowledge their delinquency. His plan proved successful, a voluntary covenant being agreed for men to divorce their foreign wives and put aside children of these marriages. On pain of ostracism and confiscation of property, all people were ordered to Jerusalem to receive Ezra's rebukes and to abide by the rulings of a commission investigating cases of marriage. After three months work, all mixed marriages were dissolved (Ezra 10:14–44).

Ezra's reforms seem to have been completed within a year. The Law that he delivered originated from what became the Torah, the Law of Moses—Genesis, Exodus, Leviticus, Numbers, and Deuteronomy. Ezra was a spiritual figure of outstanding importance. Moses had founded Israel, but Ezra reconstituted Israel and gave the Jews their faith in a form that would survive into the future. Before Nehemiah and Ezra, Israel had ceased to be a nation and could never hope to regain its national institutions. Ezra helped give the Jews a definable identity based upon the Law as a religious constitution.

"NOW WHEN EZRA HAD PRAYED, AND WHEN HE HAD CONFESSED, WEEPING AND CASTING HIMSELF DOWN BEFORE THE HOUSE OF GOD, THERE ASSEMBLED UNTO HIM OUT OF ISRAEL A VERY GREAT CONGREGATION OF MEN AND WOMEN AND CHILDREN: FOR THE PEOPLE WEPT VERY SORE. "AND SHECH-A-NI-AH THE SON OF JE-HI-EL, ONE OF THE SONS OF E-LAM, ANSWERED AND SAID UNTO EZRA, WE HAVE TRESPASSED AGAINST OUR GOD, AND HAVE TAKEN STRANGE WIVES OF THE PEOPLE OF THE LAND: YET NOW THERE IS HOPE IN ISRAEL CONCERNING THIS THING."   EZRA 10:1–2

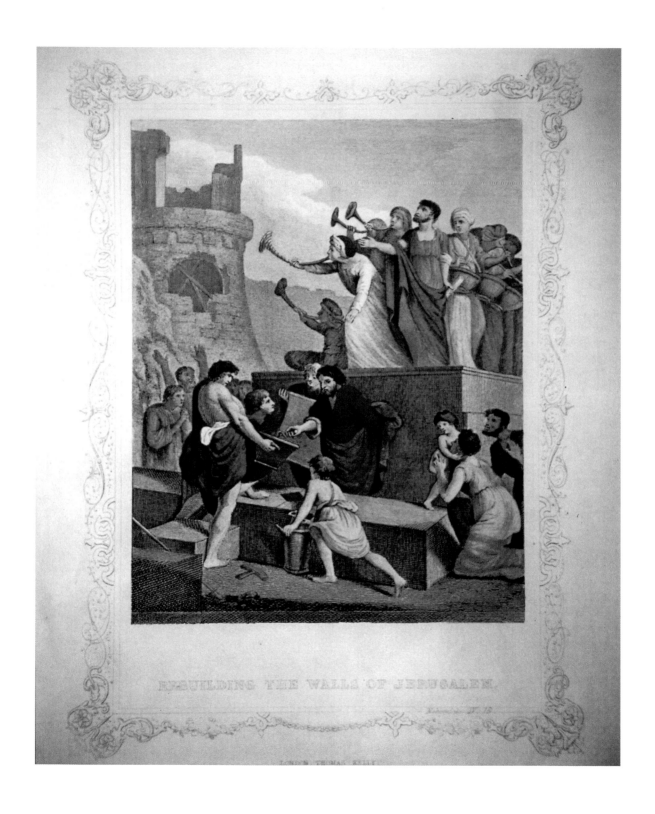

REBUILDING THE WALLS OF JERUSALEM.

ALEXANDER'S EMPIRE

"SO HE ADVANCED TO THE ENDS OF THE EARTH, PLUNDERING NATION AFTER NATION ... HE ASSEMBLED VERY POWERFUL FORCES AND SUBDUED PROVINCES, NATIONS AND PRINCES, AND THEY BECAME HIS TRIBUTARIES."   1 MACCABEES 1:3–5

Alexander inherited two things from his father, Philip II of Macedon: a large and capable army, and a plan to conquer Persia. In the spring of 334 BC, he crossed the Hellespont with 35,000 men. He attacked an army of Persians and Greek mercenaries at the River Granicus, defeating it with little loss to his own forces. His victory ensured the eventual submission of all the states in Asia Minor. Alexander refused to engage the substantial Persian fleet and resolved to defeat it by occupying all coastal cities and ports in the Persian Empire. Accordingly, after reducing Lycian and Pisidian hill tribes in western Asia Minor, he advanced southward and soon met Darius and the main Persian army in northeastern Syria at Issus (333 BC). Macedonian pikemen punched a hole through the Persian forces, generating a complete rout, turned into a disaster by the relentless pursuit of Alexander's cavalry. After capturing Darius's family, who he treated with respect, Alexander marched south to Syria and Phoenicia and moved into Egypt, thus securing control of the whole eastern Mediterranean and ensuring strategic control at sea.

On the Nile estuary, Alexander founded the city of Alexandria, which became a center for science, philosophy and trade. Alexander moved north to attack Babylon. Crossing the Euphrates and Tigris, he again met Darius, defeating him at Gaugamela (331 BC). Darius fled and was eventually murdered by his own generals. When Alexander reached Persepolis, the Persian capital, he burned Xerxes' palace in revenge for the destruction of the Acropolis in 480 BC.

With Darius dead, Alexander could legitimately claim to be the Great King. He only needed to gain the submission of the Persian satraps. His empire now extended beyond the Caspian Sea to present-day Afghanistan and Baluchistan and northward to Bactria and Sogdiana. Thinking to acquire the remaining

ALEXANDER IN BATTLE AGAINST DARIUS *(left)*
Alexander the Great's campaigns increased the influence of Greek civilization in Judah and its neighboring states. This detail is from the famous Alexander Mosaic in Pompeii, which depicts the Battle of Issus.

oddments of the Persian Empire, Alexander crossed the Indus and fought his last great battle on the Hydaspes against the kingdom of Porus (in the Punjab). When his troops mutinied and refused to go any further, Alexander followed the Indus to the Arabian Sea and arrived in Babylon in 323 BC. He died of fever in the summer of that year, reputedly in the palace of Nebuchadrezzar II. Alexander achieved much militarily, but he failed to organize his empire. No provision was made for his succession.

Alexander's campaigns between 334 and 323 BC quickened the pace of Hellenization. Alexander worked hard to unite Greek and non-Greeks, encouraged inter-marriage, founded Hellenistic cities wherever possible and named for himself, and settled Greek colonists. However, the former Persian Empire, including Palestine, was not flooded with Greek settlers. As part of this process, Greek

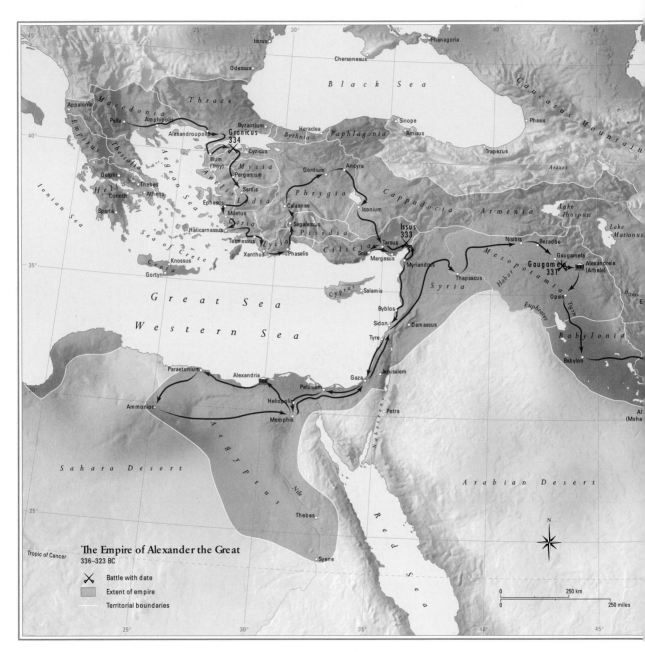

The Empire of Alexander the Great
336–323 BC

✕ Battle with date

Extent of empire

Territorial boundaries

EMPIRE OF ALEXANDER
Alexander took the Greek
language and civilization to the
limits of the known world.
His ceaseless energy gave
in to his rebellious troops
on the Indus River. He died
in Babylon in 323 BC.

influence was felt in Judah. During the 7th Century BC, Greek mercenaries served their Egyptian masters along the Philistine coast. During the 5th Century BC, Greek traders from Tyre made their appearance at Nehemiah's court in Jerusalem and by the next century Judah was using coins originating from Attica (Athens).

Judah's interest in seaborne trade is brought to life by graffiti dating from the 2nd Century BC in

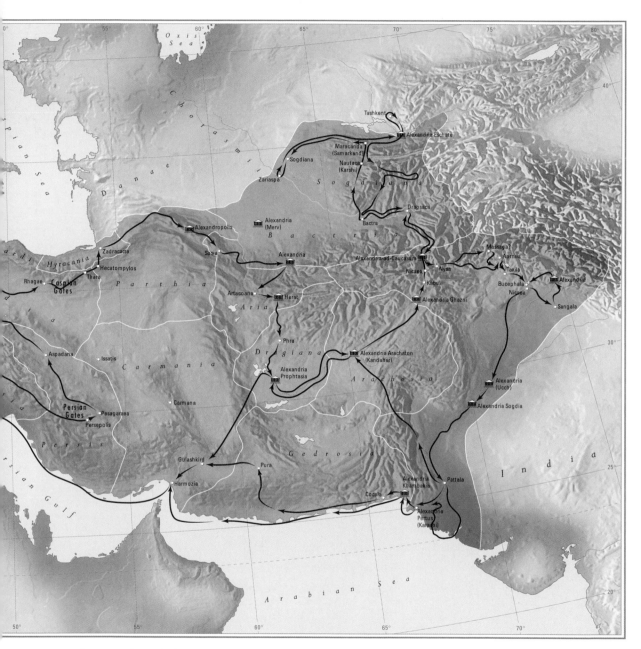

Jason's tomb in Jerusalem, which shows a Greek warship chasing a cargo ship.

The Maccabees were well aware of the Hellenistic world. Judus Maccabeus sent an envoy to Rome
(1 Maccabean 8:17) and Jonathan entertained diplomatic relationships with Sparta.

ALEXANDER'S SUCCESSORS

AFTER ALEXANDER'S DEATH IN 323 BC, HIS GENERALS DIVIDED UP HIS EMPIRE AND FOUGHT AMONGST THEMSELVES. IN THE PROCESS THEY DESTROYED THE PROSPERITY OF THE GREAT TRADING PORTS OF GREECE. THE CENTER OF WEALTH SHIFTED TO ALEXANDRIA, WHERE BOTH HELLENISTIC AND JEWISH CULTURE THRIVED.

Alexander the Great died at the age of 32 in Babylon, master of an Empire spanning the Near and Middle East. It's influence remained in the 20 or so cities named Alexandria scattered throughout his collapsing empire. Other cities were named after his companions. Many cities were replanned along Greek lines and given new names, such as Ptolemais for the Palestinian port of Acco.

The easternmost parts of the Empire in north-west India survived only briefly as independent kingdoms, although the Greek influence remained. At the other extreme, in Greece itself, the generals fought each other for control of Macedonia and of the cities of central and southern Greece. In the process they destroyed the prosperity of the great trading ports, including Athens. Migrating Gallic tribes plundered their way through Greece and on into Asia Minor. then they created the Kingdom of Galatia, which was later to become the nucleus of the Roman province of Galatia, which features in the New Testament. By the time some sort of order was restored, after 50 years of chaos, some strong and wealthy ports had emerged, including Rhodes, Ephesus and Smyrna.

Immediately after Alexander's rule, the major part of the Empire was divided among Alexander's main generals—Antigonus ruled Asia Minor, Syria, and Palestine; Seleucus ruled Mesopotamia, Persia, and the eastern parts to the border of India; and Ptolemy ruled Egypt and Libya. That division only lasted to the Battle of Ipsus in 301 BC, when Seleucus added Asia Minor and Syria to his possessions. Greek became the common tongue of the educated as the cities established schools,

PTOLEMAIC GRAVE PAINTING
This picture, from the Ptolemaic period, shows the deceased between the gods Osiris and Anubis. The Ptolemies treated Egyptian sensibilities with greater consideration than the Persians had previously done. The body of Alexander was brought back to Egypt for burial and his followers sacrificed to Egyptian deities. However their culture remained Egyptian, the only major administrative change was to impose Greek as the language of government.

theatres, Greek temples, and gymnasiums, while the Persian official language, Aramaic, continued to be used in the countryside—the situation still found in New Testament times. The Seleucids only managed to hold such a vast expanse of territory for some 50 years before the Parthians took control of eastern Mesopotamia—and eventually of most of the eastern parts of the Seleucid Kingdom around the end of the 3rd Century BC. The Parthian Empire eventually prevented Roman expansion into the east. Egypt remained under the control of the Ptolemies until the Romans conquered Egypt in 30 BC. Under Ptolemaic rule, Alexandria became the greatest trading port in the ancient world, and a major center of learning with a great library, museum, and a community of scholars exempt from taxation and maintained at royal expense. The city became a multiracial society where the Jewish community

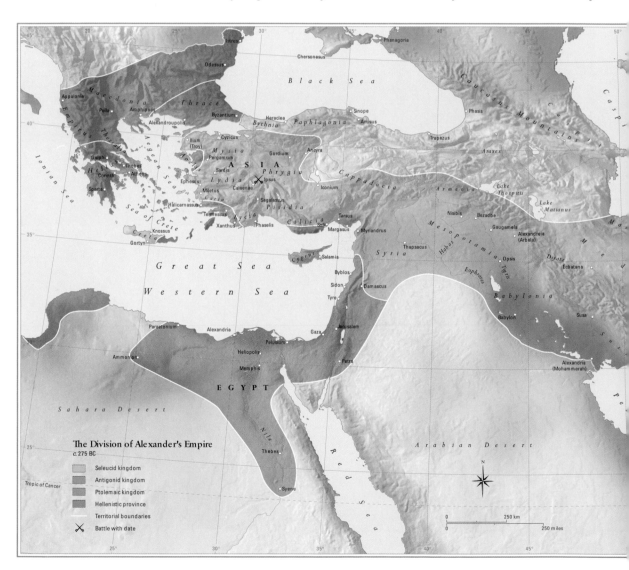

The Division of Alexander's Empire
c. 275 BC

- Seleucid kingdom
- Antigonid kingdom
- Ptolemaic kingdom
- Hellenistic province
- Territorial boundaries
- ✕ Battle with date

could live by their own customs and law within the city's constitution. Officially, Palestine had been allocated to the Seleucids after the Battle of Ipsus, but once again it was a vital frontier area between two great powers and was, in fact, under Egyptian control until the end of the 3rd Century BC. This helps account for the growth and influence of the Jewish population of Egypt in settlements all over the country. By this time, the "dispersed" Jews far outnumbered those living in Palestine, and Hebrew had become a dead language for everyday purposes. To meet the needs of Jews who could no longer read Hebrew, the Jewish sacred books, the Old Testament, began to be translated into other languages, particularly Greek as so many Jews now used it.

THE DIVISION OF ALEXANDER'S EMPIRE

At the death of Alexander at the age of 32, his Empire was divided between his senior generals.

TETRADRACHM
This coin minted in the reign
of Ptolemy I (305–283 BC).
The reverse of some coins of
Ptolemy I celebrated the
campaigns of his great friend
Alexander the Great, with
whom he had a successful
military career.

THE PTOLEMIES

Ptolemy I Soter (305–283 BC)

Ptolemy II Philadelphus
(283–246 BC)

Ptolemy III Euergetes I
(246–221 BC)

Ptolemy IV Philopator
(221–204 BC)

Ptolemy V Epiphanes
(204–180 BC)

Ptolemy VI Philometor
(180–145 BC)

> **with Ptolemy VIII Euergetes II
> and Cleopatra** (170–104 BC)

> **with Cleopatra II** (163–145 BC)

**Ptolemy VIII Euergetes II
(restored)** (145–116 BC)

**Cleopatra III and Ptolemy IX Soter II
(Lathyrus)** (116–107 BC)

**Cleopatra III and Ptolemy X
Alexander I** (107–101 BC)

**Ptolemy X Alexander I and Cleopatra
Berenice** (101–88 BC)

Ptolemy IX Soter II (restored)
(88–81 BC)

**Cleopatra Berenice and Ptolemy XI
Alexander II** (80 BC)

Ptolemy XII Neos Dionysus (Auletes)
(80–58 BC)

**Berenice IV (at first with Cleopatra
Tryphaena)** (58–56 BC)

Berenice IV and Archelaus
(56–55 BC)

**Ptolemy XII Neos Dionysus
(restored)** (55–51 BC)

Cleopatra VII Philopator (51–30 BC)

THE SELEUCIDS

Seleucus I Nicator (305–281 BC)

Antiochus I Soter (281–261 BC)

Antiochus II Theos (261–246 BC)

Seleucus II Callinicus (246–226/225 BC)

Seleucus III Soter (226/225–223 BC)

Antiochus III Megas ("the Great")
(223–187 BC)

Seleucus IV Philopator
(187–175 BC)

Antiochus IV Epiphanes
(175–164 BC)

Antiochus V Eupator (164–162 BC)

Demetrius I Soter (162–150 BC)

Alexander Balas (150–145 BC)

Demetrius II Nicator (145–140 BC)

Antiochus VI Epiphanes (145–142/141
or 139/138 BC)

Antiochus VII Sidetes (138–129 BC)

Demetrius II Nicator (restored)
(129–126/125 BC)

Cleopatra Thea (126/25–123 BC)

Antiochus VIII Grypus
(126/125–96 BC)

Seleucus V (126 BC)

Antiochus IX Philopator (Cyzicenus)
(114/113–95 BC)

Seleucus VI (95 BC)

Antiochus X Eusebes Philopator
(95 BC)

Demetrius III Philopator Soter
(95–88 BC) in Damascus

**Antiochus XI Epiphanes
Philadelphus** (95 BC) in Cilicia

Twins {
Phillip I (95–84/83 BC) in
Cilicia
Antiochus XII Dionysus
(87 BC) in Damascus

Phillip II (84/83 BC)

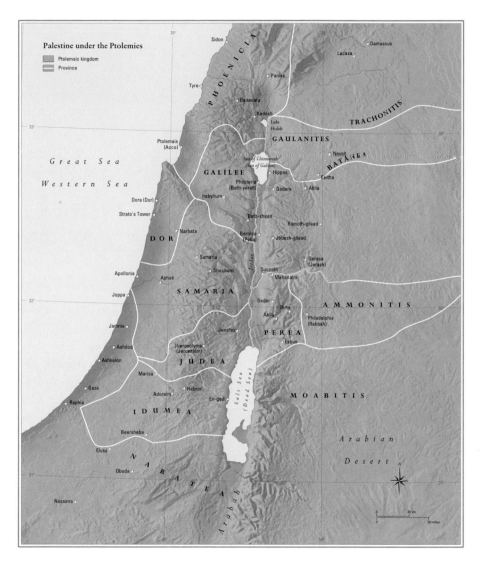

Palestine under the Ptolemies

- Ptolemaic kingdom
- Province

Sidon

PHOENICIA

Damascus

Lacasa

Panias

Tyre

Baitariata

Kedesh

Lake
Huleh

TRACHONITIS

GAULANITES

Ptolemais
(Acco)

Great Sea

Western Sea

Sea of Chinnereth
(Sea of Galilee)

GALILEE

Naveh

BATANEA

Hippos

Eeitha

Philoteria
(Beth-yerah)

Itabyrium

Gadara

Abila

Dora (Dor)

Strato's Tower

Beth-shean

Ramoth-gilead

DOR

Narbata

Bernice
(Pella)

Jabesh-gilead

Samaria

Gerasa
(Jerash)

Apollonia

Aphek

Shechem

Succoth

Mahanaim

Joppa

SAMARIA

Gedor

Birtu

AMMONITIS

Abila

Jamnia

Jericho

Philadelphia
(Rabbah)

PEREA

Ashdod

Hierosolyma
(Jerusalem)

Esbus

Ashkelon

JUDEA

Gaza

Marisa

Salt Sea
(Dead Sea)

Adoraim

Hebron

MOABITIS

Raphia

En-gedi

IDUMEA

Arabian

Beersheba

Desert

Elusa

NABATEA

Oboda

Nessana

Arabah

0   20 km
0   20 miles

LIFE UNDER THE PTOLEMIES

Alexandria was famous for its trading port, but ilt also hosted two of the glories of ancient civilization: the Lighthouse of Alexandria (one of the Wonders of the Ancient World) and the Library of Alexandria, the largest collection of books in the world.

GERASA

Gerasa was one of the numerous Hellenistic cities founded in Palestine. It was a member of a group of self-governing cities in the Decapolis.

MACCABEAN REVOLT

ALEXANDER'S VAST EMPIRE WAS DISMEMBERED BY HIS GENERALS.
PTOLEMY SEIZED EGYPT AND SELEUCUS I ESTABLISHED CONTROL
OF AN EMPIRE STRETCHING FROM THE MEDITERRANEAN SEA TO
THE RIVER INDUS IN THE EAST.

Under the Ptolemies, the Jews enjoyed considerable religious freedom, peaceful times allowing several Old Testament books to reach their final drafts. However, conflict between the Egyptian and Seleucid empires led the latter's Antiochus III (223–187 BC) to defeat Egypt at the Battle of Paneoin (eventually called Caesarea Philippi). Palestine was now acquired by the Seleucids and the Jewish population had to deal with a new ruler who was not an advocate of religious toleration.

Antichus sought to rebuild the old Alexandrine Empire. Pursuing territorial claims in Macedonia brought him into conflict with Rome and military defeat at Magnesia in 190 BC in western Asia Minor followed by naval defeat at Myonnesus. The peace terms required a 12- year financial indemnity and the loss of Asia Minor. Armenia then broke away, as did Bactria. Hostages, too, were taken, including a Seleucid son who later became Antiochus IV. Supporting Carthage's Hannibal did the Syrians no favors. Now, blocked in the west, the Seleucid monarch sought expansion elsewhere, but was so strapped for cash – to pay Rome and his mercenary armies—that he attempted to recoup his losses by looting wealthy temples. His son and successor, Seleucus IV (187–175 BC), tried but failed in his claim to the wealth of the Jewish Temple in Jerusalem as the property of the state but he failed. However, his brother, Antiochus IV (175–164 BC) exacerbated Jewish-Hellene antipathy by using violence.

Several political and religious circumstances affected Antiochus IV Epiphanes (god manifest). He desired to rid the world of any non-Hellene, non-conformist faith, Judaism being a prime target. The Seleucids desired to spread and consolidate Hellenism and Judah was an enclave of religious turbulence requiring forceful hellenisation. In 174 BC, Antiochus deposed the High Priest, Onias,

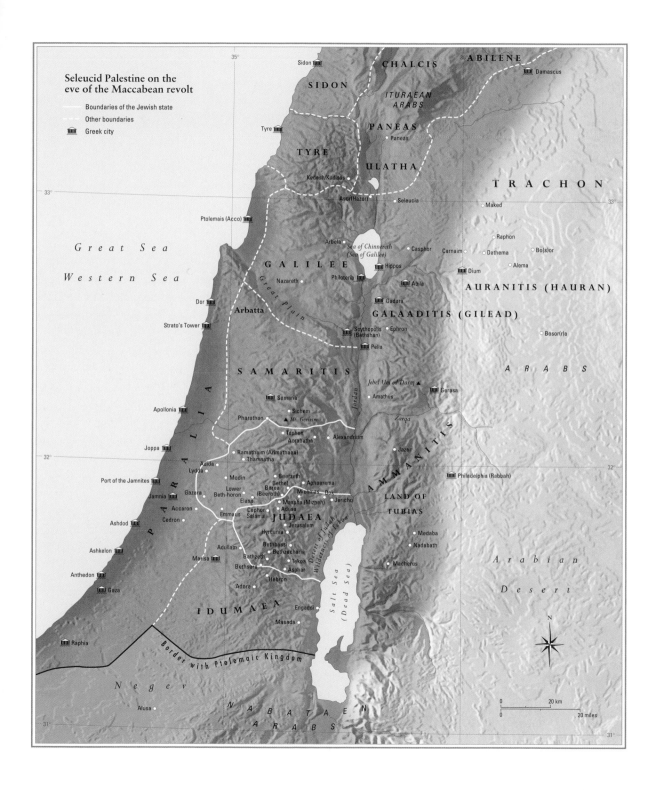

Seleucid Palestine on the eve of the Maccabean revolt

Boundaries of the Jewish state
Other boundaries
Greek city

35°

Sidon
SIDON
CHALCIS
ABILENE
Damascus

ITURAEAN ARABS

Tyre
TYRE
PANEAS
Paneas

ULATHA

Kedesh/Kudisos

TRACHON

33°   33°
Asor(Hazor)
Seleucia

Ptolemais (Acco)
Maked

Great Sea

Arbela
Sea of Chinnereth (Sea of Galilee)
Casphor
Raphon
Carnaim
Bo(s)or
Dathema

Western Sea

GALILEE
Hippos
Alema
Dium

Nazareth
Philoteria
Abila
AURANITIS (HAURAN)

Dor
Gadara

Strato's Tower
Arbatta
Scythopolis (Bethshan)
Ephron
Bosor(r)a
GALAADITIS (GILEAD)

Pella

SAMARITIS
Jebel Um ed Daraj
ARABS
Gerasa

Samaria
Amathus

Apollonia
Pharathon
Sichem
Mt. Gerizim

Jazer

Joppa
Taphon
Acrabatha
Alexandrium

32°
Ramathaim (Arimathaea)
Thamnatha
AMMANITIS
32°

Adida
Lydda
Modin
Beerzeth
Bethel
Aphaerema
Dok
Philadelphia (Rabbah)

Port of the Jamnites
Lower Beth-horon
Barea (Beeroth)
Michmias
Jericho

Jamnia
Gazara
Elasa
Maspha (Mizpeh)
LAND OF TUBIAS

Accaron
Emmaus
Caphor Salama
Adesa
JUDAEA

Cedron
Jerusalem

Ashdod
Hyrcania
Medaba

Adullam
Bethbassi
Nadabath

Ashkelon
Bathzeth
Bethzacharia

Marisa
Bethsura
Tekoa
Macherus

Anthedon
Adora
Asphar
Hebron

Arabian

Gaza
Desert

IDUMAEA
Engaddi
Salt Sea (Dead Sea)

Raphia
Masada

Border with Ptolemaic Kingdom

Negev
N

NABATAEN ARABS

Alusa

0   20 km
0   20 miles

31°   31°

P A R A L I A

Jordan
Zarqa

Great Plain

Desert of Judah
Wilderness of Tekoa

replacing him with one of his brothers, known as Jason. This new High Priest commenced building a gymnasium, an icon of Hellenization. People began to wear Greek dress and the broad-brimmed hat known as the *petasos*, which was the headgear of Hermes, the god of the gymnasium. Jews were forced to use the gymnasium where all were naked, so they could not hide their circumcision and were punished. The short Greek tunic incurred horror as it left the legs bare. The Greek obsession with the human body and its physique plunged old and young Jews into new Greek ideas.

> "THERE WAS SUCH AN EXTREME OF HELLENIZATION AND INCREASE IN THE ADOPTION OF FOREIGN WAYS BECAUSE OF THE SURPASSING WICKEDNESS OF JASON, WHO WAS UNGODLY AND NO HIGH PRIEST, THAT THE PRIESTS WERE NO LONGER INTENT UPON THEIR SERVICE AT THE ALTAR. DESPISING THE SANCTUARY AND NEGLECTING THE SACRIFICES, THEY HASTENED TO TAKE PART IN THE UNLAWFUL PROCEEDINGS IN THE WRESTLING ARENA AFTER THE CALL TO THE DISCUS."   2 MACCABEES 4:13-14

The Jews believed Hellenism to be mere nature worship, a continuation of Canaanite religion with Antiochus as a new Baal embodying Canaanite god-qualities of hate, lust, anger, greed, and envy. This Greek world view conflicted with Israel's raison d'être, the requirement to operationalise the revelation of God by building an ordered society that was ruled by God's love and justice, not by man's greed and aggression. Jewish loyalty to a revealed religion and the Word of God was antithetical to Antiochus' "god manifest," the god in human guise. When Jason failed to move beyond cultural affairs, Antiochus deposed him in favor of Menelaus, thereby generating conflict between the supporters of three High Priests—Onias, Jason, and Menelaus; but no rebellion broke out.

Antiochus now felt able to continue his foreign policy plans as Rome in the West and Parthia in the East were not perceived as a threat. In 174 BC, he marched into Egypt and despite early successes was forced to retreat when a Roman fleet arrived unexpectedly at the mouth of the Nile. His prestige maimed, Antiochus turned toward Judah. The Egyptian defeat saw Jason depose Menelaus, but the Seleucid king reversed this action and robbed the Temple of its treasures, plundered and burnt parts of Jerusalem, and established a citadel, the Accra, on a hill overlooking the Temple (167 BC). Antiochus next sought to enforce the state of Hellenism. The Temple at Jerusalem was consecrated to Olympian Zeus and the Samaritan sanctuary of Mount Gerezim was given to the worship of Zeus, the Friend of Strangers.

> "NOW THE FIFTEENTH DAY OF THE MONTH CASLEU, IN THE HUNDRED FORTY AND FIFTH YEAR, THEY SET UP THE ABOMINATION OF DESOLATION UPON THE ALTAR, AND BUILDED IDOLS THROUGHOUT THE CITIES OF JUDA ON EVERY SIDE; AND BURNT INCENSE AT THE DOORS OF THEIR HOUSES, AND IN THE STREETS. AND WHEN THEY HAD RENT IN PIECES OF THE LAW WHICH THEY FOUND, THEY BURNT THEM WITH FIRE."   1 MACCABEES 1: 54-56

The rebellion began in the small village of Modin, north-west of Jerusalem. A Syrian official and a Jew were going to offer sacrifice on a pagan altar. The apostasy so insensed a priest, Mattathias and his five sons that they killed the Syrian and the apostate. They then fled into the Judaean wilderness of hills, wadis and caves where they might survive attacks from Seleucid forces

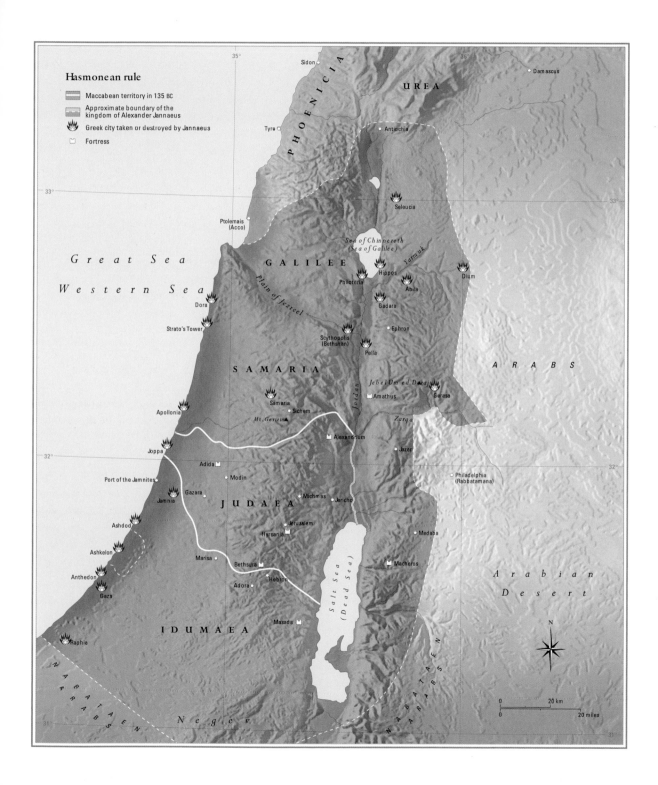

Hasmonean rule

Maccabean territory in 135 BC

Approximate boundary of the
kingdom of Alexander Jannaeus

Greek city taken or destroyed by Jannaeus

Fortress

Sidon

UREA

Damascus

PHOENICIA

Tyre

Antiochia

Seleucia

Ptolemais
(Acco)

Great Sea

Western Sea

Sea of Chinnereth
(Sea of Galilee)

GALILEE

Yarmuk

Hippos

Dium

Philoteria

Abila

Dora

Plain of Jezreel

Gadara

Strato's Tower

Ephron

Scythopolis
(Bethshan)

Pella

SAMARIA

ARABS

Jebel Um ed Daraj

Samaria

Amathus

Gerasa

Apollonia

Sichem

Mt. Gerizim

Zarqa

Joppa

Alexandrium

Jordan

Jazer

Adida

Modin

Philadelphia
(Rabbatamana)

Port of the Jamnites

Gazara

Michmas

Jamnia

JUDAEA

Jericho

Ashdod

Jerusalem

Hyrcania

Medaba

Ashkelon

Marisa

Bethsura

Anthedon

Adora

Hebron

Macherus

Gaza

Arabian
Desert

IDUMAEA

Masada

Salt Sea
(Dead Sea)

N

Raphia

NABATAEN ARABS

Negev

0   20 km

0   20 miles

JEWISH INDEPENDENCE

FOR THE FIRST TIME SINCE 587 BC JUDAH WAS UNDER THE RULE

OF A JEWISH KING. THE KINGDOM EXPANDED DRAMATICALLY.

THE SELEUCID RULER, DEMETRIUS II, EXEMPTED JUDAH FROM

TRIBUTE THUS GRANTING VIRTUAL INDEPENDENCE.

JEWISH EXPANSION UNDER THE HASMONEAN DYNASTY
(far right)
It would inaccurate to state that the victories of the Maccabees ushered in peace and tranquility for the Jews of Jerusalem during the 1st Century BC. Different factions within the Jewish state, centered on Jerusalem, fought bitterly. Although the Jews managed to extend their rule to the borders of the old Davidic Empire, internal tensions reached a state of civil war, both sides appealing to the Romans to restore order.

The rulers who sprang from the Maccabee line became known as the Hamoneans, because the historian Flavius Josephus (c. AD 37–101) claimed that Simon Maccabee's grandfather was called Hasmon. Simon, like so many Maccabees died a violent death. Abubus, Simon's son-in-law and commander of the Dor fortress was persuaded by the Syrian King to murder Simon and two of his sons at a meal while visiting him.

This rebellion failed. Simon's third son John Hyrcanus (134–104 BC), was in Gezer, west of Jerusalem, when the crime was committed. Learning of the murder, he traveled straightaway to Jerusalem, where he was immediately acknowledged as Simon's lawful successor. Meanwhile, Syrian forces arrived to aid John's brother-in-law, but John had been unable to organize his troops and was forced to withdraw into Jerusalem. The subsequent Syrian siege would have succeeded had not Rome interfered; the Syrians retreated. Power, therefore, remained in John's hands. Nevertheless, he raised a large army to aid Seleucid Antiochus VII Euergetes Eusebes Soter Sidetes (benefactor, pious, savior) in his campaigns against Parthia to regain Mesopotamia, suggesting that John owed Syria some type of tribute. John returned home before winter and was absent when the Parthian ruler, Phraates II, surprised the Seleucid army at Ecbatana, defeating it and killing Antiochus. John renounced his allegiance to Syria and rebuilt

"SO WHEN SIMON AND HIS SONS (MATTATHIAS AND JUDAS)

HAD DRUNK LARGELY, PTOLOMEE AND HIS MEN ROSE UP

AND CAME UPON SIMON INTO THE BANQUETING PLACE,

AND SLEW HIM, AND HIS TWO SONS, AND CERTAIN OF HIS

SERVANTS."   1 MACCABEE 16:16

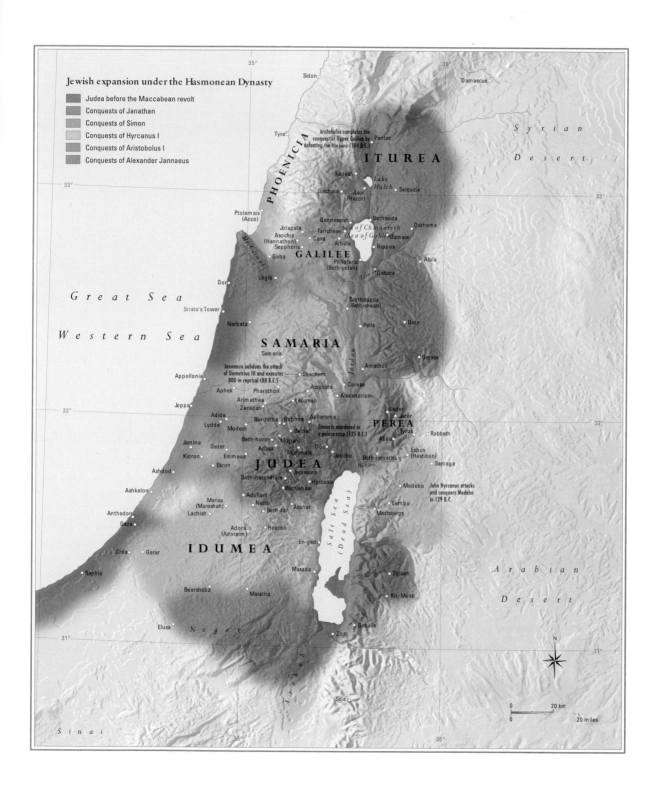

Jewish expansion under the Hasmonean Dynasty

- Judea before the Maccabean revolt
- Conquests of Janathan
- Conquests of Simon
- Conquests of Hyrcanus I
- Conquests of Aristobolus I
- Conquests of Alexander Jannaeus

35° 36°

Sidon

Damascus

S y r i a n

Tyre

Aristobulus completes the
conquest of Upper Galilee by
defeating the Itureans (104 B.C.)

Panias

PHOENICIA

ITUREA

D e s e r t

33° 33°

Kedesh

Gischala

*Lake
Huleh*

Asor
(Hazor)

Seleucia

Ptolemais
(Acco)

Gennesaret

Bethsaida

Dathema

Jotapata

Taricheae

*Sea of Chinnereth
(Sea of Galilee)*

Asochis
(Hannathon)

Cana

Arbela

Gamaia

Sepphoris

Hippos

Abila

Geba

GALILEE

Philoteria
(Beth-yerah)

Great Sea

Dor

Legio

Yarmuk Gadara

Strato's Tower

Scythopolis
(Beth-shean)

Western Sea

Narbata

Pella

Dion

SAMARIA

Samaria

Amathus

Gerasa

Appollonia

Jannaeus subdues the attack
of Demetrius III and executes
800 in reprisal (88 B.C.)

Shechem

Aphek

Pharathon

Acrabeta

Coreae

Jordan

Joppa

Arimathea

Lebonah

Alexandrium

Zeredah

32° 32°

Adida

Ber-zetha

Gophna

Apherema

Gedor

Jazer

Lydda

Modein

Bethel

PEREA

Tyrus

Jamina

Beth-horon

Mizpah

Dion

Simon is murdered in
a palace coup (135 B.C.)

Abila

Gezer

Adasa

Michmash

Rabbath

Kidron

Emmaus

JUDEA

Jericho

Beth-ramatha

Esbus
(Heshbon)

Ashdod

Ekron

Jerusalem

Samaga

Beth-haccherem

Hyrcania

Medeba

John Hyrcanus attacks
and conquers Medeba
in 129 B.C.

Ashkelon

Bethlehem

Adullam

Asphar

Lemba

Marisa
(Mareshah)

Nezib

Beth-zur

Machaergs

Anthedon

Lachish

*Salt Sea
(Dead Sea)*

Gaza

Adora
(Adoraim)

Hebron

A r a b i a n

Orda

Gerar

IDUMEA

En-gedi

D e s e r t

Raphia

Masada

Eglaim

Beersheba

Malatha

Kir-Moab

Elusa

Neg eb

Gabalis

31° 31°

Zoar

A r a b a h

N

Sela

0 20 km

0 20 miles

Sinai

35° 36°

GREEK INFLUENCE
The fashion for things Greek
was so powerful that even the
Jews of Palestine embraced it
enthusiastically. Many of the
cities were rebuilt in the
Greek style and in some parts
of the area Greek colonies
were established. Eventually,
the Old Testament had to be
translated into Greek for the
Hebrew language was no
longer in everyday use.
However this relationship
became strained as Jews
considered that their beliefs
were infringed by continued
Greek interference under the
Seleucids, especially with the
Temple in Jerusalem and its
Jewish rights, coupled with
demands that the Seleucid
king should be worshipped as
a god.

Jerusalem's walls that Antiochus had torn down in the siege. Hyrcanus further fortified his position by renewing the treaty of friendship with Rome, an insurance against possible future Syrian aggression. Again, after 129 BC, John Hyrcanus ruled an autonomous state. Coins were issued inscribed thus: "Yehohanan the high priest and the congregation of the Jews," intimating that Hyrcanus was a typical Hellenistic ruler (his eldest sons bore Greek names), emphasizing his High Priesthood, and suggesting that he governed with a council rather than becoming an autocrat.

Hyrcanus then proceeded to attack his weaker neighbors to enlarge his domains. Two main targets were Samaria and Shechem. These strongholds contained Samaritan worshippers of Adonai making sacrifices at a temple on Mount Gezerim. This alternative temple-cult was anathema to the priests in Jerusalem. Both cities were destroyed and a rivulet diverted over the ruins of Samaria (128 BC). Galilee, occupied by Aramaic-speaking gentiles was next on the agenda. Hyrcanus forced these Galileans (Ituraeans) to Judaise, insisting that males were circumcized. In the south, Idumaea (Edom) was conquered and its inhabitants were Judaised too. The town of Medeba, east of the Dead Sea, was taken thereby threatening Nabatean trade routes to the north. On the northern frontier, cities such as Pella, Dion, Gadera, and Hippos, all east of the Jordan, (eventually leaguing with others to form the Decapolis), were made tributary. These Greek cities remained intact and the people were not compelled to Judaise. Instead, trade served to benefit the Hasmonean state, which began to adopt a

new religious view that Judaism and Hellenism were compatible.

Alexander Janneus

In 104 BC, Hyrcanus died and was succeeded by his son Aristobulos I. He ruled for just one year, being followed by Alexander Janneus (103–76 BC). Aristobulos was paranoid and imprisoned most of his brothers and even his mother, who allegedly starved to death in prison. His favorite brother was killed by the royal bodyguard by mistake, an event which evidently hastened Aristobulos' current sickness into death after vomiting blood. Alexander Janneus was freed from prison by his mother and made king, according to the evidence of his minted coins.

Alexander was militarily minded like his father and, despite failing in an attempt to capture Ptolemais, seized all the port cities of Palestine, taking Gaza with great brutality. Sensibly, he remained on good terms with the Ptolemaic Egyptian Queen, who was quite capable of summoning Roman aid if she felt threatened. Alexander also captured several towns in Galaditis, Gaulanitis, and Syria. However, the southern Nabataeans continued to raid and threaten Judea and ultimately involved themselves in Hasmonean internecine family strife. Alexander remained concerned about his southern and eastern borders, evidenced by the forts at Hyrcania, Masada, and Machaerus. These were linked to further fortifications at Beth-zur, Gezer, Alexandrium and Dok.

Foreign success did not necessarily make Alexander Janneus popular among his own people. Like his father, he used many mercenaries so the Jews did not particularly feel part of the expansionist plans. Conflict grew with the orthodox religious party, the Pharisees. The latter's devotion to the Law meant spurning the pomp, power, and prestige of the Hasmonean dynasty. Further, this family had the temerity to dub themselves kings when they were not part of the Davidic line. The Pharisees also disliked Alexander's behavior; he was High Priest, but failed to observe the Law. Janneus was pelted with lemons at the Feast of the Tabernacles, leading him to massacre his opponents. The Pharisees begged help from Seleucid Demetrius III. This and several scandals provoked resistance and Alexander is said to have crucified 800 rebels in Jerusalem. Flavius Josephus claims that Alexander ordered that the rebels' wives and children be brought out and slaughtered before the eyes of the dying men.

The Pharisees maintained that while dying from a wound acquired while besieging a

Greek city, Alexander advised his wife, Alexandra Salome (76–67 BC), to mend fences with the Pharisees. Alexandra Salome became Queen rather than a son succeeding Janneus. Historians have argued that the older of his sons, Hyrcanus, was impaired, but the Queen did not wish to pass over him to the younger Aristobulos lest there be argument and even civil war. Alexandra Salome appointed Hyrcanus High Priest thus pleasing the Pharisees who now felt that their views could be imposed upon the weak-minded Hyrcanus. Since she could not preside over the Sanhedrin, the Jewish high counsel, she placed her brother in this post. Alexandra Salome was in a secure position: the Seleucids and Ptolemies were both weak and, internally, her détente with the Pharisees won her much popular Judean support. When places were left vacant in the Sanhedrin, she filled them with Pharisees rather than Sadducees, an extremely conservative group that only recognized the Torah as religious texts. Also, scribes were preferred to priests. In reality, Alexandra Salome was Queen in name only, the Pharisees holding the real power, but the country was quiet and her reign was later regarded as a Golden Age.

Peace was shattered when the Queen died in 67 BC. Conflict broke out and the dispute eventually led to the destruction of the entire Jewish state. The Pharisees supported Hyrcanus II as king and High Priest. The Sadducees backed Aristobolus, who was already in control of some parts of Judea. A civil war ensued; Hyrcanus' defeat resulted in Aristobulos usurping the monarchy and High Priesthood. Hyrcanus accepted his defeat and submitted to his brother's authority. However, a new personality entered the arena. When Alexander Janneus seized Idumaea and forcibly converted the population to Judaism, he appointed a local as governor of the region. This man's son, Antipater, possessed territorial designs and ambitions. Accordingly, he became an adviser to Hyrcanus and persuaded him to seek a restoration of his position in Judea. So, in 65 BC, the two escaped to the Nabataean capital of Petra. The Nabataeans had schemes of projecting their power into the north-west to gain control of trade routes in the area. Antipater found it easy to persuade Aretas, the Nabataean ruler, to assist Hyrcanus in returning to Jerusalem to recover his kingship. Aristobulos had not yet consolidated his resources and could not counter the enemy advance having to withdraw inside the walls of Jerusalem.

Judea's internal affairs were now in chaos. Three parties contested power. Aristobulos was contained in Jerusalem with his coterie of priests and important Jewish families. Outside the walls were Hyrcanus, Antipater, and their Nabataean allies. The Pharisees comprised the third party and they ideally sought the eradication of both Hasmoneans and a return to the rule of Law. Aristobulos knew he required outside help to withstand a siege and therefore went to Damascus, which had just been occupied by a Roman army under Pompey. Roman power had emerged from the central and western Mediterranean into the Asian world.

The Hand of Rome

The Hasmonean Kingdom had bumped into Rome's foreign policy drive toward the east. Roman ambitions had embarked upon eastern politics during the Second Punic War (264–241 BC) when Philip V of Macedon allied with Hannibal. Two Roman-Macedonian wars followed with a crushing defeat of Philip at Cynoscephalae in 197 BC. A few years later Attalos II, King of Pergamon, requested aid against his eastern neighbor, the Seleucid ruler, Antiochus III. The Romans crushed the Seleucid navy at Myonnesus (191 BC) and its land forces at Magnesia (190 BC). These defeats led to the total breakaway of Armenia (under Artaxias) and Bactria from the Seleucid Empire.

The Macedonians returned to the fray under Philip's son, Perseus, being defeated at Pydna (168 BC). Macedonia was turned into a Roman province. Greece was swallowed up in 146 BC when Rome destroyed the chief Greek city, Corinth. In 130 BC, the last King of Pergamon died bequeathing his kingdom to Rome. Thus, Rome acquired its province of Asia, its first territory beyond the Aegean. Pamphilia followed in 103 BC, and Cilicia was established as a Roman province in 101 BC in the perennial problem of eradicating piracy. Rome continued its policy of seeking to

> "NOW JUDAS HEARD OF THE FAME OF THE ROMANS, THAT THEY WERE VERY STRONG AND WERE WELL-DISPOSED TOWARD ALL WHO MADE AN ALLIANCE WITH THEM, THAT THEY PLEDGED FRIENDSHIP TO THOSE WHO CAME TO THEM, AND THAT THEY WERE VERY STRONG. MEN TOLD HIM OF THEIR WARS AND OF THE BRAVE DEEDS WHICH THEY WERE DOING AMONG THE GAULS, HOW THEY HAD DEFEATED THEM AND FORCED THEM TO PAY TRIBUTE, AND WHAT THEY HAD DONE IN THE LAND OF SPAIN TO GET CONTROL OF THE SILVER AND GOLD MINES THERE." 1 MACCABEES 8:1–3

weaken any strong power in the east while bolstering small states. At this point in time, Asia Minor contained other kingdoms such as Bithynia, Pontus, and Cappadocia, which were still ruled by Iranian princes, the remnants of satraps holding power under the old Persian Achaemenids.

These states became Hellenized and even founded cities along Greek lines, such as Nikomedia in Bithynia. The most noteworthy independent state was Pontus under the Persian, Mithridates VI Eupator. This ambitious king locked horns with Rome when he commenced a campaign of conquest by capturing Colchis and the Crimea from Scythia. He attempted to cement control in Paphlagonia and Cappadocia, but was prevented by Rome; his plot to depose Nicomedes III of Bithynia collapsed. In 88 BC, Nicomedes raided Pontus, encouraged by Rome, instigating the First Mithradatic War. Mithradates occupied Roman Asia and marched upon Greece. Between 86 and 85 BC, he was defeated by the Roman generals Gaius Flavius Fimbria and Lucius Cornelius Sulla. The Roman invasion of Pontus in 83 BC during the Second Mithradatic War was repulsed in 82 BC. Rome attempted to seize Bithynia (which Mithradates had occupied) in the Third Mithradatic War. 73 BC witnessed Mithradates' defeat by Roman general Lucius Licinius Lucullus and he was driven out of Bithynia and Pontus into Armenia. Lucullus also crushed Mithradates' father-in-law, Tigranes of Armenia, who had conquered Mesopotamia, Media, parts of Asia Minor and north Syria where he was approaching Damascus.

Appointed a Roman Consul in 70 BC, Pompey (Gnaeus Pompeius Magnus), jointly with Crassus, was empowered to finally destroy piracy in the eastern Mediterranean. While settling pirates as peaceful farmers, Pompey was given extraordinary powers to take over the command against Mithradates and to make peace and war and to organize the entire Roman east. A final defeat was inflicted upon Mithradates who committed suicide in 63 BC. Tigranes surrendered to Rome, was shorn of all conquests and fined 6000 talents. Pompey was now free to plan the consolidation of the eastern territories and to set up buffer client-states. He established four provinces: Asia remained intact; Bithynia-Pontus (eastern Pontus was excluded); Cilicia, including Pamphylia and Isauria; and Syria, the area around Antioch. The client kingdoms were eastern Pontus, Cappadocia, Galatia (under King Deitarus), Lycia, and Judaea. The buffer states, friends (amici) or allies (socii) of Rome, were a barrier against Parthia. In northern Mesopotamia, some territory was given to Tigranes. In the south, a Jewish Judea remained as did Arab Chalcis (Ituraea) and Nabataea.

The survival of Judea and the Arabic-speaking Nabataeans had depended upon the various embassies that the Levantine states had sent to Pompey. Two delegations came from Jerusalem: Hyrcanus II and Antipater were here supported by the Pharisees; the other embassy, including Sadducees, claimed that Aristobulos was the more effective of the two brothers and should be recognized as king. Some other Pharisees asked Pompey to abolish the Judean kingdom and re-establish a theocratic constitution as had existed in the times of Ezra and the Maccabees. Pompey supported Hyrcanus and he returned to Jerusalem as King (64 BC). The Nabataeans were instructed to vacate Judea.

The year 63 BC saw Pompey threatening Aretas' Nabataeans by marching two legions south. While the Romans were engaged at Petra, Aristobulos attempted to snatch back the Judean kingship. Pompey returned swiftly to Jerusalem and laid siege to the Temple precinct where Aristobulos' followers sought refugee. The siege lasted three months before the Roman legions entered the precinct and killed the rebels. Aristobulos was sent to Rome. Hyrcanus was re-established as High Priest, but Pompey reinforced his authority by violating the Temple protocols by entering the Holy of Holies, which only the High Priest was allowed to see. Even the Seleucid kings had observed religious scruples, but Pompey trampled over Jewish sensibilities and his behavior damned him forever in Jewish eyes.

Jewish morale was shattered further when Pompey decided to reduce the area of the Judean state and to abrogate the title of "king" in Hasmonean lands. The enlarged Jewish state of Alexander Janneus was truncated. The Greek city states in the northeast were placed outside Judaean control and comprised a league known as the Decapolis. The cities on the Palestinian coast from Dor southward to Gaza were given limited autonomy. Territories in the north were ceded to Ituraea and Ptolemais. These two regions were placed under the loose jurisdiction of the new Roman province of Syria. The Samaritans were allowed a small state around Shechem and the temple on Mount Gerizim. Hyrcanus II received the title of High Priest and Ethnarch. The diminished title demonstrated in no uncertain terms to the people of Judaea that they were now a subordinate Roman client-state, and their leader kept his title at the whim of the government in Rome.

Antipater became adviser to Hyrcanus and between 63 to 40 BC steered him in his religious

FORTIFICATION OF JERUSALEM *(far right)*
Although of much later date, these fortifications in Jerusalem still give an idea of how strong the city could be made in ancient times. Whenever it was vigorously defended, Jerusalem was able to stand long sieges by great military powers.

THE ROMAN EMPIRE

Throughout Europe, and particularly around the Mediterranean, there is still visible evidence of Roman civilization. During New Testament times, the Empire was beginning to reach its greatest extent and Rome was at the peak of its power. Palestine was incorporated into a Roman province by Pompey (106–48 BC), who deposed the last of the Seleucid kings in 64 BC, and, in the following year, captured Jerusalem.

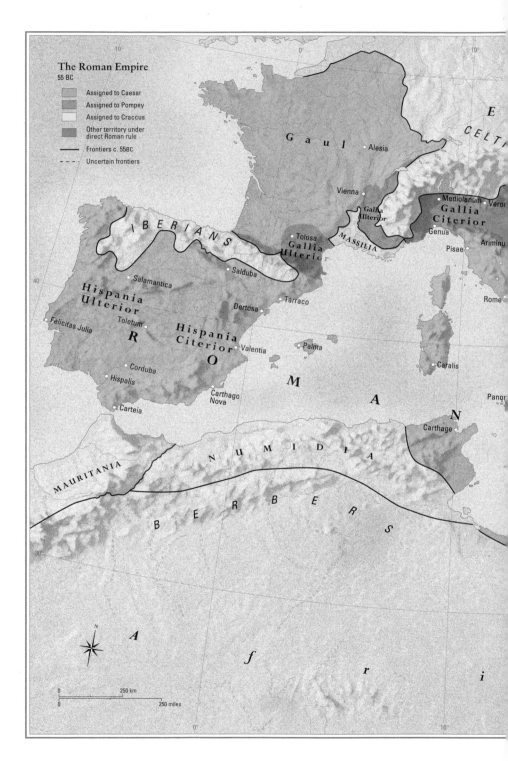

The Roman Empire
55 BC

- Assigned to Caesar
- Assigned to Pompey
- Assigned to Craccus
- Other territory under direct Roman rule
— Frontiers c. 55BC
-- Uncertain frontiers

Gaul
Alesia
Vienna
Gallia Ulterior
MASSILIA
E
CELTI
Mediolanum
Veron
Gallia Citerior
Genua
Ariminu

IBERIANS
Tolosa
Gallia Ulterior
Salduba
Dertosa
Tarraco
Rome
Salamantica
Pisae

Hispania Ulterior
Toletum
Hispania Citerior
Valentia
Palma
Felicitas Julia
R
O
Caralis

Corduba
Hispalis
M
Carthago Nova
A
Carteia
N
Panor
Carthage

MAURITANIA
N U M I D I A
B E R B E R S

A

f

r

i

0   250 km
0   250 miles

SLAVS

ro pe

IRANIAN PEOPLES

OPLES

DACIA

Olbia

Tyras

BOSPORAN
KINGDOM

Heraclea

CAUCASIANS PEOPLE

Tomi

Danube

Black Sea

Sinope

Trapezus

Salonae

Narona

Heraclea Pontica

PONTUS

ARMENIA

Stobi

Byzantium

Nicomedia

Asia

apolis

oli

Brundisium

Tarentum

Thessalonica

Demetrias

Pergamum

Smyrna

Dorylaeum

GALATIA

Antiochia

Iconium

CAPPADOCIA

COMMAGENE

SOPHENE

OSRHOENE

CORDUENE

Zeugma

Tarus

PARTHIAN
EMPIRE

Catana

Syracuse

Patrae

Corinth

Athens

Sparta

Halicarnassus

Attaleia

Side

LYCIA

Rhodes

RHODES

Antioch

Syria

Apamea

elite I.

E

M

P

I

R

E

Cyprus

Salamis

G r e a t   S e a

Gortyn

Melite I.

W e s t e r n   S e a

DECAPOLIS

INDEPENDENT
TOWNS

JUDAEA

ARABS

Cyrene

Alexandria

NABATAEA

Memphis

Nile

Red Sea

EGYPT

c

a

Thebes

Tropic of Cancer

and secular duties. Josephus says that Marcus Crassus seized 2,000 talents of gold from the Temple to finance an anti-Parthian expedition, but Antipater and Hyrcanus prevented the Jews from rebelling. The major problem confronting the two leaders was the support for Aristobulos, allegedly fostering an anti-Roman feeling after Aristobulos and his family had been sent to Rome in 62 BC. Here he became a plaything in the contest for power between Julius Caesar and Pompey, and this crisis was not concluded until the period of civil disorder ended in 27 BC. Then, Octavian, Caesar's nephew, received the title "Augustus," and extraordinary constitutional powers and control over the most important armies and provinces. Rome now had an Emperor.

During the Pompey-Caesar conflict, the civil war between Brutus and Cassius versus Octavian and Mark Antony, Hyrcanus continued in his position becoming a client of Pompey, then Julius Caesar, of Cassius, and then Octavian and Mark Antony. However, political decisions were made by Antipater who consolidated his power by moving his two oldest sons into powerful political positions. These were Phasael and Herod.

When Antipater died in 43 BC, Sadducees and opponents to Hyrcanus II sought an alternative Hasmonean candidate in Antigonus II, the surviving son of Aristobulos and nephew to Hyrcanus. He and his partisans were driven from Jerusalem, Herod being rewarded with the hand of Mariamme, Aristobulos' grand-daughter. Antigonus found Parthian backing during the Roman civil war because Parthia wished to fish in troubled waters and maybe win over the hundreds and thousands of Jews in Mesopotamia, which the Parthians had seized in the 140s BC. The Parthians entered Jerusalem, killed Phasael and arrested Hyrcanus. Josephus claims that Antigonus cut off Hyrcanus' ears, thereby making unfit to remain High Priest, and sent him to Babylon. Herod escaped to Rome via Arabia and Egypt. In 39 BC, the Roman Senate declared Herod King of Judaea. He was sent with mercenaries and a Roman force under Sosius to Judaea which he seized, capturing Antigonus in 37 BC and executing him. Herod retrieved the aging Hyrcanus II from Rome bringing him to Jerusalem. Octavian confirmed Herod as client-king in 31 BC. Hyrcanus, however, became involved in a conspiracy against Herod, was found guilty and executed in 30 BC. This same year witnessed Herod in control of Judaea (with Idumaea), Samaria, Galilee, and Peraea. He was also granted rule over Greek cities in Samaria (Hippus and Gadara) and all the coastal cities except Ascalon.

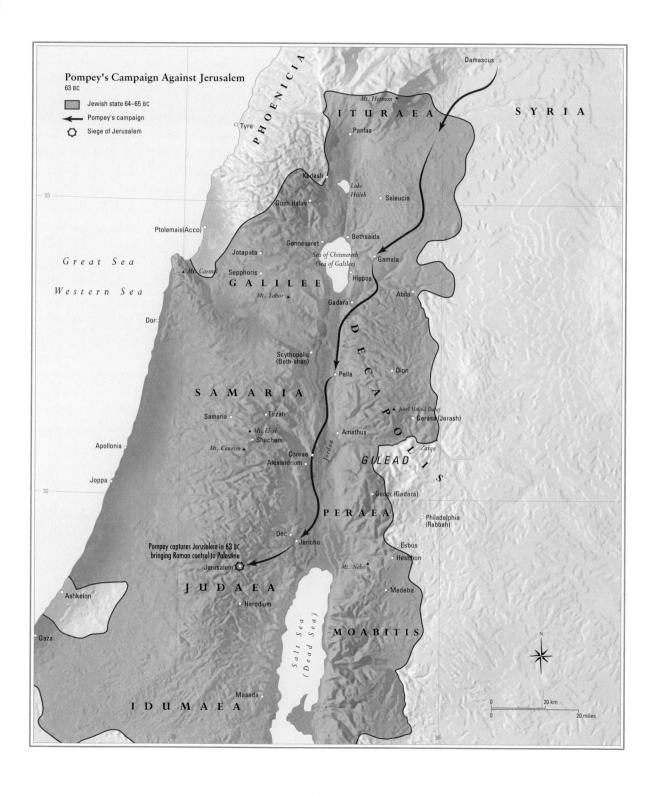

Pompey's Campaign Against Jerusalem
63 BC

- Jewish state 64–65 BC
- Pompey's campaign
- ⬡ Siege of Jerusalem

Damascus

PHOENICIA

ITURAEA

SYRIA

Mt. Hermon ▲

Tyre

Panias

Kedesh

Lake Huleh

Seleucia

Gush Halav

Ptolemais(Acco)

Bethsaida

Gennesaret

Sea of Chinnereth (Sea of Galilee)

Gamala

Jotapata

Mt. Carmel ▲

Sepphoris

Hippos

GALILEE

Abila

Mt. Tabor ▲

Gadara

Great Sea

Western Sea

Dor

DECAPOLIS

Scythopolis (Beth-shan)

Pella

Dion

SAMARIA

Jebel Um ed Daraj ▲

Gerasa (Jerash)

Samaria

Tirzah

Mt. Ebal ▲

Shechem

Amathus

Apollonia

Mt. Genzim ▲

Coreae

Jordan

Zatqa

GILEAD

Alexandrium

Joppa

Gedor (Gadara)

PERAEA

Philadelphia (Rabbah)

Doc

Jericho

Esbus

Pompey captures Jerusalem in 63 BC bringing Roman control to Palestine

Heshbon

Jerusalem ⬡

Mt. Nebo ▲

JUDAEA

Ashkelon

Herodium

Medeba

Gaza

MOABITIS

Salt Sea (Dead Sea)

N

IDUMAEA

Masada

0   20 km
0   20 miles

TRADE BETWEEN EMPIRES

INDIAN AMBASSADORS CAME BEARING GIFTS TO THE EMPEROR
AUGUSTUS AT SAMOS AS EARLY AS 20 BC. A ROMAN WAS DRIVEN
BY A STORM TO CEYLON ABOUT 50 AD, AND A FEW YEARS LATER
THEY SENT A DELEGATION TO NERO'S ROME TO ESTABLISH
DIPLOMATIC RELATIONS.

Despite the Romans conquering all the countries on the Mediterranean coast by the end of the 1st Century AD, and the Empire eventually extending to the River Rhine and to northern Britain, it was not a self-contained Roman world. Most of the provinces were self-supporting, and all basic requirements could be met within the Empire itself. Gallia, or France, was perhaps the richest province; the Empire was also a market place for luxury goods from outside its permeable borders. The ties of trade were important in holding the Empire together and allowing avenues for Christianity to spread itself within the state and even beyond. The Roman world was not the only civilization in existence at this time. Important empires existed in India and China, some of which traded with Rome. In the Americas, civilizations were extent in modern Mexico and the Yucatan, and the highly organized and technologically advanced Paracas people thrived in the region bordering Chile and Peru. Their world is evidenced by ceramics and textiles and mummy bundles enveloped in decorative cloth and buried in multiple tombs. These communities on the American continents were unknown to the Romans.

The lands and peoples outside the Empire were important as sources of furs, slaves and other goods, but all were recognized as dangerous and potential threats to the stability and security of the state. The development of Roman military strength on its frontiers shows the enemies most feared by army headquarters. Three main sectors can be ascertained.

Firstly, three legions (each containing 80 men), ten percent of the Imperial army, were located in Britain confronting the Picts and Scots who attacked by both land and sea from behind Hadrian's and Antonine Walls. In Europe, Rome faced the German tribes living beyond the Rhine and Danube rivers. Their large population and aggressiveness made them extremely dangerous, but they were

THREADS OF COMMERCE
Precious and beautiful goods created by the spinning of silk from cocoons brought trade links between the Roman Empire and empires of the Far East and China, along the trade route known as the Silk Road.

divided into small, uncoordinated groups. However, by the 3rd Century, German leagues were being formed. The Alemanni faced the angle formed by the upper reaches of the Rhine and Danube. Behind the middle and lower Rhine awaited the Franks, while the Goths were moving toward the south and south-east.

The military situation was deteriorating, this being reflected in the movement of the Roman legions. Four legions defended the borders against the German tribes, while 13 secured the provinces existing between Switzerland and the Black Sea. In the north-east, the Sarmatian tribes were under threat from the Huns and the Goths. Some moved into the Roman Empire, while others merged with the Goths. A number of tribes, such as the Jazyges and the Alans, sought to preserve their independence. The remnants of the latter group now formed the core of the Ossetians in the Caucasus.

Secondly, danger existed in the East. Persia, formerly Parthia, was a large, organized state capable of checking Rome in a balance of power, but ten legions stood facing them. It was a threat to trade since part of the Silk Road passed through its territory carrying expensive and precious goods from

RUGGED TRAILS
Trade between empires flourished despite the often inhospitable terrain it was necessary to cross, such as the dangerous mountain passes of what is now Afghanistan.

the Far East and China. Between Rome and Persia existed the unruly state of Armenia, which both powers wanted as a client state. The Persian dynasties changed frequently, culminating in the arrival of the Sassanids in AD 226. This dynasty wanted to re-establish the Archaemenid imperial tradition and regain the territories once ruled by Darius and Xerxes. They developed a heavily armored cavalry, the cataphracts, a terrifying threat to the Romans. By AD 272, the Persians had conquered much of Syria from the Romans, capturing Emperor Valerian in the process. Sassanid King Sharpur I (AD 241–272) was intolerant in a religious sense, enforcing Zoroastrianism on his people while massacring Jews, Buddhists, Hindus, and Christians.

The third zone of concern was the southern frontier, but little danger existed there except for mobile nomadic peoples, especially those south of Aswan who could threaten Egypt. The development of the state of Aksum, modern-day northern Ethiopia and Eritrea, was based upon trade with Rome and India rather than war. The kingdom converted to Christianity in the early 4th Century, and the Bible was translated into their language, Ge'ez. Elsewhere, in north-west Africa, the Berbers lived on either side of the borders, on the edges of the desert or in the mountains in a kind of equilibrium remaining until the spread of Islam.

Roman trade with the East developed swiftly, especially after the 2nd Century BC when Greeks from the powerful commercial center of Bactria, in today's Afghanistan, crossed the Hindu Kush Mountains into the northern Indus Valley. Trade was aided by the Kushans (c. 1st Century BC AD 230), who controlled the Punjab for the next two centuries. The Silk Road trade between Rome and China thrived under this dynasty, and ambassadors were exchanged between the Kushan Kings and the Roman Emperors. This trade diminished when the Kushan Empire disintegrated, with Sassanian Persia grabbing the territories that controlled the Silk Road.

The history of Roman-Chinese relations goes back to when Emperor Wu Di (140–87 BC) of the Han Dynasty sent an ambassador westward in an attempt to build an alliance with various nomadic tribes against the marauding Xiongnu from the north. He escaped after being captured, and on his return to the Han capital at Ch'ang An told tales of a great empire in the West that received Chinese silk. The Orient fascinated Rome, and a trading station was established in Arikmedu in Eastern India, amongst the Chola civilization. Archaeological evidence suggests the Romans used the port from the 1st Century to the 2nd Century AD. Roman pottery, beads, glass, and terracotta, and gold coin hoards have been found in the Deccan. Trade was so great that Pliny (AD 62–133), a governor of Bithynia, complained that India was depleting Roman gold reserves.

Archaeologists from UCLA and the University of Delaware have excavated a long-abandoned Egyptian port at Berenice on the Red Sea near the border with Sudan. Evidently, the inhabitants recycled teak timber from Indian ships that were no longer seaworthy; this was timber that was found only in India and Myanmar. A variety of ancient goods have been uncovered, including 16 pounds of black pepper dating from the 1st Century, similar to peppercorns from the same vintage found in Germany. Basketry, matting, sailcloth, batik cloth, and coconuts from the 1st and 2nd Centuries have been found with sapphires and glass beads, apparently from Sri Lanka. Roman texts have suggested that the relative cost of shipping was 20 times cheaper than moving goods overland. Berenice appears to have been a transfer port between the Orient and Alexandria with goods being moved from the former port to the Nile by camels or donkeys. Trade was also facilitated by the growth of the Gupta Empire (AD 320–480) in India. This classical Hindu civilisation exported spices, sandalwood, precious stones, perfume, indigo, and herbs while imports comprised Chinese silk, Ethiopian ivory, and Arabian and Bactrian horses to keep the state cavalry bloodlines strong. Indian ships sailed across the Indian Ocean and the Arabian and China Seas, using square-rigged, two-masted vessels. This was truly a global trading system.

Mediterranean peoples rapidly learnt how to travel to China and when the Romans sacked Jerusalem in 70 AD, many Jews emigrated to China during the Han Dynasty. Jewish communities were well-established at Kaifeng, and Jewish merchants eventually played an important role in linking China with the West. The Chinese wanted to establish direct links with Rome, but were blocked by the Parthian Empire, which turned back an ambassador to Rome. Ptoloemy relates how an expedition despatched by Titianus of Macedonia reached China in 100 AD. *The Hou Han Shou*, the histories of the Han Dynasty, tells how a band of musicians and jesters came to China from Rome in about 120 AD. They had arrived from the eastern regions of the Roman Empire, known as Ta Ch'in in China. Chinese sources also report a number of Roman merchants landing in Vietnam in 166, at Nanjing in 226 and at Luoyang in 284.

The Hou Han Shou describes the Roman Empire: "This land is very extensive and embraces a great number of subjugated nations. The walls of the houses are built of stone, and inns are to be found along the streets. The inhabitants cut their hair and wear beautiful clothing. In warfare they have drummers, standards, and tents. The capital is 100 li in circumference and contains ten palaces, all of them at a distance of ten li from one another. All pillars in these palaces are of crystal... The country has much gold, silver, and precious stones, and the inhabitants are very rich, especially by reason of their trade with Indians and Parthians. All that is costly comes from this kingdom. The inhabitants are of straightforward and righteous character, and their merchants never have two prices. Grain is always cheap. The economy of the country rests on a well-filled treasury. When ambassadors come to the borders of this kingdom they are taken by guards to the capital, where they are given gold coins as a gift."

HEROD'S KINGDOM

KING HEROD RULED PALESTINE ON BEHALF OF ROME FROM 40 BC, AND HIS FAMILY REMAINED A MAJOR FORCE IN THE AREA FOR THE NEXT 130 YEARS. ALTHOUGH THERE WERE DEEP DIFFERENCES BETWEEN JEWISH FACTIONS DURING THE ENTIRE PERIOD, THEY EVENTUALLY REBELLED AGAINST THE ROMANS IN AD 66.

The politics of Palestine in the 1st Century AD form a complex and changing pattern as different groups manoeuvred and fought for control. The Romans imposed an uneasy peace on the warring factions, having first entered the arena at the request of two groups of Jews locked in civil war, with one group besieging the other in Jerusalem. when Pompey (106–48 BC) captured Jerusalem in 63 BC, he made Palestine part of the Roman province of Syria, ruled by a Roman legate, and limited the religious authority of the high priest to the parts of Palestine where the Jews recognized the Temple in Jerusalem. Some parts of Palestine, such as Samaria, observed a different form of Hebrew religion.

The brief period of peace was short lived, as Rome itself slid into civil war again and consequently its rule over Palestine weakened. But then the Roman Senate named the politically astute Herod, who was probably half Jewish, King of Judaea in 40 BC. Herod conquered his kingdom three years later with the aid of Roman soldiers and ruled it for the next 31 years as a puppet king of Rome. He subdued his unruly kingdom and his own treacherous family with ruthless cruelty, backed by his own army and established fortresses in many parts of his kingdom, where he could find security in times of trouble.

During his uneasy period of peace, Herod built new cities, and provided buildings for every kind of different civic need, from baths, theaters, and gymnasiums to a temple for emperor worship and, above all, a magnificent rebuilding of the Temple itself, the central symbol of Hebrew religion. It was all done through forced labor and extortionate taxation. The diversity of buildings points to the deep differences between Jewish groups during the whole New Testament period. The Herods and their supporters, the Herodians, remained a major force in Palestinian politics until the Jewish War of AD 66–70, but most of Hebrew Palestine, Judaea and Samaria, was put under the direct rule of Roman procurators in AD 6.

The other main groups, who were normally at variance with each other, were the Pharisees, Sadducees and the Essenes. At the extreme of fanatical nationalism were the Zealots, called "sicarii" (stabbers) by the Romans because of their reputation for stealthy assassination. The Pharisees believed in meticulous obedience to Hebrew law, which brought every detail of daily life within the province of religion, but they took account of changing circumstances and oral traditions of interpreting the law, which made them more flexible that the other main group, the Sadducees. Paul was a Pharisee before becoming a Christian, and this flexibility can be seen in his approach to problems. The Sadducees were violently opposed to the Pharisees and rejected any attempt to adapt

HEROD'S PALACE IN JERICHO

A reconstruction of Herod's magnificent palace built on the Wadi Qilt, south of Jericho. Many features were in the Roman style.

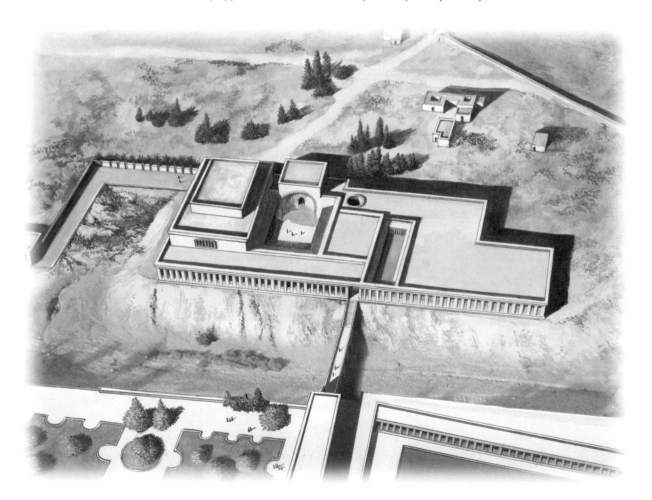

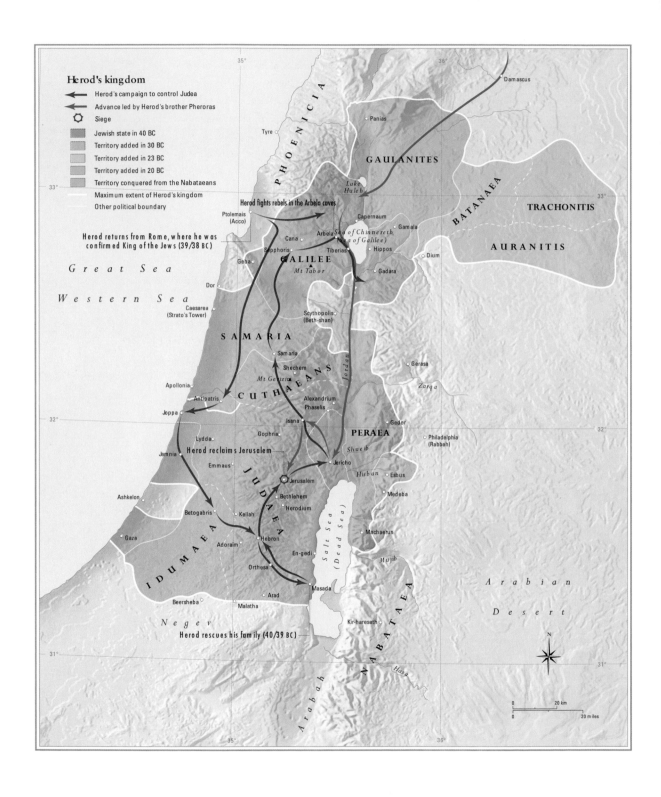

Herod's kingdom

→ Herod's campaign to control Judea

→ Advance led by Herod's brother Pheroras

⬡ Siege

Jewish state in 40 BC

Territory added in 30 BC

Territory added in 23 BC

Territory added in 20 BC

Territory conquered from the Nabataeans

Maximum extent of Herod's kingdom

Other political boundary

Herod returns from Rome, where he was confirmed King of the Jews (39/38 BC)

Herod fights rebels in the Arbela caves

Herod reclaims Jerusalem

Herod rescues his family (40/39 BC)

PHOENICIA

GAULANITES

BATANAEA

TRACHONITIS

AURANITIS

Damascus

Panias

Tyre

Lake Huleh

Capernaum

Gamala

Arbela Sea of Chinnereth (Sea of Galilee)

GALILEE

Hippos

Dium

Ptolemais (Acco)

Cana

Sepphoris

Tiberias

Geba

Mt Tabor

Gadara

Great Sea

Western Sea

Dor

Caesarea (Strato's Tower)

Scythopolis (Beth-shan)

SAMARIA

Samaria

Shechem

Mt Gerizim

Gerasa

Zarqa

Jordan

Apollonia

CUTHAEANS

Alexandrium

Phaselis

Antipatris

Joppa

Isana

PERAEA

Gedor

Gophna

Shueib

Philadelphia (Rabbah)

Lydda

Jericho

Jamnia

Emmaus

JUDAEA

Jerusalem

Hisban

Esbus

Ashkelon

Bethlehem

Medeba

Betogabris

Kellah

Herodium

Gaza

Hebron

En-gedi

Machaerus

Adoraim

IDUMAEA

Orthesa

Salt Sea (Dead Sea)

Mujib

Arabian

Desert

Beersheba

Arad

Masada

Malatha

Negev

Kir-hareseth

NABATAEA

Hasa

Arabah

N

0   20 km

0   20 miles

the written law to new situations, but their opposition was intensified by their political stance and their religious privileges. Most of the priests in Jerusalem belonged to this party, which tended to support occupying powers such as the Romans for the sake of political stability. Although the high priest of the Temple had to be chosen from certain priestly families, the appointment was made by whomever ruled Palestine at the time, whether a Herod or a Roman procurator. there is no mention of the Essenes in the New Testament, because they played no part in mainstream Hebrew religious practices or politics. Similarly, the Samaritans, in the hilly area north of Jerusalem, practised their own form of the Hebrew religion and kept to themselves. After the Jewish War (AD 66–70) the synagogues and their rabbis became more prominent but the mould of Jewish politics in Palestine had been broken.

The Dead Sea Scrolls and Qumran

The excavated ruins of Khirbet Qumran have revealed an extensive complex of buildings and caves that were occupied by a strict Jewish sect during the early years of Christianity. Biblical manuscripts and scrolls that throw light on contemporary religious attitudes in Palestine were also discovered there.

The Bible sometimes gives the impression that Jewish religion was uniform in practice, closely controlled and strictly regulated by the priests of Jerusalem. However, actual evidence suggests otherwise—and nowhere more than at Qumran. In 1947 the discovery of ancient biblical manuscripts and other Hebrew writings in caves near the northern end of the Dead Sea, changed modern knowledge about religion in Palestine during the 1st Centuries BC and AD. Within the next ten years, hundreds of complete scrolls and fragments of scrolls came to light, and the ruins of Khirbet Qumran nearby were thoroughly excavated.

The excavations and the evidence of the scrolls revealed a Jewish community occupying an extensive complex of buildings on a spur overlooking the Dead Sea and 25 caves in the steep sides of the cliffs nearby. The buildings with their eight courtyards, included a refectory, kitchen, assembly rooms, a laundry, two potteries and eight water cisterns of various sizes, some of them with steps leading down into them. There was evidence of a dam in a large gully in the cliffs, and channels to lead water from the dam to the cisterns. Stone writing tablets which had fallen from an upper storey were also discovered. Objects found in the excavations, especially coins, made it possible to date the occupation periods accurately. The community started at Qumran in the early part of the 1st Century BC and abandoned the site after an earthquake in 31 BC. Herod the Great ruled at the time, and this may be why the community did not return to the site until after his death in 4 BC. It continued there until the summer of AD 68, when the community hid its manuscripts in caves and fled with the arrival of Roman General Vespasian (AD 9–79) and the Tenth Legion, who destroyed most of the buildings.

The vast collection of writings unearthed at Qumran included books or fragments from the whole Hebrew Bible (except for Esther), other religious writings similar to parts of the Bible and documents about the organization and life of the community itself. The discoveries provided biblical manuscripts many centuries earlier than any that had previously survived, but they differed in many

HEROD'S KINGDOM
(far left)
Herod the Great consistently added to the territory under his rule (40–4 BC) and as a gift to his long-suffering people, began to rebuild the Temple in Jerusalem on a magnificent scale. However, six years after its completion, the new Temple was destroyed during the climax of the Jewish War with Rome in AD 70.

STORAGE JAR
The scrolls made at the Qumran settlement were stored in pottery jars. The jars and the extremely dry climate of the area, ensured that the scrolls were still in perfect condition when they were discovered after 2,000 years.

HEROD'S BUILDING PROJECTS
(far right)
Herod was a great builder, creating remarkable structures across his kingdom.

THE TEMPLE OF HEROD THE GREAT
Herod the Great's reconstruction was based on the same plan as Solomon's original building, though on a grander scale. This is the Temple that Jesus attended.

palaces from the ones authorized by the main Jewish authorities.

The community lived a strict life with joint ownership of all possessions, rituals of purification by water, public prayers, and religious meals. It kept a calendar of religious festivals different from the official calendar of the Jerusalem Temple. The members believed that the real meaning of the scriptures had been revealed by a "Teacher of Righteousness" at the beginning of the communities existence, and that they were chosen by God to be "Sons of Light" in the conflict with all 'Sons of Darkness' until God finally sent a Prophet and two Messiahs to bring victory and judgement. It seems certain that the members of the community were Essenes, a strict Jewish sect. Their beliefs and practices are of first importance for the light they throw on religious attitudes in Palestine during the early years of Christianity.

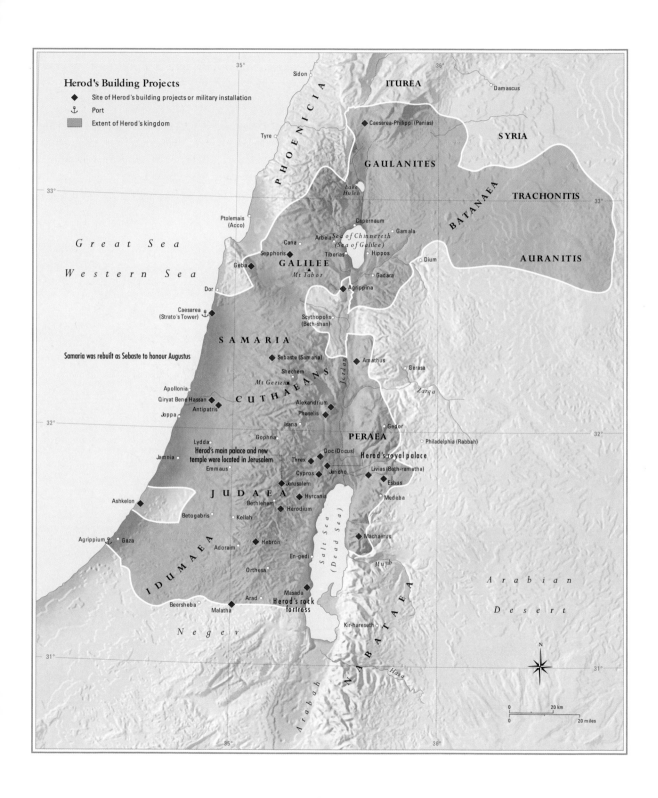

Herod's Building Projects

◆ Site of Herod's building projects or military installation

⚓ Port

▨ Extent of Herod's kingdom

Great Sea

Western Sea

Samaria was rebuilt as Sebaste to honour Augustus

Herod's main palace and new temple were located in Jerusalem

Herod's royal palace

Herod's rock fortress

PHOENICIA

ITUREA

SYRIA

GAULANITES

BATANAEA

TRACHONITIS

AURANITIS

GALILEE

SAMARIA

CUTHAEANS

PERAEA

JUDAEA

IDUMAEA

NABATAEA

Arabian Desert

Negev

Sidon
Damascus
Tyre
Caesarea-Philippi (Panias)
Lake Huleh
Ptolemais (Acco)
Capernaum
Gamala
Arbela *Sea of Chinnereth (Sea of Galilee)*
Cana
Sepphoris
Tiberias
Hippos
Geba
Mt Tabor
Gadara
Dium
Dor
Agrippina
Caesarea (Strato's Tower)
Scythopolis (Beth-shan)
Sebaste (Samaria)
Amathus
Shechem
Gerasa
Mt Gerizim
Jordan
Zarqa
Apollonia
Qiryat Bene Hassan
Alexandrium
Joppa
Antipatris
Phaselis
Isana
Gedor
Gophna
Philadelphia (Rabbah)
Lydda
Threx
Doc (Docus)
Jamnia
Cyprus
Jericho
Livias (Beth-ramatha)
Emmaus
Esbus
Jerusalem
Bethlehem
Hyrcania
Medeba
Ashkelon
Betogabris
Kellah
Herodium
Agrippium
Gaza
Hebron
Adoraim
En-gedi
Salt Sea (Dead Sea)
Mujib
Orthesa
Machaerus
Beersheba
Arad
Malatha
Masada
Kir-hareseth
Arabah
Hasa

0   20 km
0   20 miles

N

BIRTH OF JESUS

THE NEW TESTAMENT STARTS WITH THE THREE "SYNOPTIC GOSPELS" (MATTHEW, MARK AND LUKE), WHICH GIVE A BROAD VIEW OF THE LIFE OF JESUS, THOUGH THERE IS CONSIDERABLE OVERLAP IN THE CONTENT.

The major sources of information about Jesus' life are the Gospels, compiled in the last half of the 1st Century to enable Christianity to spread through Europe, the Mediterranean Basin and the Fertile Crescent. The Acts of the Apostles and St. Paul's Epistles also provide information about Jesus. He is mentioned in Tacitus' Annals and by Josephus, the Jewish historian, in Antiquities where he mentions the stoning in AD 62 of "James, the brother of Jesus, who was called Christ." Other works exist in the Infancy Gospels such as the Protoevangelium of James which was condemned by St. Jerome, along with much other old and authentic early Christian literature, and so came under a Papal ban. Extracanonical literature about Jesus was revealed in the Coptic Gospel of Thomas written by Gnostic Christians. Found at Naj' Hammadi in Egypt, it contains 114 sayings of Jesus, but no historical context.

Jesus was born at a time when the Jewish people had endured constant foreign domination with loss of political independence. The Romans had divided Herod I's kingdom among his sons, and by AD 6, the lands of Archelaus—Judaea, Jerusalem, Samaria, and Idumaea—were integrated into Roman administration. The Jesus story is concerned mainly with Galilee, where much of his ministry took place. Regarded with scorn by Judaeans, Galilee contained settlements of foreign colonists while its ruler, Herod Antipas, Hellenized the region. Individual Jewish settlements existed and there was a Jewish urban populace pursuing their own religious traditions. Monitoring the entire region was the Roman Empire, which often had the co-operation of the priest-aristocracy in Jerusalem.

In religious terms, Judaism was riven by different groups. The Pharisees have received a bad press in the Gospels, but, in reality, they originated under the Maccabees, or even earlier, and sought strict adherence to the Law (Torah) in order to create a pure Israel for God. Scrupulously observing ritual commandments for prayer, fasting, purity rituals, and avoidance of the unclean, they desired the promised Messiah of David's line who would take over Jerusalem and destroy pagan power. A second religious party was the Sadducees, a priestly Jerusalem caste. They were extremely conservative, rejecting all written additions to the Torah and having a strong voice in the religious and judicial institution, the Sanhedrin. The Gospels also mention the scribes, a teaching class that interpreted the Law for daily life. Addressed as rabbi, they were carefully trained, engaging in philosophical and religious debates. During the time of Jesus, they were linked to the Pharisees who controlled religious education in the synagogues. Two remaining groups deserve mention. The Zealots were an extremely militant nationalist group desiring a theocracy based on the Law, their political aspirations also desiring rule by the promised Messiah. The final religious group was the Essenes, normally identified with the sect living at Qumran. This monastic-style community has sometimes been described as similar in thought to Jesus and John the Baptist, but there are diametrically opposed views, especially Jesus'

MASSACRE
Fearing the birth of "the anointed one," Herod ordered the killing of all the male babies in Bethlehem under the age of two. This painting of this "massacre of the innocents" is by the Italian painter Giotto (c. 1267–1337), housed in the Scrovegni Chapel in Padua.

commandment of love to all, including outcasts and sinners.

The precise date of the birth of Jesus is unknown. Matthew locates it toward the end of Herod the Great's reign (c. 4 BC), while Luke links it to an unrecorded census ordered by the Emperor Augustus, associating this with the tax registration ordered by Quirinius, which occurred in AD 6. There is also evidence of a census implemented around 8 BC. Two Gospels, Matthew and Luke, give us some information about Jesus' birth and childhood, providing genealogies tracing Jesus' descent through Abraham, David, and his father, Joseph. One assumes that this is proof of Jesus' messiahship. Tradition has Bethlehem as Jesus' birthplace, King David's home town. In Matthew, Bethlehem is considered as Joseph and Mary's original residence, but they moved to Nazareth because of the Herodian threat. Luke, however, has the couple living in Nazareth but traveling to Bethlehem as Joseph was obliged to register at the Davidic place of origin. Both Gospels are, therefore, linking Jesus with the Old Testament Messiah as the hope of Israel.

Bethlehem's provenance is interesting, being mentioned in a prophecy from the Book of Micah, possibly dating from just after the fall of Jerusalem and the Davidic line in 587 BC:

"Now gather thyself in troops, O daughter of troops: he hath laid siege against us: they shall smite the judge of Israel with a rod upon the cheek. But thou, Beth-lehem Ephratah, though thou be little among the thousands of Judah, yet out of thee shall he come forth unto me that is to be ruler in Israel; whose goings forth have been from old, from everlasting. Therefore will he give them up, until the time that she which travaileth hath brought forth: then the remnant of his brethren shall return unto the children of Israel. And he shall stand and feed in the strength of the Lord, in the majesty of the name of the Lord his God; and they shall abide: for now shall he be great unto the ends of the earth" (Micah 5: 1–4).

According to the Gospels, Mary was an unmarried woman residing in Nazareth in Galilee where she was betrothed to Joseph, a carpenter, presumably an accomplished artisan. The archangel Gabriel told her she would conceive a child by the Holy Spirit. Joseph, received an angelic instruction to marry her. Mary and Joseph's journey from Nazareth to Bethlehem in Judaea only seems likely if Joseph was originally resident there with his family being property owners. Matthew has them in a "house" (Matthew 2:11), and that there was not enough space in the extended family's "room" or inn (Luke 2:7). Mary placed Jesus in an animal's food trough, which was sometimes placed near the entrance of 1st-century houses. Perhaps they stayed near the front of the type of cave house known to have been used in Bethlehem at the time. There may have been a previous link with Bethlehem. Extracanonical evidence of a kind can be seen in the early 2nd-Century Infancy Gospel of James, a mainly legendary collection of tales about the origin of Jesus. Mary is the virgin daughter of a prosperous Jerusalem couple named Anna and Joachim. The gospel states she grew up in the Temple, which is possible if she had priestly descent. Her 'relative', Elizabeth, was a descendant of Aaron and married to Zechariah the priest. (Luke 1:5)

The virginal conception of Jesus can be neither proved nor disproved. Acceptance of the case affirms the power and glory of God's work rather than dealing with the bitter consequences of an unplanned pregnancy and single motherhood. Interestingly, the doctrine of the virgin birth takes on and mocks an objection from Jesus' opponents. "Howbeit we know this man whence he is: but when Christ (Messiah) cometh, no man knoweth whence he is" (John 7:27).

Baby Jesus was taken to the Temple at Jerusalem to be presented to God where he was recognized as the Messiah by two elderly religious people: Simeon, who had been promised by God that he would not die before he had seen the Messiah, and the prophetess Anna.

Herod the Great, that cruel and insecure ruler, learnt that wise men (magi) from the East were nearby. They told him that they were following a star which they believed was a sign that the King of the Jews had been born, and Herod's priests confirmed that it was prophesied that the Messiah would be born in Bethlehem. Herod told the magi to go to the village and find the baby because he wanted to worship the child. They traveled to Bethlehem, finding Jesus and giving him presents of gold, frankincense, and myrrh. Returning home, they were warned in dream not to report back to Herod. This story is plausible; astrology was highly esteemed in the ancient world, especially Babylonia. A type of Jewish horoscope was attested in the Dead Sea Scrolls. We don't know whether Herod did kill all the male babies in Bethlehem. There is no evidence of the "massacre of the innocents," but if so, the number would have been so small that it probbaly received scant attention.

Jesus, Mary, and Joseph escaped Herod's fury by fleeing to Egypt, a logical refuge. Home to approximately one million Jews, this was the largest Jewish diaspora community, with a vibrant life, especially in Alexandria. Returning to Palestine, the family settled in Nazareth. There is little coverage of Jesus' childhood, but Mark (Chapter 6) describes his family and his brothers have purely Jewish

JESUS QUESTIONING THE TEACHERS

One of the few recorded events from the childhood of Jesus—his conversation with the teachers in the Temple at Jerusalem—is portrayed here by Jacopo Bassano (1517–92).

names: James (Jacob), Joseph, Judas, and Simon; his sisters are unnamed. Presumably, Jesus was raised in obedience to the Torah, and he certainly took part in annual pilgrimages to Jerusalem as evidenced in the story of the boy Jesus in the Temple.

"Now his parents went to Jerusalem every year at the feast of the Passover. And when he was 12 years old, they went up to Jerusalem after the custom of the Feast. And when they had fulfilled the days, as they returned, the child Jesus tarried behind in Jerusalem; and Joseph and his mother knew not of it. But they, supposing him to have been in the company, went a day's journey; and they sought him among their kinfolk and acquaintance. And when they found him not, they turned back again to Jerusalem seeking him. And it came to pass, that after three days they found him in the temple, sitting in the midst of the doctors, both hearing them, and asking questions. And all that heard him were astonished at his understanding and answers. And when they saw him, they were amazed: and his mother said unto him, 'Son, why hast thou thus dealt with us? Behold, thy father and I have sought thee sorrowing.' And he said unto them, 'How is it that ye sought me? Wist ye not that I must be about my Father's business?' And they understood not the saying which he spake unto them. And he went down with them, and came to Nazareth, and was subject unto them: but his mother kept all these sayings in her heart. And Jesus increased in wisdom and stature, and in favour with God and man" (Luke 2: 41–52).

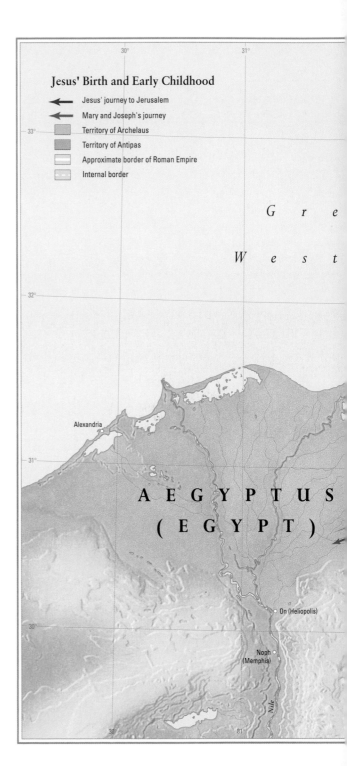

Jesus' Birth and Early Childhood

Jesus' journey to Jerusalem
Mary and Joseph's journey
Territory of Archelaus
Territory of Antipas
Approximate border of Roman Empire
Internal border

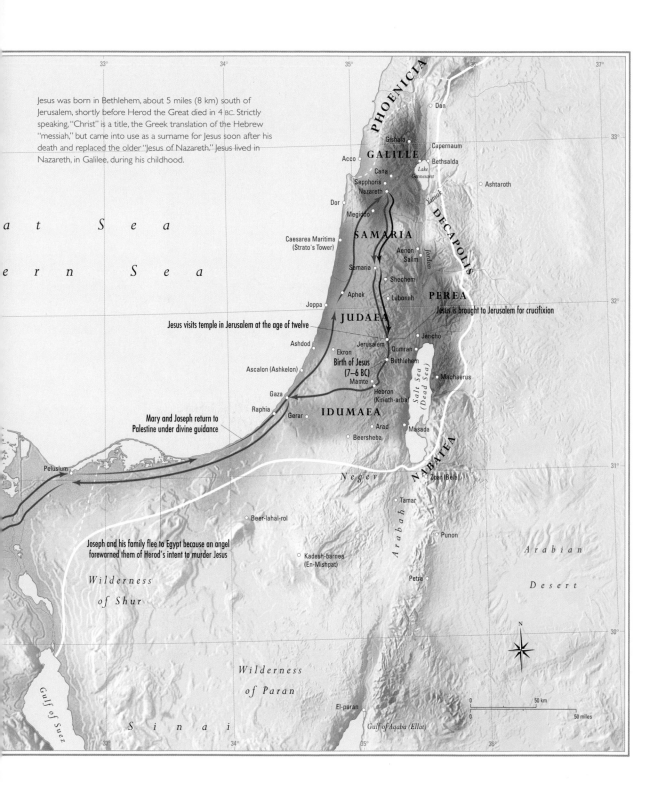

Jesus was born in Bethlehem, about 5 miles (8 km) south of Jerusalem, shortly before Herod the Great died in 4 BC. Strictly speaking, "Christ" is a title, the Greek translation of the Hebrew "messiah," but came into use as a surname for Jesus soon after his death and replaced the older "Jesus of Nazareth." Jesus lived in Nazareth, in Galilee, during his childhood.

PHOENICIA

Dan

Gishala
Capernaum
GALILEE
Acco
Bethsalda
Cana
Lake
Gennesaret
Sepphoris
Nazareth
Ashtaroth
Dor
Megiddo
DECAPOLIS
Yamuk
SAMARIA
Caesarea Maritima
(Strato's Tower)
Aenon
Salim
Samaria
Jordan
Shechem
Aphek
PEREA
Joppa
Lebonah
Jesus is brought to Jerusalem for crucifixion
JUDAEA
Jesus visits temple in Jerusalem at the age of twelve
Jericho
Ashdod
Jerusalem
Qumran
Ekron
Birth of Jesus
Bethlehem
Ascalon (Ashkelon)
(7–6 BC)
Mamre
Machaerus
Gaza
Hebron
Salt Sea
(Dead Sea)
Raphia
(Kiriath-arba)
Gerar
IDUMAEA
Arad
Masada
Mary and Joseph return to
Palestine under divine guidance
Beersheba

Pelusium
Negev
Zoar (Bela)
NABATEA

Tamar

Beer-lahal-rol
Punon
Arabian

Joseph and his family flee to Egypt because an angel
forewarned them of Herod's intent to murder Jesus
Kadesh-barnea
(En-Mishpat)
Desert
Wilderness
Petra
of Shur
Arabah

N

Wilderness
of Paran

El-paran
Gulf of Aqaba (Ellat)
0   50 km
0   50 miles

Gulf of Suez

S i n a i

at Sea

ern Sea

JUDAEA AND GALILEE

WHEN HEROD DIED IN 4 BC, HIS WILL DIVIDED HIS KINGDOM INTO THREE PARTS. ARCHELAUS, HEROD'S SON BY A SAMARITAN WIFE, WAS TO BE KING IN JERUSALEM OVER JUDAEA, IDUMEA, AND SAMARIA. THIS REGION INCLUDED THE HELLENIZED CITIES OF SEBASTE AND CAESAREA.

H erod Antipas, Archelaus' younger brother, was made tetrarch of Galilee and Perea, lands separated by the cities of the Decapolis. Their half-brother Philip—son of Cleopatra, one of Herod's Jewish wives (he had ten wives in total)—was made tetrarch of the predominantly gentile areas north and east of the Sea of Galilee, a sizeable but relatively poor area. Salome, Herod's sister, acquired Jamnia, Azotus, Phaselis, and Herod's palace in the free city of Ascalon. The Hellenized cities of Gaza on the coast and the inland cities of Gadara and Hippus in Transjordan were placed under the governor of Syria. This hotchpotch heritage had many political units, but no real power. Overseeing the entire area was Rome.

In order to have the will ratified by Augustus, Archelaus went to Rome from Caesarea leaving the region in ferment. In Jerusalem, the inhabitants protested against Herod's recent execution of two rabbis. Archelaus, failing in pacifying the crowds, called out troops to stop rioting that left 3,000 of his subjects dead. Even Herod had not managed such a shambles. Philip was left to defuse the situation. Antipas also went to Rome claiming that a previous will made him the ruler of all Herod's kingdom. Philip turned up in time to support Archelaus and his own interests.

Meanwhile, a riotous Jerusalem fomented trouble in the countryside forcing Varus, Roman governor of Syria, to impose control and stability. He left a legion to keep the peace when he returned to Syria, but his main financial official, Sabinus, exacerbated the situation by attempting to grab Herod's treasure and hold it in safe-keeping for the emperor. Archelaus' troops prevented this causing an even more difficult situation. At the Feast of Pentecost, pilgrims from all over Herod's former kingdom flooded the Jerusalem streets and

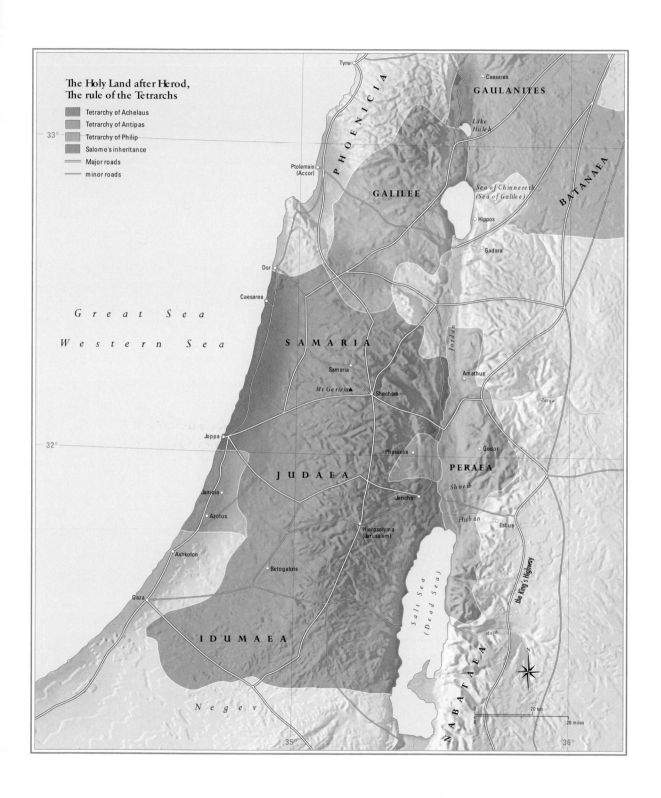

The Holy Land after Herod,
The rule of the Tetrarchs

Tetrarchy of Achelaus
Tetrarchy of Antipas
Tetrarchy of Philip
Salome's inheritance
Major roads
minor roads

33°

32°

Great Sea

Western Sea

PHOENICIA

GALILEE

Tyre

Ptolemais
(Accor)

Dor

Caesarea

SAMARIA

Samaria

Mt Gerizim ▲ Shechem

Joppa

JUDAEA

Jamnia

Azotus

Ashkelon

Betogabris

Gaza

IDUMAEA

Negev

GAULANITES

Caesarea

Lake Huleh

*Sea of Chinnereth
(Sea of Galilee)*

Hippos

Gadara

BATANAEA

Jordan

Amathus

Zarqa

PERAEA

Gedor

Shueib

Jericho

Phasaelis

Hierosolyma
(Jerusalem)

Hisban

Esbus

*Salt Sea
(Dead Sea)*

Mujib

the King's Highway

NABATAEA

0   20 km
0   20 miles

fighting spread through the city. Many of Herod's veteran soldiers joined the rebels while Roman soldiers and 3,000 auxiliaries, mainly from Sebaste, attempted to crush them.

Violent outbreaks occurred all over the country demonstrating its instability. Judaea witnessed 2,000 Herodian veterans driving loyal troops led by Herod's cousin, Achiab, from the plains into the hills. Athronges, a shepherd, claimed kingship and engaged in guerrilla warfare. In Galilee, a thief named Judas terrorized the population and with other bandits captured Sepphoris, plundering the city and its royal palace. Simon, a former slave of Herod, burned the royal palace at Jericho and was probably responsible for torching that at Beth-ramatha. Simon was caught and beheaded, but violence continued in Perea with the Amathus palace being incinerated.

Varus returned from Syria with two legions and cavalry, together with a sizeable Nabatean cavalry and infantry force loaned by Aretas IV. He placed his son in command of an armed detachment to liberate western Galilee. Roman forces captured Sepphoris, selling its inhabitants into slavery and burning the city. Varus spared Sebaste, making camp at Arus to serve as a springboard in an attack against Jerusalem. As Varus marched on Jerusalem, his Nabatean allies torched Arus. They went on to the village of Sappho, as Varus burnt Emmaus. He rapidly cleared Jerusalem, liberating Roman troops held under siege inside the city. Rebels were hunted down and captured; 2,000 were crucified. Achiab persuaded 10,000 men to surrender, their leaders being sent to Rome where they were subsequently released unless they were related to Herod.

THE SYMBOL OF THE SEVEN LAMPS
This symbol derives from a command that Moses was to create for the original Hebrew shrine. The seven lamps joined to a single stem may have symbolized the seven days of creation.

Meanwhile, in Rome, Augustus accepted Herod's will, but reduced Archelaus from king to ethnarch, still a higher rank than that of tetrarch, given to his brothers. Archelaus reigned for nearly ten years when a delegation of Jews and Samaritans complained to Augustus about his harsh rule. The ethnarch was summoned to Rome, deposed and exiled to Gaul. Samaria, Judaea, and Idumea were united as the Roman province of Judaea (AD 6).

Antipas ruled for nearly 43 years bringing peace and prosperity to Galilee and Perea. He succeeded in not offending his Jewish subjects and even managed to acquire the support of the Herodians, a pro-Roman group who preferred

"AND AS SOON AS HE KNEW THAT HE BELONGED UNTO HEROD'S JURISDICTION, HE SENT HIM TO HEROD, WHO HIMSELF ALSO WAS AT JERUSALEM AT THAT TIME.

"AND WHEN HEROD SAW JESUS, HE WAS EXCEEDING GLAD: FOR HE WAS DESIROUS TO SEE HIM OF A LONG SEASON, BECAUSE HE HAD HEARD MANY THINGS OF HIM; AND HE HOPED TO HAVE SEEN SOME MIRACLE DONE BY HIM."   LUKE 23:7-8

indirect rule from Rome through their tetrarch. Antipas rebuilt recently destroyed cities renaming Sepphoris Autocratoris and Beth-ramatha as Livias in honour of the emperor's wife. He also built Tiberias, renowned for its warm springs.

Antipas divorced his first wife, a daughter of Aretas IV of Nabatea and married Herodias, former wife of his half-brother Herod, thereby instigating a war with Aretas in which Antipas was defeated. John the Baptist criticised his marriage, resulting in his being beheaded after the manipulation of Antipas by Herodias and her daughter, Salome. After persistent harassment by his wife, Antipas went to Rome demanding that Emperor Caligula make him king. Caligula promptly deposed him, exiling him to Lugdunum (Lyons) in Gaul. It is to Herod Antipas that Pontius Pilate, procurator of Judaea, sent Jesus (Luke 23: 7–15).

Philip was the most successful heir to Herod. His land was the rugged north, mountainous, with rough steppe and plateaux. The mainly gentile population was ruled in a gentle, moderate fashion. He enlarged Paneas, making it his capital and renaming it Caesarea Philippi. Near where the Jordan flows into the Sea of Galilee, he turned the fishing village of Bethsaida into a town he called Julias. Bethsaida was the home of Jesus' disciples, Peter, Andrew and Philip. He lived quietly with his wife Salome, the same who was responsible for the death of John the Baptist.

The peace established by Antipas and Philip continued during the first three Roman governors. Caesarea Maritima took over from Jerusalem as the capital and the only armed force present were 3,000 auxiliaries drawn from the local populations of non-Jewish Sebaste and Caesarea. The comfortable existence was shattered when Valerius Gratus, the first governor of Emperor Tiberias, came to Judaea in AD 15. He deposed the High Priest, Annas, the post eventually going to his son-in-law Joseph Caiaphas. This hostile personality worked with Governor Pontius Pilate, a man who failed to understand the national pride and religious convictions of Jews, and who gave way to the Sanhedrin, sentencing Jesus to death.

THE MINISTRY OF JESUS

JESUS DID NOT BEGIN HIS MINISTRY UNTIL HE WAS 30 YEARS OLD, HOWEVER THE PREACHING OF JOHN THE BAPTIST PREPARED THE WAY FOR HIM.

BAPTISM OF CHRIST
This mosaic from the Arian Baptistry in Ravenna dates from the 5th Century AD. The Holy Spirit in the form of a dove descends onto the figure of Jesus. The figure on the right is John the Baptist; the figure on the left may represent God the Father.

Zacharias was a priest, and he and his wife Elisabeth were godly people, but elderly and childless. The archangel Gabriel appeared to Zacharias and told that his wife would have a son, who would be called John and be a great man of God. Zacharias could not believe that he and Elisabeth could have a child at their age and because of his disbelief he was temporarily made dumb, but his affliction left him after Elisabeth gave birth to John.

John became a preacher, living an ascetic life in the desert. His message centered on the need for repentance and baptism, and he spoke of a greater one who would come after him. John baptised many people in the River Jordan, including Jesus. At the moment John baptised Jesus, the Holy Spirit descended in the form of a dove and a voice from heaven said, "Thou art my beloved son. In thee I am well pleased."

John's uncompromising preaching made him enemies and when he criticised Herod (son of Herod the Great) for marrying his brother's wife Herodias, he was imprisoned. On Herod's birthday, Herodias's daughter, Salome, came in and danced for him and she pleased her stepfather so much that he promised to give her anything she asked for. After consulting her mother, Salome asked for the head of John the Baptist on a dish. Herod kept his promise and John was beheaded. After his baptism, Jesus went into the desert and fasted for 40 days and nights. The Devil tempted him, suggesting that if Jesus were God's son he could turn the stones into bread, but Jesus resisted him. The Devil then tempted Jesus with

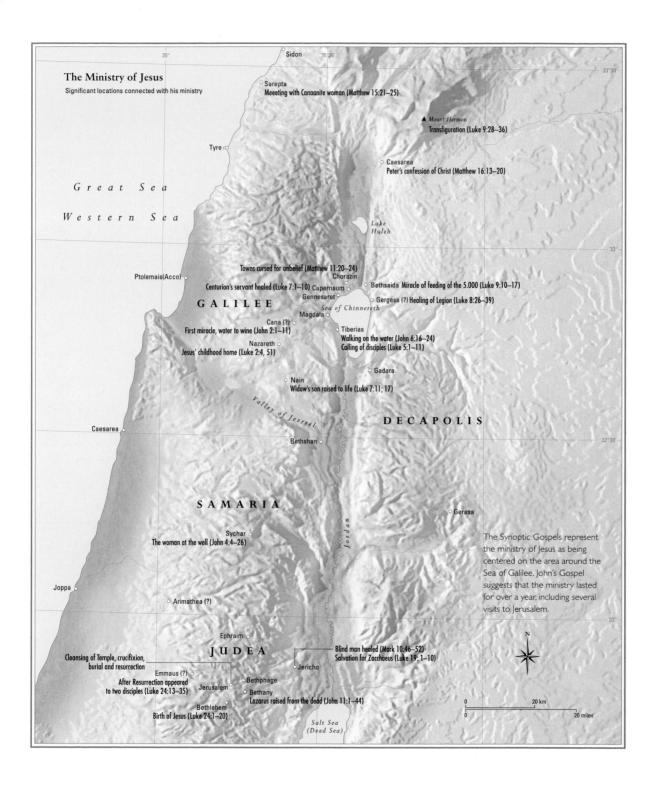

The Ministry of Jesus
Significant locations connected with his ministry

Sidon

Sarepta
Meeeting with Canaanite woman (Matthew 15:21–25)

▲ *Mount Hermon*
Transfiguration (Luke 9:28–36)

Tyre

Caesarea
Peter's confession of Christ (Matthew 16:13–20)

Great Sea

Western Sea

Lake Huleh

Towns cursed for unbelief (Matthew 11:20–24)
Chorazin
Ptolemais(Acco)
Centurion's servant healed (Luke 7:1–10)   Capernaum
Bethsaida Miracle of feeding of the 5.000 (Luke 9:10–17)
Gennesaret
GALILEE   Gergesa (?) Healing of Legion (Luke 8:26–39)
Sea of Chinnereth
Cana (?)   Magdala
First miracle, water to wine (John 2:1–11)
Tiberias
Nazareth   Walking on the water (John 6:16–24)
Jesus' childhood home (Luke 2:4, 51)   Calling of disciples (Luke 5:1–11)

Gadara

Nain
Widow's son raised to life (Luke 7:11; 17)

Valley of Jezreel

DECAPOLIS

Caesarea

Bethshan

SAMARIA

Gerasa

Jordan

Sychar
The woman at the well (John 4:4–26)

The Synoptic Gospels represent
the ministry of Jesus as being
centered on the area around the
Sea of Galilee. John's Gospel
suggests that the ministry lasted
for over a year, including several
visits to Jerusalem.

Joppa

Arimathea (?)

Ephraim

JUDEA
Cleansing of Temple, crucifixion,   Blind man healed (Mark 10:46–52)
burial and resurrection   Salvation for Zacchaeus (Luke 19: 1–10)
Emmaus (?)   Jericho
After Resurrection appeared   Bethphage
to two disciples (Luke 24:13–35)   Jerusalem
Bethany
Bethlehem   Lazarus raised from the dead (John 11:1–44)
Birth of Jesus (Luke 24:1–20)

*Salt Sea
(Dead Sea)*

N

0   20 km
0   20 miles

power and wealth, but Jesus resisted him. Jesus was led to Jerusalem, to the highest point of the Temple, where the Devil prompted him to throw himself down to test whether God would same him, but again Jesus managed to resist temptation.

Jesus now began his ministry in Galilee, preaching and healing, and immediately he began to attract crowds who recognized his gifts and authority. He began to collect a following and called 12 men to be his particular disciples and accompany him everywhere. The first of these were two pairs of brothers, Peter and Andrew and James and John. These four were all fishermen and Jesus called them from their boats and nets to follow him. Another of the disciples, Matthew, was a tax collector. This was a despised profession, but Jesus called Matthew from his office all the same.

Jesus delivered his message to different types and size of audience: to individuals, to the intimate group of his disciples, to the congregation in a synagogue, and to huge crowds gathered in the open air. The content of his preaching also varied widely, but the main themes were the fatherhood and authority of God and the need for personal righteousness and selfless love. It was mainly with his disciples that he spoke of his role as the Son of God and predicted his own death and resurrection.

Probably the most memorable of Jesus' sermons was the Sermon on the Mount, delivered to his disciples and a large crowd that had gathered to listen. It is a revolutionary sermon, starting with the Beatitudes, where Jesus states that happiness lies, not in wealth, health or success, but in humility, mercy, peacemaking, and spiritual hunger. He went on to suggest that anger is as great a sin as murder, and lustful thoughts as bad as adultery. He urged love for one's enemies, disregard for money and possessions and attention to our own sins, rather than condemnation of the sins of others. He warned his hearers to avoid hypocritical, ostentatious worship and prayer, and taught them the prayer that has come to be known as the Lord's Prayer.

One of the most striking aspects of Jesus' preaching was his habit of conveying his message by means of parables: short allegorical stories of everyday life that illustrated the spiritual points that he wished to make. Many striking parables are related in the Gospels; the best known are probably the stories of the Good Samaritan and the Prodigal Son. The former tells the story of a man who was attacked and robbed by thieves and left wounded on the road. First a priest and then a Levite came along the road and saw him, but both passed by on the other side. Then a Samaritan man came along. Jews and Samaritans were traditionally hostile to each other, but this Samaritan tended to the injured man, bound his wounds and paid for him to be cared for at the local inn.

The story illustrated the doctrine that we should love our neighbors, and that our neighbor is anyone in need. The parable of the prodigal son illustrated the fatherly love and mercy of God with a story of a young man who leaves home and squanders all his inheritance on riotous living until he is reduced to penury and degradation. When he shamefully returns home, he is joyfully welcomed and forgiven by his father.

In his three-year ministry, Jesus performed many miracles, the majority of which were concerned with healing of either physical or mental sickness. He restored sight to the blind, speech to the dumb, and hearing to the deaf (e.g. Matthew 9:27–33; 12:22; 20:29–34). He healed people suffering with leprosy, paralysis and epilepsy (e.g. Matthew 8:2–3; 9:2–7; 17:14–18). He delivered people from demonic possession (e.g. Luke 4:33–35; 8:27–35; 11:14). He was able to heal from a distance, without

JESUS' FIRST MIRACLE
(far right)
This early 14th-century
Byzantine mosaic portrays the
miracle at the wedding in
Cana, when Jesus transformed
water into wine.

even seeing the sick people (John 4:46–54). On three occasions he raised people from the dead: a widow's son and Jairus's young daughter (Luke 7:11–15; 8:41–42, 49–56); and Lazarus, Jesus' friend, who was raised after having been dead and buried for four days (John 11:1–44).

There were also miracles that involved a supernatural mastery over natural forces. Many of these miracles happened on the sea: the calming of the storm (Matthew 8:23–27); Jesus walking on the water (John 6:19–21); two miraculous catches of fish (Luke 5:1–11; John 21:1–11); and the coin found in the fish's mouth (Matthew 17:24–27). Other miracles in this category include the feeding of the 5,000, when a vast crowd was fed by the multiplication of five loaves and two small fishes (Matthew 14:15–21), and the transformation of water into wine when drink ran out at a wedding feast at Cana (John 2:1–11).

The people who were closest to Jesus, once his ministry had started, were undoubtedly his disciples. The men whose relationship with Jesus were the most intimate were apparently Peter, James, and John. John is described as "the disciple whom Jesus loved." Besides these, there were several women who were close to Jesus, particularly Mary Magdalene, whom he had healed of demonic possession, and the two sisters from Bethany, Martha and Mary, whose brother, Lazarus, was raised from the dead by Jesus. In his attitude toward Mary of Bethany, Jesus demonstrated his disregard for the conventions of the day, when women were not expected to attend to religious teaching. Martha was annoyed when her sister sat at Jesus' feet listening to his teaching, rather than helping with the domestic chores, but Jesus gently rebuked Martha for fussing, and commended Mary's choice (Luke 10:38–42). Jesus' love and compassion for the family at Bethany is shown by his tears over the death of Lazarus (John 11:33–36).

Another example of Jesus' disregard for the conventions of both sex and race is his conversation with a Samaritan woman (John 4:4–26); it was unheard of for a Jewish teacher to speak to a strange woman, and Jews and Samaritans did not mix. His concern for individuals is shown again in his encounter with the notoriously fraudulent tax collector, Zacchaeus (Luke 19:1–10), who climbed a tree to get a better view when Jesus came to Jericho. Jesus called Zacchaeus down and said that he was going to stay at his house, and Zacchaeus repented of his cheating.

Jesus was happier in the company of repentant tax collectors and prostitutes than with the religious leaders and teachers of his day, particularly the strict legalistic sect of Pharisees. He often rebuked them for their hypocrisy, and they constantly sought to catch him out in flouting the law. This often involved Jesus' attitude to the Sabbath; traditionally this was a day of rest from work, but Jesus thought that healing on this holy day was legitimate. The story of the woman taken in adultery (John 8:1–11) illustrates Jesus' conflict with the Pharisees and compassion for individual sinners. The Pharisees had caught an adultress and asked Jesus why she should not be stoned to death, as the law strictly demanded. Jesus' reply was to challenge the Pharisees: "He that is without sin amongst you, let him first cast a stone at her," and the woman's accusers went away one by one.

THE LAST DAYS OF JESUS

"FOR MINE HOUSE SHALL BE CALLED AN HOUSE OF PRAYER
FOR ALL PEOPLE"   ISAIAH 56:7

"IS THIS HOUSE WHICH IS CALLED BY MY NAME, BECOME A DEN
OF ROBBERS IN YOUR EYES? BEHOLD, EVEN I HAVE SEEN IT, SAITH
THE LORD"   JEREMIAH 7:11

While in Galilee, Jesus had created a movement allowing a circle of disciples and followers to share in his ministry and wanderings. Tradition has identified the latter group with the Apostles. Their number symbolizes the 12 tribes of Israel. If Jesus did appoint these men, then he made an eschatological claim on the whole of Israel. According to Matthew 19:28 and Luke 22:30, he conferred on the 12 the task of ruling and judging a perfected Israel when the New Age dawned.

Jesus went to Jerusalem probably several times, as John's Gospel alleges, but he decided to go there for what was his last Passover in order to reach a wider audience, calling the people of Israel together to teach of the coming Kingdom of God. Conflict with religious authorities was highly likely, and Jesus must have been aware of this possibility. He, maybe, even imagines his arrest and execution. Possibly, he wished to proclaim his message before being silenced for ever.

Jesus would face both Pharisees and Sadducees in Jerusalem, the latter controlling the Sanhedrin and using wide powers under the Romans. They certainly opposed any apparently political activity amongst the population, seeing such as a threat to the Romans and themselves. Maybe, Jesus had locked horns with these groups in Galilee. Certainly, his ministry would have become news. He taught in the city and there are vignettes of him "that on one of those days, as he taught the people in the Temple and preached the gospel, the chief priests and the scribes came upon him..." (Luke 20:1).

What is interesting is the violent way in which Jesus sought to cleanse the Temple by driving out the traders and money changers. Mark claims he upset the tables while John reports he made a whip of cords to lash these people in his drive to clear the building. His actions were an attempt to end the secularisation of the Temple. The money changers were there to exchange Greek and Roman coinage for Jewish currency, which would be used to pay Temple dues. Possibly, Jesus objected to the manner of sacrifice. Detailed regulations governed such rituals with the implication that following rules was sufficient to worship God. Jesus was witnessing the perceived economic and spiritual injustice in the "corrupt" operation of the Temple. Interestingly, the merchants business was transacted in the large outer court of the Temple, the only part of the Temple where Gentiles might go. Qumran texts also allude to the Temple as a seat of robbers. There is an accusation reportedly levelled at Jesus' trial that "We heard him say, I will destroy this temple that is made with hands, and within three days I will build another made without hands." (Mark 14:58). Layered upon this is the prediction of Jesus' own resurrection after three days, which would signal the new age and the Kingdom of God. Whatever the case, Jesus was not arrested because of the people's sympathy. "And he taught, saying unto them, Is it not written, My house shall be called of all nations the house of prayer? But ye have made it a den of thieves. And the scribes and chief priests heard it, and sought how they might destroy him: for they feared him, because all the people was astonished at his doctrine" (Mark 11:17–18). "And could not find what they might do: for all the people were very attentive to hear him" (Luke 19:48). Jesus was appealing to the Biblical prophets and their condemnation of moral injustice in the cult of Yahweh, interpreting the present corruption of the priestly caste as doomed to destruction.

Jesus was acting very much like a Jeremiah causing offence and political liability to the priestly hierarchy and to many others in Jerusalem whose social and material status depended upon the Temple trade. Jesus also disputed with the chief priests, the scribes, the Pharisees, and the Sadducees' questions about his authority, tribute to Caesar, and the Resurrection.

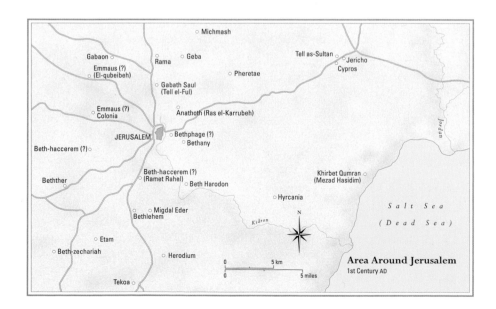

Area Around Jerusalem
1st Century AD

"Is it lawful for us to give tribute unto Caesar, or no? But he perceived their craftiness, and said unto them, Why tempt me ye? Shew me a penny. Whose image and superscription hath it? They answered and said, Caesar's. And he said unto them, Render therefore unto Caesar the things which be Caesar's, and unto God the things which be God's" (Luke 22:22–25).

Jesus also told his disciples the signs that would usher in the second coming, the Parousia. Jesus went to Bethany just before Passover and was anointed with spikenard in preparation for his burial (Matthew 26:6–13; Mark 14:3–9).

When Jesus finally entered Jerusalem, the crowds publicly acclaimed him, calling him the Messiah, very much as the old kings of Israel were acclaimed after being anointed. Some even shouted "God bless the King of Israel."

"ON THE NEXT DAY MUCH PEOPLE THAT WERE COME TO THE FEAST, WHEN THEY HEARD THAT JESUS WAS COMING TO JERUSALEM, TOOK BRANCHES OF PALM TREES AND WENT FORTH TO MEET HIM, AND CRIED, HOSANNA: BLESSED IS THE KING OF ISRAEL THAT COMETH IN THE NAME OF THE LORD. AND JESUS, WHEN HE HAD FOUND A YOUNG ASS, SAT THEREON; AS IT IS WRITTEN, FEAR NOT DAUGHTER OF SION: BEHOLD, THY KING COMETH, SITTING ON AN ASS'S COLT." (JOHN 12:12–15)

Despite attempts to disassociate himself from politics, Jesus was increasingly identified with the desired national Messiah who would free Israel from Roman rule and re-create a Jewish state. Certainly his popular support was visible, volatile, and potentially explosive, so the authorities were bound to arrest him for sedition or some trumped-up charge.

As Jesus' popularity grew, the chief priests and scribes saw him as increasingly dangerous and they were determined to kill him. Just before the Passover, they met to plot against him. Judas Iscariot, one of the 12 disciples, went to them and agreed to betray his master in exchange for 30 pieces of silver. Jesus and his 12 disciples gathered in a room of a house in Jerusalem to eat the Passover meal. During the repast, Jesus made two predictions. He said that one of their number would betray him and that Peter would deny him three times before the cock crowed next morning. Historians have disputed the exact sequence of events taking into account Jewish Law and the date of the Passover, but the meaning of events is more significant than an exact chronology. The chances are, without entering a complicated argument, that the chronology of John is more likely, that the meal, the trial and crucifixion took place on the day preceding the Passover.

While they were eating, Jesus broke the bread, gave thanks, handing it to his disciples, saying, "Take, eat; this is my body." Then he gave them wine to drink, saying, "This is my blood ... shed for many for the remission of sins" (Matthew 26:28). The testament can be regarded as a new covenant with God and this ritual, the Eucharist, has been repeated by Christians in services ever since, becoming the central sacrament in the Christian churches. The historicity of the Last Supper is uncertain and not all historians accept that Jesus meant there to be any major ritual meaning in his actions. However, the meal is mentioned in the Gospels, being symbolic of the group's "communion" with God. Additionally, Jesus knew Jewish religious books, or he would not have used the words of Isaiah and Jeremiah regarding the Temple. Surely, since he publicised himself in prophetical terms, he would cleanse the Temple and enact a new covenant with God as had occurred so often in Jewish history. The Last Supper is part of the Christian tradition and is mentioned by St. Paul in his letters (1 Corinthians 11:23–26).

Jesus went with Peter, James and John to Gethsemane, a garden on the slopes of the Mount of Olives. He was in a state of deep sorrow, "being in an agony" (Luke 22:44), and retreated to pray by himself, begging God to take the burden of suffering from him.

When he returned to the disciples, they had fallen asleep. He spoke to them, and they observed Judas Iscariot approaching, with an armed crowd. Judas went up to Jesus and kissed him, as a sign that this was the man that they were to arrest. Jesus was seized and taken to the high priest's house; his disciples ran away.

Jesus was accused of blasphemy and physically abused and mocked. Meanwhile, Peter stayed in the courtyard of the high priest's house to see what would happen. As he sat there, a servant girl approached him and asked if he was one of the men who were with Jesus. Peter denied knowledge of Jesus. Another servant girl asked the same question, Peter again denying Jesus. One of the men there insisted that Peter was one of Jesus' friends because his Galilean accent gave him away. Yet again, Peter denied all knowledge of Jesus; then, the cock crowed.

The high priest was Caiaphas who retained his position from AD 18–36, although his father-in-law, Annas, deposed from the position, called the shots from behind the scenes. The Sanhedrin, sitting in judgement over Jesus, comprised, apart from the high priest, 70 members drawn from three different groups in society. The first group were known as "the high priests," these being priests and laymen directed by the high priest, being in charge of the day-to-day administration of religious affairs. The second group, "the elders," were the heads of distinguished families. Their contribution gradually diminished because they became increasingly incapable of dealing with religious schisms. The final group had an increasing influence. These scribes, men who had studied and could interpret the Law and apply it to everyday affairs. In the Sanhedrin, the Pharisees and Sadducees had various supporters, the Sadducees being dominant. Their supporters could be found amongst "the high priests" and "elders" whereas the Pharisees were strong with the scribes who represented the Pharisaic school. The composition of the Sanhedrin bode ill for Jesus, who could expect neither sympathy nor mercy.

Jesus would also face Pontius Pilate, the Roman governor, who understood nothing of Jewish culture or religion. He was merely concerned with the authority of Rome, trampling on everybody's feelings. He allowed his troops to enter Jerusalem carrying insignia showing the Emperor's image. Octavian, Augustus Caesar, had previously promised the Jews that he would grant Jerusalem immunity from any sign of the cult of the ruler. Pilate would only listen to people's demands when they became exceedingly vociferous. He even took money from the Temple money chest to pay for a water conduit that was to lead from the pools of Solomon to Jerusalem. In AD 36 when disturbances erupted in Samaria, he used so much brutality and violence that the Emperor had him removed. This, then, was the personality that Jesus would face.

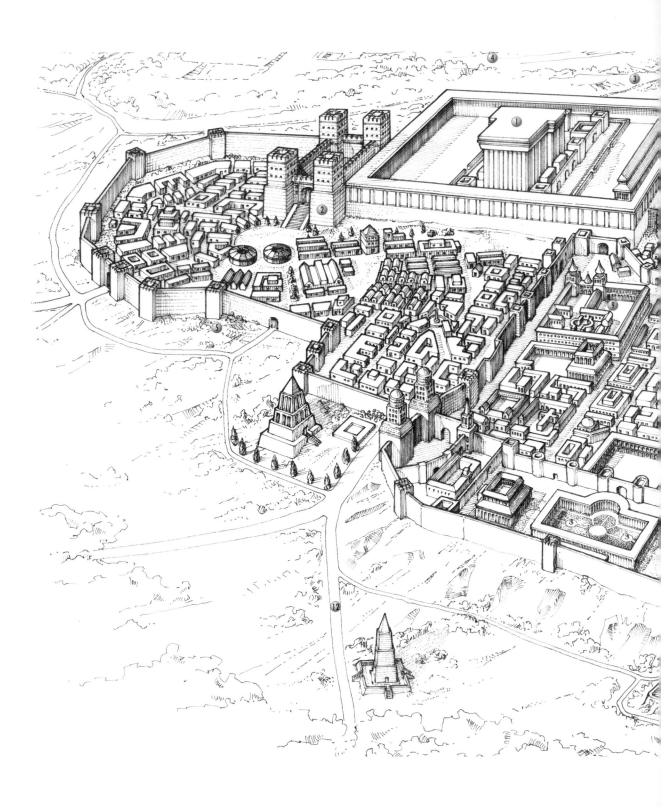

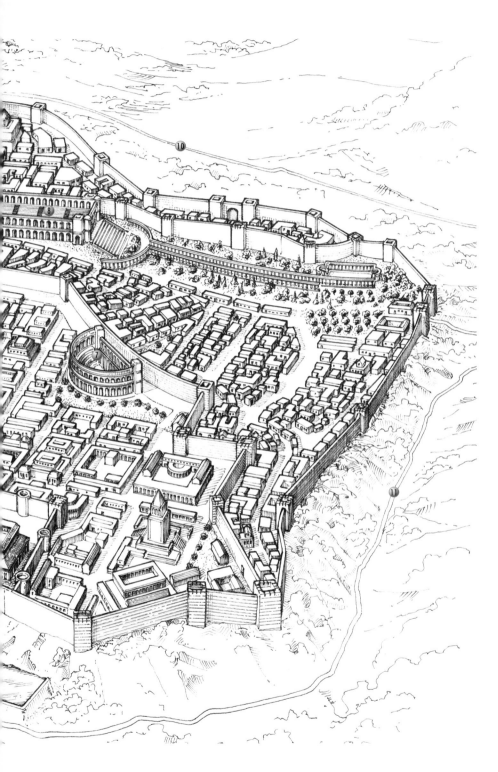

JERUSALEM
This illustration shows the city
of Jerusalem in the time of Jesus.
The impression is based on
archaeological finds, though the
exact layout of the city will
never be known.

1. The Temple
2. Fortress of Antonia
3. Garden of Gethsemane
4. Mount of Olives
5. Calvary (Golgotha)
6. Herod's Palace
7. Theater
8. Hippodrome
9. Hasmonean Palace
10. Kidron Valley
11. Hinnom Valley
12. Bethlehem Road

DEATH OF JESUS

"THE PASSION" IS THE TERM APPLIED TO THE SUFFERINGS OF
JESUS FROM HIS PRAYERS IN THE GARDEN OF GETHSEMANE, TO
HIS ARREST, TRIAL, JOURNEY TO CALVARY, AND HIS CRUCIFIXION.
IT IS SOMETIMES EXTENDED TO INCLUDE THE LAST SUPPER. ALL
THESE EVENTS TOOK PLACE IN JERUSALEM, BUT THERE HAS BEEN
MUCH DISPUTE AS TO THE EXACT LOCATION.

According to John (18:13–24), Jesus was taken before Annas for investigation. The Synoptic Gospels fail to mention this occurrence, stating that Jesus was taken before the Sanhedrin. Here, Caiaphas asked Jesus to say whether he was "the Christ (Messiah), the Son of God" (Matthew 26:63). His "affirmation" (Mark 14:62) caused the Sanhedrin to condemn Jesus to death for blasphemy. However, only the Roman Governor, Pilate, was empowered to use capital punishment. So Jesus was possibly taken to the fortress by the Temple Mount, the traditional site for the trial, near what is now the Ecce Homo (Behold the Man) arch where Pilate is believed to have shown Jesus to the crowd. Pilate asked him if he was King of the Jews. Jesus replied, "You have said so" (Mark 15:2). Pilate tried several times to save Jesus, but finally left the decision to the priests and rabble. When the people demanded his death, Pilate ordered him to be executed (Matthew 27:24).

PONTIUS PILATE WASHES HIS HANDS *(far right)*
This famous scene in the life of Jesus is portrayed by a 15th-Century Italian artist who shows Pontius Pilate washing his hands in front of the crowd.

Jesus was whipped and mocked by Roman soldiers who made him a crown of thorns. He was taken to the place of crucifixion—Calvary, or Golgotha—where he was nailed to the cross and left to die, along with two criminals who were being similarly punished. The traditional route to Golgotha is the Via Dolorosa and the place of execution was where the Church of the Holy Sepulchre now stands. Crucifixion was the normal Roman punishment for political offenders and criminals. On the cross above Jesus' head was a statement saying "This is Jesus the King of the Jews" (Matthew 27:37).

Later, the body was taken down, and owing to the approach of the Sabbath, was quickly put in a nearby tomb by Joseph of Arimathea, and, according to John, by Nicodemus.

Early, the following Sunday, Mary Magdalene and Mary, the mother of James, went to the tomb to anoint Jesus' body for a proper burial, but found the tomb empty. Mark claims that a young man clothed in white was in the tomb, announcing that Jesus had risen. According to John (21:11–18), Mary Magdalene saw two angels and then the risen Jesus. Later on the same day, Jesus apparently appeared to disciples in various places around Jerusalem. Most disciples knew what they had seen, but Thomas doubted. The Resurrection of Jesus became the most compelling doctrine of Christianity because, by rising from the dead, Jesus gave hope of a life after death in the Kingdom of Heaven. All the Gospels state that after the Resurrection, Jesus continued to teach his disciples about the Kingdom of God. He also said, "Go ye therefore, and teach all nations, baptising them in the name of the Father, and of the Son, and of the Holy Ghost: Teaching them to observe whatsoever I have commanded you: and, lo, I am with you always, even unto the end of the world. Amen" (Matthew 28:19–20). Eventually, according to Luke, at Bethany, Jesus was seen by his disciples to ascend into the heavens. The Acts of the Apostles claim that the ascension took place 40 days after the Resurrection.

The Gospels of the New Testament were written about 15 years after these events. Previously, Jesus' teachings were transmitted orally by people who had known him. The disciples and witnesses of the Crucifixion and Resurrection saw themselves as the chosen people who were offering salvation to the world by trying to live as Jesus had done. They continued to worship in the Temple and synagogues of Judaism, but their experience of the Eucharist led them to a new interpretation of the Passover, the new covenant.

The disciples started to preach, as described in the Acts of the Apostles. The general structure and contents of the apostles' sermons and speeches are reflected in the Letters of the New Testament. Those who listened to the apostles heard that God's revelations in the Old Testament had reached their climax and fulfilment in the life, death and resurrection of Jesus. He was the Messiah, the Christ. He had come from God and had now returned to Him to be "Lord of the whole creation," as both man and God. Through the Holy Spirit, Jesus Christ now shared his powers with the members of the Christian community, which was open to all who were prepared to turn to God, to accept Jesus as Lord, and to receive baptism. They were told to act swiftly because God would soon bring his whole plan of salvation to its completion with the second coming of Jesus and a general judgement of all people.

The apostles supported their preaching and teaching with recollections of Jesus' life as they had witnessed it. They told of the things he had done and related, particularly details of his final days in Jerusalem, leading up to his Crucifixion and Resurrection. Christianity was still based on word of mouth, but the people who had known Jesus personally began to die or be killed. Hence, the Gospels were written down to record the apostles' experiences of Jesus. Some of this material may have been written down earlier, but it was not until about AD 65 that the first of the Gospels (probably Mark) was written in the form that is familiar today. This was some 35 years after the death of Jesus. During the next 20 years, the other three Gospels were written. The Gospels differ: the Synoptic Gospels of

CRUCIFIXION OF JESUS
This representation of the
Crucifixion is a woodcut by
the German artist Albrecht
Dürer (1471–1528).

Matthew, Mark, and Luke emphasise the messianic vocation of Jesus and concern themselves with everyday religious and ethical matters. In addition, John states the nature and purpose of Jesus from the start of the Gospel and expresses Jesus' divine nature and relationship to God. The New Testament Letters date from about AD 45 to the end of the 1st Century.

CONVERSION OF SAUL

"AND SAUL, YET BREATHING OUT THREATENINGS AND SLAUGHTER AGAINST THE DISCIPLES OF THE LORD, WENT UNTO THE HIGH PRIEST, AND DESIRED OF HIM LETTERS TO DAMASCUS TO THE SYNAGOGUES, THAT IF HE FOUND ANY OF THIS WAY, WHETHER THEY WERE MEN OR WOMEN, HE MIGHT BRING THEM BOUND UNTO JERUSALEM."

ACTS 9:1–2

THE CONVERSION OF SAUL
(far right)
Saul journeyed from his home in Tarsus to Jerusalem as a zealous follower of Judaism. It was in Jerusalem that he defended the tradition of his fathers, believing that Jesus' message was undermining his ancient faith. While in Jerusalem, Saul secured authority from the High Priest to travel to Damascus in order to root out any followers of Jesus he found there. The road to Damascus would change his life.

Saul of Tarsus, an enthusiastic youthful Pharisee, was born into a strict Jewish family in the town of Tarsus in Cilicia. He enjoyed Roman citizenship, inherited from his father, also a worthy and committed Pharisee. Saul was considered capable of further education and traveled to Jerusalem to study under the great teacher, Rabbi Gamaliel. Saul was an eager student ready to follow and confirm the ancient faith of his forefathers. The message of Jesus seemed to Saul to undermine all of his beliefs, leading him to oppose Jesus, his teachings and his followers with extreme ferocity. He was happy to hunt down the followers of Jesus in and around the city of Jerusalem.

He was an approving witness to the stoning of Stephen. As Stephen was laid in his grave, Saul continued to ravage the followers of Jesus. While in Jerusalem, Saul was able to secure the necessary authority from the High Priest to travel to Damascus to search out and punish any followers of Jesus found in the synagogue there. With this heartfelt objective he hurried north from Jerusalem.

As Saul approached Damascus, he experienced a blinding vision, "Saul, Saul, why do you persecute me?" a voice clearly called out. Saul asked who it was who called. Saul heard the challenging words, "I am Jesus, whom you are persecuting; but rise and enter the city and you will be told what you are to do." The blinded Saul was led by his companions into Damascus where he lay for three days refusing food and drink.

The disciple Ananias was instructed, in a vision, to lay his hands on Saul in order to restore his sight. "Something like scales fell from his eyes." Saul arose and was immediately baptized. In the synagogues of the city, Saul began to proclaim Jesus as the Son of God. There was immediately confusion among Saul's personal followers and among the Jews who knew of Saul's previous anti-Christian fervor. His friends hatched a plot to kill him. Although Saul managed to escape from them, he now had new enemies. Saul was lowered over the city walls in a basket and made good his escape southwards into Arabia, into the hands of the Nabateans under their King, Aretas.

Some three years later Saul, whom we can now call Paul, reappeared in Jerusalem. He was received with some reluctance by the disciples, but

"BUT BARNABAS TOOK HIM, AND BROUGHT HIM TO THE APOSTLES, AND DECLARED UNTO THEM HOW HE HAD SEEN THE LORD IN THE WAY, AND THAT HE HAD SPOKEN TO HIM, AND HOW HE HAD PREACHED BOLDLY AT DAMASCUS IN THE NAME OF JESUS."
ACTS 9:27

he was soon preaching fearlessly and, in so doing, earned the anger of Jerusalem's conservative Hellenists. He fled the dangers of Jerusalem to Caesarea, then by ship to his home in Tarsus. He remained there until he went with Barnabas to Antioch where they worked tirelessly for a year to build the new Church. By now the disciples were, for the first time, called Christians.

Some time later famine struck Judaea, and the church in Antioch decided to send relief, which was taken south by Paul and Barnabas. At about this time the infant Christian community was subject to various bouts of persecution. Herod Agrippa decided to strike at the Christian leadership, hoping this would destroy the whole community. At Passover the apostle Peter was thrown into prison and James was killed.

The night before Peter's trial he miraculously escaped, eventually leaving Jerusalem for a safe hiding place. The Christian leadership, with Paul amongst them, survived. Later, during a public spectacle, according to Josephus, Agrippa was overcome by intense pains and died shortly afterwards. The Christians regarded this as divine judgement for his persecution of their Church.

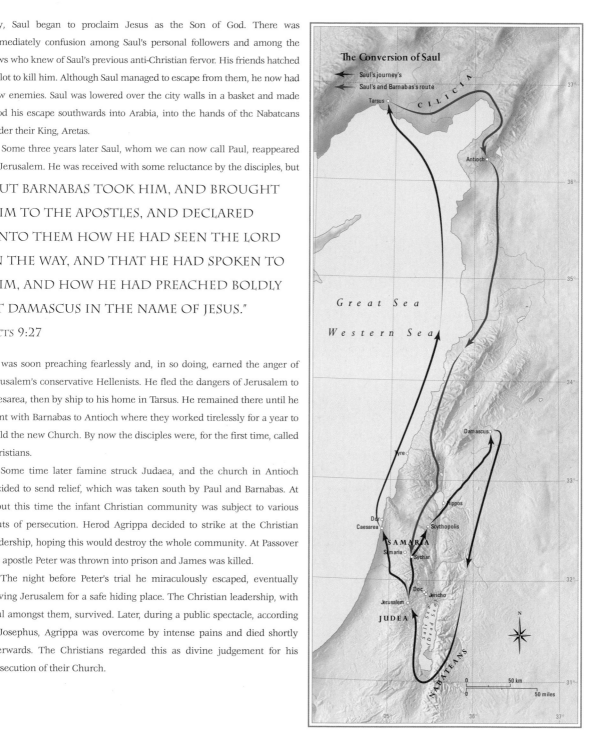

Paul's Missionary Journeys

SOON THERE WERE CHRISTIAN CHURCHES IN ASIA MINOR AND GREECE, WHERE PAUL HAD CONCENTRATED HIS MISSIONARY EFFORTS BETWEEN ABOUT AD 49 AND 58. HIS LETTERS TO HIS CONVERTS WERE GENERALLY IN RESPONSE TO SPECIFIC PROBLEMS AND HE CHIDED, PRAISED, SHOWED ANGER, AND EVEN ENGAGED IN SELF-ANALYSIS.

The meeting of Church leaders in Jerusalem, which thrashed out the difficulties of non-Jews who became Christians, took place in AD 48, 18 years after the death of Jesus. Almost all the available information in the New Testament now concentrates on the journeys of Paul into Asia Minor and Europe, until he reached Rome in AD 61. Undoubtedly there was much Christian activity before the war between the Jews and the Romans from AD 66 to 70, which led to the destruction of Jerusalem. By then, there were Christian churches in many places in the Near East and in Rome, only some of which had been founded by Paul on his first missionary journey, which took him to the island of Cyprus and the southern part of Asia Minor. The traditional belief that Peter started the Church in Rome should be seen in this context.

Paul set out on his second missionary journey in AD 49, only intending to revisit the places where he had founded churches on his first journey. He and his companions traveled by land into Galatia again, where Paul changed his plans by going to Troas, the busy port near the old site of Troy. From Troas, Paul and his party—including Luke—sailed to Neapolis, on the main land route from Italy to the east, and began their dramatic mission through Macedonia and Greece. Paul's letters show that he succeeded in forming small Christian groups in the towns he visited, but the reception he and his companions received was mixed, and occasionally violent.

At Philippi, where they went after Neapolis, Paul's party ran into trouble which reveals much about the political problems of provincial towns in the Roman Empire. Paul and Silas were arrested, flogged and

Engraved for The Revd. Dr. Southwell's Family Bible.

The priest of Jupiter
would have done sacrifice, &c.
ACTS. XIV. 13.

Corneille pinx.

Royce sculp.

PAUL & BARNABAS reputed as GODS.

PAUL AND BARNABAS
In this engraving produced for a family Bible, the scene depicted is of Lystra when Paul and Barnabas were mistaken for the Greek gods Hermes and Zeus.

PAUL'S JOURNEYS
(far right)
Christianity began as a Jewish movement and spread from Palestine through the Hebrew groups dispersed in the main cities of the Roman Empire. Paul was largely instrumental in this success.

imprisoned to await trial on a charge of advocating practices unlawful for Romans. However, the two men were Roman citizens, a status that should have protected them from such treatment, and they were released. Citizenship was an honor that could be given by the Roman state or purchased; Paul had inherited his.

Thessalonica, a later stop, was a free city, where the Romans allowed locally elected magistrates to control affairs. Any hint of disloyalty to Rome would have ended such privileges, and Paul's party fled from the city when his new converts were accused of treason. They were again opposed in the next town, Beroea. As more trouble erupted, Paul journeyed to Athens, while the rest of his companions later left for Corinth. In Athens, Paul changed his methods and presented Christianity in terms of Greek philosophy, but the resurrection of Jesus was too much for most of his listeners, and Paul moved on to Corinth.

As a great port and capital of the Roman province controlling southern Greece, and center of the Aphrodite religion, Corinth was a large and cosmopolitan city. There, Paul and his helpers found the more positive response they had hoped for, and they stayed for 18 months. Paul's two Letters to the Thessalonians, probably written during this stay in Corinth, show that the Christian Church he founded there had a hard time after he left. His Letter to the Galatians reveals a different problem.

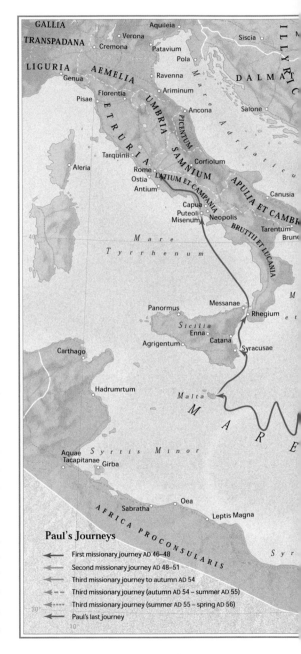

That Church was insisting that Christians had to keep the Jewish laws as well. Paul feared that all his work among them would be undone. His letter—or epistle—to them is the angriest of all the letters he wrote.

Paul returned to Caesarea, the main Roman administrative center for Judaea, by way of Ephesus. It was a logical route to use for the safest sailing, with busy sea routes available across the Aegean to Ephesus, and

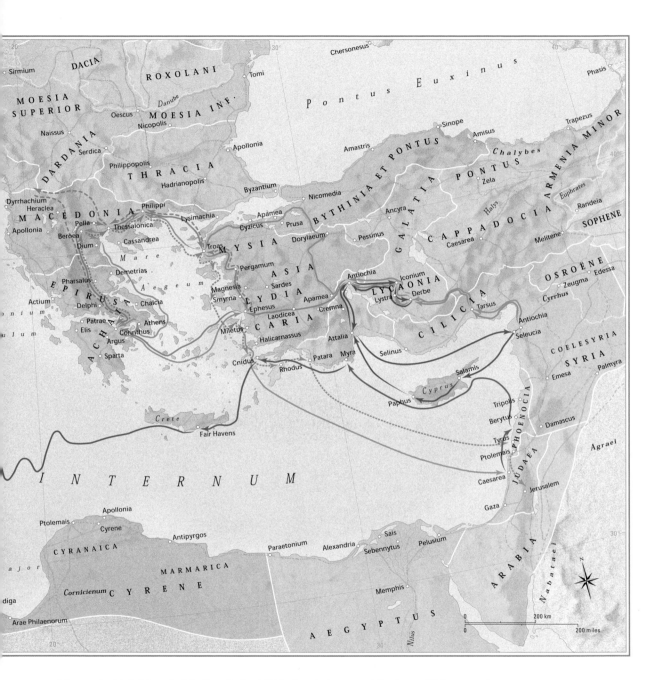

round the coast of Asia Minor to Palestine. Paul established contacts amongst the Jews of Ephesus, and promised to return.

He kept his promise quickly, after a short time at his home church of Antioch. Paul set off again and took the overland route through Galatia and Phrygia once more, but Ephesus was his main destination, and

"AND IT CAME TO PASS, THAT, WHILE A-POL-LOS WAS AT CORINTH, PAUL, HAVING PASSED THROUGH THE UPPER COASTS CAME TO EPH-E-SUS: AND FINDING CERTAIN DISCIPLES,

"HE SAID UNTO THEM, HAVE YE RECEIVED THE HOLY GHOST SINCE YE BELIEVED? AND THEY SAID UNTO HIM, WE HAVE NOT SO MUCH AS HEARD WHETHER THERE BE ANY HOLY GHOST.

"AND HE SAID UNTO THEM. UNTO WHAT THEN WERE YE BAPTIZED? AND THEY SAID, UNTO JOHN'S BAPTISM.

"THEN SAID PAUL, JOHN VERILY BAPTIZED WITH THE BAPTISM OF REPENTANCE, SAYING UNTO THE PEOPLE, THAT THEY SHOULD BELIEVE IN HIM WHICH SHOULD COME AFTER HIM, THAT IS, IN CHRIST JESUS.

'WHEN THEY HEARD THIS, THEY WERE BAPTIZED IN THE NAME OF THE LORD JESUS."

ACTS 19:1–5

when he reached it he stayed for more than two years. According to Acts 19, Paul met with great success both in Ephesus and among the people of the surrounding area. So great, indeed, was Paul's success that it threatened the trade in silver copies of the famous statue of Diana of the Ephesians, to whom the city's main temple was dedicated. Rioting broke out, and Paul decided to leave for Macedonia, by way of Troas again.

While in Ephesus, Paul had written to the Church he had founded on the other side of the Aegean at Corinth. The consequences also contributed to his decision to move on. Paul's First Letter to the Corinthians starts with a series of rebukes for various matters that had been related to him about his Corinthian Christians. There were factions in the Church there, law suits, a case of incest and members who were still worshipping at the Temple of Aphrodite. The letter continues with comments on various questions raised in a letter he had received from Corinth. It reveals concerns about marriage, social relationships with non-Christian friends, details of Church order, and the Resurrection. Both the rebukes and the worries throw light on the experience of being a Christian in such a varied and busy city as ancient Corinth. But Paul's response to the situation in Corinth had startling repercussions for him. The Corinthian Christians were so angry that they came close to rejecting him. This may be the deeper reason for Paul leaving Ephesus. The sequence of events is not

clear. He may have written another letter and paid a swift visit by sea, which only made matters worse. In the end, he sent his companion Titus to heal the breach, and was then so anxious that he crossed from Troas to Macedonia to meet Titus on his way back from Corinth.

Titus had succeeded and Paul wrote his Second Letter to the Corinthians to send on ahead as he made his way there. It is a very different letter from the first one, full of reflection on the experience of preaching Christianity. It reveals more about Paul than anything else he wrote, and about the experience of commitment to Jesus Christ. The three months Paul now spent in Corinth were the occasion for his most systematic exposition of his beliefs—his Letter to the Romans, in which he sets out his understanding of the

SCENES FROM THE LIFE OF PAUL *(far right)*
One half of this 4th-Century Florentine diptych shows scenes from the life of Paul. He is seen disputing with philosophers from Athens, bitten by a viper at Malta and healing the sick on the island.

Christian faith. He intended to make Rome the base for the next phase of his work, and this letter formed his personal introduction to the Christians who were living there.

Paul and at least six companions retraced their steps through Macedonia to Philippi, and so by stages back to Jerusalem. He little knew that his next journey would be to Rome—under arrest, with a guard of Roman soldiers to stand trial before Nero.

Paul: Disciple in Captivity

The Jerusalem to which Paul returned in AD 58 was in ferment. Eight years later it erupted into the disastrous war between Jews and Romans in which Jerusalem was destroyed. Some of this turmoil can be seen in the events that led to Paul's arrest, his long wait for his case to be heard, and his demand to be tried by the Emperor in Rome. Innocently enough, Paul went to the great Jewish Temple in Jerusalem to pray and to show that he did not encourage Jewish Christians to abandon their traditions. Rumor had it that he had taken a non-Jew into the Temple with him. Such desecration of the Temple carried the death penalty in Hebrew law, recognized by the Romans, and a crowd quickly gathered to lynch him.

Immediately alongside the wall of the Temple area stood the main guard tower of Jerusalem, which had been enlarged by Herod the Great and was now used by the Roman garrison. That too was an offence to strictly orthodox Jews. The Roman guard stopped the riot by arresting Paul, and he would have been interrogated under the lash if he had not told them that he held the privileges of Roman citizenship. The next move was a request for Paul, as a Jew, to be tried before the Sanhedrin, the main religious council, but word reached him that there was a plot to assassinate him on the way. The senior Roman officer in Jerusalem decided to move Paul to the safety of Caesarea, the main Roman administrative center, which was well away from Jerusalem. They sent him there with a strong escort. At Caesarea, Paul could be tried by Felix, the procurator of Palestine, whose harshness towards the Jews under his rule was a major cause of the coming rebellion.

If Paul had been tried by Felix the charges against him would certainly have been dismissed, but Felix kept him waiting two years, and then he was replaced by a new procurator, Festus. By

this time, Paul had had enough. Although Festus was cast in a different mould from Felix, Paul exercised his rights as a Roman citizen to have his case transferred to Rome. Perhaps Paul was influenced by the actions of the current King Herod, Agrippa II (AD 50–c. 100)—who had had James executed and Peter imprisoned. Even a Roman citizen might be sacrificed in the jungle of Palestinian politics.

Paul's voyage to Rome, in the charge of a centurion and a detachment of Roman soldiers, took the best part of a year. A coastal vessel took the group to Myra, where they joined one of the great grain ships which sailed regularly between Egypt and Italy. Headwinds delayed progress and forced the ship down to Crete; then a storm drove them westwards for a fortnight until they ran aground on Malta where the ship broke up. It was three months before the voyage could be resumed in another Egyptian corn ship, which called at Syracuse in Sicily and Rhegium on the toe of Italy, before finally reaching Putcoli near Neapolis (Naples). Paul found there were Christians at Putcoli, and stayed a week there, then traveled with his escort along the Appian Way to Nero's Rome. It was AD 61, three years before the great fire of Rome and the beginning of Nero's persecution of Roman Christians.

When Paul first reached Rome there were no signs of hostility from any Roman officials towards Christians. Paul himself looked to the Roman administration for protection, so that he could be free to spread his beliefs, and in his Letter to the Romans he even wrote that "... since all government comes from God, the civil authorities were appointed by God" (Romans 13:1). The Roman Empire was near the height of its power with control over the whole Mediterranean area, Spain, most of Europe, southern Britain, and Egypt. Rome itself was a tightly knit maze of narrow streets and lanes, contrasting with large open spaces and imposing state buildings and temples. Nearly a million people lived in the city, for the distribution of free food and the public amusements provided by prominent citizens or the state, and the wealth of the city attracted people from many parts of the Empire. The final chapter of Romans shows that Paul already knew many of the Christians in Rome when he first arrived there.

The Acts of the Apostles ends with Paul's arrival in Rome, and meetings he arranged with leading members of the Jewish community. It says that he spent "the whole of the two years in his own rented lodgings" (Acts 28:30), where he would be under custody while waiting for his case to be heard, but neither Romans nor Acts says what happened to him. Later Christian writings, some of them very near to New Testament tomes, say that he was freed at the end of the two years mentioned in Acts. If this was the case, he could have carried out his plan to extend his missionary work into the western parts of the Roman Empire, particularly Spain.

Four of Paul's letters mention that he was imprisoned when he wrote them. Even at the time of his Second Letter to the Corinthians, he wrote that he had often been imprisoned, so it is far from certain that his "captivity letters" were all written from Rome. One of them, Philemon, written to a fellow Christian, gives a vivid glimpse of the change Christianity could bring to human values and social differences. The letter urges Philemon to receive back an escaped slave, whatever wrongs he may have committed. At this time there was no legal restraint on an owner's treatment of his slave, but Paul urges the slave to be received "as a brother in the Lord" and to "welcome him as you would me" (Philemon 16f). Philippians was written to the Christians in Philippi, which Paul first visited 11 years before his arrival in Rome. The contents of the letter suggest that it belongs to an earlier stage of Paul's thinking. Colossians and Ephesians, on the other hand, deal with the problems arising from a new philosophical and religious movement that

VICTORIOUS EMPEROR
Across the Roman Empire, the glory of victorious emperors was proclaimed by setting up triumphal arches and monuments. Here the emperor, surrounded by his officers, receives the submission of conquered barbarians.

was attracting Christians. Evidence suggests that Ephesians was written to a number of Christian churches around Ephesus, so the whole area may have been influenced.

The new religion of these many different churches formed a patchwork of beliefs and practices taken from a wide range of religions and philosophies. However, Paul remained steadfast in his insistence that only Jesus Christ could give full salvation.

ROME
Ruins of the Forum seen from the Capitoline Hill, the nerve center of the most powerful empire in the ancient world. Paul's Letter to the Romans gives a clear exposition of the doctrine of justification by faith.

PERSECUTION OF CHRISTIANS

"I ASKED THEM WHETHER THEY WERE CHRISTIANS OR NOT? IF
THEY CONFESSED THAT THEY WERE CHRISTIANS, I ASKED THEM
AGAIN.... IF THEY PERSEVERED IN THEIR CONFESSION, I ORDERED
THEM TO BE EXECUTED; FOR I DID NOT DOUBT BUT, LET THIS
CONFESSION BE OF ANY SORT WHATSOEVER, THIS POSITIVENESS
AND INFLEXIBLE OBSTINACY DESERVED TO BE PUNISHED."

PLINY THE YOUNGER TO EMPEROR TRAJAN IN 112 AD

The early Christian community was severely persecuted by Jews well before the well known attacks by the Romans under Emperor Nero. Originally, Christians were brought up under Judaism, being merely a sect of Judaism. A sectarian conflict began within Judaism, as Jews persecuted other Jews who were Christians. This inter-faith strife might be understood; Christians were preaching about the imminent return of the King of the Jews and the establishment of his kingdom. The Pharisees persecuted Christians because they mistook the kingdom to be political rather than spiritual. The Romans had granted Jews a degree of autonomy and the Jewish leaders were obliged to collect taxes for Rome and maintain civil order. Jesus appeared to the Pharisees as a seditious political figure who might bring the wrath of the Romans down upon the Jewish leadership. Failure to dampen down or suppress sedition meant that the Jewish leaders would be sent to Rome for trial and possible execution. Therefore, the Pharisees wanted to localize the problem for their own survival.

Whereas other Jewish sects such as the Essenes were left alone, Jesus was crucified, and his followers were persecuted after his death. The Jewish leadership under the high priest Annas and his family, Caiphas, John and Alexander imprisoned Peter and John after disliking Peter's sermon to a mass outside the Temple but then released them because they could not find their acts punishable (Acts 4: 1–21). Eventually, all the apostles were imprisoned by the high priest and Sadducees.

THREAT TO FAITH
Having faith in God could be a dangerous life choice for many early Christians, who could suffer terrible persecution at the hands of unbelievers. The memory of Christ's crucifixion - as depicted in this 11th century stained glass window - and what it represents has always buoyed followers in their resolve.

"And laid their hands on the apostles, and put them in the common prison.

But the angel of the Lord by night opened the prison doors, and brought them forth, and said,

Go, stand and speak in the temple to the people all the words of this life."

(Acts 5: 18–20)

The apostles were brought before the Sanhedrin where the high priest commanded them not to teach in Jesus' name lest you "intend to bring this man's blood upon us" (Acts 5:28), a possible reference to the fear of Roman retribution. Gamaliel, a learned Pharisee, and doctor of law, said that the apostles should be given space: "... Refrain from these men, and let them alone: for if this counsel or this work be of men, it will come to nought: But if it be of God, ye cannot overthrow it; lest happily ye be found even to fight against God" (Act 5:38–39). The apostles were beaten and released, and warned not to speak in the name of Jesus. They did, in the Temple and elsewhere.

The first Christian martyr was Stephen, who was stoned to death by members of the Sanhedrin. "And cast him out of the city, and stoned him: and the witnesses laid down their clothes at a young man's feet, whose name was Saul" (Acts 7:58). This Saul of Tarsus, a Pharisee, implemented a major persecution of Christians. Saul, or Paul as his Greek name, was trained in Jewish Law in preparation to be a rabbi. He excelled in the Law and his zeal in its cause led him to persecute Christians. "For ye have heard of my conversation in time past in the Jews' religion, how that beyond measure I

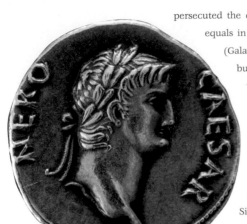

persecuted the church of God, and wasted it; And profited in the Jews' religion above many my equals in mine own nation, being more exceedingly zealous of the traditions of my fathers" (Galatians 1:13–14). He regarded the Christians as a Jewish sect that should be destroyed, but on his way from Jerusalem to Damascus saw a vision that convinced him that Christ was God's call to all the world, outside of the needs of Judaism itself. His sudden conversion was difficult to accept, with people trying to kill him in Damascus (Acts 9: 22–25), and other attempts on his life recorded in Acts 9: 26–27 and 29.

Persecution by Romans is a well-recorded historical fact. Eleven of the Apostles were killed, murdered, executed or martyred, except for John, son of Zebedee and Salome, and writer of the Book of Revelations. Paul was stoned by Jews from Antioch and Iconium and left for dead (Acts 15: 19). Later, Paul and his companion, Silas, were whipped and placed in stocks at Philippi before being freed when an earthquake struck (Acts 17: 22–26). Christian tradition has it that Paul was beheaded in Rome.

ROMAN SCOURGE
Under Emperor Nero (as depicted on this coin) Christians would suffer crucifixion or violent death in the gladiatorial arena, as the Roman authorities sought a scapegoat for local unrest.

Persecution by the Roman Empire commenced under Emperor Nero (AD 37-68). Different forms of execution were used by the authorities, including systematic murder, crucifixion with crosses being set alight to provide nightlights in the dark, and feeding Christians to lions and other wild animals. The historian Tacitus wrote: 'They were killed by dogs by having the hides of beasts attached to them and worse' (Annals XV: 44). He also states that 'a vast multitude, were convicted, not so much of the crime of arson as of hatred of the human race.' The official persecution of Christians in Rome was then taken up by officials in the provinces who wanted someone to blame for local problems. By the middle of the second century, anti-Christian mobs could be organized without much effort. This was witnessed during persecutions in Lyons in AD 177, during the reign of the Emperor Marcus Aurelius (161–180), when there were assaults, robberies, and stonings, demonstrating the intensity of anti-Christian feeling.

Records show two more Empire-wide persecutions. The Emperor Decius (AD 249–251) launched a systematic attack on Christianity in 250 demanding that all citizens signify their willingness to worship pagan gods. Victims of this persecution included Pope Fabian (AD 236–250) and Cyprian, the bishop of Carthage (AD 200–258), who was exiled and later martyred and beheaded under Emperor Valerian (AD 253–260). Church father and renowned biblical scholar Origen (c. AD 185–c. 254) was imprisoned and tortured. Decius had become emperor during a period of imperial usurpations and used the wave of persecutions to shroud the inherent instability of his reign. After he died, Christian leaders argued about the fate of those followers who had accepted the orders of Decius and then wished to return to the fold. Cyprian argued for leniency towards these *lapsi* (Christians who had relapsed into heathenism). The next wave of persecution occurred under Emperor Diocletian (AD 284–305), who ordered all churches and Christian books to be destroyed, and followed this with the execution of Christians for the subsequent eight years. Christianity was saved when the joint Emperors Constantine (c. AD 306–337) and Licinius (308–314) gave the faith legal recognition by the Edict of Milan in 313. Christian churches were hereby recognized as legal corporations. Persecutions still went on, however, when Romans failed to understand Christian rituals, and still considered Christians as corrupt and anti-

Roman. However, such hostility gradually diminished.

An explanation for the persecutions reveals a plethora of reasons. Firstly, Christians denied the basis for Roman rule by stating that their God was the only real God. This denied the existence of the Roman pagan gods, including the divinity of the Emperor. This denial, as far as Roman commoners or aristocracy, was concerned was an attack upon the "peace of the gods" and upon Rome itself. Christians were also accused of corrupting public morals by participating in Mass, mistaken as cannibalism. Christians were also feared for seeking martyrdom. Saint Ignatius of Antioch (35–107), condemned to death, wrote to the Roman: "Grant me no more than you let my blood be spilled in sacrifices to God, while yet there is an altar ready." Romans thought that the Christian desire for death was again corrupting public morals. The Romans failed to comprehend the Book of Revelation, viewing it as an attack on Rome because they thought the references to Babylon really meant Rome. Thus, the book was deemed anti-Roman propaganda. A final accusation levelled at Christians was that they failed to honor their ancestors and their authority. Romans continued to worship their own gods, believing that this enhanced social and political stability. The Christians did not acknowledge their Jewish ancestors and the books of the Old Testament. This "new" approach was a double crime because Christians not only denied their own ancestors but the Roman gods too. Hence, they were oppressed, a policy exacerbated by Roman magistrates who followed public opinion and its antipathy towards Christians.

THE SHADOW OF ROME

A SERIES OF NATURAL AND MILITARY DISASTERS AROUSED
SUSPICIONS THAT NERO WAS OUT OF FAVOR WITH THE GODS.
IN ABOUT AD 65, AND NEEDING SCAPEGOATS, HE HAD MANY
CHRISTIANS PUT TO DEATH WITH SADISTIC CRUELTY. THIS
CREATED A PRECEDENT FOR WIDESPREAD PERSECUTION.

**POMPEY'S SETTLEMENT OF
THE HASMONEAN JEWISH
STATE (64–40 BC)** *(far right)*
Under the rule of the Maccabees,
the Jews entered into an alliance
with Rome to protect their
newly won independence. When
the Jewish state collapsed in civil
war, both sides called for the
Romans to restore peace. From
56 BC onwards Palestine was
ruled by Rome, which appointed
native kings under a Roman
governor. Herod the Great was
the first such puppet king of the
Jews, and retained his throne until
his death in 4 BC. Herod and his
family ruled ruthlessly and held
their power, with Roman help,
from five great fortresses—
Masada, Herodium, Machaerus,
Alexanrium, and Hyracania.

Nero, the Roman Emperor to whom Paul appealed, began his 14-year reign in AD 54
with assassinations and executions to secure his power and finance his
extravagances, but there was no attempt to discredit or suppress Christians. Nero's
predecessors had centralized power and increased the efficiency of the Roman civil service
until the Emperor's actions were beyond any control—provided the army remained loyal to
him. Emperors began to be honored as divine, and the 16-year-old Nero encouraged the cult.
Such absolute power could only be sustained by strong rulers, and Nero was not cast in that
mold. A series of natural disasters in Italy, and military crises on the borders of the Empire,
aroused the suspicion that Nero was out of favor with the gods. In Britain, a rebellion led by
Queen Boadicea very nearly drove the Romans out of the province they had only conquered
some 18 years earlier. At the eastern extreme of the Roman Empire, the Parthians inflicted a
decisive defeat on a Roman army, and Nero had to agree to peace terms. In AD 63, an
earthquake destroyed most of Pompeii, anticipating its final destruction 16 years later.

Fire broke out in Rome itself near the Circus Maximus in the summer of AD 64. The
congested city was familiar with fires, but this one spread rapidly for six days until all the
southern part of the city had been destroyed as far as the Tiber and the Servian wall, then it
broke out again and spread through the northern districts. By the time it finally died down, it

had burned through ten of the city's 14 wards. Nero was widely blamed for the fire, which was said to have been started on his orders. Even the rebuilding of the city caused unpopularity, as the rest of Italy and the provinces were squeezed to pay for the work. A plague in the following year added to the misery. The Christians in Rome were convenient scapegoats, and Nero had as many as could be found put to death with sadistic cruelty, punished both for the fire and on the charge that they were "haters of the human race" who refused to take part in other religious activities.

The persecutions of Christians under Nero seem to have been confined to Rome, as a distraction from the suspicions about his own involvement in the fire and other disasters, but it did create a precedent for Roman officials in other parts of the Empire and it ended any possibility of the Christian Church coming to a similar agreement with Rome as that enjoyed by Jews, whose exclusive religion was recognized by the state and respected, without any suggestion that it smacked of treason. There could be no hope of that for Christianity in the foreseeable future, especially as Jesus himself had been condemned by a Roman magistrate on a treason charge, and executed. It would no longer be possible for Christians such as Paul to hope that Roman citizenship would provide protection from trouble. This formed the background to the last years of Paul and Peter.

Paul's three Letters to Timothy and Titus are usually called the pastoral letters, because they are addressed to individual leaders of local churches, and contain advice about church organization and worship. Timothy was in Ephesus and Titus in Crete. These are the last letters attributed to Paul and show that two of the earlier threats to Christians beliefs had now combined—an insistence that all Christians must express their Christianity in Jewish form, and belief in a system of secret knowledge that guaranteed salvation and allocated a subordinate role to Jesus. This belief, called Gnosticism, from the Greek *gnosis* meaning knowledge, dogged Christianity throughout the rest of the New Testament period and beyond.

Information about Paul's last years and death is very sparse, in contrast to the wealth of detail provided by Acts about his arrest in Jerusalem and his struggles to have his case tried properly. Acts ends with Paul staying two years in Rome under house arrest, but does not say what happened to him then. It was still only about AD 63, before Nero began his attacks on Christians, and the charges against Paul would certainly have been dismissed at that time if he had received a fair trial.

If Paul was in fact released, he probably went back to Macedonia, and to Asia Minor and Crete where his old companions Timothy and Titus were in charge of churches. He then returned—or was taken—to Rome again after the great fire to a more severe form of imprisonment and to death. This would account for passages in the pastoral letters about Paul's movements and his expectation of death. They would have been written during the second imprisonment in Rome, which ended with Paul's execution near the end of Nero's reign.

Alternatively, Paul might have been executed after the two years imprisonment described in Acts, and someone else wrote these three final letters to give the kind of teaching and advice Paul would have given to leaders of local churches. So it seems likely that Paul was executed before

Nero committed suicide in AD 68. He was taken outside the southern walls of the city of Rome and beheaded, as befitted a Roman citizen. Early Church tradition asserts that Peter was crucified during the same period in the Vaticanum, an area west of the River Tiber.

Nero's reign ended in chaos, amidst events that created a completely new situation for the Christian churches. His death marked the end of a dynasty and resulted in a year of civil war in Rome. Whatever the Roman constitution said, real power lay with the military—the praetorian guard in Rome and the great armies guarding the frontiers of the Empire. During the bloody struggle for political power, Rome itself was stormed by Roman troops, the Capital was burned, three emperors were proclaimed and overthrown and, finally, Vespasian emerged as victor. He reigned as emperor from AD 69–79.

In this period, the situation in Palestine deteriorated swiftly. Even before the death of Nero, war had broken out between Rome and the Jews of Palestine and this was to have disastrous effects on the privileges Jews enjoyed throughout the Empire, on their economic and political power, and on their cultural influence.

FORTIFIED PILLARS
The strength of Rome's military power can be appreciated from the number of great fortresses it captured. In many cases provincial kings drew their inspiration from the Romans themselves, only to discover to their cost, that the strength of Rome lay in the iron discipline of its troops rather than fortified positions.

Under the corrupt rule of the last of the Roman procurators, Florus, a comparatively small protest grew to open rebellion when Jerusalem Jews compelled Florus and his soldiers to retreat to Caesarea, the Roman administrative center for Judaea. The Governor of Syria, Gallius, then marched on Jerusalem with the Roman Twelfth Legion and was, in turn, repulsed with heavy losses at the end of AD 66. The rebellion had turned into a war, and Nero sent one of his most able generals, the future emperor, Vespasian, with 60,000 men.

Vespasian began a systematic campaign to subdue Palestine, beginning with Galilee. He drove the Zealots before him to take refuge in Jerusalem, where they murdered Jewish opponents and moderates. By the end of AD 68 all Judaea and Idumaea had been subdued, and only such strongholds as Jerusalem and Masada held out. It was at this time that the Jewish community at Qumran hid its library in caves and fled to Masada.

When Vesparian was proclaimed Emperor in AD 69, his son Titus carried on in his place, and began the full siege of Jerusalem early in AD 70. That part of the war was over by September, with the city and its Temple

destroyed, and the Jews of Jerusalem killed or sold into slavery. Titus celebrated his victory with sacrifices to the standards of the Roman Legion in front of the ruins of the Temple. The following year Vesparian and Titus had their victory proclaimed by a "triumph," a huge procession in Rome in which treasures from the Jerusalem Temple were carried and Jewish captives walked in chains. The occasion is vividly portrayed in the carvings of the Arch of Titus.

Further strongholds fell one by one during the years AD 70–73. These included: the Herodium, south of Jerusalem; Machaerus, east of the Dead Sea; and, finally, the massive fortress of Masada, where Jewish slaves built a ramp to its summit, more than 1,000 feet (300 m) above the shore of the Dead Sea. On the night before the final assault, the defenders killed their families and themselves. This marked the end of the war.

The Christians of Jerusalem had fled the city before the siege closed, and settled at Pella in

CAESAREA
This artist's impression shows the town in its heyday, founded by Herod the Great in 22 BC and named in honor of the Emperor Augustus Caesar. The port appears in the Bible as the place where St Paul was imprisoned for two years.

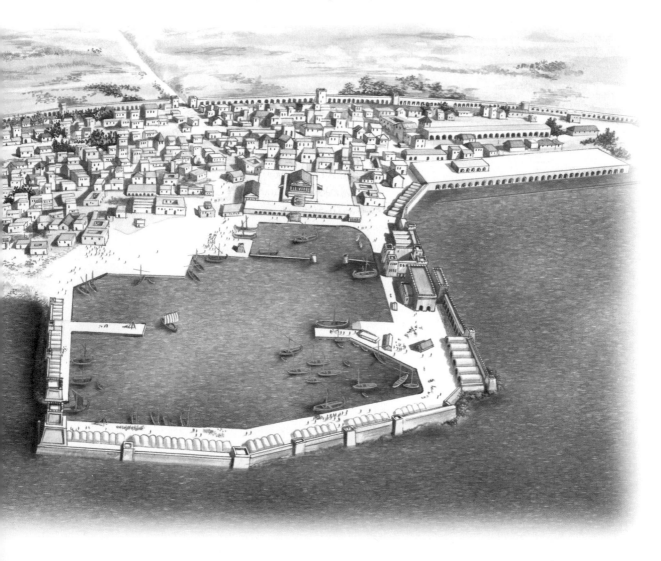

EMPEROR NERO
Roman Emperor from AD 54, during his unstable reign, Rome suffered a great fire in AD 64. This was widely blamed on the Christians, who he subsequently persecuted. After various plots and revolts to end his rule, he committed suicide in AD 68, leaving the Empire in disarray.

the Jordan Valley. This had quite a wide-ranging effect on the early Christian Church; the Christians of Jerusalem could no longer be a center of authority and stability for the growing number of followers of their faith elsewhere in the Roman Empire. The Jewish Christians who left Jerusalem came under fire from both Jews and Romans, but the only serious persecution occurred was later in the reign of Domitian (AD 81–96).

In the New Testament, three letters that are difficult to date may best be understood as belonging to the period of radical rethinking for Christians, which followed the destruction of Jerusalem. The Second Letter of Peter was probably written after Peter's death to show how he would have guided Christians in the new situation, and it has many similarities to the Letter of Jude, which deals with problems of false teachers and worries about the delay in the expected return of Jesus. The long and remarkable Letter to the Hebrews differs radically from anything else ascribed to Paul, and the authorship has been questioned from very early times. It presents the work of Jesus in terms of the Hebrew priesthood and sacrifices. These are ways that would particularly appeal to Jewish Christians after the destruction of the Temple.

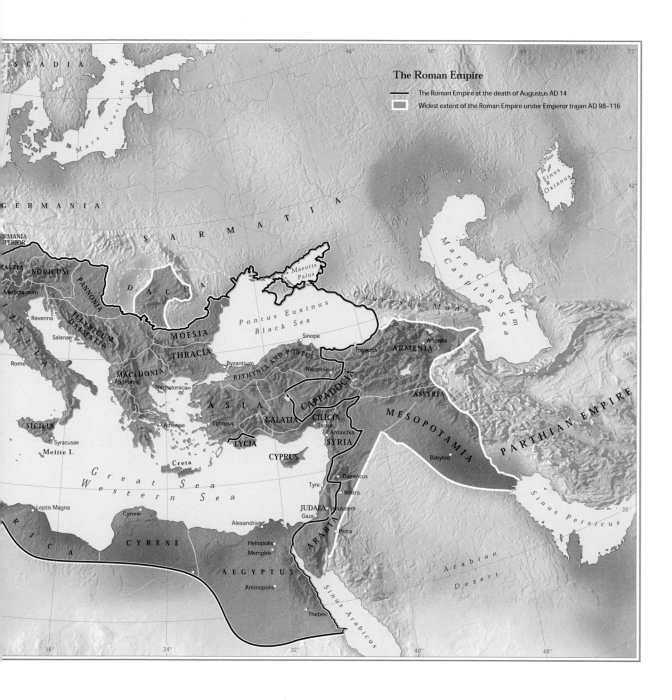

The Roman Empire

— The Roman Empire at the death of Augustus AD 14

▭ Widest extent of the Roman Empire under Emperor trajan AD 98–116

EVANGELISING CHRISTIANITY

AFTER CHRIST'S RESURRECTION, HIS FOLLOWERS RESTRICTED THEMSELVES TO EVANGELISING AMONGST THE JEWISH POPULATION, A CAPTIVE AUDIENCE. MANY CONVERTS TRAVELED WITH THE DIASPORA SPREADING THE CHRISTIAN WORD THROUGHOUT THE ROMAN EMPIRE.

The spread of early Christianity was aided by several factors. Firstly, a unifying language and culture existed, certainly in an urban sense, from Italy to India. Alexander the Great's empire and its successor states established common Greek, or *koine,* as the main imperial language. A second factor enabling missionaries to travel was the *Pax Romana* (the Roman peace), founded by Augustus Caesar. Safe travel had been possible by sea, since Pompey's eradication of piracy turned the Mediterranean into a Roman lake, and via a network of brilliantly engineered roads.

A third major factor was the extent of the Jewish diaspora, which allowed target audiences for the new Jewish message being spread by Jesus' supporters. Large communities of Jews had existed outside Palestine since the fall of the kingdoms of Israel and Judah. However, the greatest Jewish diaspora occurred after the Alexandrine conquest of the Persian Empire freed up movement in the Fertile Crescent. Whatever the causes of the diaspora, trade certainly played a major part in establishing Jewish communities in many of the cities along the east Mediterranean coastline. This massive movement was enhanced when Jewish captives were sold into slavery after the two Jewish revolts of AD 66–70 and AD 132–135. By AD 100, the philosopher Philo claimed there were a million Jews, either by birth or conversion, in Egypt.

The New Testament, especially the Acts of the Apostles, constantly mentions Jews, often Christians, living in Syria, Asia Minor and Greece. Evidence about Jews in Egypt is extant, owing to surviving papyri and some archaeological excavations of synagogues, although the majority originate from later centuries. The exiles' religious worship remained constant to Judaism with its notion of ethical superiority. Concern was mainly expressed over the Temple and the Law. The latter was most

RUINS OF EPHESUS
Ephesus was the capital of the
Roman province of Asia, on
the west coast of what is now
Asiatic Turkey. It flourished
under the Romans in the early
centuries AD. The photograph
shows a fountain built in the
reign of Augustus. Ephesus
was also the site of one of the
earliest Christian churches.

THE EARLY SPREAD OF THE GOSPEL
(far right)

The Gospel seems to have spread into Samaria and then along the coastal plain, although the chronology of this early spread is unclear. Philip, one of the seven deacons of the early Church, traveled from Jerusalem into Samaria where he enjoyed success when preaching the Gospel. His later travels took him from Jerusalem to Gaza and then north along the coastal plain. Peter proclaimed the Gospels to the Gentiles as well as to the Jews and at Lydda he cured a cripple. He also brought a woman back from the dead during his travels to Joppa.

important, all Jews preserving the traditional food restrictions and observing the Sabbath as a rest day.

The Law became the focus of life as did the local synagogues, which became sacred buildings, often of architectural note, since the Temple was in Palestine. Leaders of synagogues were not only important in religious life, but often acted as magistrates within their congregations, settling disputes without reference to Gentile authorities. In some cases, the local sovereign power would acknowledge this autonomy as convenient or consider that the community was more likely to control its deviants and rebels through excommunication rather than official local sanctions. Such self-concern often led to isolation, the requirement of the Law in dietary terms and hostility towards mixed marriages occasionally causing resentment in some cities. Endemic anti-Semitism became vicious in Alexandria where local Greeks were angry at Jews seeking full city citizenship while refusing to join in local pagan cults or allow city authorities to police their religious community. First-century Alexandria was prone to communal fighting, culminating in a Jewish uprising in AD 117–119, as in Cyrene and Cyprus.

Christianity commenced as a movement within Judaism. Jesus was a Jew, as were his Apostles. His adherents accepted him as the "Christ" sent to fulfil God's promise to Abraham, Isaac and Jacob. Jesus' message was awaited since Palestine was in turmoil after the formal annexation by Rome in AD 6, with a variety of contending sects like the spiritual Essenes or nationalists (like the later Zealots). Enter Christ, the Messiah, a liberator? In this situation, Jewish authorities regarded Jesus with suspicion, as another troublemaker, and more so as his adherents increased after the Resurrection. The good news of God's reigning power, this revelation, was first presented in an exclusive Judaic context. A major issue confronting this situation was whether Gentiles would be allowed to pursue Christ's doctrines without accepting Judaic Law.

After Christ's Resurrection, his supporters restricted themselves to evangelising among Jews. Thousands of Jews surged into Jerusalem for the most important religious festivals, a captive audience. Undoubtedly, many converts then returned to their homes in the diaspora, spreading the Christian word throughout the Roman Empire. Otherwise how would Paul have found converts wherever he traveled? However, some Jerusalem Christians were more progressive, seeking to spread the new teachings beyond orthodox Jewry. Hellenized Jews were quick to digest the new message as compared with Aramaic-speaking Jews. While the Apostles were out preaching, they required people to administer Church funds, given by such people as Barnabas. Seven men were ordained as deacons for this purpose. One, Stephen, thought the faith was for all people, and not just orthodox Jews, or Pharisees. His views attacked conservatism and led to ideological conflict within Judaism. Stephen was seized by the High Priest and the Jewish Supreme Court, being accused of blasphemy, disavowing the Temple cult, and the Jewish claim to be the sole authority in religious belief, he was condemned to death by stoning, becoming a martyr and eventually a saint.

The expansion of the early Christian Church in Palestine can be laid at the feet of Philip, Peter and John as shown in the Acts of the Apostles (4–11). Philip, another Hellenist, went to the city of Samaria, and commenced evangelising amongst these despised, unorthodox Jews. Samaritan scriptures consisted of Moses' five books, and that of Joshua, but not the prophets, their temple on Mount Gezerim, near Shechen claiming to possess legitimate Zadokite descent. Mass conversions resulted, causing Peter and John to travel to Samaria to confirm new disciples in their faith. Philip also preached

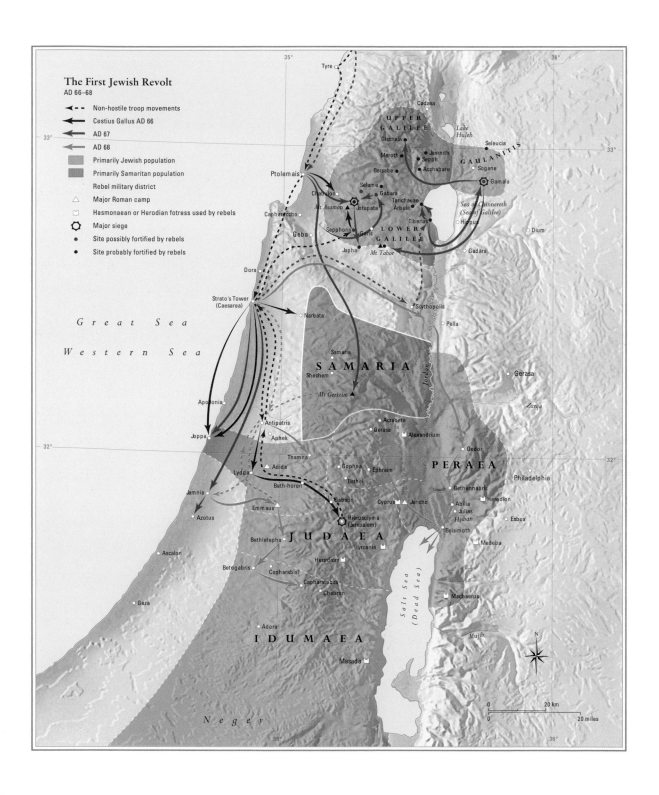

The First Jewish Revolt
AD 66–68

◄- - Non-hostile troop movements
◄— Cestius Gallus AD 66
◄— AD 67
◄— AD 68
▨ Primarily Jewish population
▨ Primarily Samaritan population
- - - Rebel military district
△ Major Roman camp
⌂ Hasmonaean or Herodian fotress used by rebels
◉ Major siege
• Site possibly fortified by rebels
• Site probably fortified by rebels

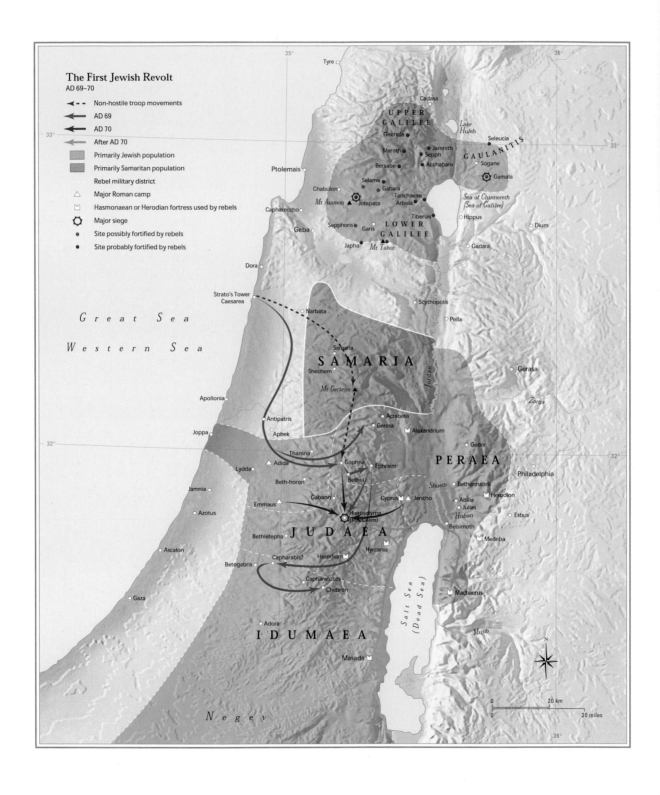

The First Jewish Revolt
AD 69–70

◄--- Non-hostile troop movements
◄— AD 69
◄— AD 70
◄— After AD 70
▨ Primarily Jewish population
▨ Primarily Samaritan population
---- Rebel military district
△ Major Roman camp
⌂ Hasmonaean or Herodian fortress used by rebels
⬡ Major siege
• Site possibly fortified by rebels
● Site probably fortified by rebels

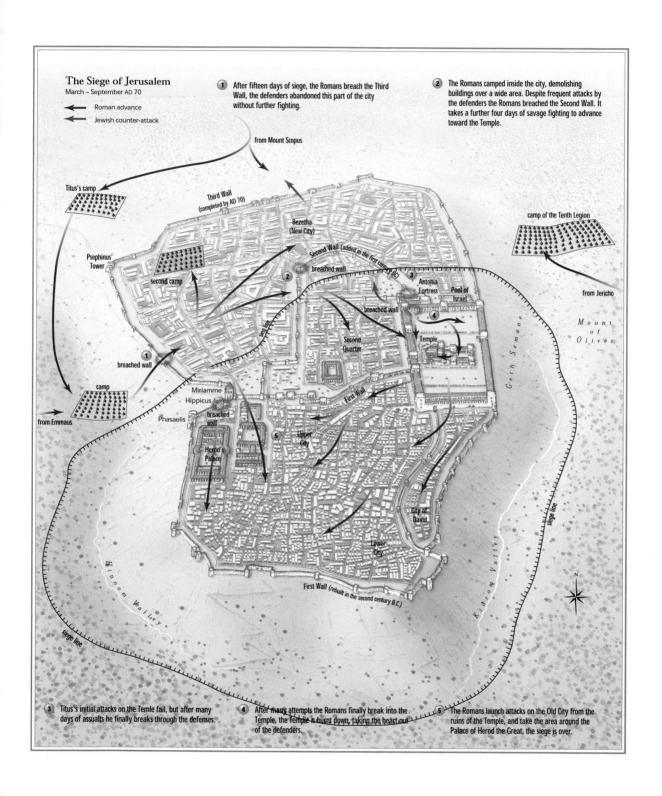

The Siege of Jerusalem
March – September AD 70

→ Roman advance
→ Jewish counter-attack

1 After fifteen days of siege, the Romans breach the Third Wall, the defenders abandoned this part of the city without further fighting.

2 The Romans camped inside the city, demolishing buildings over a wide area. Despite frequent attacks by the defenders the Romans breached the Second Wall. It takes a further four days of savage fighting to advance toward the Temple.

from Mount Scopus

Titus's camp

Third Wall
(completed by AD 70)

Bezetha
(New City)

camp of the Tenth Legion

Psephinus'
Tower

Second Wall (added in the first century BC)

breached wall

Antonia
Fortress

Pool of
Israel

from Jericho

second camp

2

3

*Mount
of
Olives*

breached wall

4

Temple

Geth Semane

siege line

Second
Quarter

1

breached wall

First Wall

camp

Miriamme
Hippicus

Phasaelis

breached
wall

5

Upper
City

from Emmaus

Herod's
Palace

Hinnom Valley

City of
David

siege line

Lower
City

First Wall (rebuilt in the second century B.C.)

Kidron Valley

N

siege line

3 Titus's initial attacks on the Temle fail, but after many days of assualts he finally breaks through the defenses.

4 After many attempts the Romans finally break into the Temple, the Temple is burnt down, taking the heart out of the defenders.

5 The Romans launch attacks on the Old City from the ruins of the Temple, and take the area around the Palace of Herod the Great, the siege is over.

THE SIEGE OF JERUSALEM

(previous page right)
Vespasian's son, Titus, took over the siege of Jerusalem when his father was proclaimed Emperor, and captured the city in AD 70. Jerusalem was levelled and its surviving citizens sold into slavery. The Romans rebuilt Jerusalem, but they forbade Jews to live there and the Temple has never been rebuilt. The Christians of Jerusalem fled the city before the Romans besieged it and settled at Pella, in the Jordan Valley near where the river leaves the Sea of Galilee. From now on, Jerusalem would no longer be the main center of authority for the Christians of the Roman Empire.

so this initial stage of the war was directed by leading Pharisees and Sadducees. Evidence concerning the insurrection can be found in *The Jewish War* by Flavius Josephus, in which he said the country was divided into revolutionary military districts. Jerusalem was placed in the hands of its former High Priest, Ananus, son of Anunus, and Joseph, son of Gorion. Idumaea was entrusted to two chief priests, Jesus son of Sapphias, and Eleazar. The region of Jericho was placed in the hands of Joseph, son of Simon, and Peraea (Transjordan) under Manasseh. The west and north of Judaea (the districts of Thamna, Lydda, Joppa, and Emmaus) were governed by John the Essene. John, son of Ananias, led northeastern Judaea (Gophna and Acrabeta), and both Galilee and the area of Gamal in Gaulantis were given to Josephus, son of Matthias, the author.

Josephus, then Joseph ben Matthias, immediately began to organize the defence of his command, despite fierce armed opposition from an extreme nationalist, John from Gischala. In Gaulantis, Josephus agreed that the walls of Gamla should be repaired and Seleucia and Sogane fortified in Upper Galilee. Meroth, Jamnith, and Acchabare were circumvallated and the three cities of Taricheae, Tiberias, and Sepphoris were fortified, together with several villages: the Cave of Arbele, Bersabe, Selame, Jotapata, Capchareccho, Japha, Sigoph, and Mount Tabor. A few of these fortifications were intended to be obstacles blocking the roads from Roman bases at Ptolemais (Sigoph, Capchareccho) and Scythopolis (Mount Tabor), or from Phoenicians (at Bersabe, Selame, Meroth) and from Agrippa's base at Caesarea Philippi (Jamnitj, Seleucia, Sogane). Others defended large population centres (Taricheae, Tiberias, Sepphoria, and Japha). The remainder of the fortresses were major strongholds (Jotapata, Acchabare, and Gamala).

In December, AD 66, Emperor Nero sent Vespasian to restore order and the authority of Rome. Vespasian acted cautiously and assembled troops in Syria while his son, Titus, was sent to Egypt to seek reinforcements. In spring, AD 67, Vespasian marched on Galilee from Antioch via Ptolemais, where Titus, with his Egyptian force, joined him. In total, the two generals commanded 60,000 legionaries and auxiliary troops. Galilean resistance cracked, Sephoris joined the Romans immediately, but Jotapata was besieged for two months, its garrison being slaughtered. Josephus' army at Garis fled and all of Lower Galilee fell immediately, Josephus retreating to Tiberias and then Jotapata. The latter was captured, Josephus surrendering. Of the fortresses, only Gamala continued to resist before being captured. The end of AD 67 witnessed the conquest of northern Palestine. Vespasian then sent his legions to winter at Caesaria and Scythopolis, thus keeping Galilee cut off from the area still resisting Rome.

The next phase of the war saw civil unrest between various Jewish factions, between the fanatical supporters of John of Gischalla, allied to the Idumaeans, and the aristocractic leaders of the revolt who were accused of dragging their heels in the fight against Rome. Vespasian chose to let the Jerusalem factions destroy each other while turning on Peraea where he soon occupied the whole area as far south as Macherus. By late spring, Antipatris, Lydda, and Jamnia were taken. A legion was stationed outside Emmaus, and after traveling through Samaria, the Romans entered Jericho.

While Vespasian's forces were traveling to Caesaria to prepare the siege of Jerusalem, Nero's suicide was announced. Vespasian ceased military activity while the political situation settled down. Finally, in the summer of AD 69, the armies in the eastern part of the Empire proclaimed Vespasian as

emperor. Faced by the rise of a new rebel leader, Simon bar Giora, Vespasian completed the subjugation of Judaea, controlling Acrabeta, Bethel and Ephraim, together with Hebron in the south. Only Jerusalem, Macherus, Herodium and Masada still held out against Rome. He then journeyed to Rome via Alexandria leaving Titus to end the rebellion.

The Jerusalem civil war continued. One faction of aristocratic patriots, of whom Josephus had been one, controlled a hill in the south-west of the city while the Zealots under John of Gischala held the eastern city and a major area of the Temple court. The aristocrats requested Simon bar Giora's help, but he conducted a reign of terror amongst the aristocrats, killing anyone who mentioned surrender. In the spring of AD 70, Titus marched on Jerusalem, building a siege wall around the city, and then attacking its north wall. Titus broke into the city and drove out final, fanatical resistance by fire, the Temple being torched. Within a month the Romans occupied the city, capturing Simon bar Giora and John of Gischala. These two men formed part of Titus' triumphal procession in Rome in AD 71, the event being commemorated on the triumphal Arch of Titus which still stands in Rome.

Lucilius Bassus, Palestinian governor, began the final clearing-up operation against the remaining Zealot strongholds. Herodium, near Bethlehem, surrendered. Macherus on the Dead Sea followed after some resistance. Masada, Herod's awesome palace on its high rock plateau, remained under the

ROMAN FORT AT MASADA
The Romans surrounded Masada with walls and forts. They were determined to destroy the last stronghold of the Jewish revolt.

leadership of Eleazar, son of Jair, a descendant of the Zealot founder, Judas the Galilean. The new governor of Judaea, Flavius Silva (AD 73–81) started the siege. The fortress sat on a steep, craggy outcrop rising from the western shore of the Dead Sea. The only route to the top was a narrow trail, known as the "snake path," zigzagging its way to the top for two miles, and a shorter, much steeper, path. This was a possible route, but dangerous on the western side. The plateau rim was circumscribed by an 18-foot-high wall, 12-feet broad with 37 towers, much of it wooden. The approximately 20 acre-plateau could be brought under cultivation, water being collected in huge cisterns that held some 200,000 gallons (909,000 litres). The 1,300-foot (396-metre) high eminence required skillful attention, a circumvallation was built to prevent escape or reinforcements. The Romans then built a siege ramp and mound on the west side where a battering ram could be brought into play, the wall soon collapsed, the Romans entering to silence. The insurgents had decided to die rather than surrender. The men killed their wives and children first, then the men drew lots to kill each other. In all, some 960 died; only two women and five children escaped this terrible fate.

"(The Romans) ... came within the palace, and so met with the multitude of the slain, but could take no pleasure in the fact, though it were done to their enemies. Nor could they do other than wonder at the courage of their resolution, and at the immovable contempt of death which so great a number of them had shown, when they went through with such an action as that was." (F. Josephus, *The Jewish War*, Chapter 10) Jewish resistance continued intermittently. About AD 116, during Emperor Trajan's reign, a revolt occurred but little is known about the uprising, probably because it was crushed quickly. Elsewhere, between AD 115–117, the Jews of Egypt, Cyrenaica, Mesopotamia and Cyprus rose, the latter uprising commencing with a massacre of the ruling Greeks, which was crushed by the Romans. The Jews next rose again during the reign of the Emperor Hadrian (AD 117–138). Two main causes have been offered by historians for this revolt. Firstly, Hadrian had attempted to ban circumcision in the Empire in all subject nations, irrespective of their faith. Secondly, and perhaps more importantly, was the plan to build a new city on Jerusalem's ruins; this Aelia Capitolina was to be pagan. Hadrian was present in Syria and Egypt between AD 129–131, his departure signalling the beginning of an uprising. The second Jewish revolt erupted in AD 132.

The leader of the revolt was known as Simeon bar Kokhba to his friends, and Simeon bar Kosiba (son of the lie—false Messiah) to his enemies. His real name and title as discovered in documents found in the caves of the Wadi Murabba'at and Nahal Hever in the Judaean desert are recorded as Simeon bar Kosiba, Prince of Israel. The first designation "son of the star" emanates from rabbi Akiba ben Joseph (AD 40–c. 135), who perfected the school of Biblical interpretation known as Midrash. After he met Simeon bar Kokhba, Akiba was impressed with his power and sense of destiny, seeing him as the promised Messiah. "This man is destined to lead us as it is written" (Numbers 24:17). "And a star (Kokhba) shall rise out of Jacob and sceptre from Israel and shall smite the corners of Moab and destroy the children of Seth." Akiba was criticised for being wrong; there is no record of Simeon being involved in the revolt after his proclamation.

When the revolt began, Jerusalem was not a fortified city and was faced by the camp of the Tenth Legion. Jerusalem was easily captured from Tinneius Rufus, the Roman governor, and the rebels held out against the Romans for two years. The insurgents minted coins in the first year of the rebellion with legends such as "liberation of Israel," "liberation of Jerusalem," and "the priest Eleazar", the latter suggesting a possible revival of the Temple cult. Hadrian then called for Julius Severus, from Britain, to command forces against the rebels.

The main concentration of rebels was in the Judaean desert centered around Herodium, Tekoa, Qiryat Arabayya, En-gedi, and the unidentified Beth Mashko, the last three being centres of rebel government. Papyri have ascertained the names of several rebel leaders: Joshua ben Galgula, Judah bar Manasseh, Jonathan bar Ba'ayan, and Masabala bar Simon. One Roman historian, Cassius Dio, stated that the Roman soldiers could not fight the Jews in open combat owing to the rough countryside. Guerrilla warfare ensued, with the Romans hunting down the insurgents in small groups, ferreting them out of caves, or holding areas to intercept supplies, thereby starving them to death.

Archaeological and manuscript evidence has been found in numerous caves in the Judaean desert. From north to south, they are found from Wadi Murabba'at, Nahal Hever, Nahal Mishmar, and Nahal Ze'elim. Four caves discovered in the northern wall of Wadi Murabba'at, just over 12 miles (19.3 km) south of Qumran, have offered up Hebrew, Aramaic, Greek, and Latin papyri fragments together with lamps, jars, weapons, tools, domestic objects, sandals, cloth, and dresses, and coins dating from the revolt. The best known letter from Simeon bar Kokhba states: "From Simeon ben Kokhba to Joshua ben Galgolah, and to the men of your company, peace! I call heaven to witness that if one of the Galileans whom you have taken under your wing should cause us any trouble, I will clap your feet in irons, as I did with the son of Aplul. Simeon ben Kokhba, ruler of Israel."

In four caves on the northern side of Nahal Hever, domestic vessels and bones of sheep and

ARCH OF TRIUMPH
Titus' victory in the Jewish-Roman War and his conquest of Jerusalem in AD 70 are commemorated by this triumphal arch erected by his brother, Domitian, at the old entrance to the Palatine in Rome. It still stands today.

goats have been found. In the fifth, the Cave of Letters, were preserved papyri fragments and 19 human skeletons. The south side Cave of Horrors indicated that 40 men, women, and children starved to death. This cave also held food containers, cooking pots, lamps, and the remnants of the scroll of the Twelve Minor Prophets in Greek. These victims could not escape since some caves were overlooked by a Roman camp on each side of the defile. A leather bag containing papyri texts and one text on a strip of wood provides letters to two men at En-gedi called Jonathan and Masabala. They were commanded, in a very dictatorial fashion, to provide Simeon with provisions and troops.

Two caves in the south wall of Nahal Mishmat were used as hiding places by several families, while a third was a store containing papyri fragments, glass vessels, and good-quality lamps and stone utensils. The single occupied cave in the south wall of Nahal Harduf contained a water cistern and pottery but no human remains. On the north face of Nahal Ze'elim, the Cave of Skulls revealed seven skeletons with pottery and a coin of Trajan; the Cave of Arrows, arrows and pottery; and the Cave of Scrolls, fragments of a leather scroll, papyri and a phylactery (a small leather box containing Hebrew texts worn by Jewish men at morning prayer).

In AD 135, Bether, a mountain fortress south of Jerusalem, where Simeon bar Kokhba was killed, witnessed the final battle of the insurgency. The siege lasted nearly a year, the entire war three and a half years. Roman losses were so severe that Hadrian reported to the Senate ignoring the traditional phrase, "I and the legions are well." The historian Cassio Dio recorded the disaster overwhelming the Jews. "Fifty of their most important outposts and nine hundred and eighty-five of their most famous villages were razed to the ground. Five hundred and eighty thousand men were slain in the various raids and battles, and the number of those who perished by famine, disease and fire was past finding out. Thus, nearly the whole of Judaea was made desolate." Reports show that, owing to the market place being swamped by Jewish prisoners, the price of a Jew in the Hebron slave market fell below that of a horse. Surplus captives were removed to Gaza, then Egypt. Little wonder a Roman coin from Hadrian's reign was inscribed "Judaea Capta" with the depiction of an enslaved woman.

After the revolt was crushed, Jerusalem was rebuilt into a Roman provincial city named Colonia Aelia Capitolina, a pagan city inhabited only by Gentiles, Romans, Greeks, and other peoples from the Empire, Jews being forbidden to live there on pain of death. Only on the anniversary of the destruction of the Temple were Jews allowed in to bewail the loss of their Temple. The southern gate of Jerusalem, facing toward Bethlehem, portrayed the carved image of a pig. On the Temple hill, a sanctuary rose to Jupiter Capitolinus and the province of Judaea was renamed Syria Palaestina. In Judaea, the Jews were apparently exterminated, but they survived in Galilee, which, like Samaria, seemed not to have been involved in the revolt. Tiberias in Galilee became the residence of Jewish patriarchs who there completed the Mishnah, the Talmud, and other early rabbinic texts.

The Roman Administration of Judaea—Emperors, Governors, and High Priests

ROMAN EMPERORS

Augustus (16 January 27 BC–19 August AD 14)
Tiberius (17 September 14–16 March 37)
Gaius (16 March 37–24 January 41)
Claudius (24 January 41–13 October 54)
Nero (13 October 54–9 June 68)
Galba (10 June 68–15 January 69)
Otho (15 January 69–14 April 69)
Vitellius (2 January 69–20 December 69)
Vespasian (1 July 69–24 June 79)
Titus (24 June 79–13 September 81)
Domitian (14 September 81–16 September 96)
Nerva (16 September 96–25 January 98)
Trajan (25 January 97–8 August 117)
Hadrian (11 August 117–10 July 138)

ROMAN GOVERNORS OF JUDAEA (AD 6–135)

Prefects/Procurators subject to supervision by the
Imperial Legate in Syria (AD 6–66):
Coponius (c. 6–9)
Marcus Ambibulus (c. 9–12)
Annius Rufus (c. 12–15)
Valerius Gratus (15–26)
Pontius Pilate (26–36)
Marcellus/Marullus (36–41)
King Herod Agrippa (41–44)
Cuspius Fadus (44–46?)
Tiberius Iulius Alexander (46?–48)
Ventidius Cumanus (48–c. 52)
Antonius Felix (c. 52–60?)
Porcius Festus (60?–62)
Lucceius Albinus (62–64)
Gessius Florus (64–66)
(Jewish Revolt (66–70))
Commanders of the Legio X Fretensis with praetorian
rank (AD 70–120?): Only isolated names are known:
Sex. Vettulenus Cerialis (70–71?)
Lucilius Bassus (71?–73)
L. Flavius Silva (73–?)
Cn. Pompeius Longinus (80)
Sedx. Hermetidius Campanus (93)
Atticus (99/100?–102/103?)
C. Iulius Quadratus Bassus (c. 102/103–104/105)
Q. Roscius Coelius Pompeius Falco (c. 105–107)
? Tiberianus (c. 114)
Lusius Quietus (c. 117)

Governors of consular rank when the Legio VI Ferrata
was also stationed in Judaea (AD 120?–135):
Q. Tineius Rufus (132)
C. Quninctius Certus Publicius Marcellus (?)
Sex. Iulius Severus (235)

HIGH PRIESTS

Appointed by King Herod the Great (37–4 BC)
Ananel (37–36, and again from 34 BC)
Aristobulus III (35 BC)
Jesus son of Phiabi (to c. 23 BC)
Simon son of Boethus (c. 23–5 BC)
Matthias son of Theophilus (5–4 BC)
Joseph son of Ellem (one day)
Joazar son of Boethus (4 BC)
Appointed by the Tetrarch Archelaus (4 BC–AD 6)
Eleazar son of Boethus (from 4 BC)
Jesus son of See (to AD 6)
Appointed by Quirinius, Legate of Syria (AD 6)
Ananus/Annas son of Sethi (AD 6–15)
Appointed by Gratus, Procurator of Judaea (AD 15–26)
Ismail son of Phiabi (c. 15–16)
Eleazar son of Ananus (c. 16–17)
Simon son of Camithus (c. 17–18)
Josephus Caiaphas (c. 18–37)
Appointed by Vitellius, Legate of Syria (AD 35–39)
Jonathan son of Ananus (two months in 37)
Theophilus son of Ananus (from 37)
Appointed by King Agrippa (AD 41–44)
Simon Cantheras son of Beothus (from 41)
Matthias son of Ananus (?)
Elionaeus son of Cantheras (c. 44)
Appointed by Herod of Chalcis (AD 44–48)
Joseph son of Kami (?)
Ananias son of Nedebaeus (47–c. 59)
Appointed by King Agrippa II (AD 50–92?)
Ismael son of Phiabi (c. 50–61)
Joseph Cabi son of Simon (61–62)
Ananus son of Ananus (three months in 62)
Jesus son of Damnaeus (c. 62–63)
Jesus son of Gamaliel (c. 63–64)
Matthias son of Theophilius (65–?)
Appointed by people during the Revolt (AD 66–70)
Phannias/Phanni/Phanasos son of Samuel (?)

THE JEWISH DIASPORA

"BY THE WATERS OF BABYLON,

THERE WE SAT DOWN, YEA, WE WEPT,

WHEN WE REMEMBERED ZION.

WE HANG OUR HARPS UPON THE WILLOWS IN THE MIDST THEREOF.

FOR THERE THEY THAT CARRIED US AWAY CAPTIVE REQUIRED OF US

A SONG;

AND THEY THAT WASTED US REQUIRED OF US MIRTH, SAYING,

SING US ONE OF THE SONGS OF ZION.

HOW SHALL WE SING THE LORD'S SONG IN A STRANGE LAND?"

PSALMS 137: 1–4

The spread of Christianity was aided by missionaries targeting Greek-speaking Jewish communities outside Palestine. This Jewish Diaspora, or 'exile', was a dispersion of Jews throughout old Babylonia and the Roman Empire, the numbers of Jews increasing by further migrations or conversions. The first dispersion took place after 931 BC, when Jewish tribes in the north split from their southern kin and formed the kingdom of Israel, while the southerners established the kingdom of Judah. Israel collapsed in 722 BC when King Shalmaneser V of Assyria attacked and deported some of the tribes to Khorasan. Nebuchadnezzar II, King of Babylon (630–562 BC), attacked Judah in 597 BC and laid siege to Jerusalem, which left the city and the Temple in ruins. He deported a portion of the Jewish population, including King Jehoiachin, to Babylon and the valley of the Euphrates.

Many Jews fled to Alexandria and Elephantine in Egypt, with the former turning into a major Jewish center. Jews moved about freely in Greek colonies and settlements: the Black Sea saw them in action at Kallatis, Tyras, Olbia, Tanais, Phanagoria and inland in Asia Minor at Trapezunt and Gerasus. Massilia (Marseille), Emporion and Hemeroscopion were other trading centres. The Jews also played a key role as traders in the Carthaginian Empire, establishing vibrant communities. In 536 BC, King

Cyrus of Persia (c. 576–530 BC), who conquered Babylonia, allowed the exiles to return. Many did, but some chose to remain in exile. The entire story is encapsulated in II Chronicles.

The end of the Babylonian captivity is captured in the words of Ezra:

'... THUS SAITH CYRUS KING OF PERSIA. THE LORD GOD OF HEAVEN HATH GIVEN ME ALL THE KINGDOMS OF THE EARTH; AND HE HATH CHARGED ME TO BUILD HIM AN HOUSE AT JERUSALEM, WHICH IS IN JUDAH. WHO IS THERE AMONG YOU OF ALL HIS PEOPLE? HIS GOD BE WITH HIM, AND LET HIM GO UP TO JERUSALEM, WHICH IS IN JUDAH, AND BUILD THE HOUSE OF THE LORD GOD OF ISRAEL (HE IS THE GOD), WHICH IS IN JERUSALEM' (EZRA 1: 2–3).

Nevertheless, some Jews rebelled against Persia in the regions of Babylon, Cutha and Sura. The failure of the revolt witnessed some Jews fleeing north to Hycarnia on the Caspian Sea and toward the Caucasus, while others fled east toward India. By 175 BC, Jews were established in Mumbai. In 320 BC, Egyptian rulers settled 30,000 Jews on the Sinai and Cyrenaican (at Cyrene, Barca, and Ptolemais) borders, and in Cyprus to protect Egypt from attack. Jews were also active in converting tribes to Judaism in modern-day Morocco (in 200 BC), at Sale and Volubilis.

Under Greek Seleucid rule and the later Hasmonean princes, Jews dispersed throughout the known world, as they did under Roman rule after Pompey invaded Jerusalem in 63 BC. As early as the middle of the 2nd Century BC, a Jewish author in the third book of the Oracula Sibyllina recognized that the Jews were present in every land. Works by the period's greatest writers—Greek historian, geographer and philosopher Strabo, the Greek-speaking Jewish philosopher Philo, the Roman philosopher Seneca, and Josephus, the Jewish historian who wrote *Antiquities of the Jews*—all bear witness to the dispersion of the Jewish people.

In a letter to Emperor Caligula (AD 12–41), King Agrippa I of Judea (c. 10 BC–AD 44) stated which Roman provinces were Jewish communities, but ignored the settlement in Rome and Cyrene. Josephus maintained that after Palestine and Babylonia, Syria was host to the densest Jewish population, Antioch and Damascus in particular. Philo claimed that one million Jews inhabited Egypt, comprising one-eighth of the population. Alexandria was the most important Jewish community in Egypt, inhabiting two out of five quarters in the city, according to Philo. The large Jewish community was classified as Politai (citizens) and therefore enjoyed the protection of civil laws. The Jews were a distinct group—below the Greeks, but above the native Egyptians. Alexandrine Jews had not been citizens of the old Greek polis, nor did they wish it. Retention of their status was essential; citizenship would have meant losing their Jewish identity. Considering the number of Jews massacred in 115 BC, the numbers living in Cyrenaica, Cyprus and Mesopotamia must have been very large. In Rome, at the accession of Caesar Augustus (Octavian) to the imperial throne in 27 BC, 7,000 Jews were known to be living in Rome. This is an accurate figure, since this was the number of delegates demanding the deposition of the Hasmonean Prince, Archelaus. Tax records also show 45,000 Jewish males paying taxes in Asia Minor. First Century estimates suggest that 5,000,000 Jews lived outside Palestine, four-fifths of them within the Roman Empire.

Roman rule over Palestine was shaken by a Jewish revolt from AD 66–70 led by the Zealots and finally crushed with the capture of their last stronghold at Masada. One outcome was the destruction of the Temple, the focus of the Temple cult and center of national and religious life. Another result was the creation of several Greek and Roman colonies in Judea, an attempt to dilute Jewish national aspirations. Titus, the Roman victor, exterminated a quarter of the Jewish population and enslaved a further ten per cent, thereby reducing the Jewish population to such an extent that they were almost a minority in their own land. Despite destroying the military power of the Zealots, the Jewish faith remained a powerful unifying force. In the villages and towns of Judea and the Diaspora communities, the teachings and rituals of Judaism continued and a Jewish underground grew. Many Jews hoped a messianic leader would restore their independence, and plotted for that eventuality.

A major Jewish exodus then commenced with Jewish élites fleeing to Mesopotamia, then part of the Parthian Empire. In AD 114, Roman Emperor Trajan attacked the Parthians, invading Mesopotamia. The Roman legions smashed the Parthians, but faced fierce resistance from the large Jewish settlements. These settlers were enraged that the destroyers of the Temple were now attacking them again. Jewish troops were recruited at Nisibis. Queen Helena of the semi-independent Kingdom of Adiabene had converted to Judaism, both supported the revolt in Judea and allowed Jewish forces to be recruited in her lands.

The conflict in Mesopotamia signalled a general Jewish revolt in the Roman Empire. Risings commenced in Cyrene (modern Libya), spreading to Alexandria and Cyprus. Judea saw unrest but no actual rebellion. The Romans crushed the revolts with great difficulty, exterminating the Cypriot Jewish community and burning the main synagogue in Alexandria. Trajan's successor, Hadrian, withdrew from Parthia allowing peace for the Mesopotamian Jews.

A second Jewish revolt lasting from AD 132–135 under Simon bar Kokhba ended in defeat with his last supporters being hunted down in the caves of the Dead Sea region. Some half a million Jews were massacred during this war and thousands sold into slavery. Judea became known as Syria-Palaestina and Jerusalem was dedicated to Jupiter. Even so, Jewish communities remained in the Negev, Galilee and the Jordan Valley. Gamaliel III became head of the Jewish community and leader of the Sandedrin while he established an academy at Usha in Lower Galilee. He and his successors compiled part of the Torah, comprising the Psalms and Proverbs, the Song of Songs and the Books of Job, Ruth, Lamentations, Ecclesiastes, Esther, Daniel, Ezra, Nehemiah and the Chronicles—collectively known as the Writings or Hagiography (Ketuvim).

The destruction of the Temple saw the final dispersion of the Jews throughout the world. The Jews sold as slaves ended up everywhere, as did captives generally. Diaspora Jews were eventually accepted into the Roman Empire. Other Jewish communities were expelled from Judea and despatched to various Roman provinces in the Middle East, Europe and

ROUTES OF DISPERSAL
(*right*) The main diaspora of the Jews began in the 8th-6th centuries BC. The number of Jews that were dispersed was greater than that living in Israel. After this period Jews were dispersed broadly throughout the Roman Empire and the world beyond.

The Jewish Diaspora, c. 1300 B.C.E. – c. 300
- Extent of the Roman Empire, c. 300 C.E.
- Kingdom of David, 10th century B.C.E.
- Kingdom of Israel, 931 – 722 B.C.E.
- Kingdom of Judah, 931 – 587 B.C.E
- Probable route of the Exodus, 13th century
- Route of Babylonian exile, 587 B.C.E.
- Jewish dispersion routes, c. 70 B.C.E. – c.30

North Africa. With the rise of Christianity, however, came restrictions, especially as Jewish communities became a major focus of Christian missionary work. Jews in Babylon enjoyed a different life, becoming the center of Judaism. In the 3rd Century AD, a religious academy was established in Babylon with another founded at Pumbetia in Mesopotamia. These centres became significant in creating the most important version of the Talmud, and Sua and Pumbetia became the major centres of Judaic thought until the 9th Century. Interestingly, these eastern Jews enjoyed relatively autonomy whether living under the rule of the Assyro-Chaldeans, the Persians, the Parthians and, eventually, the Muslims.

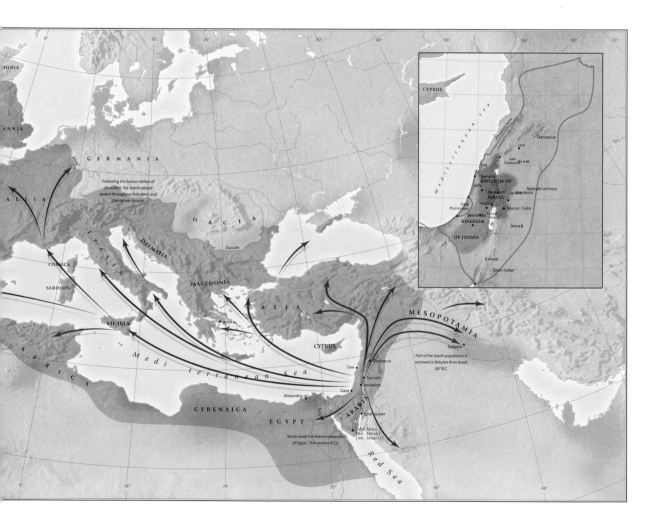

EARLY CHRISTIAN DEVELOPMENT

"WE BELIEVE IN ONE GOD, THE FATHER, THE ALMIGHTY, MAKER OF HEAVEN AND EARTH, OF ALL THAT IS SEEN AND UNSEEN. WE BELIEVE IN ONE LORD, JESUS CHRIST, THE ONLY SON OF GOD, ETERNALLY BEGOTTEN OF THE FATHER, GOD FROM GOD, LIGHT FROM LIGHT, TRUE GOD FROM TRUE GOD, BEGOTTEN, NOT MADE, OF ONE BEING WITH THE FATHER ..."   (NICENE CREED)

The Greek culture and language dominating the eastern Mediterranean region assisted the spread of Christianity beyond the boundaries of Palestine. The dispersed Jewish communities in towns spread throughout the Middle East spoke Greek, possessed a Greek translation of the Old Testament and provided the first Christian missionaries with points of contact with the local population. The initial, speedy expansion of Christianity during New Testament times was northward into the Greek cultural zone of Syria, Asia Minor, and Greece, and into the Greek speaking areas of North Africa, particularly Alexandria and Cyrene. Until the end of the 2nd Century, the lists of the Bishops of Rome show them to be Greek-speaking, and the New Testament was first written in Greek.

Syrian Edessa was the portal through which Christianity would spread beyond the borders of the Roman Empire into Mesopotamia, where Syriac became the language of Christian worship and devotion. From there Christianity reached slowly into Persia and India. Once Christianity had spread into the Western, Latin-speaking areas of the Roman Empire, Christianity advanced swiftly. By the 3rd Century AD, there were more than one hundred bishops in Italy, while Christianity established itself in Gaul and Spain. After the Romans gave Christianity official recognition in AD 313, there were at least three bishoprics in Britain and, elsewhere, St. Patrick's mission to Ireland started about AD 432.

HOLY SETTLEMENTS
Christians at first met in
private homes, but in time
began to construct chapels for
worship, and entire religious
communities based around
the church, such as Iona, a
small island off Scotland,
which was founded as a
Celtic monastery in 563AD
by Columba.

During this expansion, Christians engaged in the holy meal of bread and wine—the Eucharist (thanksgiving)—which was, and still is, regarded as a sacrament, a conduit for divine grace to permeate the recipient with the spirit of Christ. Converts were initiated into the Church via baptism through which God's grace washed away all sins. Interestingly, for obscure or hidden reasons, the wide range of written texts telling the story of the Christian faith had been whittled down to those ascribed to Matthew, Mark, Luke, and John, which became the core of the New Testament. Christians were also inspired by the lives of saints, whose written tradition is known as hagiography.

Initially, Christian communities met in private homes, but eventually purpose-built churches became the norm. A distinction grew up between the clergy and laity. The former governed the Church and administered the sacraments, while the latter were the recipients. The clergy became ordained into the priesthood and became divided into ranks: the priests administered the Eucharist, while the bishops supervised priests and led Christian urban communities. Archbishops supervised the bishops, and were sometimes known as metropolitans. The most important bishops were those of the greatest and most influential cities, such as Rome, Antioch, Alexandria, Jerusalem, and Constantinople. These bishops were known as patriarchs. Of these, only one lived in the West, and claimed to have pre-eminence—Peter. The most important of the apostles, Peter lived out his last years in Rome and was martyred there. He was held to be the first pope and later popes considered themselves his successors. However, the other patriarchs refused to acknowledge Rome's authority until centuries later.

The Christians were convinced that they possessed the absolute truth and totally rejected all other religions. This certitude and arrogance resulted in intermittent waves of persecution, which finally ended when joint Emperors Constantine and Licinius granted Christians official toleration and protection in 313. The Roman emperors nourished Christianity and several councils of bishops were held in the fourth century to iron out doctrinal disputes and set out rules of behavior, and gradually things began to change. Magnificent and awesome Christian churches were built. The emperors ended gladiatorial combat in the arena and replaced it with chariot races. The abandonment of babies was prohibited, but slavery continued for so-called economic reasons. Constantine's activities won him the support of the Church, which led to imperial legitimation.

The Christian faith won over massive numbers of converts and became the dominant religion in the Mediterranean, but its character changed for the worse. The Church became controlled by the wealthy, aristocratic families, thereby diminishing its initial equality and women's roles were curtailed that weakened their earlier role in church formation. The institutionalized Church became ever more patriarchal, rigid, and much spirituality withered on the vine.

The Church now switched its fight against paganism and Roman gods to enemies within the fold. Issues of doctrine became paramount, with disagreements between schools of thought being fought out as conflicts between orthodoxy and heresy. The most noticeable confrontation was between orthodox Trinitarianism and Arianism. Arianism was condemned at the Council of Nicaea in 325 and the reign of Emperor Theodosius I (AD 378–395) witnessed the state adding to the ban on Arianism by outlawing its teachings and making Christianity the official religion of the Roman state. Arians based their views on those of Arius, a Libyan who studied at the school of Lucien of Antioch. Despite his views being outlawed, they survived amongst the Germanic tribes into the late sixth century.

Arius contended that God was unbegotten and without beginning, whereas Christ was begotten, and could not be God in the sense of God the Father. Christ the Son was not created from the divine substance of the Father; he did not exist from all eternity, but was formed out of nothing like all other creatures, and existed by the will of the Father. In other words, the relationship of the Son to the Father was not natural, but adoptive. A letter from Arius to Eusebius of Nicomedia, Patriarch of Constantinople (AD 339–342), stated, "We are persecuted, because we say that the Son has a beginning, but that God is without beginning."

The Council of Nicea formulated the Nicene Creed, which remains intact and is still used by Roman Catholic, Orthodox, Anglican, and some Protestant services. The Creed affirms that Father and Son are of one being. Arius was exiled as were the Libyan bishops Theonas of Marmarica and Secundus of Ptolemais. These events failed to end controversy. Constantine wanted leniency to exist regarding Arius and his Arians. Arius was rehabilitated and his main accuser, Athanasius, Bishop of Alexandria, banished. This man was rehabilitated and exiled several times, but is now a saint. Constantine's son Constantius II (AD 351–361) attacked adherents of the Nicene Creed, preferring Arianism. However, supporters of Arius splintered into various groups who sought to reconcile their differences in 18 councils. Theodosius sought to end all confrontation at the ecumenical council at Constantinople in 381. Henceforth, the Nicene Creed was accepted by the Roman peoples, excepting the Germans.

As Arianism began to flourish in Constantinople, a Goth convert named Ulfilas was despatched as a missionary to the Gothic tribes across the River Danube, this being seen as a means of diminishing the Goth threat if they converted. Ulfilas was incredibly successful in teaching, preaching and converting the Germanic tribes to the Arian brand of Christianity. These Germans, having now been Christian for over a century, eventually entered the Roman Empire and founded successor states in the western part, such as Lombardy in Italy. In these Arian Germanic kingdoms, the Germanic Arian élite co-existed with their Nicene subjects. Parallel Church hierarchies worked with the élites, holding on to Arianism in order to keep their identity amidst the majority Nicene peoples. The Germans tolerated Nicene beliefs, except in North Africa where the Nicene clergy and their institutions were persecuted. The Arian German kingdoms included the Ostrogoths, the Visigoths, Vandals, Burgundians, and Lombards. The Franks converted to Nicene Christianity immediately and their leader, Pepin, supported the Pope in his search for secular lands to protect Rome and in turn was anointed King of the Franks, thereby usurping the traditional Merovingian rulers. By the beginning of the Eighth Century, these Germanic kingdoms had been either converted or conquered by their neighbors, or, like the Visigoths and Lombards, they had accepted Nicene Christianity.

Elsewhere, a division within Nicene Christianity occurred that mirrored the divisions of the old Roman Empire into East and West. Western Christians looked to the Pope in Rome for authority as he claimed authority over all Christians, using the term catholic (universal) to categorise his faith. Eastern Christians rejected this claim, and regarded the Byzantine Emperor and the patriarch of Constantinople as their leaders. This division between Catholic and Eastern Orthodox Christians developed over several centuries with various issues being disputed, but the year 1054 is usually accepted as the date of the schism between East and West because Pope Leo IX (1049-1054) and Patrirach Michael Cerularius (1043–58) excommunicated each other.

The Western Church is particularly important in another sense. It digested Roman political organisation, administration, and law. The Pope assumed the ancient Roman title of pontifex maximus (supreme pontiff), and kept going much of the ritual of the late imperial courts. Canon law, that is Church law, is modelled on Roman civil law and in this sense the early medieval church was a specter of the Roman Empire. Perhaps the greatest difference however, is that Church allowed the masses to participate in common rituals, providing a sense of involvement and identity, which had never happened under the Roman Empire.

THE SPREAD OF CHRISTIANITY

DESPITE INTERMITTENT PERIODS OF PERSECUTION,
CHRISTIANITY EXPANDED RAPIDLY, WAS GIVEN ROMAN LEGAL
STATUS IN 313, AND WAS HELPED BY THE MONASTIC MOVEMENT.
HOWEVER, ABOUT 750, MOHAMMED'S ISLAMIC RELIGION, WHICH
RECOGNIZED ALLAH AS THE ONLY GOD, CONTROLLED SOME
MEDITERRANEAN AREAS AND THE EAST AS FAR AS INDIA.

D uring the early days of Christianity, the authors of the New Testament saw the rapid spread of
the new faith as miraculous. It provided direct evidence of the divinity of Jesus. The final
phase of God's plans to save the world must have begun, clearly shown by the Christian
groups that sprang up and survived in the towns from Palestine to Rome. The movement was helped by a
number of factors, particularly the peace imposed by Rome on her Empire, which by now included all the
peoples of the Mediterranean and Black Sea areas, the whole of Europe as far east as the River Rhine, and
most of Britain. Wherever the Romans gained control they created safe, efficient communications by both
land and sea, in order to move administrators and troops swiftly, and to supply the needs of Rome's
teeming population.

The official religions of the Empire were extensions of Roman power that tended to confirm and justify
its rule and the divine authority of the Emperor. Christianity, on the other hand, offered its members a sense
of freedom, equality, and community, which transcended all differences of race, social class, and legal
status. The destruction of Jerusalem by the Romans in AD 70 helped to free Christianity from its Jewish
origins so that it could make a more universal appeal and meet the needs of non-Jewish converts without
the restrictions of the Hebrew religious laws.

From the time of Alexander the Great's triumphant reign (336–323 BC), Greek culture and language had
dominated the eastern Mediterranean region, and this also assisted the spread of Christianity beyond the

RESURRECTED CHRIST
(far right)
The first appearance of the
resurrected Christ was
to Mary Magdalene. This
painting of the scene, from
the Scrovegni Chapel,
Padua in Italy, is by
Giotto (1276–1337).

THE EXPANSION OF CHRISTIANITY

From its centers in the Greek-speaking world, Christianity spread into Mesopotamia, Persia and India. It was soon firmly established in western Europe, including Britain, and for most of the time Christians were allowed to practice their religion without interference, even though there are records of two widespread persecutions by the Roman authorities in AD 250 and 303. In AD 313 the joint Roman Emperors, Constantine and Licinius, gave legal recognition to Christianity. When Constantine moved the capital of the Roman Empire from Rome to Constantinople in AD 331, he hoped that Christianity would unite all his subjects, for the Empire was beginning to disintegrate. The differences between Greek-speaking Christians and Latin-speaking Christians had become more serious. In AD 325 a council held at Nicea tried to close the widening breach with a creed that set out the basic beliefs of Christianity. Six more ecumenical councils during the following four and a half centuries would try to establish a form of Christianity faithful to its founder and agreed by all Christians.

The Spread of Christianity

- Christian by AD 45
- Christian by AD 100
- Christian by AD 185
- Christian by AD 325
- Roman Empire c. 300

SARMATIA

DACIA

MOESIA

THRACIA

MACEDONIA

Byzantium

BITHYNIA AND PONTUS

Maeotis Palus

Pontus Euxinus
Black Sea

Sinope

Trapezus

Nicopolis

CAPPADOCIA

ARMENIA

Artaxata

Caucasus Mountains

Sinus Oxianus

Mare Caspium
Caspian Sea

ASIA

GALATIA

CILICIA

Ephesus

Athenae

LYCIA

CYPRUS

Creta

Tarsus

Antiochia

SYRIA

ASSYRIA

MESOPOTAMIA

Babylon

PERSIAN EMPIRE

Cyrene

Mare   Internum

Tyre

Damascus

Bostra

JUDAEA   Jerusalem

Gaza

Alexandria

Heliopolis

Memphis

ARABIA

Arabian

Desert

Sinus Persicus

CYRENE

AEGYPTUS

Antinopolis

Thebes

Sinus Arabic

N

0   500 km

0   500 miles

MEMPHIS MOSAIC
The old town of Memphis is
depicted in this detail of a
mosaic in the church of St. John
in Khirbet El-Samra in Jordan.

confines of Palestine. The scattered Jewish communities in towns throughout the Near East spoke Greek, had a Greek translation of the Old Testament, and provided the first Christian missionaries with convenient points of contact with the population. The first rapid expansion of Christianity during New Testament times was northward into the Greek world of Syria, Asia Minor, and Greece, and into the Greek-speaking areas of northern Africa, particularly Alexandria and Cyrene. The lists of the early bishops of Rome show that until the end of the 2nd Century they were all Greek-speaking and, indeed, the New Testament was originally written in Greek.

Edessa in Syria was the gateway for Christianity to reach beyond the borders of the Roman Empire into Mesopotamia, where Syriac became the language of Christian worship and devotion, and from there Christianity spread slowly into Persia and India. Once it had penetrated effectively into the western, Latin-speaking areas of Roman rule, Christianity made rapid advances. By the 3rd Century AD, there were more than a hundred bishoprics in Italy, and Christianity was firmly established in Gaul and Spain. In the following century, when the Romans gave Christianity official recognition, there were at least three bishoprics in Britain (London, York, and either Colchester or Lincoln) while St. Patrick's mission to Ireland began about 432.

Persecution of Christians by the Roman authorities was usually spasmodic and localised, typified by Nero's notorious cruelty to them in Rome following the great fire of AD 64. However, the martyrdoms at Lyons in 177, during the reign of the Emperor Marcus Aurelius (161–180), show how intense such local persecutions could be. There are records of two more universal persecutions—the Emperor Decius (249–251) mounted a systematic attack on Christianity in 250, and a subsequent period of tolerance ended abruptly in 303 when the Emperor Diocletian (284–305) ordered all churches and Christian books to be destroyed and followed this with the execution of Christians during the next eight years. The first main phase of Christian expansion ended with the Edict of Milan in 313, when the joint Emperors Constantine (c. 306–337) and Licinius (308–314) gave Christianity legal recognition. From that date, Constantine, as senior Emperor, forged close links between Christianity and the Roman state.

In granting recognition to Christianity in 313, the Emperor Constantine hoped that Christianity would unite all his subjects in a common faith and help withstand the barbarian incursions, for the Roman Empire was beginning to disintegrate. In 331, Constantine moved the capital of the Empire from Rome to Constantinople (Istanbul), the new city he had built to command the sea passage from the Mediterranean to the Black Sea. As the western parts of the Empire crumbled, so the cultural differences between the eastern, Greek-speaking Christians, and the western, Latin-speakers became more obvious. The uncertainties of intermittent persecution and tolerance had helped unite Christians but the new period of official recognition brought differences out into the open.

Freedom from fear of official interference allowed resentments to surface against Christians who had submitted to the Roman laws against Christianity, even though a Church synod ruled that there should be no rejection of the lapsed who wished to return. A more serious split amongst Christians developed from Alexandria, where a controversy raged about the exact status of Jesus Christ as God, and spread throughout the eastern churches. The Emperor Constantine convened a council at Nicea in 325, which set out the basic beliefs of Christianity in a creed for universal acceptance. Nicea was followed by six more ecumenical councils during the following four and a half centuries to try to settle further controversies and establish a

"I AM THE TRUE VINE, AND MY FATHER IS THE HUSBANDMAN.

"EVERY BRANCH IN ME THAT BEARETH NOT FRUIT HE TAKETH AWAY: AND EVERY BRANCH THAT BEARETH FRUIT, HE PURGETH IT, THAT IT MAY BRING FORTH MORE FRUIT.

"NOW YE ARE CLEAN THROUGH THE WORD WHICH I HAVE SPOKEN UNTO YOU.

"ABIDE IN ME, AND IT IN YOU. AS THE BRANCH CANNOT BEAR FRUIT OF ITSELF, EXCEPT IT ABIDE IN THE VINE; NO MORE CAN YE, EXCEPT YE ABIDE IN ME.

"I AM THE VINE, YE ARE THE BRANCHES: HE THAT ABIDETH IN ME, AND I IN HIM, THE SAME BRINGETH FORTH MUCH FRUIT: FOR WITHOUT ME YE CAN DO NOTHING."
JOHN 15:1–5

form of Christianity agreed by all Christians. They met at Constantinople (381), Ephesus (431), Chalcedon (451), Constantinople again (553 and 680) and Nicea (787).

Inevitably, the Christians adopted much of the administrative organisation of the Roman Empire, if only because it provided convenient and natural geographical division and symbols of authority—even in such matters as ceremonial dress familiar to all. A diocese was originally a larger administrative region of secular government within the Roman Empire, containing a number of provinces. In time the term was applied to the larger areas of ecclesiastical jurisdiction, containing a number of bishoprics, and finally to the smaller area ruled by each bishop. An important stage in the recognition of special influence by the Bishop of Rome was reached at the time of the Council of Chalcedon (451), when the Bishop of Constantinople appealed to Leo, Bishop of Rome, for help and received a summary of the Christian faith, the "Tome of Leo," which was given official status by the Council.

Even before the recognition of Christianity by Constantinople, a new movement developed first in Egypt and then in other places which was to have lasting effects on the spread of Christianity. Christian hermits who had withdrawn to the desert in Egypt became so numerous that they organized themselves into communities with a common rule, which recognized the individualism of the hermits' ideals but provided for shared worship. The movement, monasticism, spread in modified forms to Arabia, Asia Minor, north Africa, Spain, and Britain, where Patrick made it the means of consolidating Christianity in Ireland. In the following century, Columba took monasticism from Ireland to Scotland, establishing a monastery at what was then a center of communications on the island of Iona, and consolidated the work begun by Ninian nearly two centuries earlier.

The form of monasticism most familiar in the West stems from Benedict, who transformed the hermit type of monasticism in Italy into a thoroughly integrated and organized form of community life controlled by his famous Rule. Benedict's twin principles of "stability"—commitment to the community and to the Rule—quickly gained followers. The Benedictine form of monasticism spread rapidly within Italy, and was introduced into Britain by Augustine of Canterbury in 597. Eventually, it became the normal form of monasticism in the West and one of the main means of extending the influence of Rome within Christianity.

ROCK TOMB *(far right)*
Jesus' body was taken down from the cross and laid in an empty rock tomb similar to this one. The rolled-back circular stone door was the first sign of Jesus' Resurrection from the dead.

With the collapse of the western parts of the Roman Empire under barbarian attacks, and the gradual conversion of the invading peoples, it might have seemed that Christianity would prove to be a unifying force to replace the old military might of Rome. However, an important setback to such an ideal came from an unexpected area in the Arabian Desert to the east of the Red Sea.

The main religion of the nomads of the Arabian Desert, and the people of the isolated towns on the main caravan routes, was a polytheism of many gods associated with particular localities or various aspects of nature and of human need. All that was changed dramatically by Mohammed, who was born into a prominent family in Mecca about 570. The first 40 years of his life were in no way extraordinary. Mohammed traveled with the caravans from Mecca as far as Syria as a merchant, and married. His call as a prophet came to him at the age of 40, and he began his preaching some three years later in Mecca.

Both Judaism and Christianity had penetrated into Arabia, and the caravans came into contact with them at the great trading centres in Syria and Mesopotamia, but Mohammed preached a monotheism that identified Allah, the chief god of Mecca, as the sole God of the universe who alone must be worshipped. The main practical consequence for believers was acceptance of the equality of all people before God, and the duty of all to care for the less fortunate.

Mohammed claimed that he was only the last of a line of prophets sent by God, which included Abraham, Moses, and Jesus, but to Mohammed God dictated a sacred book through an angel that contains all that is needed for belief, the regulation of personal life and the organization of society. This book, the Koran (or Qu'ran), is in Arabic and is divided into 114 chapters or suras. It is so sacred for Islam that strict Muslims will not recognize any translation of it. The pattern of life derived from the Koran is expressed in five "pillars of faith"—belief in Allah as the only God, and Mohammed as his prophet; prayer five times each day; alms-giving; fasting during daylight hours in the month of Ramadan; and a pilgrimage to Mecca.

From the beginning, Mohammed had to assert the supremacy of his teaching by force, to overcome the antagonism of the families that controlled western Arabia, particularly Mecca. War remained a legitimate means of spreading God's revelation if people would not accept it peacefully. But the religion preached by Mohammed and perpetuated through the Koran would never have achieved such remarkable success if it had not been so attractive. To the believer, it provides a simple, systematic and coherent way of life.

With remarkable speed, the new religion embarked on a great campaign of conquest, first within Arabia itself and then into the surrounding areas of Syria, Palestine, Mesopotamia, Egypt and northern Africa. By the middle of the 8th Century it had expanded into India and had control of most of Spain. Much of this was achieved within 20 years of the death of Mohammed in 632. Breathtakingly beautiful shrines were erected, such as the Dome of the Rock in Jerusalem. It was built in 691 over the place where Muslims believe that Mohammed began his "night journey" in which the glories of heaven were revealed to him. Traditionally, this is also the place where Abraham was prepared to sacrifice Isaac (Genesis 22), and the site of the Hebrew Temple before its destruction by the Romans in AD 70.

THE DOME OF THE ROCK
Seen from the Mount of Olives, the Temple area dominates Jerusalem. The main feature is the great stone platform for the Temple courtyards, built by Herod the Great. The Temple itself stood on the site of the domed building, a Muslim shrine that protects the bare rock of the hill sacred to Jews and Muslims. The Jerusalem of King David's time lay to the left of the present Temple area and the city spread beyond the Temple, where modern Jerusalem has continued to expand.

PEOPLE OF THE BIBLE

ALL OF THE MOST IMPORTANT—AND INTERESTING—
CHARACTERS IN THE OLD AND NEW TESTAMENTS HAVE BEEN
SELECTED FOR THIS "WHO'S WHO" OF THE BIBLE. CHARACTERS
ARE LISTED IN THE ORDER IN WHICH THEY APPEAR AND MAJOR
BIBLE REFERENCES ARE GIVEN.

ADAM

The first man, Adam was created out of dust by God and was given the task of naming and ruling over all the animals. He and his wife, Eve, were placed in the beautiful and fruitful garden of Eden and told that they could eat fruit from every tree, except the tree of the knowledge of good and evil. First Eve and then Adam succumbed to temptation and ate this fruit, as a result of which they became aware of their nakedness and made themselves clothes from fig leaves. When God accused him of disobedience, Adam blamed Eve, but God cast them both out of the garden.
Meaning of name: Earth, man
Bible reference: Genesis 2–3; 4:1, 25; 5:1–4

EVE

The first woman. According to one account she was made in God's image at the same time as man; another account has her created from Adam's rib. Eve was deceived by the serpent into disobeying God's commandment and she ate the forbidden fruit and then offered it to Adam. Before God cast them out of the garden, He told Eve that she would now suffer in childbirth and be subject to her husband.
Meaning of name: Life
Bible reference: Genesis 2:18–4:2

CAIN

The eldest son of Adam and Eve and the first murderer in the Bible. Cain was jealous when his brother Abel's offering of a lamb was preferred by God to his own offering of crops, and he killed his brother. When God asked him where Abel was, Cain replied, "Am I my brother's keeper?" God told Cain that from then on he would become a permanent fugitive, but set a mark upon him so that he should not be killed.
Meaning of name: Acquisition
Bible reference: Genesis 4

ABEL

The second son of Adam and Eve. He became a shepherd and God was pleased with the offering of his first-born lamb as a sacrifice. Abel was subsequently murdered by his angry brother Cain, whose own offering to God had been rejected.
Meaning of name: Meadow, breath, or vanity
Bible reference: Genesis 4:2–9

NOAH

An early patriarch. Noah was a good and just man at a time of great wickedness. God regretted having created

humankind and planned to destroy all living things by a flood, but He decided to save Noah and his family. He gave Noah instructions for building an ark to accommodate himself, his wife, his sons and their wives, and two of each animal. Noah built the ark and when the rains came he, his family and the animals were saved but everyone else was destroyed. After seven months the ark came to rest on the top of Mount Ararat. Noah sent out a dove and it returned with an olive leaf, so they knew that the flood had abated. God made a covenant with Noah that He would never again destroy the world by flood and the sign of the covenant was a rainbow.
Meaning of name: Rest
Bible reference: Genesis 5:28–9:29

ABRAHAM
Abraham was a descendent of Noah. He was born in Ur in Babylonia, but his family moved to Haran. Abraham prospered there, but when he was 75-years-old God told him to leave Haran and travel to Canaan. God promised Abraham that he would become the father of a great nation and, as a sign of this covenant, Abraham and all his male descendants were to be circumcised.
    Abraham's wife Sarah was barren but her servant Hagar had borne him a son, Ishmael. At last, when Abraham and Sarah were both very old, God promised them a son, and Isaac was born. When Isaac was a young man God tested Abraham's faith and obedience by commanding him to take Isaac up a mountain and offer him as a sacrifice. Abraham obeyed but as he was about to kill his son he was stopped by an angel and God provided a ram to be sacrificed in Isaac's place.
    Abraham was the ancestor of all the Hebrew people and Isaiah 41 refers to him as God's friend.
Meaning of name: Father of a multitude
Bible reference: Genesis 11:27–25:10

LOT
Nephew of Abraham. He accompanied Abraham to Canaan, but they separated and Lot elected to live in the fruitful Jordan Valley, where he settled among the notorious people of Sodom. However he was rescued by angels when the city was destroyed by God. Lot protected the angels whom he was entertaining from the lust of the men of Sodom, but his virtue is diminished by the fact that he offered his daughters instead. When they escaped the destruction of the city, Lot's wife looked back and turned into a pillar of salt. Making their father drunk, Lot's daughters conceived sons by him, who became the ancestors of the Moabites and the Ammonites.
Meaning of name: Covering or concealed
Bible reference: Genesis 11:27, 31; 12:5, 13; 14:12–16, 19

SARAH
Wife of Abraham. Sarah was also Abraham's half-sister and on two occasions during their travels Abraham pretended she was his sister, for he was afraid that her great beauty might endanger his safety. Sarah was childless for many years but when she was an old woman Abraham entertained three angels who declared that she would have a son. Sarah laughed when she heard this, but she gave birth to Isaac. (*Also see* Hagar, Ishmael.)
Meaning of name: Princess
Bible reference: Genesis 11:29–30; 12:11–20; 16:1–6; 17:15–19; 18:1–15, 20; 21:1–10; 23:1–2, 19

HAGAR
Egyptian handmaid of Sarah. When Sarah was unable to conceive, she gave Hagar to Abraham as a concubine. Hagar became pregnant, which made her despise her mistress. Sarah treated her harshly and Hagar fled, but she met an angel who told her to return. Hagar had a son, Ishmael, but after her own son was born Sarah cast Hagar and Ishmael out. In the wilderness they ran out of water and Hagar left her son, for she did not want to witness his death. Then God spoke to her and she saw a well of water; she and Ishmael drank and were saved.
Meaning of name: Flight
Bible reference: Genesis 16, 21:9–21

ISHMAEL
Son of Abraham and Hagar. When Hagar fled from Sarah (*see* Hagar), the angel who appeared to her told her that the son she would bear would be called Ishmael, and would be a wild man whom everyone would oppose. When Isaac was weaned, his father gave a feast and Sarah saw Ishmael mocking. He and his mother were cast out to wander in the wilderness. Ishmael grew up, became an archer and married an Egyptian woman.
Meaning of name: God hears
Bible reference: Genesis 16:3–4, 15; 17:18, 20, 23–27; 21:9–21; 25:12–18; 28:9

REBEKAH
Wife of Isaac. Abraham sent his more trusted servant to look for a wife for Isaac and when he stopped at a well, Rebekah offered him water and hospitality at her father's house. The servant realised that she was related to his master and he arranged a marriage between her and Isaac. Rebekah was barren for 20 years until she gave birth to the twins Esau and Jacob. Rebekah loved Jacob best and it was she who planned the tricking of Isaac over Esau's blessing (*see* Esau).
Meaning of name: Noose
Bible reference: Genesis 24:15–67; 25:20–24, 28; 26:35; 27:5–17, 42–46

ESAU
Elder son of Isaac and Rebekah. Esau became a hunter and his father's favorite. Being the first-born of twins, Esau was entitled to the birthright, but he sold it to his brother, Jacob, in return for some lentil stew. Esau was then tricked out of

his father's blessing by Jacob and Rebekah. Isaac had asked Esau to bring venison and make him a stew from it, so he could eat and then bless his son before he died. But Rebekah made a stew and covered Jacob in goat skin so that he would feel hairy like his brother. Jacob then pretended to be Esau and obtained the blessing. Esau hated Jacob for this, and wanted to kill him, but eventually the brothers were reconciled.
Meaning of name: Hairy
Bible reference: Genesis 25:21–34; 26:34–27:46; 28:6–9, 32–33; 35:29–36:19

JACOB

Second son of Isaac and Rebekah. He cheated his twin brother out of his birthright and his father's blessing (*see* Esau). After the latter episode, Jacob fled from Esau's wrath to take refuge with his uncle Laban. On his way he dreamed that he saw a ladder reaching up to heaven and that God promised to be with him. Jacob fell in love with Laban's younger daughter, Rachel, but Laban tricked him into marrying her as well (*see* Leah). Jacob became very rich and had 12 sons by his two wives and two concubines. After 20 years he and his family left Laban to return to Canaan; on the way Jacob wrestled with a strange man, apparently an angel, who renamed him Israel.
Meaning of name: Follower, supplanter
Bible reference: Genesis 25:21–34, 27–35; 37:1, 3, 10, 31–35; 42:1–4, 29–38; 43:1–14, 46–49

RACHEL

Wife of Jacob. When Jacob traveled to Haran to stay with his uncle Laban, the first person he met was Laban's younger daughter, Rachel, who was taking her father's sheep to water. Rachel was beautiful and Jacob fell in love with her, but was tricked into marrying her sister first (*see* Leah). Rachel was childless for many years, although Jacob fathered sons on her handmaid, Bilhah, but at last she gave birth to Joseph. Rachel did not share her husband's devotion to God for, when they left Laban, she stole her father's household gods and when he pursued them she hid the images so he could not find them. Rachel died giving birth to Benjamin, the youngest of Jacob's sons.
Meaning of name: Ewe
Bible reference: Genesis 29:6–30:1–24; 31:4–19, 33–35; 33:1, 7; 35:16–20; Jeremiah 31:15

LEAH

Wife of Jacob. Leah was the elder daughter of Laban. Jacob fell in love with her sister Rachel and agreed to serve Laban for seven years to earn her. After this time Jacob claimed Rachel as his wife but on the wedding night Laban substituted Leah for her sister—a trick that Jacob did not realise until the morning. Jacob was allowed to marry Rachel too, but had to serve Laban another seven years for her. There was considerable jealousy between the sisters, Leah envying Rachel because Jacob loved her best and Rachel envying Leah her fertility.
Meaning of name: Cow
Bible reference: Genesis 29:16–35; 30:9–21: 49:31

JOSEPH

Son of Jacob and Rachel. Joseph incurred the hatred of his older brothers because of his father's favoritism and because of his own dreams, in which he appeared to be prophesying that he would rule over them. They considered killing him but finally sold him to merchants, although they told Jacob that he had been killed by animals.

Joseph was taken into Egypt and sold to Potiphar, one of the Pharaoh's officers. He found favor with Potiphar and was promoted to overseer, but when he rejected the advances of Potiphar's wife she pretended he had assaulted her and he was imprisoned. While in prison he successfully interpreted his fellow prisoners' dreams and when the Pharaoh had a dream Joseph was summoned to interpret it. The interpretation was that there would be plentiful years followed by famine, and Joseph advised the Pharaoh to store grain during the good years. The Pharaoh agreed and appointed Joseph as governor. He became rich and powerful, and when his brothers arrived in Egypt to buy corn they failed to recognize him. Joseph eventually revealed himself and told his brothers he forgave them because God had blessed him so greatly.
Meaning of name: God increases
Bible reference: Genesis 30:22–24, 37, 39–50

MOSES

Leader and lawgiver. Adopted by the Pharaoh's daughter (*see* Miriam), Moses had a privileged upbringing, but he identified with his own people and resented their oppression by the Egyptians. He was forced to flee to Midian after killing an Egyptian who was beating a Hebrew slave. While he was in Midian, God spoke to Moses from a miraculously burning bush, and told him to return to Egypt and liberate his people.

Moses asked the Pharaoh to let the people leave Egypt but when he refused, God visited the Egyptians with plagues of frogs, flies, locusts, boils, and hailstorms. The rivers turned to blood, there was darkness over the land and all the animals died. However it was not until God killed all the first-born sons of the Egyptians did Pharaoh agree to let the Hebrew people go. After they left, the Egyptians pursued them to the Red Sea. God told Moses to hold his hand over the sea. The waters divided and the Hebrews crossed the sea, but when the Egyptians followed they were drowned.

At Mount Sinai God gave Moses the laws that the people were to obey, including the Ten Commandments. Moses led the people through the desert for 40 years as spiritual and military leader, until they reached the land God had promised them, but Moses himself did not enter the land.
Meaning of name: Child or drawn forth
Bible reference: Exodus 2–40; Leviticus 1:1; Numbers 1–36; Deuteronomy 1–34

AARON

The elder brother of Moses. He was chosen by God to be Moses' spokesman because of his eloquence, and was the first High Priest of Israel. It was Aaron who was responsible for making the golden calf that the Israelites worshipped while Moses was on Mount Sinai.

Meaning of name: Mountain
Bible reference: Exodus 4:14–16; 5:1; 17:12, 28, 29, 32; Numbers 12, 17–20

MIRIAM

Sister of Moses and Aaron. The family lived in Egypt, and Moses was born at a time when the Pharaoh had ordered all male Hebrew babies to be killed. Their mother hid Moses in a basket and left it by the river. When the Pharaoh's daughter discovered the baby, Miriam offered to find him a nurse, and fetched her mother to nurse Moses. Miriam became a prophetess and led the women in celebrating their crossing of the Red Sea. Miriam and Aaron later rebelled against Moses, and God punished Miriam with leprosy, but healed her after seven days.
Meaning of name: Beloved or bitter
Bible reference: Exodus 2:4–8; 15:20–21; Numbers 12; 20:2; Deuteronomy 24:9; Micah 6:4

JOSHUA

Soldier and leader. Joshua was chosen as a helper by Moses. He was one of the spies sent to report on the land of Canaan and only he and Caleb urged Moses to go in and possess it. He was appointed as successor to Moses and led the people after Moses' death, commanding several successful campaigns against the Canaanites. Joshua's military feats were matched by his trust in God, which resulted in some spectacular events, such as the fall of the walls of Jericho, and the sun and moon standing still at Joshua's command.
Meaning of name: God is salvation
Bible reference: Exodus 17:9–16; 24:13; 33:11; Numbers 13:1–16; 14:6–9; 27:18–23; Deuteronomy 31:23; Joshua 1–24

RAHAB

A prostitute of Jericho. Joshua sent out two spies to Jericho and they lodged with Rahab. The king heard that they were there and sent to Rahab's house for them. Rahab believed that God had given the Israelites the land of Canaan and she wanted them to succeed in their attempt to seize it. She lied to those who came in search of the spies and helped the men escape, letting them out through a back window. She asked only that she and her family should be saved when the city was destroyed, and Joshua saw that this was done.
Meaning of name: Broad
Bible reference: Joshua 2, 6:17, 22–25

DEBORAH

Judge and prophetess. Deborah was the fifth of the leaders of Israel appointed by God after the invasion of Canaan and before the monarchy was established. Most of these "judges" were military leaders, but Deborah acted as a civil judge, too. She was a fervent patriot who commanded the warrior Barak to go to Mount Tabor to fight against Sisera's army. Barak refused to go unless Deborah went with him. Sisera's whole army was killed and Deborah's song celebrates this event.
Meaning of name: Bee
Bible reference: Judges 4–5

GIDEON

Fifth judge of Israel. Gideon was of obscure birth; although his father was a worshipper of Baal, he himself believed in God. Informed by an angel that God had chosen him to defeat the Midianites, who were ruling Israel at that time, Gideon gathered an army together. To make quite sure that God was really going to use him, Gideon asked God for a sign. He placed a fleece on the ground and told God that if, in the morning, there was dew on the fleece but not on the ground, he would believe he was chosen. This happened, but Gideon asked God to reverse the miracle. Next morning there was dew on the ground, but not on the fleece. God then told Gideon that his army was too large. Following God's instructions, Gideon reduced it to 300, and with this tiny army he defeated the Midianites.
Meaning of name: Hewer
Bible reference: Judges 6–8

SAMSON

Judge of Israel. At the time of the Philistine oppression an angel appeared to a barren Hebrew woman and told her that she would bear a son who must never cut his hair as he would be dedicated to God and would deliver Israel from the Philistines. The son was Samson who became an extraordinarily strong man and judge of Israel. His marriage to a Philistine woman grieved his parents and resulted in the slaughter of a thousand Philistines. Later he fell in love with Delilah who betrayed him (*see* Delilah). His hair was cut off and he was captured by the Philistines. The rulers met to celebrate Samson's downfall and decided to have him brought out of prison to entertain them. Samson's hair had grown again while he was in prison and he had regained his strength. After praying for revenge, he pushed against the pillars that held the building up. The building collapsed, killing Samson and 3,000 Philistines.
Meaning of name: Of the sun
Bible reference: Judges 13–16

DELILAH

A Philistine woman, mistress of Samson. Samson, judge of Israel, fell in love with Delilah. She was bribed by his enemies, the Philistine kings, to find out the secret of his strength, so they could overpower him. Three times Delilah asked Samson to tell her the secret of his strength and each time he gave her a false answer. Delilah complained that Samson did not really love her and nagged him so much that at last he revealed that his strength was in his hair, which had never been cut. Delilah lulled Samson to sleep. While he slept, his enemies cut off his hair and he was captured and blinded.
Meaning of name: Delicate
Bible reference: Judges 16:4–22

RUTH

A Moabite woman, great-grandmother of David. When Naomi decided to leave Moab to return to Bethlehem (*see* Naomi), she expected her daughters-in-law to remain and remarry. But Ruth insisted on going with Naomi, saying, "thy people shall be my people, and thy God my God." Ruth went to glean corn in the field belonging to Boaz (*see* Boaz). Obeying Naomi, Ruth lay at Boaz's feet as he slept and, when he woke, claimed his protection as a kinsman. After a nearer kinsman had rejected the opportunity, Boaz redeemed the property of Naomi's husband, Elimelech, and married Ruth.
Meaning of name: Friend
Bible reference: Ruth 1–4

NAOMI

Mother-in-law of Ruth. She came from Bethlehem but her family moved to Moab in a time of famine and her sons married Moabite women, Ruth and Orpah. Naomi's husband and sons died and she resolved to return to Bethlehem alone, but Ruth insisted on going with her. Naomi planned the marriage between Ruth and Boaz and when their son Obed was born she took on the responsibility of his care.
Meaning of name: Pleasant, my delight
Bible reference: Ruth 1–4

BOAZ

Husband of Ruth. Boaz was a rich landlord related to the father of Ruth's first husband who had died. Ruth's mother-in-law, Naomi, sent Ruth to glean corn in Boaz's field and Boaz offered her protection and hospitality. His sense of family responsibility, and also perhaps an inclination toward Ruth, led him to redeem family property when a nearer kinsman refused to do so. Boaz then married Ruth, and became the great-grandfather of David.
Meaning of name: Strength
Bible reference: Ruth 2–4

HANNAH

Mother of Samuel. Hannah was grieved because of her childlessness and she vowed to God that if he gave her a son she would dedicate him to God's service. Soon after she became pregnant and, when Samuel was weaned, she took him to the priest Eli to be brought up in the House of the Lord. Hannah visited Samuel every year, always bringing a coat she made for him; she subsequently had five more children. Hannah's song of thanksgiving exalts God for his holiness, power, and faithfulness to the weak and lowly.
Meaning of name: Grace
Bible reference: 1 Samuel 1; 2:1–10, 18–21

SAMUEL

Prophet and judge. Dedicated to God by his mother (*see* Hannah), Samuel was brought up in the house of the priest Eli. God spoke to him when he was still a boy, prophesying doom in Eli's family (*see* Eli). Samuel became judge and leader of Israel, gathering an army that defeated the Philistines. When the people demanded a king, Samuel resisted their wishes at first, but God gave him instructions to anoint Saul, which he did. Samuel fell out with Saul because of his disobedience of God's commandments and he secretly anointed David.
Meaning of name: Heard by God
Bible reference: 1 Samuel 1–3, 7–12, 15–16; 25:1

ELI

Judge and High Priest of Israel. Eli was of the tribe of Levi and his priesthood was a hereditary office. Although Eli himself lived a blameless life, his sons abused their priesthoods and behaved scandalously. Eli was grieved by their behavior, but barely reproached them for it. The child Samuel heard a message from God pronouncing the downfall of Eli and his sons because of their wickedness and his failure to rebuke them effectively. The sons were killed by the Philistines and the Ark of the Covenant was taken. When he heard this news, Eli fell from his seat, breaking his neck, and died.
Meaning of name: God is high
Bible reference: 1 Samuel 1:9–4:18

SAUL

First King of Israel. Anointed as King by Samuel, Saul became a great military leader. Though originally filled with the Spirit of God, Saul became increasingly disobedient of God's commandments and God rejected him as King. Once God's Spirit had left him, Saul became prey to fits of melancholy and the young David was summoned to play the harp to him, which soothed him. After David's victory over Goliath, and his increasing popularity with the people, Saul was consumed with jealousy and hatred for him. He sought for many years to kill David, though he was thwarted by his own son and daughter (*see* Jonathan, Michal). When his army was defeated by the Philistines and his sons were killed, Saul killed himself on the battlefield.
Meaning of name: Asked for
Bible reference: 1 Samuel 9–11, 13–24, 26–28, 31; 2 Samuel 1

JONATHAN

Son of Saul. Jonathan was a fearless soldier and his father's heir. He became a very close friend of David, never resenting the ascendancy that David gained, and risking his own relationship with his father through his love and loyalty to his

friend. He died with his father and brothers, fighting the Philistines.
Meaning of name: The Lord has given
Bible reference: 1 Samuel 13:2–3, 14; 18:1–5; 19:1–7, 20; 30:2; 2 Samuel 1

MICHAL

A wife of David; Saul's younger daughter. She fell in love with David and her father planned to use this to effect David's downfall. He offered her to David for a bride, but demanded a dowry of a hundred Philistine foreskins. The plan misfired, for David killed twice the required number of Philistines and married Michal. When Saul again attempted to kill David, Michal helped him escape, deceiving her father. While David was in exile, Saul married Michal to another man but after Saul's death David demanded her return. Michal despised David for his abandoned dancing when the Ark of the Lord was brought into the city and because of this she remained childless forever.
Meaning of name: Who is like Jehovah?
Bible reference: 1 Samuel 14:49; 18:20–28; 19:11–17; 25:44; 2 Samuel 3:13–14; 6:16–23

DAVID

Second King of Israel. Descended from Ruth, and the youngest of eight brothers, David was brought up as a shepherd. When God rejected Saul as King, Samuel secretly anointed David. David first came to King Saul's attention as a musician (*see* Saul) and then found fame when he killed the Philistine Goliath (*see* Goliath). Saul's son became David's closest friend and Saul's daughter became his wife (*see* Jonathan, Michal) but Saul subsequently turned against David, who spent many years in exile fleeing from the king.

When Saul and Jonathan were killed in battle, David became King and reigned for some 40 years. He was noted for his skill as a warrior as well as for his gifts as a prophet and poet. He was devoted to God and recovered the Ark of the Covenant, bringing it to Jerusalem. The psalms that David wrote reveal his great love for and closeness to God, but his saintliness was marred and the episode of Uriah (*see* Bathsheba. Uriah) was a shameful one (*see also* Abigail, Absalom, Joab).
Meaning of name: Beloved
Bible reference: 1 Samuel 16–31; 2 Samuel 1–24; 1 Kings 1:1–2:11; 1 Chronicles 11–29

GOLIATH

Giant of Gath. Goliath was a huge man, around 10 feet (3 m) tall, who was fighting for the Philistine army. Heavily armed, he demanded a champion from the Israelites to fight him in single combat. He issued the challenge every day for 40 days, until the young David volunteered to fight him. Goliath mocked when he saw the unarmed boy coming toward him but David, using a sling, hit Goliath on the forehead with a stone, breaking his skull and killing him.
Meaning of name: Exile
Bible reference: 1 Samuel 17

ABIGAIL

A wife of David. Abigail was a beautiful and intelligent woman, married to a drunken, churlish man called Nabal. Nabal angered David by rudely refusing him and his men hospitality, but Abigail tactfully apologized for her husband and offered David generous provisions. Nabal had a stroke and died shortly after, and David married Abigail.
Meaning of name: Father of joy
Bible reference: 1 Samuel 25

JOAB

David's nephew and captain of his army. An ambitious and able man, Joab rose to become commander-in-chief over Israel. When David's captain, Abner, reluctantly killed Joab's brother in self-defence, Joab avenged him by murdering Abner. He understood David well, conniving with him in the affair of Uriah (*see* Uriah) and acting as peacemaker between David and Absalom, although it was Joab who was eventually responsible for Absalom's death (*see* Absalom). After this David appointed Amasa as commander but Joab killed Amasa and was reinstated. However, David bore Joab grudges for these murders. Before David died he told Solomon to avenge them and Solomon had Joab killed.
Meaning of name: Jehovah is father
Bible reference: 2 Samuel 2:12–32; 3:22–31, 10–11, 14, 18; 19:1–8, 20; 24:1–4; 1 Kings 1:7, 19; 2:5–6, 22, 28–34; 1 Chronicles 11:6, 8

ABSALOM

Third son of David. He was a handsome, charming young man and his father's favorite and heir. His half-brother, Amnon, fell in love with Absalom's sister Tamar and, after tricking her into visiting him at his house, raped her. Absalom arranged for Amnon to be killed and then fled. David forgave him but Absalom plotted against his father and organized a rebellion against him. Pursued by his father's men, Absalom got caught by his long hair in an oak tree and was killed by David's captain, Joab, and his followers. When David heard of his death he wept, crying "O my son Absalom, my son, Absalom! Would God I had died for thee, O Absalom, my son, my son!"
Meaning of name: Father of peace
Bible reference: 2 Samuel 3:3, 13–18

BATHSHEBA

Bathsheba was a beautiful woman married to Uriah, one of David's soldiers. When David saw her bathing, he was attracted to her and sent for her. Bathsheba slept with the King and when she later told him she had become pregnant, David had Uriah killed (*see* Uriah). Bathsheba married David but the son born to them died. Their second son was

Solomon; when David was an old man, Bathsheba persuaded him to choose Solomon to succeed him.
Meaning of name: Seventh daughter
Bible reference: 2 Samuel 11–12:24; 1 Kings 1:11–31; 2:13–22

URIAH
Husband of Bathsheba. Uriah the Hittite was one of David's generals. When Bathsheba became pregnant (*see* Bathsheba), David sent for Uriah and encouraged him to go home, hoping that he would sleep with his wife and that the pregnancy could be attributed to him. When this ploy failed, David sent Uriah with a letter to Joab telling him to put Uriah in the forefront of the battle and leave him defenceless. Joab obeyed and Uriah was killed. The prophet Nathan opened David's eyes to the wickedness of this deed and he repented of it.
Meaning of name: Jehovah is light
Bible reference: 2 Samuel 11–12:15; 23:39; 1 Kings 15:5

SOLOMON
Son of David and Bathsheba, and King of Israel. After Solomon had succeeded David as King, God appeared to him in a dream and told him to ask for any gift. Solomon chose wisdom and God promised him not only wisdom but riches and honor. Solomon's finest act was the building of the Temple in Jerusalem. Though he achieved great things in his 40-year reign, Solomon finally turned away from God. He had an enormous harem of foreign wives and concubines and they led him into idolatrous worship.
Meaning of name: Peaceable
Bible reference: 2 Samuel 5:14; 1 Kings 1:10–53, 2–11; Nehemiah 13:26; Proverbs 1:1

AHAB
Seventh king of Israel. He was a successful warrior but, under the influence of his wife Jezebel, he introduced idolatry into the kingdom. God's prophets were persecuted under his reign, and worship of Baal was encouraged. Ahab's greed and disregard for justice are illustrated in the story of Naboth's vineyard (*see* Jezebel).
Meaning of name: Father's brother
Bible reference: 1 Kings 16:28–33; 18:1–19:1; 20:2–22:40

JEZEBEL
Wife of Ahab. A follower of Baal and Asherah, she encouraged their worship in Israel and was furious when Elijah killed the prophets of Baal (*see* Elijah). Ahab became depressed because he coveted a vineyard belonging to a man called Naboth who had refused to sell it to him. Jezebel arranged to have Naboth falsely accused of cursing God and the King, and he was stoned to death. Ahab then took possession of the vineyard, but was denounced by Elijah. Elijah prophesied a horrible death for Jezebel and the prophecy was fulfilled by Jehu (*see* Jehu).
Meaning of name: Chaste
Bible reference: 1 Kings 16:31; 19:1–2; 21:1–25; 2 Kings 9:7–10, 30–37

ELIJAH
Prophet during the reign of Ahab. Elijah was notable for his fearlessness in speaking to the King (*see* Jezebel) and for several miracles. Among these were the raising of the widow's son and the relief of the drought in Israel that had lasted three years. In this dramatic incident Elijah challenged the prophets of Baal on Mount Carmel to see whose god could answer their prayers with fire. When Baal had failed, Elijah built an altar and placed a sacrifice on it, soaking it in water, and God sent fire to consume it. Elijah then killed the prophets of Baal and the same evening the rains came. Elijah did not die, but was taken up into heaven in a whirlwind.
Meaning of name: Jehovah is God
Bible reference: 1 Kings 17–19; 21; 2 Kings 1–2:15; Malachi 4:5

ELISHA
Prophet of Israel. He served under Elijah and inherited his ministry when Elijah was taken up to heaven, though he was less fiery as a prophet than his predecessor, Elisha's ministry was also marked by miracles, including healings and raising from the dead. He was a prophet for 50 years.
Meaning of name: God is salvation
Bible reference: 1 Kings 19:16–21; 2 Kings 2:1–9:3; 13:14–21

JEHU
King of Israel. He was anointed by Elisha to replace Ahab as King. His first action was to drive furiously in his chariot to seek out Ahab's son Joram, King of Judah, and kill him. He then had Ahab's wife Jezebel killed by ordering her servants to throw her out of the window, where she was smashed to pieces and trodden underfoot. Jehu continued to slay every remaining member of Ahab's family. He also killed all the worshippers of Baal and burned every image of the god, but he was not a sincere follower of God for he did nothing to stop the worship of golden calves.
Meaning of name: Jehovah is he
Bible reference: 2 Kings 9–10

NEBUCHADNEZZAR
King of Babylon. A powerful ruler and military leader, Nebuchadnezzar conquered many nations. He captured Jerusalem, destroying the Temple and taking captives back to Babylon. He promoted Daniel for interpreting his dreams but continued in wickedness and idolatry. His pride was punished by a seven-year fit of madness, when he was driven out from the people and lived like an animal, eating grass. When he recovered, Nebuchadnezzar repented and praised God. (*See also* Daniel, Shadrach)

Meaning of name: Nebo (a Babylonian god) protect the boundary
Bible reference: 2 Kings 24–25; Jeremiah 21:2, 7; Ezekiel 26:7; 29:18–19; Daniel 1–4

AHASUERUS

Persian king, almost certainly identical to Xerxes I. He deposed his Queen, Vashti, when she refused to appear to display her beauty to his drunken friends. He then married Esther, not knowing that she was Jewish. Urged on by Haman his chief minister, Ahasuerus planned to destroy all the Jewish people in his kingdom. This plan was averted (*see* Esther) but Ahasuerus' change of heart and punishment of Haman indicate the capriciousness of his character rather than genuine repentance.
Meaning of name: King or mighty man
Bible reference: Esther 1–10

ESTHER

A Jewish woman who became Queen of Persia. She was an orphan and was brought up by her cousin, Mordecai. When King Ahasuerus was looking for a new wife (*see* Ahasuerus), Mordecai entered Esther for what was virtually a beauty contest to select a queen. Esther was married to Ahasuerus, but continued to accept Mordecai's advice.

Mordecai attracted the enmity of the king's chief minister Haman, by refusing to bow to him, which led Haman to obtain the King's permission to order the destruction of all the Jews. Haman prepared a gallows upon which to hang Mordecai but the King discovered that Mordecai had once been responsible for averting an assassination plot against him, so he had Mordecai publicly honored. Esther organized a banquet for the King and Ahasuerus told her to ask him for anything she wanted. She then interceded for her people and begged the King to stop the massacre. Haman was hanged on the gallows he had prepared for Mordecai but the royal proclamation against the Jews had already gone out. Ahasuerus allowed Esther and Mordecai to send out letters, with the royal seal, warning the Jews to defend themselves. Having prepared and armed themselves, the Jews were able to kill their enemies.
Meaning of name: Star
Bible reference: Esther 1–10

JOB

A man living in Uz. Job was an upright, godly and prosperous man. God allowed Satan to test Job's faith and he was visited by various disasters, losing his ten children and his property and, finally, being struck down by a dreadful disease. Despite his suffering and the unhelpful advice of his wife and friends, Job remained faithful to God. Eventually his health and wealth were restored and he had ten more children.
Meaning of name: Pious, afflicted
Bible reference: Job 1–42

DANIEL

One of the major prophets. Of noble descent, Daniel was taken as a captive to Babylon and trained in the King's service. He gained prominence as a scholar and an interpreter of dreams, but persisted in his adherence to the Jewish religion. Having interpreted the dreams and visions of Nebuchadnezzar and Belshazzar, Daniel was promoted to the highest office under the next King, Darius. Other officials denounced Daniel to the King for praying to God, and Daniel was cast unto a den of lions. When the lions did not harm the prophet, Darius decreed that Daniel's accusers should be thrown to the lions and that Daniel's God should be worshipped throughout the Empire. (*See also* Belshazzar, Nebuchadnezzar, Shadrach)
Meaning of name: God is my judge
Bible reference: Daniel 1–12

SHADRACH

Companion of Daniel. When Daniel was taken into Babylon, three other Jewish youths were taken with him, Hananish, Mishael and Azariah, who were given the Babylonian names of Shadrach, Meshah and Abednego. They found favor with Nebuchadnezzar because of their wisdom and were given high office. However, the King made a gold image and ordered everyone to worship it. Shadrach, Meshach and Abednego refused to bow down to the image and Nebuchadnezzar threatened to throw them into a fiery furnace if they persisted in their disobedience. They remained resolute and were thrown into the furnace, but were totally unscathed. The King praised their God and promoted the three men.
Meaning of name: Command of Aku (moon god)
Bible reference: Daniel 1:7; 2:49; 3

MESHACH

See Shadrach
Meaning of name: Agile
Bible reference: Daniel 1:7; 2:49; 3

ABEDNEGO

See Shadrach
Meaning of name: Servant of light
Bible reference: Daniel 1:7; 2:49; 3

BELSHAZZAR

King of Babylon. Belshazzar gave a great feast for a thousand of his lords. He took precious vessels belonging to God's Temple and used them for the wine with which they toasted false gods. Suddenly a hand appeared and wrote on the wall of the palace the words "Mene, Mene, Tekelm Upharsin." The King was terrified and offered rich rewards to anyone who could interpret this mysterious writing. Daniel was brought in; he rebuked Belshazzar for his ungodly conduct, telling

him that the message on the wall meant that his kingdom was doomed. That same night Belshazzar was killed.
Meaning of name: Bel protect the king
Bible reference: Daniel 5

JONAH

A minor prophet. God told Jonah to go to Nineveh and denounce the people's wickedness, but Jonah was afraid to do this and boarded a ship going to Tarsish instead. There was a tempest and the ship was in danger. Jonah admitted that he must be the cause because he was trying to escape from God, so he was thrown overboard by the crew. He was swallowed by a large fish and remained in its belly for three days. after the fish vomited him out, Jonah obeyed God and preached to the people of Nineveh who repented and were spared punishment. Jonah resented God's mercy to them, but God taught him the need for compassion.
Meaning of name: Dove
Bible reference: 2 Kings 14:25; Jonah 1–4

MARY

Mother of Jesus. An obscure young woman living in Nazareth, Mary was betrothed to Joseph when the angel Gabriel visited her. She was told that she had found favor with God and would bear a child by the Holy Spirit. Mary humbly accepted this extraordinary situation and eventually gave birth to Jesus in a stable in Bethlehem. Mary knew, from the circumstances of his birth, the visits of the shepherds and wise men, and the prayers of Simeon and Anna, who Jesus was. It was Mary who encouraged him to perform his first miracle at Cana. After Jesus left home to begin his ministry, Mary rarely appears, but she was at the foot of the Cross and continued to meet with the disciples after Jesus' Crucifixion and Resurrection. (*See also* Joseph, John, Simeon, Anna)
Meaning of name: Beloved or bitter
Bible reference: Matthew 1:18–24; 2:11; 12:46–47; 13:55; Luke 1:26–56; 2; John 2:1–12; 19:25; Acts 1:14

JOSEPH

Husband of Mary, mother of Jesus. Joseph was a carpenter, betrothed to Mary when she became pregnant. An angel told him in a dream that Mary's child was "conceived of the Holy Spirit" and would be the Savior, so Joseph married her; she subsequently gave birth to Jesus. In another dream Joseph was warned to escape Herod the Great's wrath by fleeing to Egypt and, after Herod's death, another angelic visitation brought him back to Israel where he settled with his family in Nazareth. Joseph acted as a father to Jesus, but was apparently dead before Jesus' ministry began.
Meaning of name: God increases
Bible reference: Matthew 1:18–25; 2:13–15, 19–23; Luke 2:4–5

ELISABETH

Mother of John the Baptist. She was a pious woman from a priestly family and was married to a priest, Zacharias. They were old and childless but after her husband had a vision (*see* Zacharias), Elisabeth became pregnant. When Mary, who was a relation of Elisabeth, came to her house, the baby leapt in Elisabeth's womb. Filled with the Holy Spirit, she said to Mary, "Blessed art thou among women, and blessed is the fruit of thy womb." Mary stayed at the house for three months and then Elisabeth gave birth to the son who was to became John the Baptist.
Meaning of name: God is my oath
Bible reference: Luke 1:5–7, 24–26, 36, 39–45, 57–61

ZACHARIAS

Father of John the Baptist. Zacharias was a priest and he and his wife Elisabeth were godly people, but childless. The angel Gabriel appeared to Zacharias in his old age and told him that Elisabeth would have a son who must be called John and who would be a great man of God. Zacharias could not believe that he and Elisabeth could have children at their age. Gabriel said that, because of his disbelief, Zacharias would be struck dumb until the prophecy was fulfilled. When John was born it was assumed that he would be named after his father, but Zacharias wrote down, "His name is John." Then at once his affliction left him; he praised God and prophesied about John's mission.
Meaning of name: Jehovah is renowned
Bible reference: Luke 1:5–24, 57–79

SIMEON

A devout man of Jerusalem. God had told Simeon that he would not die before he had seen the Messiah. He was in the Temple in Jerusalem when Mary and Joseph brought Jesus to present him to God. Simeon took the baby in his arms and praised God, saying that now he had seen Jesus he was happy to die. He prophesied that Jesus would be a light to the Gentiles and a glory to Israel. (*See also* Anna)
Meaning of name: Hearing
Bible reference: Luke 2:25–35

ANNA

A prophetess, Anna was an old woman who had been widowed for many years. She spent her time in the Temple in Jerusalem, fasting and praying, waiting for the Messiah to come. When Mary and Joseph brought Jesus to the Temple, Anna recognized the baby as the Messiah, and gave thanks to God. She subsequently spoke of the child to all those who, like her, were waiting for God's redemption. (*See also* Simeon)
Meaning of name: Grace
Bible reference: Luke 2:36–38

HEROD THE GREAT
King at the time of Jesus' birth. When his wise men announced the birth of a king in Bethlehem, he sent them to search for the child. When they failed to return, Herod ordered the slaughter of all the children under the age of two in the Bethlehem region.
Meaning of name: Son of the hero
Bible reference: Matthew 2

JOHN THE BAPTIST
Prophet and preacher. Born to the elderly Elisabeth and Zacharias, he grew up in the desert and lived an ascetic life. He was a fiery preacher and gained fame for his message that centered upon the need for people to repent of their sins and be baptized. He baptized many people in the Jordan, including Jesus himself. John recognized that he was the forerunner of a greater man, preparing the way of Jesus. His forthright preaching made him many enemies and he was eventually beheaded (*see* Salome).
Meaning of name: God is gracious
Bible reference: Matthew 3; 11:2–29; 21:25–32; Mark 6:14–29; Luke 1:5–25, 57–80; 7:18–33; John 3:23–30

ANDREW
One of the 12 apostles. He was a disciple of John the Baptist, who introduced him to Jesus. Andrew then brought his brother Peter to see Jesus and they were later both called from their fishing boats to become disciples. It was Andrew who drew Jesus' attention to the boy with the five loaves and two fishes which fed the 5,000.
Meaning of name: Manly
Bible reference: Matthew 4:18–20; Mark 13:3; John 1:40–42, 44; 6:8–9; 12:22

PETER (CEPHAS)
One of the 12 apostles. A fisherman, originally named Simon, Peter was called to discipleship with his brother Andrew. He was one of those closest to Jesus, and was a warm-hearted and impulsive man who often acted without thinking, as on the occasion when he tried to walk on water, or when he cut off the ear of the soldier who arrested Jesus. Despite his deep love for Jesus and commitment to him, Peter often failed to understand him and his courage deserted him after Jesus' arrest when Peter denied knowledge of him three times.
After the Resurrection and the coming of the Holy Spirit, Peter became a true "rock" and the main leader of the Church. He became a bold preacher and a worker of miracles. Despite his vision that the Gospel was for the Gentiles too (*see* Cornelius), Peter was later rebuked by Paul for refusing to eat with Gentiles.
Meaning of name: Rock
Bible reference: Matthew 4:18–20; 8:14; 14:25–32; 16:13–23; 17:1–4; 26:31–40, 69–75; Luke 24:12; John 13:6–9; 18:10–11; 20:2–6; 21:7–21; Acts 1:13; 2:14–40; 3:1–4:23; 5:1–10, 15; 8:14–25; 9:32–12:18; 15:7–11; Galatians 2:11–14; 1 Peter; 2 Peter

JAMES THE APOSTLE
One of the 12 apostles and son of Zebedee. A fisherman, James was called to be a disciple at the same time as his brother John. He witnessed the Transfiguration and was among the select few disciples closest to Jesus. He was put to death by Herod Agrippa I.
Meaning of name: Follower, supplanter
Bible reference: Matthew 4:21–22; 17:1; Mark 1:29; 5:37; 10:35–41; 13:3; 14:32–40; Luke 9:54; Acts 1:13; 12:2

JOHN
One of the 12 apostles. The son of Zebedee and brother of James, John was one of the disciples closest to Jesus. He is not mentioned by name in the Gospel of John, but is assumed to be "the disciple whom Jesus loved" (John 13:23; 19:26–27) to whom Jesus entrusted the care of his mother before he died. As a leader of the early Christian church, his name is usually linked with that of Peter.
Meaning of name: God is gracious
Bible reference: Matthew 4:21–22; 17:1; Mark 1:29; 5:37; 10:35–41; 13:3; 14:32–40; Luke 9:49, 54; 22:8; Acts 1:13; 3:1–11; 4:1–23; 8:14–25; Galatians 2:9

MATTHEW
One of the 12 apostles. He is assumed to be the same person as the disciple Levi mentioned in the Gospels of Mark and Luke. Matthew was a tax collector, a despised occupation, and he was called by Jesus when sitting in the tax office. He then gave a feast for Jesus, who was criticized for eating with such people.
Meaning of name: Gift of Jehovah
Bible reference: Matthew 9:9–10; Mark 3:18; Luke 5:27–29

BARTHOLOMEW
One of the 12 apostles. Bartholomew is thought to be identical to Nathanael (*see* Nathanael).
Meaning of name: Son of Talmai
Bible reference: Matthew 10:3

NATHANAEL
One of the 12 apostles, thought to be the same person as Bartholomew. When Philip told him that he had found the Messiah, Nathanael doubted that a Galilean could be the promised one. However, when he saw Jesus, who appeared to

know him although they had never met, Nathanael hailed him as the Son of God. Jesus described Nathanael as "an Israelite indeed in whom is no guile."
Meaning of name: Gift of God
Bible reference: John 1:45–49; 21:2

PHILIP THE APOSTLE
One of the 12 apostles. It was Philip who told Nathanael that he had found the Messiah. Jesus tested Philip by asking him how to feed the 5,000 but Philip failed to anticipate the miracle and answered in practical terms.
Meaning of name: Lover of horses
Bible reference: Matthew 10:3; John 1:43–48; 6:5–7; 12:21–22; 14:8–9

THOMAS
One of the 12 apostles. When Jesus first appeared to his disciples after the Resurrection, Thomas was not with them. When they told him that they had seen the risen Jesus, Thomas said he would not believe it until he had touched the nail scars in Jesus' hands and the spear wound in his side. A week later Jesus appeared again and, when he saw Thomas, invited him to touch his hands and side. Thomas answered, "My Lord and my God."
Meaning of name: Twin
Bible reference: Matthew 10:3; John 11:16; 14:5; 20:24–28; 21:2; Acts 1:13

SIMON THE APOSTLE
One of the 12 apostles. He was known as Simon the Zealot, presumably because of his patriotic fervor.
Meaning of name: Hearing
Bible reference: Matthew 10:4; Acts 1:13

JUDAS
One of the 12 apostles. He was the treasurer and, apparently, carried out this task dishonestly. At the Last Supper Jesus said that one of his disciples would betray him; Judas had, in fact, agreed to hand him over to the authorities in return for 30 pieces of silver. Judas identified Jesus to the soldiers who came to arrest him by kissing him. According to Matthew, Judas hanged himself after Jesus' arrest, but Acts says that he purchased a field with the silver and fell there, bursting open and spilling his bowels out.
Meaning of name: Praise of the Lord
Bible reference: Matthew 10:4; 26:14–16, 20–25, 47–49; 27:3–10; John 6:70–71; 12:4–6; Acts 1:16–25

HEROD ANTIPAS
Son of Herod the Great. He had John the Baptist killed (*see* Salome) and delivered Jesus up to Pontius Pilate.
Meaning of name: Son of the hero
Bible reference: Matthew 6:14–29; Luke 9:7–9; 13:31; 23:6–12, 15

SALOME
Step-daughter of Herod Antipas. John the Baptist had enraged Herodias, Herod's wife, by criticising their marriage on the grounds that she was Herod's brother's wife. At Herodias' request, John was imprisoned. On Herod's birthday, Salome, Herodias' daughter, came in and danced for him. Her dancing pleased him so much that he said he would give her anything she asked for. She consulted her mother who told her to ask for the head of John the Baptist. Salome demanded John's head on a platter and Herod kept his promise.
Meaning of name: Peace
Bible reference: Mark 6:19–28

MARTHA
Sister of Mary and Lazarus. Martha was the practical one of the two sisters. When she complained that her sister was not helping her with serving food, Jesus gently rebuked her for her fussing. Martha's faith in Jesus was absolute. When her brother died (*see* Lazarus) she was sure that Jesus would have been able to save him had he arrived in time, and she declared her belief in Jesus as the Son of God.
Meaning of name: Lady, mistress
Bible reference: Luke 10:38–42; John 11–12:2

MARY OF BETHANY
Sister of Martha and Lazarus. while her sister busied herself with housework, Mary chose to sit at Jesus' feet and listen to his teaching and Jesus praised her for her choice. After the raising of Lazarus (*see* Lazarus) Jesus had supper with the family at Bethany. Mary took a jar of very expensive scented ointment and anointed Jesus' feet, wiping them with her hair. Judas criticized her action, but Jesus defended her.
Meaning of name: Beloved or bitter
Bible reference: Luke 10:38–42; John 11; 12:3–7

LAZARUS
Brother of Martha and Mary. This family, living at Bethany, were friends of Jesus. Lazarus became sick and his sisters asked Jesus to come to him. Jesus did not go straight away and, by the time he got to Bethany, Lazarus was dead and buried. Jesus wept with Lazarus' sisters at the grave, then asked them to take away the stone at the mouth of the cave where the body lay. He called "Lazarus, come forth," and Lazarus walked out alive.
Meaning of name: God is help
Bible reference: John 11; 12:1–17

ZACCHAEUS

A tax collector of Jericho. Zacchaeus had become rich through fraudulent dealings as a tax collector. When Jesus came to Jericho, Zacchaeus wanted to see him but he was very short and could not see through the crowds, so he climbed a sycamore tree to get a better view. As Jesus passed he looked up and called to Zacchaeus to come down, for he was going to stay at his house. People were shocked that Jesus was to be the guest of such a sinner, but Zacchaeus told Jesus that he would repay all those he had cheated and give half his goods to the poor.
Meaning of name: Jehovah is renowned
Bible reference: Luke 19:1–10

NICODEMUS

A Jewish leader. Nicodemus was a Pharisee who recognized, by the miracles he saw, that Jesus had come from God. He went to see Jesus by night but was puzzled by his teaching that people need to be born again of the Spirit. He was subsequently brave enough to speak up for Jesus to the Pharisees, and he was one of those who brought spices to anoint Jesus' body after his death.
Meaning of name: Victor of the people
Bible reference: John 3:1–10; 7:50–51; 19:39

PONTIUS PILATE

Roman governor. Jesus was delivered into Pilate's hands after his arrest. Pilate was unwilling to interfere in Jewish religious affairs and could find no fault in Jesus' conduct. His wife also warned him not to be involved because of a dream she had had. However, when his one attempt to release Jesus had failed (*see* Barabbas) Pilate publicly washed his hands to demonstrate his own innocence and then ordered Jesus to be flogged and crucified.
Meaning of name: Armed with a dart
Bible reference: Matthew 27:1–26; Luke 3:1; 13:1; John 18:28–19:23, 38; Acts 4:27

BARABBAS

A man imprisoned for sedition and murder. At the time of the Passover, it was the custom to release any prisoner of the people's choice. Pilate hoped to release Jesus in this way, but the priests organized a popular movement in favor of Barabbas. When Pilate offered the people the choice of releasing Jesus or Barabbas, they clamored to have Barabbas released and Jesus crucified, and this was done.
Meaning of name: Son of a father
Bible reference: Matthew 27:16–26

MARY MAGDALENE

A follower of Jesus. She is said to have been healed by Jesus from a sickness caused by demon possession. She was with the other women at the foot of the cross and, according to John, was the first to see the resurrected Lord. She was weeping at the tomb when he appeared, and at first she mistook him for a gardener. Jesus spoke her name and she recognized him. He told her not to touch him for he had not yet ascended to his Father, but to tell the other disciples what she had seen.
Meaning of name: Beloved or bitter
Bible reference: Matthew 27:56, 61; 28:1–10; Luke 8:2; John 20:1–2, 11–18

JAMES

Brother of Jesus. There is no evidence that James was a believer in his brother's lifetime. Jesus appeared to him after the Resurrection, and James became a prominent leader in the early Church.
Meaning of name: Follower, supplanter
Bible reference: Matthew 13:55; Acts 12:17; 15:13–21; 1 Corinthians 15:7; Galatians 1:19; 2:9, 12

BARNABAS

Apostle and missionary. He had a close relationship with Paul and accompanied him on many of his missionary journeys. Having been a believer before Paul's conversion, Barnabas originally took the lead in the partnership but Paul later became dominant. Barnabas was a good man and a dedicated missionary, but was not strong enough in character to withstand pressures from the Jewish Christians who were refusing to eat with Gentile believers. Barnabas was apparently impressive enough in appearance for the Lycaonians to mistake him for the god Jupiter.
Meaning of name: Son of exhortation
Bible reference: Acts 4:36–37; 11:22–30; 12:25; 13–15; 1 Corinthians 9–6; Galatians 2:1, 9, 13; Colossians 4:10

PHILIP THE EVANGELIST

Deacon and evangelist. He was an effective preacher, responsible for many conversions including those of Simon the magician and the Ethiopian eunuch, whom Philip baptized right away as they were traveling close to water.
Meaning of name: Lover of horses
Bible reference: Acts 6:5; 8:5–40; 21:8–9

STEPHEN

Deacon and first Christian martyr. Stephen is described as a man "full of faith and of the Holy Spirit." His preaching and miracles brought him to the attention of certain zealous Jews who had him accused of blasphemy. Stephen defended

himself by preaching on the history of Israel and the people's constant rejection of God's prophets and, finally, of the Messiah. This infuriated the council, and when Stephen looked up to heaven and said he saw Jesus standing at the right hand of God, they cast him out of the city and stoned him to death. His last words were a prayer of forgiveness for his murderers.
Meaning of name: Crown
Bible reference: Acts 6:5, 8–15; 7; 8:2

PAUL
Apostle and missionary. Originally called Saul, Paul was a zealous Pharisee and persecutor of the early Christians, witnessing and approving Stephen's murder. He was converted by a dramatic vision of Jesus when he was on the road to Damascus, and became one of the leaders of the Church. Paul spent the rest of his life in extensive and tireless missionary work, preaching the Gospel and establishing churches wherever he went. He was arrested, beaten, and imprisoned many times, and his life was often in danger.

Paul was a tentmaker by trade, but an educated man who was an eloquent preacher and clear writer. His main theological contribution to Christianity is his exposition of justification by faith.
Meaning of name: Little
Bible reference: Acts 7:58–8:3; 9:1–30; 13–18; See also Romans; 1 Corinthians; 2 Corinthians; Galatians; Ephesians; Philippians; Colossians; 1 Thessalonians; 2 Thessalonians; 1 Timothy; 2 Timothy; Titus; Philemon

SIMON THE MAGICIAN
A magician of Samaria. Simon was considered to be a man with power from God because of his sorcery but, when Philip preached the Gospel in Samaria, he was among the many who believed and were baptized. Peter and John arrived in Samaria and began to lay hands on the new believers and pray for them to receive the Holy Spirit. When Simon saw the effect of the laying on of hands he longed to have the same power as the apostles, and offered them money to give him the power. Peter rebuked him for thinking that spiritual gifts could be purchased with money.
Meaning of name: Hearing
Bible reference: Acts 8:9–24

DORCAS
A disciple living at Joppa. Dorcas was a charitable woman who helped the poor and made clothes for them. When she died her friends were deeply grieved and sent for Peter, who was in nearby Lydda. Peter arrived and prayed, then told Dorcas to get up. She sat up and Peter called all the believers to witness that she was alive.
Meaning of name: Gazelle
Bible reference: Acts 9:36–42

CORNELIUS
A Roman centurion. He is described as a "devout" man, pious, and charitable. One day Cornelius had a vision of an angel who told him to call for Peter, who would tell him what to do. He sent two of his servants to fetch Peter, who meanwhile had had a vision in which God told him that nothing was unclean that God had made clean. Peter went to Cornelius' house, although Cornelius was a Gentile, and normally Jews did not mix with Gentiles. There, he realized that his vision had meant that Gentiles were no longer to be excluded, so he preached the Gospel of Jesus to Cornelius. Cornelius and his household believed and received the Holy Spirit. When Peter heard them praising God and speaking in tongues he knew that they should be treated as Christian believers and baptized them accordingly.
Meaning of name: Horn
Bible reference: Acts 10

HEROD AGRIPPA I
Grandson of Herod the Great. A persecutor of the early Church, he had James killed and Peter imprisoned.
Meaning of name: Son of the hero
Bible reference: Acts 12:1–6, 19–21

MARK
Companion of Paul. Mark's mother was a wealthy Christian widow living in Jerusalem, and she was related to Barnabas. Mark accompanied Paul and Barnabas to Cyprus but left them at Perga. Because of this, when Barnabas wished to take him on their next journey, Paul opposed the idea. Unable to agree, they parted, Barnabas going to Cyprus with Mark. The rift with Paul was apparently later healed, for Mark accompanied both Paul and Timothy on subsequent missions.
Meaning of name: Roman surname associated with the god Mars
Bible reference: Acts 12:12, 25; 13:5, 13; 15:37–39; Colossians 4:10; 2 Timothy 4:11; Philemon 24

TIMOTHY
Companion of Paul. Timothy was the son of a Jewish mother and a Greek father, but was brought up to worship God. He was probably converted to Christianity when Paul visited Lystra on his first missionary journey. Timothy accompanied Paul on many of his missions and the apostle regarded him as a spiritual son.
Meaning of name: Honored of God
Bible reference: Acts 16:1–3; 17:14–16; 18:5; 19:22; 20:4; 1 Corinthians 4:17; 16:10–11; 2 Corinthians 1:1, 19; Philemon 2:19–23; 1 Thessalonians 3:2–6; Hebrews 13:23; *see also* 1 Timothy; 2 Timothy

LYDIA

A woman from Thyatira. Lydia was a successful businesswoman who dealt in purple dye. She was apparently a Gentile convert to Judaism and was one of a group of women who met by the river at Philippi to pray. When she heard the Gospel from Paul, Lydia believed and was baptized. She offered hospitality to Paul and his companions and when Paul and Silas came out of prison they went to Lydia's house.

Meaning of name: The Lydian woman

Bible reference: Acts 16:13–15, 40

AQUILA

See Priscilla

Meaning of name: Eagle

Bible reference: Acts 18:2–3, 18–19, 26; Romans 16:3–5

PRISCILLA

Fellow-worker with Paul. She and her husband Aquila were tentmakers by trade, like Paul, and had a close relationship with him. They accompanied him to Syria and Ephesus, where he left them and it was there that they met Apollos and made themselves responsible for instructing him in the Christian faith (*see* Apollos).

Meaning of name: Ancient, former

Bible reference: Acts 18:2–3, 18–19, 26; Romans 16:3–5

APOLLOS

An Alexandrian Jew. He appeared in Ephesus in AD 52 and preached eloquently in the synagogues. He knew about Jesus, but his knowledge was incomplete. However, instructed by Priscilla and Aquila, he went on to become a reliable and successful preacher. His influence became such that factions arose of those loyal to his preaching as opposed to Paul's but it is clear that neither man desired such party followings, and Paul regarded Apollos as a fellow-worker for the Gospel.

Meaning of name: From Apollonia

Bible reference: Acts 18:24–19:1; 1 Chronicles 1:12; 3:4–6, 22; 4:6; 16:12

HEROD AGRIPPA II

Son of Herod Agrippa I. When imprisoned by the governor Festus, Paul appealed to Herod Agrippa II and defended himself before him. The King declared that he could not see that Paul deserved any punishment.

Meaning of name: Son of the hero

Bible reference: Acts 25:13–26:2; 26:27–32

LUKE

Fellow-worker with Paul. Luke is described as a physician and a close companion of Paul. He was the author of the third Gospel, the most literary of the Gospels, and the Book of Acts, some of which is written in the first person.

Meaning of name: From Lucania

Bible reference: Colossians 4:14; 2 Timothy 4:11; Philemon 24

THE HOLY LAND TODAY

THE GEOGRAPHICAL AREA COVERED BY THE BIBLE TAKES IN, NOT JUST THE TRADITIONAL BIBLE LANDS, BUT STRETCHES OVER PARTS OF ASIA, AFRICA, AND EUROPE. SOME OF THE PLACES MENTIONED ARE STILL THRIVING, OTHERS HAVE BEEN UNINHABITED FOR CENTURIES. THE REGION REMAINS IN THE NEWS ALMOST DAILY.

The Holy Land has long been a route for invasion and trade, a cockpit of war over which empires have always sought dominance. Conquered by Assyrians, Babylonians, Persians, Alexander the Great, and the Ptolemaic Empire, the region finally fell to Rome in 63 BC. The Persian Sassanid Empire followed, destroying the Byzantine presence. This was in turn overthrown by the Arab conquests of the seventh century, eventually creating the Ottoman Empire. The Crusader states were a minor interim period during this process. Turkish defeat by the Allies during the First World War witnessed the Fertile Crescent becoming the bounty of the Western imperial powers. The Ottoman Empire was carved up into League of Nations' mandates. France gained control over Syria and Lebanon in 1920, the two becoming notionally independent in 1943 and 1944 respectively. Britain was awarded Palestine, Iraq, and Transjordan, the last two winning qualified independence in 1932 and 1946 respectively while Iraq, despite independence in 1932 came under the British military governance during the Second World War. Meanwhile, Britain promised Jews a national home in Palestine, embodied in the 1920 Balfour Declaration, causing great consternation among Arab nationalists.

Arab–Jewish conflict persisted, turning into outright war in the spring of 1948 as a prelude to Israel's independence in 1949. Afterwards, the Bible Lands became a byword for violence exposing local problems, which were used as an excuse for superpower involvement. Issues of conflicting nationalism, faiths, water, and property rights, the plight of Palestinian refugees fleeing to the Gaza Strip and Jordanian-controlled West Bank, have been exacerbated by great power penetration during the 1956 Suez War. French and British influence declined when the USA and USSR pursued their own foreign policy

THE DEAD SEA
Overlooked by the hills of Moab the Dead Sea, (at 1,371 feet / 418 m below sea level) has attracted interest and visitors from around the Mediterranean basin for thousands of years. It was a place of refuge for King David, and one of the world's first health resorts -for Herod the Great.

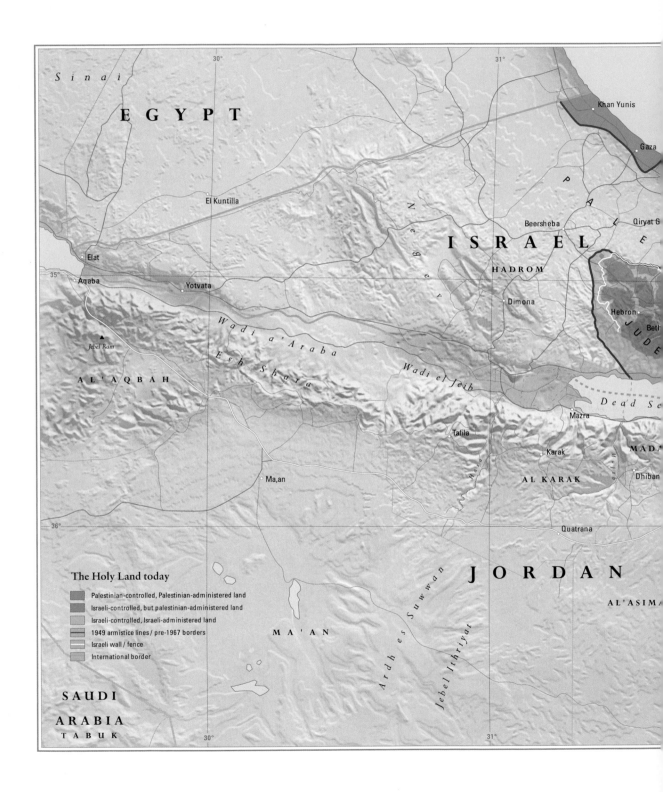

EGYPT

Sinai

Khan Yunis

Gaza

El Kuntilla

Beersheba

Qiryat G

ISRAEL

P
A
L
E

Elat

HADROM

Aqaba

Yotvata

Dimona

Hebron

JUDE

Wadi a'Araba

Beth

Jebel Ram

Esh Shara

Wadi el Jeib

AL'AQBAH

Dead Se

Mazra

Tafila

Karak

MADA

AL KARAK

Dhiban

Ma,an

Quatrana

The Holy Land today

■ Palestinian-controlled, Palestinian-administered land
■ Israeli-controlled, but palestinian-administered land
□ Israeli-controlled, Israeli-administered land
— 1949 armistice lines / pre-1967 borders
□ Israeli wall / fence
■ International border

JORDAN

AL'ASIMA

MA'AN

Ardh es Suwwan

Jebel Ithriyat

SAUDI

ARABIA

TABUK

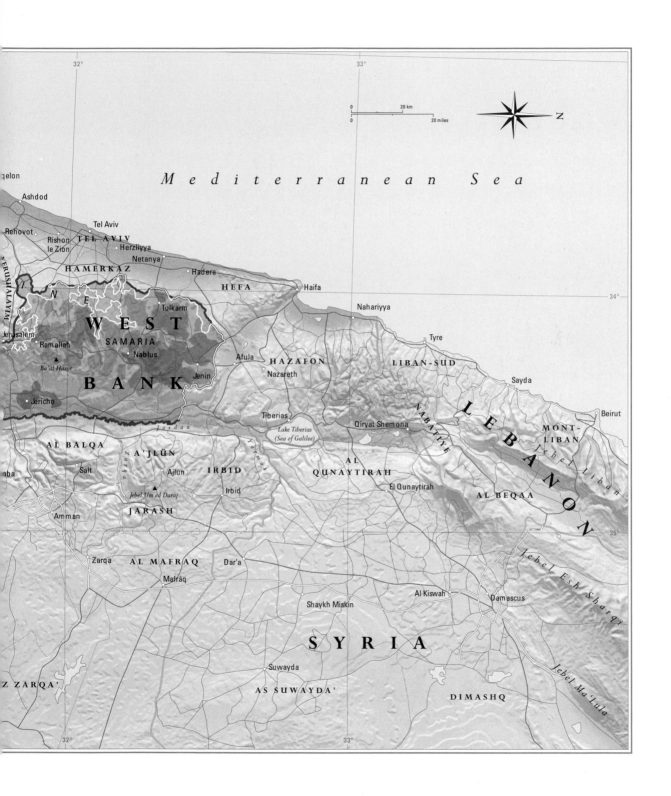

Mediterranean Sea

qelon
Ashdod
Rehovot
Rishon
le Zion
Tel Aviv
TEL AVIV
Herzliyya
Netanya
HAMERKAZ
Hadera
HEFA
Haifa
Nahariyya
Tyre
Jerusalem
Ramallah
SAMARIA
Tulkarm
Nablus
WEST
BANK
Afula
Nazareth
HAZAFON
LIBAN-SUD
Sayda
Beirut
Ba'al Hazor
Jenin
Jericho
Jordan
Tiberias
Lake Tiberias
(Sea of Galilee)
Qiryat Shemona
NABATIYE
LEBANON
MONT-
LIBAN
Jebel Liban
AL BALQA
A'JLÜN
IRBID
AL
QUNAYTIRAH
Salt
Ajlun
Irbid
El Qunaytirah
AL BEQAA
Yarmuk
Jebel Um ed Daraj
JARASH
aba
Amman
Z ZARQA'
Zarqa
AL MAFRAQ
Dar'a
Damascus
Jebel Esh Sharqi
Mafraq
Shaykh Miskin
Al Kiswah
SYRIA
Suwayda
AS SUWAYDA'
DIMASHQ
Jebel Ma'lula

0   20 km
0   20 miles

N

32°
33°
34°
35°

interests in the region. The USA has ultimately supported Israel while the Soviet Union backed Arab states creating conflicts by proxy.

The Six Day War in 1967 and the 1973 Yom Kippur War resulted in the Israeli seizure of the Gaza Strip, the West Bank, and the Golan Heights. The sudden acquisition of a large Palestinian population together with the building of Israeli settlements in Arab lands, an Israeli incursion into Lebanon, intifadas, and terrorism further soured an already embittered Arab-Israeli relationship. The two sides have sought peace accords with some success—Egypt (1978) and Jordan (1994), the latter a possible response to the end of the Cold War. A long-lasting peace with a truly independent Palestine has yet to be reached. However, 2005 saw Israeli evacuating settlements in the Gaza Strip, a sign of some promise. Meanwhile the Holy Land with all its religious sites, important to Jew, Muslim, and Christian alike, is divided among several different states.

JUDAEA AND CANAAN

Bethany

A village just outside Jerusalem, by the eastern slope of the Mount of Olives on the Jericho Road. It remains today with an Arab population, its modern name is El-Azariyah. This name is a reference to Lazarus, for Bethany was the village where Jesus' friend, lived with his sisters Martha and Mary. It was here that Jesus was anointed (Matthew 26:6–13; Mark 14:3–9); it is also here—though the name of the village is not mentioned—that Jesus was served by Martha and commended Mary for listening to his teaching and that Lazarus was raised from the dead (John 11). The Bethany on the River Jordan (sometimes rendered "Bethabara") where John the Baptist was operating (John 1:28) has not been identified by scholars.

Bethel

A small settlement about 12 miles north of Jerusalem on the watershed route. Archaeological excavations suggest that there was a prosperous city here in the Middle Bronze Age, which was destroyed in about 1550 BC and replaced by a later settlement, which was also destroyed and rebuilt. At an early stage it became an Israelite settlement and it flourished in the early days of the monarchy. The city was rebuilt as a Roman township in the first century AD. It is now an Arab village called Tell Beitin.

Bethel is first mentioned as a place where Abraham pitched his tent and built an altar (Genesis 12:8). Jacob had his vision of the ladder (Genesis 28:10–22) there, and is said to have renamed the place Bethal (House of God) from its original name, Luz. It was looked on as a holy place when the Ark was kept there but under Rehoboam it became a center of idolatrous worship (1 Kings 12–13).

Bethlehem

A town five miles south of Jerusalem. It was a Philistine garrison town and was later fortified by Rehoboam. Once famed as the City of David, it had become an obscure village at the time of Jesus' birth. It was desecrated by the Roman Emperor, Hadrian, in the 2nd Century AD but the Church of the Nativity was built by Constantine two centuries later. The town now has the Arab name Bayt Lahm, with the same meaning: "house of bread."

Bethlehem is first mentioned as being close to Rachel's burial place (Genesis 35:19), when it was called Ephrath. It was the home of Boaz who married Ruth and their descendant Jesse, David's father,

Resurrection all happened in or just outside the city. The first seven chapters of Acts describe the growth of the early Church at Jerusalem.

Joppa

Ancient city and seaport, founded in the 17th Century BC or earlier. It was given to the tribe of Dan after the Israelite conquest of Canaan, but was conquered by the Philistines and was under various foreign occupations until the Jews recaptured it in the 2nd Century BC. It is now called Jaffa and is just south of Tel Aviv.

Joppa features in the story of Jonah, as the port from which the prophet set sail for Tarshish instead of going to Nineveh (Jonah 1:3). Peter raised Dorcas at Joppa (Acts 9:36–43) and it was there he had his vision before the conversion of Cornelius (Acts 10).

Judea

Judea is the name of various Roman administrative regions, more or less corresponding to Judah, the southern kingdom after the division. It stretches from the Philistine plain to the Dead Sea. The split from Israel occurred in 931 BC, when the first separate monarchy of Judah under Rehoboam was established. The kingdom continued until 587 BC, when Judah fell to the Babylonians. After the exile, the political significance of Judah was lost, but the name remains in the words Judaism and Jew. The Roman region of Judea is sometimes used in the New Testament to denote the whole of the western Palestine area.

The reigns of the kings of Judah are described in the Books of Kings and Chronicles. Judea is referred to throughout the New Testament as: the birthplace of Jesus (Bethlehem in Judea), the area where John the Baptist preached (the wilderness of Judea, i.e. the desert to the west of the Dead Sea) and the Roman administrative region in general.

Siloam

A cistern or reservoir fed by the spring of Gihon, on the outskirts of Jerusalem. The tunnel connecting the pool to the spring was built by Hezekiah when threatened with Assyrian invasion in around 700 BC (2 Chronicles 32:30). The Old Pool was still in use in New Testament times and remains of a bath house of the period have been found on the site.

Jesus healed a man who had been blind from birth by putting clay on his eyes and sending him to wash in the Pool of Siloam. This led to a dispute with the Pharisees because the healing took place on the Sabbath (John 9). The tower of Siloam, which fell killing 18 people, is referred to by Jesus (Luke 13:4) and is thought to have been sited above the pool.

Sodom

One of the five "cities of the plain" in the Dead Sea region. The cities were destroyed by "fire and brimstone"—probably some kind of seismic event—and their exact location has never been established.

Sodom is first mentioned as the place Lot chose as a home (Genesis 13:10–13). In Genesis 14 Lot was captured when Sodom was involved in war. Genesis 19 describes how Lot entertained angels in his house and was besieged by men of Sodom, wanting sex with his visitors. Lot and his family fled from Sodom just in time to escape its destruction, but Lot's wife looked back at the city and was turned into a pillar of salt. Sodom became synonymous with sin throughout the Bible. Ezekial 16:49–51 lists the sins of Sodom as pride, haughtiness, and neglect of the poor and needy.

GALILEE AND SAMARIA

Cana

A village in the highlands west of the Sea of Galilee. There are two places which claim to be on the site of the original Cana: Kefr Kenna, a village about four miles north-east of Nazareth on the road to Tiberias, and Khirbet Kana, a ruined site some nine miles north of Nazareth.

Cana is mentioned only in John's Gospel. It was the place where Jesus performed his first miracle, turning water into wine at the wedding feast (2:1–11), and also the scene of a later miracle when Jesus healed the son of a nobleman, without even seeing the child (4:46–54). It is also mentioned as the home town of Nathanael (21:2).

Capernaum

A town on the north-west shore of the Sea of Galilee. It was a garrison town, an administrative center and a custom's post. Capernaum is thought to have been inhabited from the 1st Century BC until the 7th Century AD. Although there was a rival site at Khirbet Minyeh, modern scholars are now convinced that the city was at Tell Hum, where remains of the synagogue and other evidence of a Jewish settlement have been found.

Capernaum was Jesus' second home (Matthew 4:13; John 2:12) and it was from here that he called Peter, Andrew and Matthew, It was here, too, that Jesus met the centurion whose servant he healed (Matthew 8:5–13), and he also preached in the synagogue (Mark 1:21). Jesus walked on the water near Capernaum, and when he was back on the shore he spoke of himself as the bread of life (John 6). Jesus condemned the inhabitants of Capernaum for their disbelief, despite all the miracles he had performed there (Matthew 11:23–24).

Carmel

A mountain range about 15 miles long running north-west to south-east over an area south of the modern Israeli town of Haifa. Mount Carmel is the main ridge. It was sacred to both Baal and Yahweh, and in the 6th Century BC was sacred to Jupiter. There are records of a monastery there from AD 570, and subsequent monasteries on the site have been built and destroyed. Mount Carmel was the scene for the dramative contest between Elijah and the prophets of Baal (1 Kings 18:18–46).

The town of Carmel in Judah, where Nabel and Abigail lived (1 Samuel 25), is a few miles south-east of Hebron and is now called Khirbnet el-Karmil.

Galilee

A region in northern Israel. Its boundaries are not precise, but as a Roman province it was an area bounded on the east by the River Jordan and the Sea of Galilee, and separated from the Mediterranean coast by Syrophoenicia. The fertile area was Lower Galilee. The Sea of Galilee is a lake in the region, 14 miles long through which the Jordan flows. Being cut off from the rest of Israel by Gentile nations, the Galileans were traditionally regarded as provincial and uncouth by southern Jews. Little is known of the region's history before New Testament times, when it was under Roman domination.

Galilee is the scene for many of the Gospel narratives, as it was where Jesus lived and where most of his ministry was carried out. Isaiah prophesied that the Messiah would come from Galilee (Isaiah 9:1–2) and Jesus' preaching confirmed the prophecy (Matthew 4:12–17). The disciples Peter, Andrew, James, and John were called from their nets on the Sea of Galilee; it was on this lake that Jesus calmed the storm (Matthew 8:23–27) and walked on the water (Matthew 14:22–32); and on its shores that Jesus fed the 5,000 (Matthew 14:15–21).

Jordan

River flowing from Mount Hermon, through the Sea of Galilee, to the Dead Sea. The valley was inhabited from about 5000 BC and city states began to emerge from the end of the 4th millennium BC, though many were destroyed in nomadic invasions. The most settled areas were around Galilee; the Dead Sea area is arid and infertile.

The Jordan Valley was the territory chosen by Lot, when he and Abraham parted (Genesis 13). The Israelites' crossing of the river is described in Joshua 3–4. It was on the banks of the Jordan that Elijah was taken up to heaven (2 Kings 2:1–15) and Elisha healed Naaman of leprosy by making him bathe in the Jordan (2 Kings 5). John the Baptist's ministry was centred on the Jordan and Jesus was baptized in the river (Luke 3:1–22).

Nazareth

Town in the hills of southern Lebanon, midway between the Sea of Galilee and the Mediterranean. Nothing is known of Nazareth before New Testament times, when it was under Roman rule. The present Israeli town is probably a little to the west of the original Nazareth.

Mary and Joseph returned to Nazareth after their stay in Egypt (Matthew 2:19–23) and all Jesus' early life was spent there. At the start of his ministry Jesus preached in the synagogue at Nazareth but because they recognized him as a local man of no status, the people refused to accept him (Luke 4:16–30) and he was unable to perform miracles there (Matthew 13:53–58). Being in an area cut off from the rest of Israel (see Galilee), Nazareth was despised by many Jews. Nathanael, on first hearing of Jesus, asked, "Can any good thing come out of Nazareth?" (John 1:45–46).

Samaria

Capital of the northern kingdom of Israel; also a designation used for the surrounding area. It was situated on a hill about six miles north of what is now Nablus in Jordan. There is evidence of habitation from the Early Bronze Age, but the city was founded by King Omri in around 880 BC. The construction was continued by Ahab, in whose reign the city became a center of idolatrous worship. It was besieged by the Assyrians several times until in 721 BC the King of Assyria deported over 27,000 captives from Samaria, replacing them with colonists from the Assyrian Empire. Samaria declined and was destroyed by Alexander in the 4th Century BC, but was rebuilt by Pompey and then Herod.

The foundation of the city, its rise, and its fall, are described in the books of Kings (1 Kings 16–2 Kings 17). In New Testament times there was deep mutual suspicion and enmity between Jews and the inhabitants of Samaria. John's account of Jesus' meeting with the Samaritan woman (John 4:1–43) says that Jews have no dealings with Samaritans. It was in Samaria that Philip, Peter and John encountered Simon the Magician (Acts 8:5, 7–24).

THE LANDS TO THE SOUTH AND SOUTH-WEST

Edom

A mountainous region between the Dead Sea and the Gulf of Aqaba, the traditional home of the descendants of Esau. The capital was called Sela and was near the ancient city of Petra. There is evidence that the Edomites were not the first settlers in the territory, but became the dominant tribe and had established a kingdom before the Israelites did. Edom was conquered first by Saul, then by David, and subsequently involved in a series of wars against the Israelites, although at one time it was leagued with Israel against Assyria. Archaeological evidence is sparse, but it seems that after being conquered and overrun by Assyrians, Arabs and Nabateans, Edom had lost its identity by about the 3rd Century BC. Many of the inhabitants fled to Judah and were assimilated among the Jews.

Esau was called Edom (Genesis 25:30), in memory of the red lentils, for which he sold his birthright, because the word is similar to the Hebrew for red. His family had settled in the territory at the time Jacob left Laban (Genesis 32:3; 36:8–9). Moses sent messengers to the King of Edom asking for passage for the Israelites through their land but the request was refused (Numbers 20:14–21), thereby establishing enmity between the brother nations. Edom suffered massive casualties under David and subsequent kings of Israel and Judah (e.g. 1 Kings 11:15–16; 2 Kings 14:7). Psalm 137 records how Edom rejoiced at the fall of Jerusalem (verse 7) and many of the prophets foretold Edom's doom because of its hatred (e.g. Ezekiel 25:12–14).

Egypt

Ancient kingdom at the north-east extremity of Africa. The country is mainly desert and today 99 percent of the inhabitants live in the fertile area near the Nile and its delta, which makes up just 4 percent of the land. There have been settlers in the Nile Valley from prehistoric times but the first Pharaoh emerged in about 3000 BC and Egyptian culture began to flourish from that time, reaching a peak in the period from about 2680 to 2180 BC. After this time the power of the kings waned and foreign influences came in, but there were further peaks in Egyptian cultural and political history in 2134 to 1786 BC and then in 1552 to 1069 BC. It was during this period that the Israelite oppression and the Exodus took place. After this there was a long period of decline until Egypt was conquered, first by Alexander the Great in 332 BC and then by the Romans.

The Israelites' association with Egypt began when Joseph was sold into slavery there (Genesis 37–47). The Israelites multiplied in number and were forced into slavery by the Egyptians, who eventually attempted to control their numbers by genocide (Exodus 1). Moses escaped the slaughter, was brought up in the royal palace and finally led the Israelites out of Egypt. When Herod sought the life of Jesus, it was to Egypt that Joseph and Mary fled (Matthew 2:13–14).

Gaza

The most southerly of the five principal Philistine cities. It is situated on the Mediterranean coast near the Israel-Egypt border and is now part of Egypt. Gaza was used as a military base by Egyptian kings from 1500 BC. It was conquered by Joshua, but later came under Philistine domination. It changed hands many times over the centuries until captured by Alexander in 332 BC and it was finally desolated, although a modern city has been built on the site.

Joshua's battles with the city are recorded in Joshua 10:41 and 11:21–22. Samson visited a prostitute in Gaza (Judges 16:1–3) and his death and final revenge on the Philistines took place in Gaza (Judges 16:21–30).

Midian

A desert region around the Gulf of Aqaba, south of Edom. The Midianites were descendants of Midian, son of Abraham and his concubine Keturah (Genesis 25:1–6). Midian oppressed Israel for seven years until defeated by the army of Gideon.

The merchants to whom Joseph was originally sold were Midianites (Genesis 37:28–36). Moses fled to Midian after killing the Egyptian, and he married there and lived as a shepherd in the region for many years (Exodus 2:15–3:1). Midian later joined Moab to conspire against Israel (*see* Moab). Gideon's defeat of the Midianites is described in Judges 6–8.

Moab

A region east of the Jordan and the Dead Sea, north of Edom. It was settled by the descendants of Moab, Lot's son by his eldest daughter (Genesis 19:37), but was already inhabited before this. Moab became a well-organized kingdom with a distinctive culture. Moab oppressed Israel for 18 years during the time of the judges, but it was subdued by David. Moab continued to attack Israel, but was finally conquered first by the Babylonians and then the Persians, at which point it ceased to have an independent existence as a nation.

The King of Moab, Balak, conspired with the Midianites against the Israelites when they were traveling to Canaan, by attempting to bribe the prophet Balaam to curse Israel. Naomi and her husband migrated to Moab and their sons married the Moabite women, Ruth and Orpah. Saul, David, and Solomon all fought with the Moabites, and after the division, kings of both Israel and Judah continued to battle with Moab.

Sinai

A mountain in the peninsula between the gulfs of Suez and Aqaba (now Sinai Peninsula), also known as Horeb in the Old Testament. Its identity is disputed but both tradition and much modern scholarship points to Jebel Musa ("Mountains of Moses"—about 7,400 feet). The surrounding area was known as the wilderness of Sinai (or of Sin).

Mount Sinai's significance is as the place where Moses received the Law from God (Exodus 19), and all other Bible references to it were within this context.

THE LANDS TO THE EAST

Babylon

Babylon was the capital city of the area known as Babylonia in south-east Asia, which is now southern Iraq. The city of Babylon stood on the Euphrates River a little north of the modern town of Hillah. Although there is no archaeological evidence dating the city from before about 1800 BC, Babel is said to have been founded by Nimrod, Noah's descendant (Genesis 10:9–10), and is thought to have been on the same site as the later Babylon. For many years, Babylon struggled for independence under foreign domination, notably Assyria, until a new Chaldean dynasty was founded in 626 BC and the city was restored. The victorious Babylonian army began to take Jewish captives back to the city and plundered the Temple at Jerusalem. Babylon was a religious center where many gods were worshiped, principally

Marduk. The city flourished until 539 BC, when the Persians invaded and the King, Belshazzar, was killed; eventually it fell into ruins.

The original city of Babel is remembered by the description of the building of the tower, when the people's languages became confused (Genesis 11:1–9). The fall of Jerusalem to the Babylonian King, Nebuchadnezzar, is narrated in 2 Kings 24–25, and Babylonian captivity is described in the Book of Daniel. The captivity is lamented by many of the prophets and the destruction of Babylon is foretold (Isaiah 14:4; 21:9; Jeremiah 50–51). The Babylon mentioned in Revelations 17–18 is thought to be a symbol for the city of Rome, which was similarly oppressing God's people.

Damascus

The capital city of Syria, now and in ancient times. It is situated on the River Barada at the eastern foot of the Anti-Lebanon Mountains. Damascus is said to be the oldest continuously inhabited city in the world. It was already a well-established city in 2000 BC. It became a buffer between Assyria and the emergent kingdom of Israel, and figured for centuries in the wars between these states. The city was captured in 734 BC and lost its capital status, which was not restored until 111 BC. From 64 BC to AD 33, Damascus was under the Romans and subsidiary in importance to Antioch, but after the Arab conquest of AD 634 it regained its supremacy.

Damascus is first mentioned in Genesis, as the place to which Abraham pursued five kings (14:15), and as the home town of Abraham's steward, Eliezer (15:2). David captured the city and garrisoned it (2 Samuel 8:5–6), but it became the home of Solomon's adversary, Rezon (1 Kings 11:23–25), and grew increasingly powerful under his successors. It was as Paul traveled to Damascus that he experienced the vision which brought about his conversion and he was baptized in the city (Acts 9:1–22).

Nineveh

Ancient city of the Assyrian Empire, situated on the River Tigris, opposite what is now the town of Mosul in north Iraq. The site was occupied from prehistoric times, but the city is said to have been built by Nimrod, or Asshur (Genesis 10:11). There was a temple dedicated to the goddess Ishtar there in 2300 BC, which was restored in 1800 BC. The city flourished from about 1260 BC until its destruction in 612 BC, when it was attacked by Babylonians and Medes and left in ruins, never to be rebuilt.

The attack of the Assyrian King Sennacherib and his defeat and return to Nineveh, is described in 2 Kings 18–19. The prophet Jonah was sent by God to prophesy against Nineveh, and when he finally did so the people repented and were spared from destruction (Jonah 1:1; 3:1–10). The Book of Nahum is a celebration of the fall of Nineveh.

Ur

An ancient city, generally identified with a site now occupied by Tell el-Muqayyar on the River Euphrates in southern Iraq. Archaeological work in the site indicates occupation from 5000 BC. Remains from graves dating back to 3500 BC have been found, and the ruins of the ancient temple tower still stand. The city was ruled by the Babylonians and Chaldeans, but had ceased to be inhabited by 300 BC.

Ur is mentioned as the home of Abraham's family before they left to travel to Haran and then Canaan (Genesis 11:28–31; 15:7; Nehemiah 9:7).

GREECE AND TURKEY

Antioch

1. Antioch in Syria. Antioch is situated on the River Orontes in what is now south-east Turkey, near the Syrian border. The city was founded in about 300 BC and was the capital of the Roman province of Syria. It became the third largest city of the Roman Empire after it fell to Pompey in 64 BC. It is now called Antalya. Antioch had a very mixed population of Jews and Gentiles and became a center of early Christianity, second only to Jerusalem. During the persecution that followed Stephen's martyrdom, some Christians went to Antioch to preach to the Jews there, and when many Jews and Greeks had been converted, Barnabas and Paul were sent to Antioch. It was here that the disciples were first given the name Christians (Acts 11:19–26). Antioch was at the center of the dispute over whether Gentile converts had to be circumcised (Acts 14:26–15:35; Galatians 2:11).

2. Antioch in Pisidia. This Antioch was a Roman colony situated in an area that is now in central Turkey. The ruins of the city are to be found near the town of Yalvaj. It had been founded by 280 BC and became a free Roman city, Greek-speaking but with a mixed population, including many Jews.

Antioch was a center of civil and military administration at the time that Paul visited it on his first missionary journey. Paul preached in the synagogue there, but when he declared that the Gospel was also for the Gentiles, some of the Jews roused those in high office in Antioch to organize persecution of Paul and Barnabas. They were expelled from the city but returned later (Acts 13:14–50; 14:19–21).

Athens

Athens is the capital of modern Greece and one of the most important cities of antiquity. There appears to have been a city on the site since prehistoric times, but it was in the Classical period of the 4th and 5th Centuries BC that it became renowned as a cultural center. Athens was named for the goddess Athene, but many gods were worshiped there.

The Areopagus (hill of Ares or Mars) no longer exists, but it was once the meeting place for the Athenian tribunal, and it was from here that Paul preached his famous sermon (Acts 17:15–34) in which he condemned the superstition and idolatry he saw in Athens, and expounded the true nature of God.

Corinth

A major trading city on the isthmus between the Greek mainland and the Peloponnese. Corinth began to achieve its importance and prosperity in the 6th and 7th Centuries BC. It became part of the Peloponnesian league under Sparta, but later came under Macedonian domination. In the war with the Romans of 146 BC the city was despoiled, but it was rebuilt by Julius Caesar in 46 BC and regained its former prosperity. Corinth was the center of worship of Aphrodite, goddess of love, and was notorious for the immorality of its inhabitants. An earthquake destroyed the old town in 1858 and the subsequent modern town of New Corinth has also been the victim of earthquakes.

It was at Corinth that Paul met Priscilla and Aquila and stayed with them. Although his teaching was opposed in the synagogue, Paul stayed in Corinth for 18 months, founding the church to which he subsequently wrote the two letters to the Corinthians.

Cyprus

An island in the eastern Mediterranean, equidistant from the coasts of Turkey and Syria. In New

Testament times it was a Roman province governed by a proconsul. Cyprus became a significant area in the Bronze Age as it was a primary source of copper. The culture was influenced over the centuries by the Minoans and Myceneans. In the 9th Century BC the island was settled by Phoenicians, and it was conquered by the Egyptians in the 6th Century. It became part of the Persian Empire in 525 BC, fell to Alexander in 33 BC, and became a Roman province in 58 BC.

In the Old Testament, Cyprus (Chittim in older translations) is briefly referred to in the books of Isaiah, Jeremiah, and Ezekiel. The New Testament apostle Barnabas was a native of Cyprus (Acts 4:36) and he traveled there with Paul at the start of their first missionary journey, when they encountered the sorcerer Bar-jesus (Acts 13:2–12). After the disagreement between Paul and Barnabas over Mark, Barnabas, and Mark traveled again to Cyprus.

Ephesus

Ancient city and capital of the Roman province of Asia. It was situated at the mouth of the River Cayster, on the west coast of what is now Asiatic Turkey. The city was established in the 19th Century BC, although there was already a settlement there. From ancient times the area had been associated with the worship of a fertility goddess, who later became identified with Artemis (or Roman Diana). The city was conquered by Croesus in the 6th Century BC and came variously under Lydian and Persian domination until Alexander established democratic government in 334 BC. Ephesus was finally conquered by the Romans, under whose rule the city flourished. It declined after the 4th Century AD and has been uninhabited for centuries.

With Priscilla and Aquila, Paul helped to establish the Church here (Acts 18:19–28; 19:1–10). The popularity of Christianity caused trouble among those who made their living from the cult of Diana and they stirred up a riot (Acts 19:23–41). After Paul left Ephesus (Acts 20:17–38), he left Timothy in charge (1 Timothy 1:3). Paul wrote a letter to the Church at Ephesus. It was one of the seven Asian churches that received a message in Revelation (Revelation 2:1–7).

Haran

Haran, or Harran, was an ancient city on the main route from Nineveh to Aleppo. The name means "crossroads" and its position gave it strategic importance. Its name appears in texts from 2000 BC and it later became an important Assyrian center. It was sacked in 763 BC, but was rebuilt and became the last capital of Assyria after the fall of Nineveh. It was then captured by the Babylonians and was under Roman, then Islamic domination before it fell into ruins. The site is about 20 miles south-east of Urfa in modern Turkey.

Haran was a staging post in Abraham's journey from Ur to Canaan (Genesis 11:31–12:5). It was the home of Rebekah (Genesis 24) and of her nieces, Rachel and Leah, who both became Jacob's wives in Haran (Genesis 29–31). All Jacob's sons, except Benjamin, were born in Haran.

Lystra

A remote town in a mountainous region of the Roman territory of Lycaonia. The region is mentioned by writers from the 4th Century BC, and became a Roman province in Pompey's time. The people spoke a distinct language, which was still used in Lystra when Paul visited it. The site of the town is near the modern Hatunsaray in Turkey.

Paul and Barnabas fled to Lystra when threatened with persecution in Iconium. When Paul healed a crippled man the people of Lystra mistook the apostles for gods, but their veneration turned to persecution after Paul explained their mistake (Acts 14:6–19). Paul later returned to Lystra where he circumcised Timothy (Acts 16:1–3).

Macedonia

An important Roman province and former imperial power. The province covered modern-day northern Greece, southern Yugoslavia and Albania. The Macedonian Empire was founded by Alexander in the 4th Century BC, but the region came under the control of the Romans in 146 BC.

Paul had a vision of a man from Macedonia, asking him to come and help him (Acts 16:9), and he and Silas immediately went there. Paul later returned (Acts 20:1–2); and the Church established in Macedonia gave financial support to the Jerusalem Church (Romans 15:26; 2 Corinthians 8:1–4).

Philippi

One of the principal cities of the Roman province of Macedonia. It was situated on a steep hill on what is now the River Angista in north-east Greece. The town was developed by Philip of Macedon who conquered it in about 360 BC. It was taken by the Romans in 168 BC and in New Testament times had been colonised by Italians who were given special rights and privileges. The site is now uninhabited, although ruins of an amphitheatre and temple remain.

Philippi was the first European city to be evangelised by Paul. His first visit there was marked by the conversion of Lydia, and the imprisonment and miraculous deliverance of Paul and Silas (Acts 16:12–40). Paul's letter to the Philippians thanks them for a gift sent to him in prison.

TIMELINES

S o far the story of the Bible has been covered thematically, which can make relating one event to another problematic. The charts on the following pages give a graphic insight into the chronology of these turbulent times. The first chart locates the history of states of Israel and Judah alongside other major ancient civilisations mentioned in the Bible.

The second chart represents a slice through a mound or "tel" in this region revealing the layers of human culture that would be found from the Stone Ages through to the Islamic period. On our chart we refer to the beginning of the Bronze Age as the Chalcolithic (Copper-Stone) Age.

The timelines covering the next 12 pages gives a chronological oversight into all the major events that affected the cultures and peoples of this region from 3000 BC to AD 600.

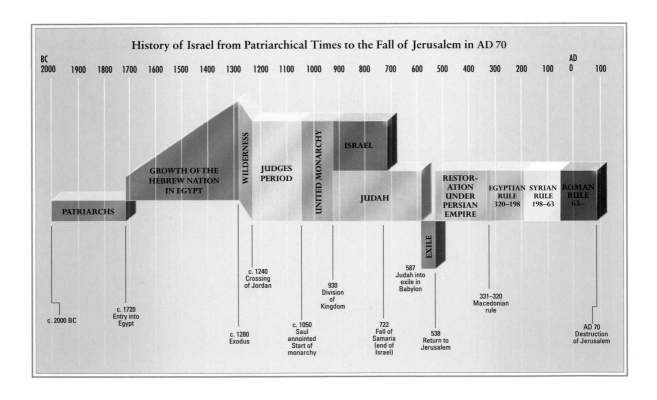

History of Israel from Patriarchical Times to the Fall of Jerusalem in AD 70

BC 2000 1900 1800 1700 1600 1500 1400 1300 1200 1100 1000 900 800 700 600 500 400 300 200 100 AD 0 100

PATRIARCHS

GROWTH OF THE HEBREW NATION IN EGYPT

WILDERNESS

JUDGES PERIOD

UNITED MONARCHY

ISRAEL

JUDAH

EXILE

RESTOR-ATION UNDER PERSIAN EMPIRE

EGYPTIAN RULE 320–198

SYRIAN RULE 198–63

ROMAN RULE 63–

c. 2000 BC

c. 1720 Entry into Egypt

c. 1280 Exodus

c. 1240 Crossing of Jordan

c. 1050 Saul annointed Start of monarchy

930 Division of Kingdom

722 Fall of Samaria (end of Israel)

587 Judah into exile in Babylon

538 Return to Jerusalem

331–320 Macedonian rule

AD 70 Destruction of Jerusalem

Archealogical Layers
Mesolithic to Islamic

ISLAMIC AD 636 –	Islamic	AD 636 –
BYZANTINE AD 324 – 636	Byzantine	AD 324 – 636
ROMAN 63 BC – AD 324	Roman III	AD 180 – 324
	Roman II	AD 70 – 180
	Roman I (Herodian)	63 BC – AD 70
HELLENISTIC 330 – 63 BC	Hellenistic II (Hasmonaean/Maccabean) 152 – 63 BC	
	Hellenistic I (Ptolemaic/Seleucid) 330 – 152 BC	
IRON AGE 1200 – 330 BC	Babylonian/Persian (Late Iron/Persian) 587 – 330 BC	
(SOMETIMES KNOWN AS ISRAELITE PERIOD)	Iron Age IIIb	720 – 587 BC
	Iron Age IIIa	800 – 720 BC
	Iron Age IIb (Middle Iron)	900 – 800 BC
	Iron Age IIa	1000 – 900 BC
	Iron Age Ib	1150 – 1000 BC
	Iron Age Ia	1200 – 1150 BC
BRONZE AGE 3150 – 1200 BC	Late Bronze IIb	1300 – 1200 BC
(SOMETIMES KNOWN AS CANAANITE PERIOD)	Late Bronze IIa	1400 – 1300 BC
	Late Bronze I (Late Canaanite)	1550 – 1400 BC
	Middle Bronze IIc	1600 – 1550 BC
	Middle Bronze IIb	1750 – 1600 BC
	Middle Bronze IIa (Middle Canaanite)	1950 – 1750 BC
	Middle Bronze I (Early – Middle Bronze Age)	2200 – 1950 BC
	Early Bronze IV (Early Canaanite IV)	2350 – 2200 BC
	Early Bronze III (Early Canaanite III)	2650 – 2350 BC
	Early Bronze II (Early Canaanite II)	2850 – 2650 BC
	Early Bronze I (Early Canaanite I)	3150 – 2850 BC
CHALCOLITHIC	Chalcolithic (Ghassulian)	4000 – 3150 BC
STONE AGE – 4000 BC	Neolithic (Pottery)	5000 – 4000 BC
	Neolithic (Pre-pottery) (New Stone Age)	7500 – 5000 BC
	Mesolithic (Middle Stone Age/Natufian)	10,000 – 7500 BC

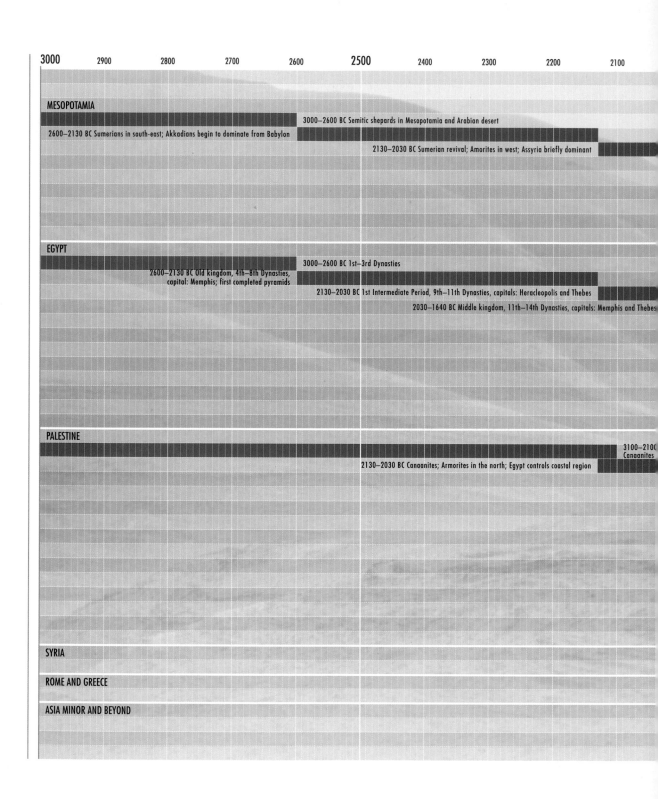

| 3000 | 2900 | 2800 | 2700 | 2600 | 2500 | 2400 | 2300 | 2200 | 2100 |

MESOPOTAMIA

3000–2600 BC Semitic shepards in Mesopotamia and Arabian desert

2600–2130 BC Sumerians in south-east; Akkadians begin to dominate from Babylon

2130–2030 BC Sumerian revival; Amorites in west; Assyria briefly dominant

EGYPT

3000–2600 BC 1st–3rd Dynasties

2600–2130 BC Old kingdom, 4th–8th Dynasties, capital: Memphis; first completed pyramids

2130–2030 BC 1st Intermediate Period, 9th–11th Dynasties, capitals: Heracleopolis and Thebes

2030–1640 BC Middle kingdom, 11th–14th Dynasties, capitals: Memphis and Thebes

PALESTINE

3100–2100 Canaanites

2130–2030 BC Canaanites; Amorites in the north; Egypt controls coastal region

SYRIA

ROME AND GREECE

ASIA MINOR AND BEYOND

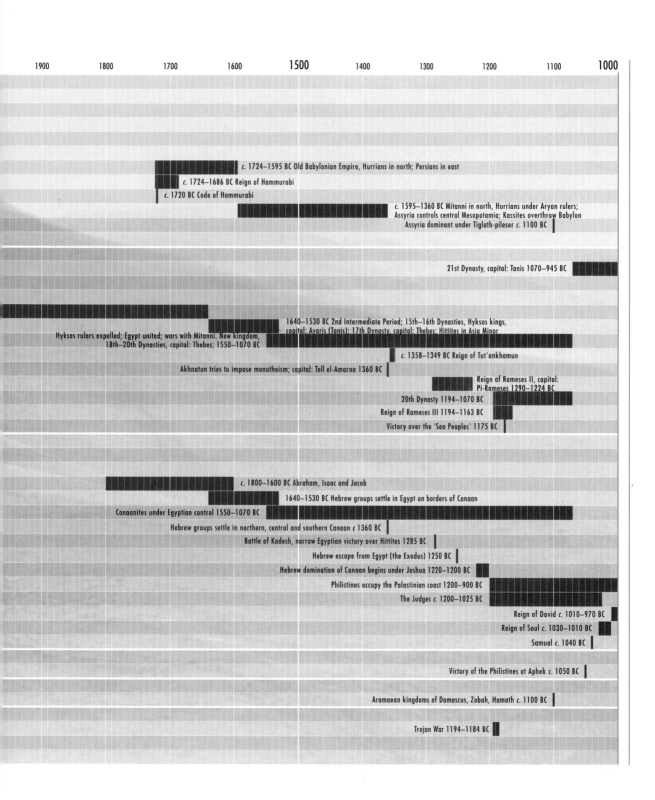

1900   1800   1700   1600   **1500**   1400   1300   1200   1100   **1000**

c. 1724–1595 BC Old Babylonian Empire, Hurrians in north; Persians in east

c. 1724–1686 BC Reign of Hammurabi

c. 1720 BC Code of Hammurabi

c. 1595–1360 BC Mitanni in north, Hurrians under Aryan rulers;
Assyria controls central Mesopotamia; Kassites overthrow Babylon
Assyria dominant under Tiglath-pileser *c.* 1100 BC

21st Dynasty, capital: Tanis 1070–945 BC

1640–1530 BC 2nd Intermediate Period; 15th–16th Dynasties, Hyksos kings,
capital: Avaris (Tanis); 17th Dynasty, capital: Thebes; Hittites in Asia Minor

Hyksos rulers expelled; Egypt united; wars with Mitanni. New kingdom,
18th–20th Dynasties, capital: Thebes; 1550–1070 BC

c. 1358–1349 BC Reign of Tut'ankhamun

Akhnaton tries to impose monotheism; capital: Tell el-Amarna 1360 BC

Reign of Rameses II, capital:
Pi-Rameses 1290–1224 BC

20th Dynasty 1194–1070 BC

Reign of Rameses III 1194–1163 BC

Victory over the 'Sea Peoples' 1175 BC

c. 1800–1600 BC Abraham, Isaac and Jacob

1640–1530 BC Hebrew groups settle in Egypt on borders of Canaan

Canaanites under Egyptian control 1550–1070 BC

Hebrew groups settle in northern, central and southern Canaan *c* 1360 BC

Battle of Kadesh, narrow Egyptian victory over Hittites 1285 BC

Hebrew escape from Egypt (the Exodus) 1250 BC

Hebrew domination of Canaan begins under Joshua 1220–1200 BC

Philistines occupy the Palastinian coast 1200–900 BC

The Judges *c.* 1200–1025 BC

Reign of David *c.* 1010–970 BC

Reign of Saul *c.* 1030–1010 BC

Samual *c.* 1040 BC

Victory of the Philistines at Aphek *c.* 1050 BC

Aramaean kingdoms of Damascus, Zobah, Hamath *c.* 1100 BC

Trojan War 1194–1184 BC

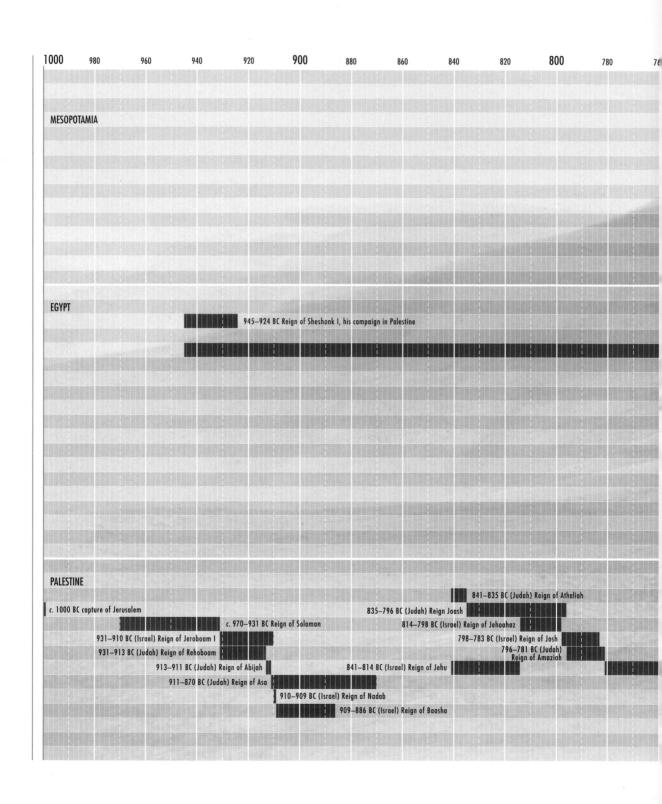

| 1000 | 980 | 960 | 940 | 920 | **900** | 880 | 860 | 840 | 820 | **800** | 780 | 7(|

MESOPOTAMIA

EGYPT

945–924 BC Reign of Sheshonk I, his campaign in Palestine

PALESTINE

841–835 BC (Judah) Reign of Athaliah

c. 1000 BC capture of Jerusalem

835–796 BC (Judah) Reign Joash

c. 970–931 BC Reign of Solomon

814–798 BC (Israel) Reign of Jehoahaz

931–910 BC (Israel) Reign of Jeroboam I

798–783 BC (Israel) Reign of Josh

931–913 BC (Judah) Reign of Rehoboam

796–781 BC (Judah)
Reign of Amaziah

913–911 BC (Judah) Reign of Abijah

841–814 BC (Israel) Reign of Jehu

911–870 BC (Judah) Reign of Asa

910–909 BC (Israel) Reign of Nadab

909–886 BC (Israel) Reign of Baasha

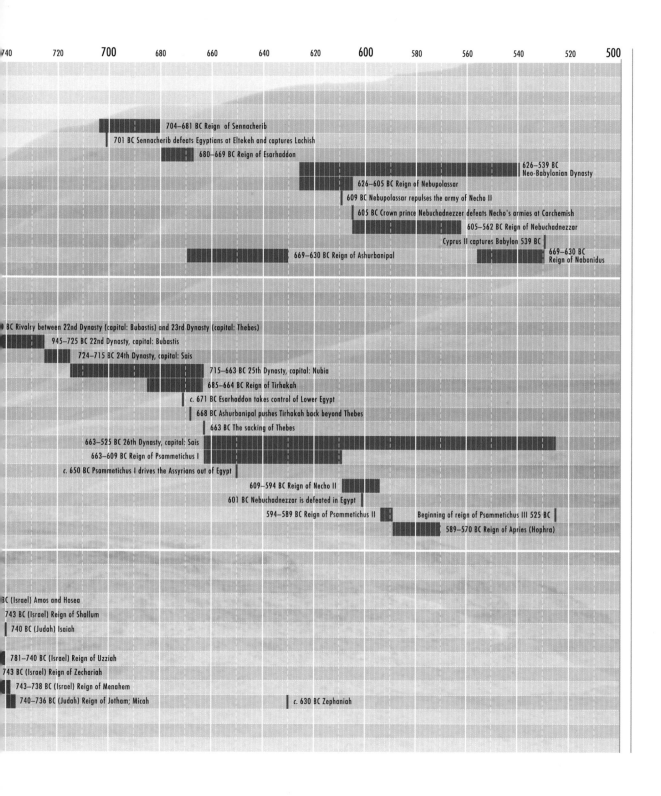

740　720　**700**　680　660　640　620　**600**　580　560　540　520　**500**

704–681 BC Reign of Sennacherib

701 BC Sennacherib defeats Egyptians at Eltekeh and captures Lachish

680–669 BC Reign of Esarhaddon

626–539 BC
Neo-Babylonian Dynasty

626–605 BC Reign of Nebupolassar

609 BC Nebupolassar repulses the army of Necho II

605 BC Crown prince Nebuchadnezzer defeats Necho's armies at Carchemish

605–562 BC Reign of Nebuchadnezzar

Cyprus II captures Babylon 539 BC

669–630 BC Reign of Ashurbanipal

669–630 BC
Reign of Nabonidus

BC Rivalry between 22nd Dynasty (capital: Bubastis) and 23rd Dynasty (capital: Thebes)

945–725 BC 22nd Dynasty, capital: Bubastis

724–715 BC 24th Dynasty, capital: Sais

715–663 BC 25th Dynasty, capital: Nubia

685–664 BC Reign of Tirhakah

c. 671 BC Esarhaddon takes control of Lower Egypt

668 BC Ashurbanipal pushes Tirhakah back beyond Thebes

663 BC The sacking of Thebes

663–525 BC 26th Dynasty, capital: Sais

663–609 BC Reign of Psammetichus I

c. 650 BC Psammetichus I drives the Assyrians out of Egypt

609–594 BC Reign of Necho II

601 BC Nebuchadnezzar is defeated in Egypt

594–589 BC Reign of Psammetichus II

Beginning of reign of Psammetichus III 525 BC

589–570 BC Reign of Apries (Hophra)

BC (Israel) Amos and Hosea

743 BC (Israel) Reign of Shallum

740 BC (Judah) Isaiah

781–740 BC (Israel) Reign of Uzziah

743 BC (Israel) Reign of Zechariah

743–738 BC (Israel) Reign of Menahem

740–736 BC (Judah) Reign of Jotham; Micah

c. 630 BC Zephaniah

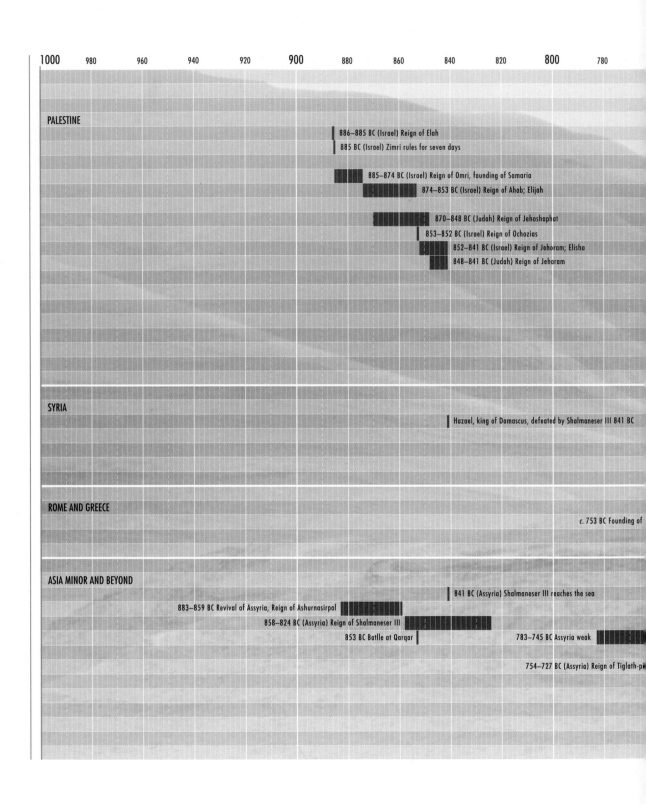

| 1000 | 980 | 960 | 940 | 920 | **900** | 880 | 860 | 840 | 820 | **800** | 780 |

PALESTINE

886–885 BC (Israel) Reign of Elah

885 BC (Israel) Zimri rules for seven days

885–874 BC (Israel) Reign of Omri, founding of Samaria

874–853 BC (Israel) Reign of Ahab; Elijah

870–848 BC (Judah) Reign of Jehoshaphat

853–852 BC (Israel) Reign of Ochozias

852–841 BC (Israel) Reign of Jehoram; Elisha

848–841 BC (Judah) Reign of Jehoram

SYRIA

Hazael, king of Damascus, defeated by Shalmaneser III 841 BC

ROME AND GREECE

c. 753 BC Founding of

ASIA MINOR AND BEYOND

841 BC (Assyria) Shalmaneser III reaches the sea

883–859 BC Revival of Assyria, Reign of Ashurnasirpal

858–824 BC (Assyria) Reign of Shalmaneser III

853 BC Batlle at Qarqar

783–745 BC Assyria weak

754–727 BC (Assyria) Reign of Tiglath-pi

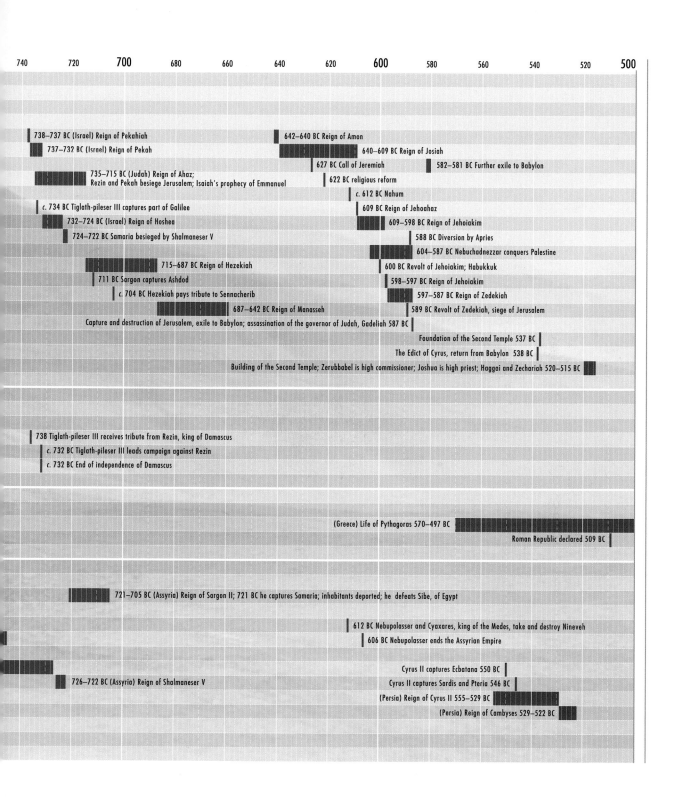

740   720   **700**   680   660   640   620   **600**   580   560   540   520   **500**

738–737 BC (Israel) Reign of Pekahiah

737–732 BC (Israel) Reign of Pekah

735–715 BC (Judah) Reign of Ahaz;
Rezin and Pekah besiege Jerusalem; Isaiah's prophecy of Emmanuel

c. 734 BC Tiglath-pileser III captures part of Galilee

732–724 BC (Israel) Reign of Hoshea

724–722 BC Samaria besieged by Shalmaneser V

715–687 BC Reign of Hezekiah

711 BC Sargon captures Ashdod

c. 704 BC Hezekiah pays tribute to Sennacherib

687–642 BC Reign of Manasseh

Capture and destruction of Jerusalem, exile to Babylon; assassination of the governor of Judah, Gadeliah 587 BC

642–640 BC Reign of Amon

640–609 BC Reign of Josiah

627 BC Call of Jeremiah

622 BC religious reform

582–581 BC Further exile to Babylon

c. 612 BC Nahum

609 BC Reign of Jehoahaz

609–598 BC Reign of Jehoiakim

588 BC Diversion by Apries

604–587 BC Nebuchadnezzar conquers Palestine

600 BC Revolt of Jehoiakim; Habukkuk

598–597 BC Reign of Jehoiakim

597–587 BC Reign of Zedekiah

589 BC Revolt of Zedekiah, siege of Jerusalem

Foundation of the Second Temple 537 BC

The Edict of Cyrus, return from Babylon 538 BC

Building of the Second Temple; Zerubbabel is high commissioner; Joshua is high priest; Haggai and Zechariah 520–515 BC

738 Tiglath-pileser III receives tribute from Rezin, king of Damascus

c. 732 BC Tiglath-pileser III leads campaign against Rezin

c. 732 BC End of independence of Damascus

(Greece) Life of Pythagoras 570–497 BC

Roman Republic declared 509 BC

721–705 BC (Assyria) Reign of Sargon II; 721 BC he captures Samaria; inhabitants deported; he defeats Sibe, of Egypt

612 BC Nebupolasser and Cyaxares, king of the Medes, take and destroy Nineveh

606 BC Nebupolasser ends the Assyrian Empire

Cyrus II captures Ecbatana 550 BC

726–722 BC (Assyria) Reign of Shalmaneser V

Cyrus II captures Sardis and Pteria 546 BC

(Persia) Reign of Cyrus II 555–529 BC

(Persia) Reign of Cambyses 529–522 BC

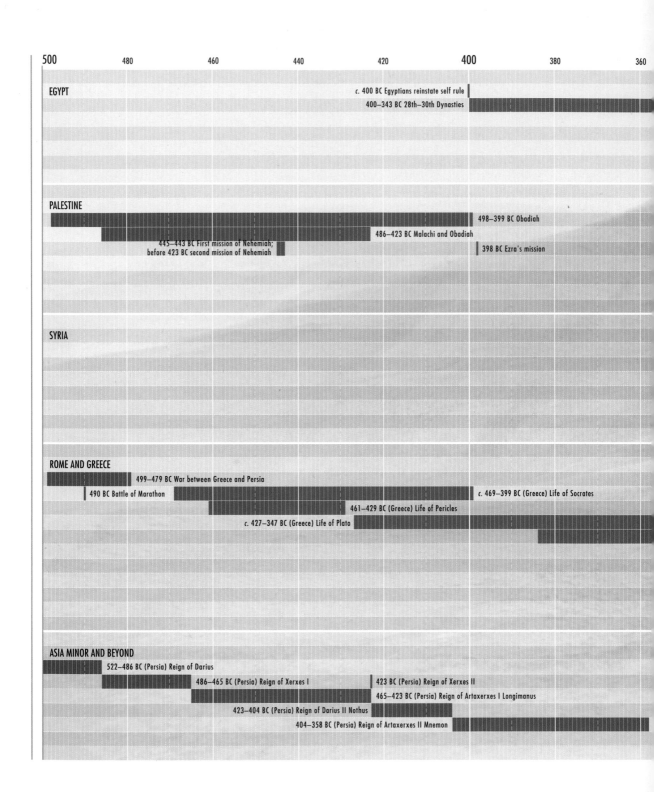

	500	480	460	440	420	400	380	360

EGYPT

c. 400 BC Egyptians reinstate self rule

400–343 BC 28th–30th Dynasties

PALESTINE

498–399 BC Obadiah

486–423 BC Malachi and Obadiah

445–443 BC First mission of Nehemiah;
before 423 BC second mission of Nehemiah

398 BC Ezra's mission

SYRIA

ROME AND GREECE

499–479 BC War between Greece and Persia

490 BC Battle of Marathon

c. 469–399 BC (Greece) Life of Socrates

461–429 BC (Greece) Life of Pericles

c. 427–347 BC (Greece) Life of Plato

ASIA MINOR AND BEYOND

522–486 BC (Persia) Reign of Darius

486–465 BC (Persia) Reign of Xerxes I

423 BC (Persia) Reign of Xerxes II

465–423 BC (Persia) Reign of Artaxerxes I Longimanus

423–404 BC (Persia) Reign of Darius II Nothus

404–358 BC (Persia) Reign of Artaxerxes II Mnemon

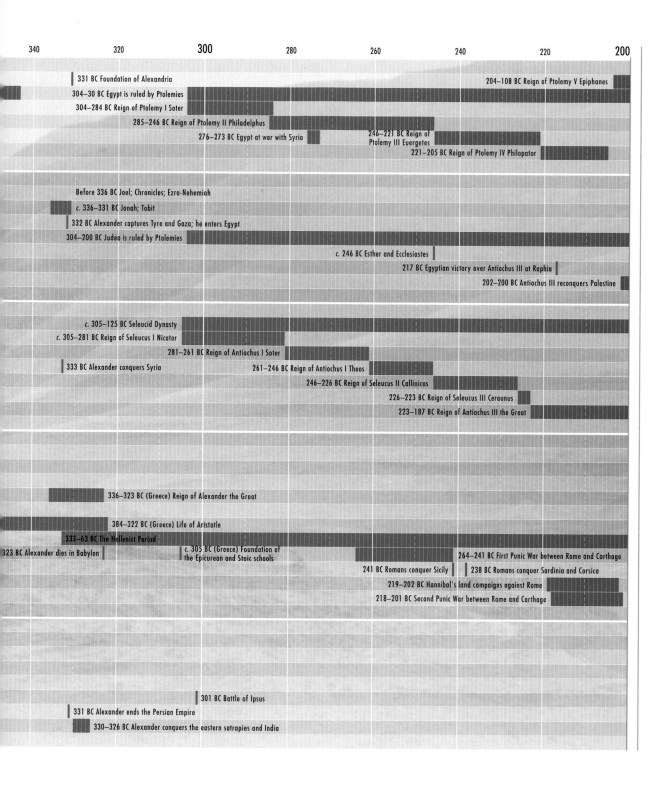

340   320   **300**   280   260   240   220   **200**

331 BC Foundation of Alexandria

204–108 BC Reign of Ptolemy V Epiphanes

304–30 BC Egypt is ruled by Ptolemies

304–284 BC Reign of Ptolemy I Soter

285–246 BC Reign of Ptolemy II Philadelphus

276–273 BC Egypt at war with Syria

246–221 BC Reign of Ptolemy III Euergetes

221–205 BC Reign of Ptolemy IV Philopator

Before 336 BC Joel; Chronicles; Ezra-Nehemiah

c. 336–331 BC Jonah; Tobit

332 BC Alexander captures Tyre and Gaza; he enters Egypt

304–200 BC Judea is ruled by Ptolemies

c. 246 BC Esther and Ecclesiastes

217 BC Egyptian victory over Antiochus III at Raphia

202–200 BC Antiochus III reconquers Palestine

c. 305–125 BC Seleucid Dynasty

c. 305–281 BC Reign of Seleucus I Nicator

281–261 BC Reign of Antiochus I Soter

333 BC Alexander conquers Syria

261–246 BC Reign of Antiochus I Theos

246–226 BC Reign of Seleucus II Callinicos

226–223 BC Reign of Seleucus III Ceraunus

223–187 BC Reign of Antiochus III the Great

336–323 BC (Greece) Reign of Alexander the Great

384–322 BC (Greece) Life of Aristotle

333–63 BC The Hellenist Period

323 BC Alexander dies in Babylon

c. 305 BC (Greece) Foundation of the Epicurean and Stoic schools

264–241 BC First Punic War between Rome and Carthage

241 BC Romans conquer Sicily

238 BC Romans conquer Sardinia and Corsica

219–202 BC Hannibal's land campaigns against Rome

218–201 BC Second Punic War between Rome and Carthage

301 BC Battle of Ipsus

331 BC Alexander ends the Persian Empire

330–326 BC Alexander conquers the eastern satrapies and India

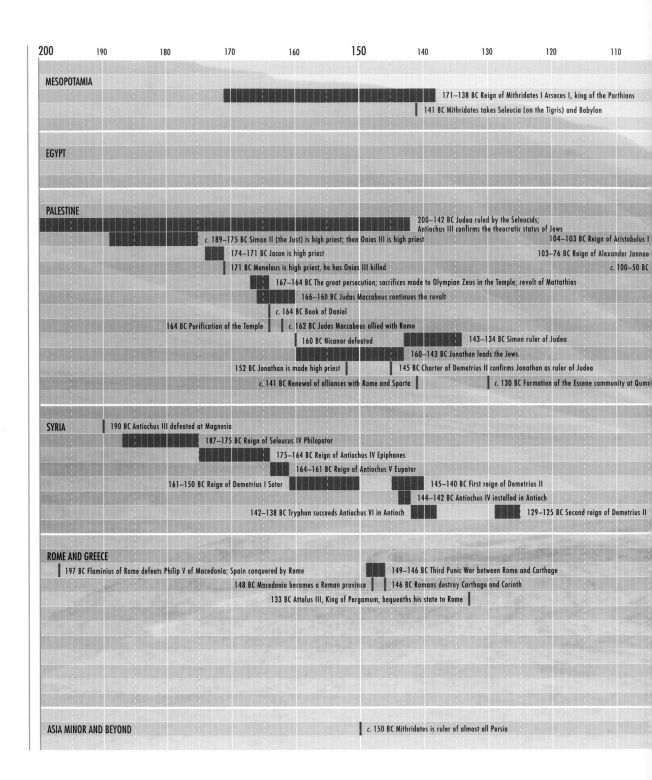

| 200 | 190 | 180 | 170 | 160 | 150 | 140 | 130 | 120 | 110 |

MESOPOTAMIA

171–138 BC Reign of Mithridates I Arsaces I, king of the Parthians

141 BC Mithridates takes Seleucia (on the Tigris) and Babylon

EGYPT

PALESTINE

200–142 BC Judea ruled by the Seleucids; Antiochus III confirms the theocratic status of Jews

c. 189–175 BC Simon II (the Just) is high priest; then Onias III is high priest

104–103 BC Reign of Aristobulus I

174–171 BC Jason is high priest

103–76 BC Reign of Alexander Jannae

171 BC Menelaus is high priest, he has Onias III killed

c. 100–50 BC

167–164 BC The great persecution; sacrifices made to Olympian Zeus in the Temple; revolt of Mattathias

166–160 BC Judas Maccabeus continues the revolt

c. 164 BC Book of Daniel

164 BC Purification of the Temple

c. 162 BC Judas Maccabeus allied with Rome

160 BC Nicanor defeated

143–134 BC Simon ruler of Judea

160–143 BC Jonathan leads the Jews

152 BC Jonathan is made high priest

145 BC Charter of Demetrius II confirms Jonathan as ruler of Judea

c. 141 BC Renewal of alliances with Rome and Sparta

c. 130 BC Formation of the Essene community at Qumr

SYRIA

190 BC Antiochus III defeated at Magnesia

187–175 BC Reign of Seleucus IV Philopator

175–164 BC Reign of Antiochus IV Epiphanes

164–161 BC Reign of Antiochus V Eupator

161–150 BC Reign of Demetrius I Soter

145–140 BC First reign of Demetrius II

144–142 BC Antiochus IV installed in Antioch

142–138 BC Tryphon succeeds Antiochus VI in Antioch

129–125 BC Second reign of Demetrius II

ROME AND GREECE

197 BC Flaminius of Rome defeats Philip V of Macedonia; Spain conquered by Rome

149–146 BC Third Punic War between Rome and Carthage

148 BC Macedonia becomes a Roman province

146 BC Romans destroy Carthage and Corinth

133 BC Attalus III, King of Pergamum, bequeaths his state to Rome

ASIA MINOR AND BEYOND

c. 150 BC Mithridates is ruler of almost all Persia

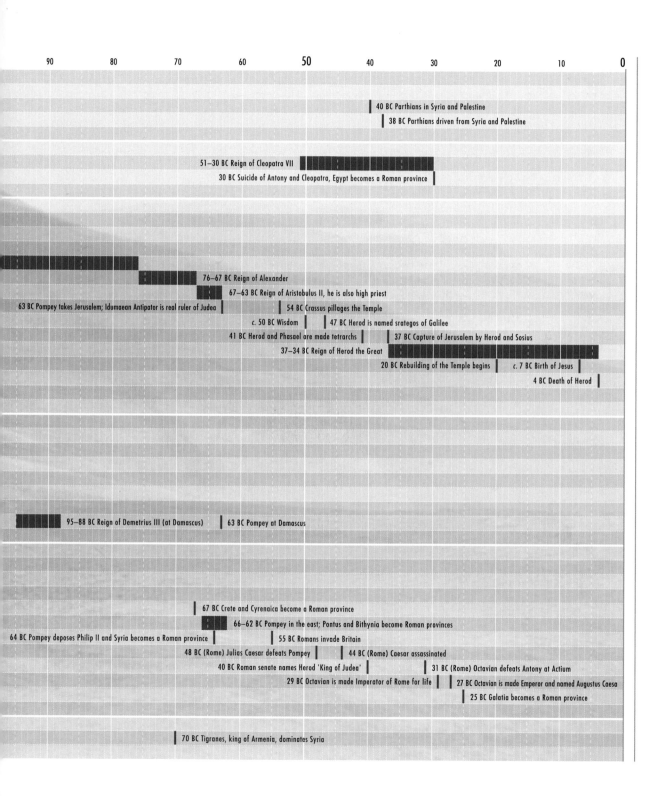

90   80   70   60   **50**   40   30   20   10   **0**

40 BC Parthians in Syria and Palestine

38 BC Parthians driven from Syria and Palestine

51–30 BC Reign of Cleopatra VII

30 BC Suicide of Antony and Cleopatra, Egypt becomes a Roman province

76–67 BC Reign of Alexander

67–63 BC Reign of Aristobulus II, he is also high priest

63 BC Pompey takes Jerusalem; Idumaean Antipator is real ruler of Judea

54 BC Crassus pillages the Temple

c. 50 BC Wisdom

47 BC Herod is named srategos of Galilee

41 BC Herod and Phasael are made tetrarchs

37 BC Capture of Jerusalem by Herod and Sosius

37–34 BC Reign of Herod the Great

20 BC Rebuilding of the Temple begins

c. 7 BC Birth of Jesus

4 BC Death of Herod

95–88 BC Reign of Demetrius III (at Damascus)

63 BC Pompey at Damascus

67 BC Crete and Cyrenaica become a Roman province

66–62 BC Pompey in the east; Pontus and Bithynia become Roman provinces

64 BC Pompey deposes Philip II and Syria becomes a Roman province

55 BC Romans invade Britain

48 BC (Rome) Julius Caesar defeats Pompey

44 BC (Rome) Caesar assassinated

40 BC Roman senate names Herod 'King of Judea'

31 BC (Rome) Octavian defeats Antony at Actium

29 BC Octavian is made Imperator of Rome for life

27 BC Octavian is made Emperor and named Augustus Caesa

25 BC Galatia becomes a Roman province

70 BC Tigranes, king of Armenia, dominates Syria

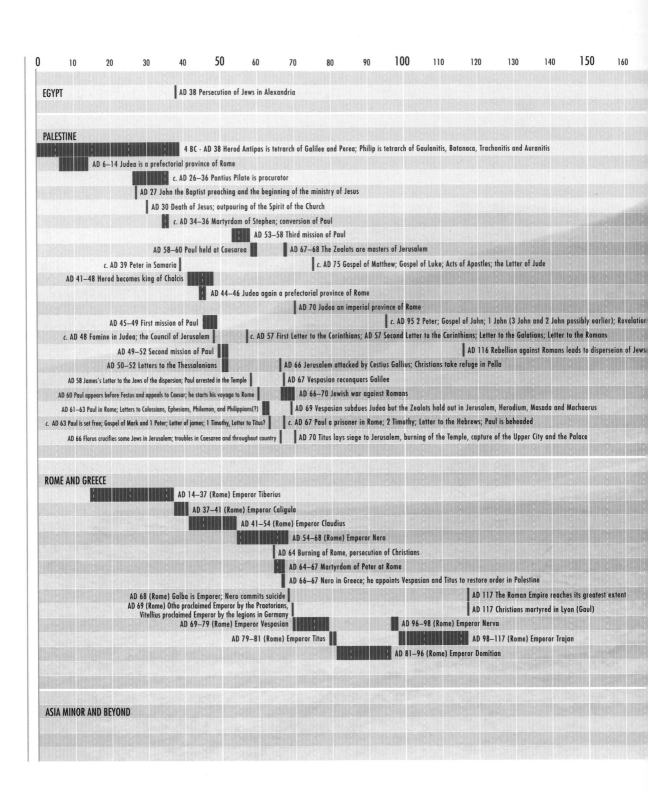

0   10   20   30   40   **50**   60   70   80   90   **100**   110   120   130   140   **150**   160

EGYPT

AD 38 Persecution of Jews in Alexandria

PALESTINE

4 BC - AD 38 Herod Antipas is tetrarch of Galilee and Perea; Philip is tetrarch of Gaulanitis, Batanaca, Trachonitis and Auranitis

AD 6–14 Judea is a prefectorial province of Rome

c. AD 26–36 Pontius Pilate is procurator

AD 27 John the Baptist preaching and the beginning of the ministry of Jesus

AD 30 Death of Jesus; outpouring of the Spirit of the Church

c. AD 34–36 Martyrdom of Stephen; conversion of Paul

AD 53–58 Third mission of Paul

AD 58–60 Paul held at Caesarea   AD 67–68 The Zealots are masters of Jerusalem

c. AD 39 Peter in Samaria   c. AD 75 Gospel of Matthew; Gospel of Luke; Acts of Apostles; the Letter of Jude

AD 41–48 Herod becomes king of Chalcis

AD 44–46 Judea again a prefectorial province of Rome

AD 70 Judea an imperial province of Rome

AD 45–49 First mission of Paul   c. AD 95 2 Peter; Gospel of John; 1 John (3 John and 2 John possibly earlier); Revelation

c. AD 48 Famine in Judea; the Council of Jerusalem   c. AD 57 First Letter to the Corinthians; AD 57 Second Letter to the Corinthians; Letter to the Galatians; Letter to the Romans

AD 49–52 Second mission of Paul   AD 116 Rebellion against Romans leads to disperseion of Jews

AD 50–52 Letters to the Thessalonians   AD 66 Jerusalem attacked by Cestius Gallius; Christians take refuge in Pella

AD 58 James's Letter to the Jews of the dispersion; Paul arrested in the Temple   AD 67 Vespasian reconquers Galilee

AD 60 Paul appears before Festus and appeals to Caesar; he starts his voyage to Rome   AD 66–70 Jewish war against Romans

AD 61–63 Paul in Rome; Letters to Colossians, Ephesians, Philemon, and Philippians(?)   AD 69 Vespasian subdues Judea but the Zealots hold out in Jerusalem, Herodium, Masada and Machaerus

c. AD 63 Paul is set free; Gospel of Mark and 1 Peter; Letter of James; 1 Timothy, Letter to Titus?   c. AD 67 Paul a prisoner in Rome; 2 Timothy; Letter to the Hebrews; Paul is beheaded

AD 66 Florus crucifies some Jews in Jerusalem; troubles in Caesarea and throughout country   AD 70 Titus lays siege to Jerusalem, burning of the Temple, capture of the Upper City and the Palace

ROME AND GREECE

AD 14–37 (Rome) Emperor Tiberius

AD 37–41 (Rome) Emperor Caligula

AD 41–54 (Rome) Emperor Claudius

AD 54–68 (Rome) Emperor Nero

AD 64 Burning of Rome, persecution of Christians

AD 64–67 Martyrdom of Peter at Rome

AD 66–67 Nero in Greece; he appoints Vespasian and Titus to restore order in Palestine

AD 68 (Rome) Galba is Emporer; Nero commits suicide   AD 117 The Roman Empire reaches its greatest extent
AD 69 (Rome) Otho proclaimed Emperor by the Praetorians,   AD 117 Christians martyred in Lyon (Gaul)
Vitellius proclaimed Emperor by the legions in Germany
AD 69–79 (Rome) Emperor Vespasian   AD 96–98 (Rome) Emperor Nerva

AD 79–81 (Rome) Emperor Titus   AD 98–117 (Rome) Emperor Trajan

AD 81–96 (Rome) Emperor Domitian

ASIA MINOR AND BEYOND

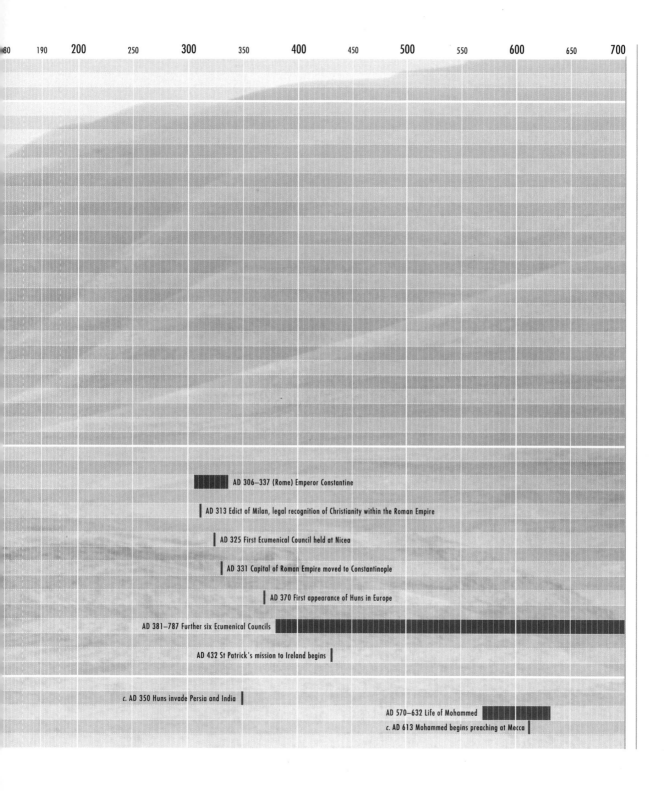

180 190 **200** 250 **300** 350 **400** 450 **500** 550 **600** 650 **700**

AD 306–337 (Rome) Emperor Constantine

AD 313 Edict of Milan, legal recognition of Christianity within the Roman Empire

AD 325 First Ecumenical Council held at Nicea

AD 331 Capital of Roman Empire moved to Constantinople

AD 370 First appearance of Huns in Europe

AD 381–787 Further six Ecumenical Councils

AD 432 St Patrick's mission to Ireland begins

c. AD 350 Huns invade Persia and India

AD 570–632 Life of Mohammed

c. AD 613 Mohammed begins preaching at Mecca

BIBLIOGRAPHY

The author readily acknowledges the work of many scholars and published works that have been consulted in preparation of this atlas. Among this selected bibliography are books recommended for further reading and study of biblical history in the times of ancient civilizations.

Ackerman, Susan, *Warrior, Dancer, Seductress, Queen. Women in Judges and Biblical Israel*, New York: Bantam, Doubleday, Dell Publishing Group Inc., 1998

Anderson, Bernard, *Living World of the Old Testament*, London: Prentice Hall, 1998

Bar-Kochva, B., *Judas Maccabaeus: the Jewish Struggle against the Romans*, Cambridge: Cambridge University Press, 2002

Black, Jeremy (ed), *The Literature of Ancient Sumer*, Oxford: Oxford University Press, 2006

Bockmuehl, M., *This Jesus, Martyr, Lord, Messiah*, Edinburgh: T and T Clark, 1994

Bosworth, A.B., *The Legacy of Alexander: Politics, Warfare and Propaganda under the Successors*, Oxford: Oxford University Press, 2005

Brettler, Marc Zvi, *The Book of Judges*, London: Routledge, 2001

Bright, John, *A History of Israel*, London: SCM Press, 1972

Bryce, Trevor, *The Kingdom of the Hittites*, Oxford: Oxford University Press, 2005

Chavalas, Mark. W., *The Ancient Near East. Historical Sources in Translation*, Oxford: Blackwell Publishing, 2006

Conder, Clause Reigner, *The Tell Amarna Tablets*, Athena University Press, 2004

Curtis, J.E. and Tallis, Nigel, *Forgotten Empire: the World of Ancient Persia*, London: British Museum Press, 2005

Daniel, Glyn, *The First Civilizations, the Archaeology of their Origin*, London: Thames and Hudson, 1968

Davies, W.V., *Egyptian Hieroglyphs*, London: British Museum Press, 1987

Deconick, April D., *Recovering the Original Gospel of Thomas*, London: Continuum International Publishing Group, 2005

De Jonge, M., *Studies on the Testaments of the Twelve Patriarchs: Texts and Interpretation*, The Netherlands, Leiden: Brill, 1975

De Vaux, R., *Archaeology and the Dead Sea Scrolls*, Oxford: Oxford University Press, 2004

Dicks, Brian, *The Ancient Persians. How They Lived and Worked*, London: David and Charles, 1979

Driver, G.R., *Semitic Writing, From Pictograph to Alphabet*, Oxford: Oxford University Press, 1976

Dunderbeg, Ismo, *The Beloved Disciple in Conflict. Revisiting the Gospels of John and Thomas*, Oxford: Oxford University Press, 2006

Ehrman, Bart D., *Peter, Paul and Mary: The Followers of Jesus in History and Legend*, Oxford: Oxford University Press, 2000

Ehrman, Bart D., *The Apostolic Fathers, Vols I and II*, London: Harvard University Press, 2003

Fairbairn, Donald, *Grace and Christology in the Early Church*, Oxford: Oxford University Press, 2006

Finkelstein, Israel and Silberman, Neil Asher, *The Bible Unearthed: Archaeology's New Vision of Ancient Israel*, New York: Simon and Schuster, 2002

Fitzmyer, S.J., Joseph A., *The Dead Sea Scrolls and Christian Origins*, Cambridge: William B. Eerdmans Publicity Company, 2000

Fohrer, Georg, *Introduction to the Old Testament*, London: SPCK, 1976

Fox, Robin Lane, *Alexander the Great*, London: Penguin Books Ltd., 2004

Frend, W.H.C., *The Rise of Christianity, Evangelical Lutheran Church in America*: Augsburg Fortress Publishing, 1986

Fuchs, Daniel and Sevener, Harald A., *From Bondage to Freedom: A Survey of Jewish History from the Babylonian Captivity to the Coming of the Messiah*, New York: Loiseaux Brothers, 1996

George, A. R., *The Babylonian Gilgamesh Epic*, Oxford: Oxford University Press, 2003

Gilbert, M., *The Routledge Atlas of Jewish History*, London: Routledge, 1993

Gilmore, Alec, *Dictionary of the English Bible and its Origins*, London: Routledge, 2001

Golden, Jonathan M., *Ancient Canaan and Israel: New Perspectives*, Oxford: ABC-Clio, 2004

Grottanelli, Christiano, *Kings and Prophets, Monarchic Power, Inspired Leadership and Sacred Text in Biblical Narrative*, Oxford: Oxford University Press, 1999

Gruen, Erich S., *Diaspora*, London: Harvard University Press, 2004

Habicht, Christian, *Hellenistic Monarchies. Selected Papers*, Chicago: University of Michigan Press, 2006

Hamilton, V., *Handbook on the Historical Books: Joshua, Judges, Ruth, Samuel, Kings, Chronicles, Ezra-Nehemiah, Esther*, Baker Book House Company, 2001

Hawks, J., *The First Great Civilizations: Life in Mesopotamia, the Indus Valley, and Egypt*, London: Penguin, 1977

Hayes, John H. and Mandell, Sara R., *The Jewish People in Classical Antiquity from Alexander to Bar Kochba*, Louisville, Kentucky, USA: Westminster John Knox Press, 1998

Josephus, *Complete Works*, London: Pickering and Inglis Ltd., 1960

Keen, Ralph, *The Christian Tradition*, London: Prentice Hall, 2004

Kent, Charles Foster, *A History of the Hebrew People from the Settlement in Canaan to the Division of the Kingdom*, Kessinger Publishing LLC, 2004

Kenyon, Kathleen, *Amorites and Canaanites*, Oxford: Oxford University Press, 2004

King, Leonard William, *Babylonian Religion and Mythology*, USA: Fredonia Books, 2003

Knoblet, Jerry, *Herod the Great*, Lanham, Maryland, USA: University Press of America Inc., 2005

Killebrew, Ann E., *Biblical Peoples and Ethnicity: An Archaeological Study of Egyptians, Canaanites, Philistines, and Early Israel, 1300–1100 BC*, The Netherlands, Leiden: Brill, 2006

Kinzl, Konrad H., *A Companion to the Classical Greek World*, Oxford: Blackwell Publishing, 2006

Kramer, S.N., *Sumerian Mythology*, Philadelphia: University of Pennsylvania Press, 1998

Kuhrt, Amelie, *The Ancient Near East, c. 3000–330 BC*, London: Routledge, 1997

Layton, Bentley, *The Gnostic Scriptures*, New York: Doubleday, 1987

Le Glay, Marcel, Voisin, Jean-Louis, Le Bohec, Yann, *A History of Rome*, Oxford: Blackwell Publishing, 1996

Lieu, J., North, J.A., and Rajak, T. (eds.), *The Jews among Pagans and Christians in the Roman Empire*, London: Routledge, 1992

Ma, John, *Antiochus III and the Cities of Western Asia*, Oxford: Oxford University Press, 2002

Malamat, Abraham, Mari and the Early Israelite Experience. The Schweich Lectures, 1984, Oxford: Oxford University Press, 1992

Mascarenhas, Theodore, *The Missionary Function of Israel in Psalms 67, 96 and 117*, Oxford: Rowman and Littlefield Publishing, 2005

Miller, J. Maxwell and Hayes, John H., *A History of Ancient Israel and Judah*, London: SCM Press, 1986

Moscato, Sabatino, *The Phoenicians*, London: I. B. Tauris, 2001

Murphy-O'Connor, Jerome, *Paul: A Critical Life*, Oxford: Oxford University Press, 1998

O'Collins, Gerald, *Jesus Our Redeemer. A Christian Approach to Salvation*, Oxford: Oxford University Press, 2001

Nakhai, Beth Alpert, *Archaeology and Religions of Canaan*, American Schools of Oriental Research, 2002

Niditch, Susan, *Ancient Israelite Religion*, USA: Oxford University Press, Inc., 1988

Pinches, Theophilus Goldridge, *The Old Testament in the Light of the Historical Records and Legends of Assyria and Babylon*, Chestnut Hill, Massachussetts: Adamant Media Corporation, 2005

Rhodes, P.J., *A History of the Classical Greek World, 478–323 BC*, Oxford: Blackwell Publishing, 2006

Rogerson, John and Davies, Philip, *The Old Testament World*, London: Continuum International Publishing Group, 2005

Rohl, David, *From Eden to Exile: the Epic History of the People of the Bible*, Arrow, 2003

Romer, Thomas, *The So-called Deuteronomistic History*, Continuum, 2005

Sandars, N., *The Sea Peoples, Warriors of the Eastern Mediterranean*, London: Thames and Hudson, 1985

Sanders, E. P., *The Historical Figure of Jesus*, London: Penguin Books Ltd., 2005

Schürer, E., *The History of the Jewish People in the Age of Jesus Christ (175 BC–AD 135)*, revised edition, 3 vols. Trans. T. A. Burkill et al., Edinburgh, 1973–87

Shanks, Hershel (ed.), *Ancient Israel. A Short History from Abraham to the Roman Destruction of the Temple*, London: SPCK, 1989

Shaw, Ian, *The Oxford History of Ancient Egypt*, Oxford: Oxford University Press, 2003

Sievers, Joseph, *The Hasmoneans and their Supporters: From Mattathias to the Death of John Hyrcanus I*, Cambridge: Scholars Press, 1990

Soggin, J. Alberto, *An Introduction to the History of Israel and Judah*, London: SCM Press, 1993

Soggin, J. Alberto, *Judges*, USA, Kentucky, Louisville: Presbyterian Publishing Corporation, Westminster John Knox Press, 1981

Spalinger, Anthony J., *War in Ancient Egypt. The New Kingdom*, Oxford: Blackwell Publishing, 2004

Sweeney, Marvin A., *King Josiah of Judah*, Oxford: Oxford University Press, 2001

Terry, Michael, *Reader's Guide to Judaism*, London: Routledge, 2000

Thompson, Thomas L., *The Historicity of the Patriarchal Narratives: The Quest for the Historical Abraham*, London: Continuum International Publishing Group

Tyldesley, Joyce, *Ramesses: Egypt's Greatest Pharaoh*, London: Penguin Books Ltd., 2001

Van de Mierop, Marc, *Cuneiform Texts and the Writing of History*, London: Routledge, 1999

Van de Mierop, Marc, *King Hammurabi of Babylon*, Oxford: Blackwell Publishing, 2004

White, Ellen G., *The Acts of the Apostles in the Proclamation of the Gospel of Jesus Christ*, Kessinger Publishing Company, 2005

Wilson, Penelope, *Hieroglyphs*, Oxford: Oxford University Press, 2004

Wiseman, D.J., *Nebuchadnezzar and Babylon*, Oxford: Oxford University Press, 1991

Yadin, Yigael, *Hazor*, Oxford: Oxford University Press, 2005

Yadin, Yigael, *Masada. Herod's Fortress and the Zealot's Last Stand*, London: Weidenfeld and Nicolson, 1966

Nomads Tented tribes who herd sheep and goats across sparse pastures.

Nubians See Ethiopians.

Obelisk A four-sided tapering shaft of stone with a small pyramid at the top. Obelisks were associated with sun worship and were often placed in pairs outside the entrances of Egyptian temples and tombs.

Oil Invariably olive oil used in cooking, medicine, cosmetics, lamps, and religious rites. See Anoint.

Palestine Strictly the coastal strip northeast of Egypt settled by Philistines but extended to refer to the land from Lebanon to the Sinai Desert.

Panathenae A Greek religious festival held annually in Athens in honor of their goddess Athena.

Pantheon Originally the term applied to the temple at Rome built in 27 BC to all the gods. It is also used to describe all the gods as a group.

Pantheism From the Greek words for "all" and "god," any religion or belief that holds that "God is all and all is God" so identifying God and the whole universe with each other.

Parthians A people famous for their archers and horsemen whose empire was at its height in the 1st Century BC. It extended from the River Euphrates as far as the Indus and the Indian Ocean. The empire fell into decline when the Persians conquered the Parthians in AD 226.

Passion The sufferings of Jesus from his arrest to his crucifixion.

Passover The oldest Hebrew festival commemorating the exodus from Egypt.

Patriarchs The main Hebrew ancestors from Adam to Joseph.

Pentateuch Literally "five books" in Greek; the first five books of the Old Testament.

Pentecost From the Greek meaning 50th; a harvest festival 50 days after that of Unleavened Bread.

Persians A people east of the Persian Gulf who overthrew the Babylonians in 540 BC; conquered by Alexander the Great in 331 BC.

Pharisees A lay Jewish group committed to a strict interpretation of the law.

Philistines The people who occupied the Palestinian coastal plain between the Mediterranean (the Great Sea) and the Shephelah. The name "Palestine" is a derivative of Philistine. Some of the Sea Peoples who invaded Egypt in the late 19th and early 20th dynasties were Philistines.

Polytheism The belief in many or more than one god.

Prefectorial province A district administered by a prefect appointed by the authorities in ancient Rome.

Priest The class responsible for oracles, law, and performing sacrifices; eventually exclusive and hereditary.

Procurator A Roman official directly responsible to the Emperor.

Prophet A person claiming to speak in God's name.

Psalm A song used in worship.

Puppet kingdom A kingdom that is more or less completely governed by and is answerable to a more powerful kingdom or state.

Qumran Site of an Essene community near the northwest shore of the Dead Sea.

Rabbi Literally "my master" in Aramaic; a teacher, especially a scribe.

Satrap A governor of a province (or satrapy) in ancient Persia.

Scroll A rolled book usually written on a long strip of papyrus or sheepskin. The Dead Sea Scrolls are the recently discovered Essene library from Qumran.

Sea Peoples See Philistines.

Semites A people from the Arabian Desert, including Hebrews, with related languages.

Septuagint The ancient translation of the Old Testament into Greek.

Sumerians A people controlling southern Mesopotamia in the 3rd Millennium BC.

Synagogue Literally "assembly place" derived from Greek; a Jewish meeting place for worship, teaching and discussion.

Tabernacle The tent-shrine of the Ark of the Covenant before the Temple was built.

Tabernacles The third harvest festival, named after the tents that harvesters used in the fields.

Tell An artificial mound indicating an abandoned settlement.

Temple Any building dedicated to gods and associated with their presence. In this book, temple with a capital "T" refers to the one in Jerusalem.

Testament Another translation of the words for "covenant." See Covenant.

Tetrarchy In the Roman Empire, a fourth part of a country or province. Each was ruled by a tetrarch.

Theocracy A form of government in which a god is recognized as supreme ruler and his laws are carried out by priests.

Unleavened bread Bread made without yeast, offered as a pure harvest sacrifice, hence the name of the first harvest festival attached to the Passover.

Vulgate The ancient Latin translation of the Bible.

Wadi A watercourse that is dry except during periods of rainfall, found in places such as Egypt.

Yahweh The modern transliteration of the Hebrew personal name of God.

Zealots A fanatical Jewish sect who rebelled against the Romans and were not accepted by other Jews. They carried out many assassinations and were responsible for numerous revolts. They were the main initiators of the Jewish-Roman war in AD 66.

Zeus The chief god of the ancient Greeks, identified as Jupiter by the Romans.

Ziggurat A Mesopotamian tower-like temple.

Zion The ancient Davidic citadel of Jerusalem. The exact location is not certain.

NAMES AND TITLES OF GOD

The Hebrew word usually translated as "God" is *elohim*, from the word *el*, which is used for gods of all kinds. Also derived from this word is the title *el elyon*, meaning "the most high God" (e.g. Genesis 14:18).

The only actual personal name of God is the Hebrew *Yahweh*, translated in English versions as "the Lord" or "Jehovah" (e.g. Genesis 12:8; Exodus 6:3). When he declared himself to Moses as "I am" (Hebrew *ehyeh*) this can be seen as a play on the word Yahweh.

Most of God's other titles or descriptions combine the word *el* or the name *Yahweh* with another word. They include: "Almighty God" (e.g. Genesis 17:1), "Lord God of Israel" (e.g. Joshua 24:2) and "the Lord of hosts" (e.g. 1 Samuel 17:45). Some titles were given on one particular occasion, for example *Jehovah-jireh* ("the Lord provides"—Genesis 23:14), *Jehovah-nissi* ("the Lord is my banner"—Exodus 17:15) and *Jehovah-shalom* ("the Lord is peace"—Judges 6:24).

Other Old Testament names include "the Holy One of Israel" (e.g. Isaiah 1:4) and "the Ancient of Days" (Daniel 7:9). Titles that are descriptions rather than names include: "Creator" (Isaiah 40:28), "Father" (Malachi 2:8) and "King" (e.g. Jeremiah 10:7). New Testament titles and descriptions, other then God and Father, are: "Father of lights" (Jas. 1:17) and "King of kings and Lord of lords" (1 Timothy 6:15).

NAMES AND TITLES OF JESUS

The name Jesus is the Greek form of Joshua, which means "God is salvation;" Saviour became one of his titles (e.g. Titus 1:4). Christ is the Greek form of Messiah, literally "anointed."

Before his birth, Jesus was named by Isaiah as "Wonderful, Councillor, the Mighty God, the Everlasting Father, the Prince of Peace" (Isaiah 9:6). Isaiah also used the name Immanuel (Isaiah 7:14, Matthew 1:23), meaning "God with us."

Jesus often referred to himself as "the Son of man" (Matthew 8:20), but he did not deny that he was the "Son of God" (Matthew 26:63–64). Many of his most striking titles are found in John's Gospel: "the word" (1:1), "the Lamb of God" (1:29), "the bread of life" (6:35), "the light of the world" (8:12), "the door" (10:9), "the good shepherd" (10:11), "the resurrection and the life" (11:25), "the way, the truth, and the life" (14:6), "the vine" (15:5). In Revelation he is called "Alpha and Omega" (1:8), "Lord of lords, King of kings" (17:14).

INDEX

INDEX

INDEX

INDEX

INDEX

Maps and Reconstructions

ACKNOWLEDGMENTS

For Cartographica Press
Design, Maps and Typesetting: Jeanne Radford, PAB Smith,
    Alexander Swanston, Malcolm Swanston, and Jonathan
    Young

Biblical advice: Reverend Roland Jones

The publishers would like to thank the following picture
    libraries for their kind permission to use their pictures and
    illustrations:

Ashmolean Library, Oxford 263
Bodlien Library 53 (upper)
Bridgeman Art Library 9, 27, 65, 95
C.M. Dixon 272, 297, 309
E T Archive 23, 333
Folkmuseum, Bygdøy 39
iStockphoto 11 (Paul Cowan), 64–65, 357 (Steven Allan), 93
    (James Margolis), 104 (Neta Degany), 105, 122–123 (Claudia
    Dewald), 131 (Dimitry Romanchuck), 253 (Jeurgen Sack),
    254 (Berthold Engelman), 320
    (Mark Weiss), 329 (BMPix)
J Catling Allen 215
Mansell Collection 291
Mary Evans Picture Library 123
Peter Newark Historical Pictures 223
Quarto Publishing Group 12 (upper), 12 (lower), 14, 18, 26, 49,
    53 (lower), 56, 70, 82, 83, 90, 106–107, 112, 142, 149, 158,
    159 (lower), 161, 165, 187, 199, 205 (inset), 206, 217, 221,
    235, 236–237, 242–243, 247, 259, 265, 270, 285, 319, 322,
    339, 340-341
RLP&P 7, 24-25, 28, 72, 134–135, 147, 151, 161, 159 (upper),
    165 (lower), 169, 174, 177, 179, 181, 189, 209, 213, 227, 231,
    282–283, 295, 296, 304, 306
University of London 33, 60–61, 145, 275, 287

Every effort has been made to contact the copyright holders
    for images reproduced in this book.
    The publishers would welcome any errors or
    omissions being brought to their attention.